THE NEW PLURALISM

THE NEW PLURALISM

WILLIAM CONNOLLY

AND THE CONTEMPORARY

GLOBAL CONDITION

edited by David Campbell and Morton Schoolman

DUKE UNIVERSITY PRESS Durham and London 2008

George Kateb's essay "Prohibition and Transgression" previously appeared
in *Patriotism and Other Mistakes* (New Haven: Yale University Press, 2006),
© Yale University Press. Reprinted with permission.

Library of Congress Cataloging-in-Publication Data appear
on the last printed page of this book.

CONTENTS

INTRODUCTION:
PLURALISM "OLD" AND "NEW"

Morton Schoolman and David Campbell

WILLIAM CONNOLLY HAS BEEN ONE of the principal architects of a "new pluralism" whose theoretical dimensions will be described and critically examined in the essays that follow. This new pluralism is not unrelated to the "old pluralism," by which we mean conventional pluralist theory as it evolved in American and British political science and sociology, especially after the Second World War. On the contrary, the old pluralism has been incorporated into the central theoretical, methodological, and political concerns of its successor. However, the new pluralism has revised and reconstructed the old pluralism in line with philosophical developments occurring during the past half-century, specifically those of poststructuralism, postmodernism, critical theory, and feminist theory. All these developments have of course also influenced the broader evolution of political theory and international relations theory in decisive ways. And although Connolly's work has been influential in transforming pluralist theory, many other political theorists and political scientists have contributed importantly to this sea change, which the critical essays we have collected both exemplify and continue to advance.

The new pluralism flows from the widest range of theoretical and philosophical arguments; it aims to overcome closures in political theory that exclude possibilities for thinking critically about existing political constellations and the multiple ways in which they can be reconfigured. The new pluralism insists uncompromisingly on including theories and practices from outside the well-governed territory of established political theory and political practice. Recognizing that there always will be a theoretical and practical "outside" eligible for inclusion in thinking and in politics, the new pluralism reflects on the normative boundaries of theory and on its own normative boundaries in ways that pluralize approaches to the understanding of politics, and to its reform and reconstitution.

Although Connolly is a chief architect of the new pluralism, he also was involved prominently in the debates surrounding the old pluralism, whose general contours can be illuminated by recalling his earliest work. Our genealogy will bring into focus the limits of conventional pluralist theory and the ways Connolly's new pluralism addresses those limits. Connolly's initial engagements with pluralist theory occurred in his first book, *Political Science and Ideology*, and in an essay, "The Challenge to Pluralist Theory," which introduced a collection that he edited entitled *The Bias of Pluralism*.[1] Pluralism for some time had been recognized as the political form and defining quality of American society and the philosophical expression of both. Pluralism, in other words, was taken to be singular evidence for democracy in America. It was an ideal widely considered the clearest expression of American ideals. Connolly affirmed the pluralist ideal, as he has since (though not without revision), and he has affirmed its prerequisites: the basic principle of constitutionalism, and the principles of universal rights and human suffrage, among others. It was at this time too that the Vietnam War had reached its nadir and inflamed a critical temper that in the American academy had already begun to contest the pluralist ideal, just as the civil rights and antiwar movements were launching critiques of American domestic and foreign policy. Connolly allied himself with the critics of pluralism inside and outside the academy, and defined as his work's threefold purpose: determining the extent to which modern democratic pluralism, notably in America, met the conditions for an ideal of pluralism formulated in the late eighteenth century and the early nineteenth; conceptualizing alternative models of pluralism better approximating the pluralist ideal; and on the basis of these models, formulating political strategies for the reform of pluralist institutions and practices.

Connolly's early work traces the intellectual heritage of the American pluralist ideal to both Madison and Tocqueville, though it is Tocqueville whom he engages most closely. The ideal pluralist system rooted in Tocqueville's thought is held by its theoretical proponents to perform multiple functions. It is believed to promote a plurality of private and public ends; it maximizes opportunities for participation in politics that nurture capacities for intelligent, effective, and responsible citizenship and promotes political efficacy and fealty to the political system as a whole; it raises the most important problems facing society and brings to bear on governmental institutions pressures to ensure their political redress; it offers equal opportunities for new groups pressing to enter the political process with new demands; and most importantly, it balances demands and policy outcomes to maintain a stable system through all conflicts.

When Connolly reviews the conditions that Tocqueville specifies for the flourishing of pluralism, however, he finds glaring discrepancies between its preconditions and the conditions that prevail in modern democratic society. Whereas Tocqueville contended that pluralism draws the citizenry from all classes and ranks into politics, Connolly notes that by some measures the level of political participation is far lower than what Tocqueville foresaw. Tocqueville's view that voluntary associations can serve as vehicles for political education, for safeguarding rights, and for aggregating and articulating political demands is also compromised by modern, large-scale organizations whose structural dynamics favor oligarchical interests over those of an organization's membership. At the same time, individuals dependent on established organizations are reluctant to pursue other associational ties at times of stress, when they are most needed, which only reinforces the position of dominant organizations and their leaderships. Labor, moreover, has become so specialized for all classes in society that it is difficult to develop through work the broader perspectives on politics and the economy historically available to the middle class. And the eclipse of the once economically independent bourgeois entrepreneur brought about by modern capitalist industry deprives society of a class with the time and intellectual resources to participate actively in associational life. The locally owned and managed free press on which the citizenry could rely for competing points of view has been replaced by a centralized media ruled by economic elites sharing similar ideas and values, while access to the media in general is reserved to those with sufficient capital. Finally, individuals and groups politically disadvantaged by the logic of this modern pluralist system no longer have the American frontier that Tocqueville held out as an escape route for those rebuffed by democratic politics. In Connolly's view, these changes thwart the possibilities for the robust pluralism that Tocqueville believed was emergent in America and bearing the fruits of modern democracy.

To be sure, Connolly reflects on the institutional developments that social scientists claim are introduced by modern democracies to compensate for or ameliorate injuries done to the earlier democratic potential foregrounded by Tocqueville. His position overall is that given their normative commitments to the existing political system, social scientists are too eager to fit the older pluralist ideal to the new conditions threatening it, with the result that they misjudge the degree to which this image obscures the degeneration of the modern democratic form. Connolly indicts conventional pluralist theory precisely for this error. When he turns to examples of social scientists who try to fit the pluralist ideal to the modern conditions under which it is constrained to operate, he takes up the work of two who have been seminal in the development of conventional pluralist theory.

Robert Dahl is selected by Connolly to illustrate the variant of pluralist theory that views government as the arena where political differences are contested and conflicts resolved. Dahl, whom Connolly admires for his persuasive interpretation of this version of pluralism, is taken to task primarily for two claims. First, although only a small minority of citizens participate actively in politics, they still represent a wider collection of groups. Second, there is an underlying normative consensus that regulates conflict among groups because it is the intersubjective product of the society as a whole. Pluralism is alleged by Dahl to remain intact for both reasons, which in different ways point to structures of representation that appear to guarantee the efficacy of a plurality of voices, values, and interests. With the ideal so protected, Dahl then can proceed to argue that pluralism achieves a stable political regime, because the rights of the majority have been respected and little coercion is necessary to constrain the minority to go along, even though its voices remain unheard. Dahl's conceptual slight of hand, which substitutes the *representation of* a plurality for its *actual participation*, likewise neglects another of the important achievements ideally attributed by Tocqueville to pluralism: namely, widespread political participation facilitates the development of capacities salient to human and political development in a way that melds together pluralism, the right, and the good. Indeed, Connolly pursues Dahl on this matter to insist that his narrowing of political participation to minority representation of pluralities belies the deeper intent of Tocqueville's pluralist ideal, which Dewey captures with his proposal that a viable pluralism must foster the expansion of political participation beyond government to the family, church, business, workplace, and school. Only such plural opportunities for participation, which Dewey's model of social democracy entails, meet the Tocquevillian imperative of fully developed human faculties. Thus in Connolly's estimation, Dahl's critique of the ruling élite model illustrates attempts by social scientists to adjust the pluralist ideal to modern conditions so that American democracy seems to be its realization.

Connolly also considers the implications for pluralist theory of the arguments made by a second leading thinker, Adolf Berle, highly regarded for his impact on New Deal theories of economic intervention and the regulation of big business. Among other issues, Berle's position that a democratic society can rely upon an underlying public consensus of values to support government constraints on business and to influence managerial behavior is problematic. Connolly argues that Berle fails to specify how that consensus would be formed, especially regarding the concerns of specialized groups such as intellectuals, the media, and politicians, who disproportionately shape the agenda that determines how power is wielded on behalf of the public interest. As with Dahl, Connolly finds Berle's notion of consensus to be undertheorized, thus leveraging a pluralist ideal that covers up the shortfalls of American democracy.

Connolly examines variants of pluralist theory more extensive than those we have discussed here. Nearly all, though, focus on the same or similar aspects of pluralist politics. Whereas, for example, pluralist theorists have concentrated on the competition among organized groups in governmental arenas, Connolly corrects the picture by showing how the larger societal context is biased in favor of certain types of groups and against others. Contextual biases run along the lines of class, organizational factors affecting the political efficacy of groups, and the power and resources at the disposal of elites and the public to determine which concerns are and are not registered in the political process and translated into policy. They also include systemic ideological biases prejudicial to individuals and groups opposed to the values that create, maintain, and reproduce the status quo. Such biases work to determine which issues, interests, norms, values, perspectives, alternatives, reforms, groups, and individuals are represented and which excluded, while they limit the extent to which biases can be eliminated without introducing dislocations that undermine the political system as a whole.

In support of this argument Connolly invokes a range of social and political theorists and economists of the day, including C. Wright Mills, Herbert Marcuse, Robert Paul Wolff, John Kenneth Galbraith, Grant McConnell, and Henry Kariel. Their critiques of conventional pluralist theory are more and less radical, as are their proposed reforms. Despite their differences, though, Connolly discerns telling similarities among them that amount to a common "critical temper" with which he explicitly identifies and that to this day continues to find expression in the left wing of the social sciences. Among the critical priorities of this group, the centrality of normative concerns in social science is first and foremost. Normative questions should guide research rather than be subordinated to the narrow methodological aims of social scientists, who conduct investigations that assume the legitimacy of the dominant values. Connolly explains that in its tacit preoccupation with the relationship between mechanisms of conflict resolution and systemic stability, conventional pluralist theory assumes the legitimacy of the underlying values served by the political system. In addition, conventional pluralists marshal untenable epistemologies to bracket values and suppress the questions that values require us to ask, accordingly remaining methodologically indifferent to their concepts' normative implications and hostile to norms not already operating in the pluralist system that they examine. Confining themselves to operationally defined concepts, social scientists prejudge their research outcomes, as the concept of "group" is employed in conventional pluralist theory, an empirical measure insensitive to the concerns of ensembles who do not meet the criteria specified by the operationalized concept of the group. Conventional pluralist theory proves the political process to be far more democratic when its advocates adopt social science methods that screen out the concerns of poor or poorly organized and otherwise marginal groups.

Thus in Connolly's view, and in the view of other theorists whose work defined the critical temper, conventional pluralist theory is biased, burdened by normative assumptions, and top-heavy with methodologies masking an ideological and institutional infrastructure that organizes socioeconomic and political power to favor certain interests and groups.

For Connolly and other theorists who share a critical temper, however, the burden of proof does not end with the demonstration of the biases of conventional pluralist theory. It is dedicated equally to developing alternative models of pluralist practice and to devising strategies for reform that bring democratic politics into conformity with the theory and practice of these models—although not entirely. As Connolly emphasizes, while proponents must be clear about the normative commitments embedded in their empirical models, their expectation and the expectation of their political allies and supporters must not be that the alternatives envisioned be fully attainable in practice. Practice always lags behind. Rather, alternative models are to provide bases for appraising the performance of the established pluralist system, including grounds to appreciate the achievements of existing pluralist practices, and they are to assist in setting goals for reform. Alternative models can also spur impulses for political reform and, importantly, create opportunities for reform by dramatizing future possibilities that can be realized through the political reorganization of already developed cultural and material resources. Put differently, alternative models can help to avoid the contented attitude toward the established political system that conventional pluralist theory often appears to encourage. Finally, alternative models also bring "the critical temper into sharper focus," which is to say that the critical temper has not completed its work until it turns back reflexively to appraise and revise as necessary every theoretical and practical aspect of critique.

Such were the intended purposes of two alternative models of pluralism developed by Connolly in new works published not long after *Political Science and Ideology* and *The Bias of Pluralism*. In *The Terms of Political Discourse* (1974) Connolly explored how key concepts in politics are constructed from a normative point of view, and how normative differences among concepts can make them "essentially contestable."[2] Connolly's larger intention here was to develop an alternative model of inquiry to the reigning positivist model, one better equipped to conceptualize both the shortcomings of modern pluralism and alternative models of pluralist politics. Indeed, in *The Politicized Economy* (1976) he and his coauthor Michael Best introduce an analysis of consumption distinguishing between consumer goods that expand inequality as they are generalized and consumer goods that reduce inequality as they are expanded to become inclusive goods.[3] Their intention with this analysis was to construct an alternative

model of pluralism able to reduce inequality and instruct political efforts
to that end.

Of course, the responsibility that the critical temper assumes is to move
through political engagement at the theoretical level to political engagement at the practical level. This conventional way to formulate the relationship between theory and practice is somewhat misleading, though,
for Connolly considers political theory generally a form of political practice, and in this context the critical temper itself instructs political strategy, for example by demonstrating the need and potential for reducing
social and economic inequality. Connolly agrees with several of the theorists whose ideas fuel the critical temper that because its work broaches
the political realm, the social science community can, like intellectuals as
a whole, become an agent for political change and a pluralizing force
within a political system whose barriers to democratic pluralism the critical temper understands well. The critical temper's political role grows out
of its academic functions. It would help to "educate a larger public to the
deficiencies of a biased pluralism," reopen "forgotten debates among social scientists, challenging the complacency of some and activating the
latent concerns of others," and exert "constructive pressures on liberals in
and around government."[4]

Connolly is neither sanguine, nor cavalier, nor highly optimistic about
improving the prospects for political reform through the allied agencies
of the critical temper and its public. He recognizes that political strategy
is the greatest challenge faced by the critics of conventional pluralist
theory, because its theoretical advocates and the modern pluralist system
of politics both work to define and limit the terms of political discourse.
Yet he also recognizes that the challenge cannot be left to the routine
politics of modern pluralism, to the positivist model of inquiry at one
time dominant in the academy, or to the belief that the promise of a
democratic pluralism will be redeemed by historical forces whose objectivity is vulnerable to the same criticism brought to bear on all other
forms of positivism.

To this point in our discussion, the "old pluralism" is in the main
composed of multiple dimensions. It is characterized by an ideal formulation of pluralist democracy rooted in the political thought of Madison
and Tocqueville; by conventional pluralist theory, whose adherents attempt to salvage the ideal by adapting it to modern conditions that call

the ideal into question; by critiques of conventional pluralist theory, including Connolly's, that illuminate the discrepancies between the ideal and the real and how efforts to conceal these discrepancies tend to exaggerate the democratic achievements of modern pluralist society; and by the emergence of a critical temper from these practices, whose agents construct alternative models of pluralist politics, as well as strategies for political action for which their models provide the guidelines. Our use of the concept of "old pluralism" signals that the contributors to this book generally agree with Connolly's framing of a formative period in the history of pluralist theory and practice. While the critical spirit of the old pluralism finds expression in Connolly's later work, his "new pluralism" is marked by important developments and qualitative differences, which can be described in general terms.

As we saw, among Connolly's contributions to the old pluralism were his demonstration that conventional pluralist theory attempted to fit the pluralist ideal to modern conditions and his proposal for alternative models able to show, to the contrary, which changes in modern conditions were required for "the practice of politics to approach the pluralist ideal," as he put it in *The Bias of Pluralism*. While this strategy is held over in the new pluralist theory that begins to take shape with a new edition of *The Terms of Political Discourse* in 1983, Connolly's new pluralism is distinguished by the continual *revision* of the pluralist ideal. Whereas Connolly's contribution to the old pluralism is based primarily on an *acceptance* of the Tocquevillian pluralist ideal, the new pluralist theory seeks to rework and reconceptualize this ideal, though not, need it be said, to adjust it to changing modern conditions. Rather, Connolly continues to develop alternative models of pluralist politics, though models of politics more likely to realize an ideal whose continual revisions are informed by ever more demanding theoretical and philosophical standards. With this fundamental shift in Connolly's normative orientation, two other changes follow.

As would be expected, Connolly's revisions of the pluralist ideal were made with the assistance of thinkers quite different from those who had sown the seeds of the old pluralism. Besides Madison and Tocqueville, Dahl and Berle, Dewey and Marcuse, Mills and Galbraith, we find Spinoza and Nietzsche, Bergson and James, Foucault and Deleuze, Virilio and Damasio and Prigogine, to name some who made the deepest impressions on Connolly. As also must be expected, with Connolly's revisions of the pluralist ideal come corresponding revisions in critical methodologies and approaches to pluralist theory and practice, and revisions in his formulation of alternative models of pluralist politics and political strategies for reform. These revisions are supported by the ensemble of thinkers whose work contributes to Connolly's revisions of the pluralist ideal.

With these generally distinguishing features of the new pluralism in mind, and without getting too far ahead of ourselves, we offer some specifics of Connolly's theoretical turn and points of demarcation to help orient the reader. The old pluralism that we reviewed above is primarily the subject of four works previously cited, *Political Science and Ideology*, *The Bias of Pluralism*, *The Terms of Political Discourse*, and *The Politicized Economy*, published in the years 1967–76. Beginning with the 1983 edition of *The Terms of Political Discourse*, as we noted, the theoretical developments that form the new pluralism begin in earnest and continue in each subsequent work—*Politics and Ambiguity* (1987); *Identity\Difference: Democratic Negotiations of Political Paradox* (1991); *The Augustinian Imperative: A Reflection on the Politics of Morality* (1993); *The Ethos of Pluralization* (1995); *Why I Am Not a Secularist* (1999); *Neuropolitics: Thinking, Culture, Speed* (2002)—through to Connolly's most recent *Pluralism* (2005).[5] In *Appearance and Reality in Politics* (1981), which is a "bridge" work, elements of the old pluralism are present, while Connolly's examination of how the quest for personal identity is connected to the politics of the welfare state is a sign of the new pluralism to come.

Each of the works from which the new pluralism springs is concerned with one or more of the following and their bearing on modern pluralist politics: (1) how identity and difference are interwoven as identity defines itself through difference and through the conversion of difference to otherness; (2) the political character of relations between identity and difference; (3) the insufficiency of both individualist and communitarian conceptions of democracy, rooted in their misunderstandings of the constitutive tension between the politics of representation and the politics of agitation, by means of which a new right, new faith, new good, or new identity is ushered into being; (4) challenges to the *necessity* of conceptions of morality grounded in law or putative universals, which are contrasted with an ethics grounded in the first instance in a gratitude for the abundance of being that exceeds the constitutions of identity; (5) an emphasis on the role that ontology plays in every political theory, which is tied to the argument for an ontology of immanent naturalism as a defensible and contestable option to be considered seriously; (6) an understanding of how every political theory implicitly and explicitly projects an image of time, and of how theory can support an image of open temporality that challenges the linear, determinist, and teleological conceptions governing most debates in political theory; (7) the need to close the gap between political theory and international relations theory through a model of democracy in which citizens' political activity proceeds at multiple levels, including the local, state, nation-state, and cross-state levels; (8) a refiguration of the global political condition and the conventions of sovereignty, territoriality, and the state attached to it, taking the pluralist ideal beyond its American frontiers; (9) challenges to the dominant theories of cosmopolitanism in light of the new dangers and possibilities produced by the globalization of contingency; (10) a reassessment of the relation between nature and culture and a willingness to bring the new neuroscience to bear upon cultural and political theory; and (11) an acknowledgment that multimedia "micropolitics" are ubiquitous in a world incompletely colonized by "macropolitics." Attention to these problems, questions, strategies, and innovations can be found throughout the following essays.

In "A Pluralist Mind: Agonistic Respect and the Problem of Violence toward Difference," Morton Schoolman traces the evolution of Connolly's pluralist theory from his early to his recent work, mapping out its main lines of argument, differentiating its theoretical strategies, explicating many of its central concepts, and demonstrating how the strands of his new pluralism converge on what has become a central problem in contemporary political theory: how to eliminate violence toward difference within a democratic society.

Taking up the theme of "Connolly's Voice," Thomas Dumm approaches Connolly's work by inquiring into the role of voice in political theory and, more specifically, into how Connolly's work makes a series of associated claims regarding affect, embodiment, and pluralization that can be folded into a theory of the politics of voice. Examining influences on Connolly's work in the writings of Bennett, Deleuze, and Thoreau, and then tying those influences to such thinkers as Cavell and Lauterbach, Dumm suggests that Connolly's ethos of pluralization is as much a work of art as of philosophy, or that it usefully crosses the lines of those two genres of writing.

Bonnie Honig's "The Time of Rights: Emergent Thoughts in an Emergency Setting" begins with an appreciation of Connolly's position on paradox. For Connolly, the paradox of politics, in which the law presupposes the subjects it has yet to produce, does not legitimate law, nor does it unsettle democratic politics. Instead, it invites democratic theorists to rethink their assumption of linear time. Honig joins Connolly in that quest, noting however that his focus on rights more than on public goods, a focus that he shares with liberal theory, tends to support the linear temporality that he seeks to disturb. Nonetheless, rights can be reconceptualized along plural timelines, Honig argues. As Honig makes clear, Connolly has been misread as an advocate of speed over the slow pace of democracy called for by deliberative democrats and also by Sheldon Wolin. The choice is not between fast and slow tempos, however. The choice is among various possible responses to a world in which the gap between the fastest and slowest tempos of life has become enlarged. Drawing on Connolly, Arendt, Wittgenstein, and others, Honig develops a response of worldliness.

Roland Bleiker's "Visualizing Post-national Democracy" addresses one of Connolly's premier concerns in international politics: the role that cross-state, non-national movements can play in developing a postnational democratic ethos. Sharing the commitment to go beyond communitarianism and cosmopolitanism, and while questioning the relevance in an age of globalization of the place that state and territory have held on the democratic imagination, Bleiker extends Connolly's gestures to new social movements and begins to flesh out the role that transnational politics can play in democratic disturbance.

In "Uncertain Constellations: Dignity, Equality, Respect, and . . . ?" Stephen White argues that at the core of modern western political thought is a commitment to a constellation of three concepts: dignity, equality, and respect. Each person possesses a basic human dignity, and because of that each is owed equal respect. As we look forward into a century in which the topics of human rights and global justice take on ever-increasing salience, this constellation is destined to bear ever more weight. But as the burden becomes heavier, it also becomes increasingly obvious that there is an unsettling amount of contention and lack of clarity surrounding the core of dignity, equality, and respect. At least this is true of perspectives that do not ground dignity in a theistic account. White tries to show that alternative, nontheistic grounds, such as the figure of the autonomous agent, are not persuasive. To be convincing, a nontheistic account must do a better job of representing human subjection to finitude. Although not formulated explicitly as a response to this specific need, William Connolly's figuration of being in a world without God proves important to White's purposes.

George Kateb's "Prohibition and Transgression" examines themes that Connolly has engaged in several of his writings, most centrally in *The Augustinian Imperative: A Reflection on the Politics of Morality*, a decisive text for understanding Connolly's pluralism. Connolly admires and is fascinated by the moral psychology propounded in some of Augustine's main texts, especially his *Confessions* and *The City of God*. Kateb explores Connolly's insights, and also aims to determine what value the moral psychology of Augustine has for a secular reader. Like Connolly, Kateb believes that the value is great, but suggests that some of Augustine's work is dominated by a theological mission that may interfere with his genuine profundity. To this end, Kateb looks at Augustine's analyses of acts of transgression, distinguishes between kinds of transgressions, and endeavors to decide which kinds Augustine identifies as crucial in the acts that he analyzes. He also discusses other kinds of transgressions, several of which play some part in Augustine's analyses.

In "Radicalizing Democratic Theory: Social Space in Connolly, Deleuze, and Rancière," Michael Shapiro reads Connolly in conjunction with Jacques Rancière and Gilles Deleuze, all in the context of literature by Michelle Cliff and Toni Morrison, among others, to problematize the boundaries of the political and the social. For Shapiro, each author offers critical purchase on the commitments that underpin social space in general, and the possibility of democratic social space in the United States in particular. With each seeing the social as an arena of discord out of which stable arrangements are made, Shapiro highlights the different ways that each reintroduces contingency as a precondition for what Connolly understands to be an agonistic, multidimensional pluralism.

Kathy Ferguson's "Theorizing Dyslexia with Connolly and Haraway" draws on Connolly's *Neuropolitics: Thinking, Culture, Speed* to put Connolly's new pluralism into creative conversation with Donna Haraway.

She does so to show how the dichotomy of nature and culture can be problematized and transgressed. Highlighting a number of commonalities between Connolly and Haraway, especially their commitment to questions of spatiality, complexity, mobility, and affect in the biosocial domain, Ferguson draws them into a reflection on how "learning disabilities" can be approached differently when one is committed to retheorizing the relations of body, brain, and culture.

In "Sovereignty and the Return of the Repressed," Wendy Brown argues that the reasons why the practice and concept of nation-state sovereignty emerged in the early modern West were, *inter alia*, to contain two other forms of power—the economic and the political. This containment, Brown proposes, occurs through the articulation and the sovereignty of the political, an autonomy and sovereignty that are mutually reinforcing. When in late modernity nation-state sovereignty is eroded, Brown maintains, theological and economic powers are resurgent as political forces—capital and theological politics are decontained, as the house of the political in nation-state sovereignty is weakened. In her view, one "progressive" response to this condition has involved attempted reassertion of the sovereignty of the political, a response that she attributes to Connolly, Étienne Balibar, Jürgen Habermas, and Michael Hardt and Antonio Negri. Brown critically engages this response for the problematic conceit of autonomy that it recuperates, and the failure to reckon with the theological and economic powers that it represents.

James Der Derian's "Becoming Connolly: Critique, Crossing Over, and Concepts" offers a personal and synoptic account of how Connolly's work, in the form of personal interventions and written texts, both reflected and influenced the turn to critical social theory in the study of international relations from the 1980s onward. Understanding Connolly's work as an exemplar of the crossover between political theory and international relations, Der Derian recounts how his prescience with regard to the relationship between language, discourse, and sovereignty in the field—which questioned the fundamentalism of mainstream theory and neoconservative practice in the era of permanent emergency and homeland security—helped to reset key terms and drew a critical response from the mainstream.

In our final essay, "Identity, Difference and the Global: William Connolly's International Theory," David Campbell draws together Connolly's many and varied contributions to international political theory to show how the global condition has been pivotal to Connolly's work. Focusing in particular on the problematic of identity\difference and the way Connolly's refiguration of this problematic recasts our understanding of the state, sovereignty, and the international, Campbell emphasizes how Connolly challenges the either/or logic that has plagued international politics, and demonstrates that neither the current condition nor future possibilities are best understood by favoring one side of the dichotomy over the other. The result is a commitment to contestation, negotiation, and struggle rather than resignation, fantasy, or flight.

Our interview with William Connolly, following these essays, is devoted partly to issues considered in this book and partly to dimensions of his thought that extend beyond the parameters of the work collected here. The interview offers new insights into how the parts of Connolly's political theory speak to each other.

This collection of essays should not be confused with a *Festschrift*, except in the sense that every critical work honors its subject. As will become evident from the arguments presented here, the intent is to explicate and evaluate the contribution to democratic pluralism made by a theorist who engages arguments at the center of political science and political theory. Our interest is to push Connolly on many fronts. Perhaps we have made some progress.

We began developing this collection of essays in the fall of 2005 and the work, which has been shared between us, has been all the more enjoyable and instructive for the enthusiastic participation of our contributors. All of us are grateful to William Connolly for his participation in the interview and the example set by his work.

NOTES

1 William E. Connolly, *Political Science and Ideology* (New York: Atherton, 1967), and *The Bias of Pluralism* (New York: Atherton, 1969).

2 William E. Connolly, *The Terms of Political Discourse* (Lexington, Mass.: D. C. Heath, 1974; 2nd edn Princeton: Princeton University Press, 1983; 3rd edn 1993).

3 With Michael Best, *The Politicized Economy* (Lexington, Mass.: D. C. Heath, 1976).

4 Ibid., 28.

5 Connolly, *The Terms of Political Discourse*; *Politics and Ambiguity* (Madison: University of Wisconsin Press, 1987); *Identity \ Difference: Democratic Negotiations of Political Paradox* (Ithaca: Cornell University Press, 1991; enlarged with new essay, "Confessing Identity\Belonging to Difference," Minneapolis: University of Minnesota Press, 2002); *The Augustinian Imperative: A Reflection on the Politics of Morality*, ed. with an introd. by Morton Schoolman (Newbury Park, Calif.: Sage, 1993; repr. Lanham, Md.: Rowman and Littlefield, 2002); *The Ethos of Pluralization* (Minneapolis: University of Minnesota Press, 1995); *Why I Am Not a Secularist* (Minneapolis: University of Minnesota Press, 1999); *Neuropolitics: Thinking, Culture, Speed* (Minneapolis: University of Minnesota Press, 2002); *Pluralism* (Durham: Duke University Press, 2005).

A PLURALIST MIND:
AGONISTIC RESPECT AND THE PROBLEM
OF VIOLENCE TOWARD DIFFERENCE

Morton Schoolman

That generous and warm feeling for living Nature which flooded my heart with such bliss, so that I saw the world around me as a Paradise, has now become an unbearable torment, a sort of demon that persecutes me wherever I go . . . There is not one moment which does not consume you and yours, and not one moment when you yourself are not inevitably destructive; the most harmless walk costs the lives of poor, minute creatures; *one* step of your foot annihilates their painstaking constructions, and stamps a small world into its ignominious grave. My heart is worn out by this consuming power latent in the whole of Nature which has formed nothing that will not destroy its neighbor and itself . . . I see nothing but an eternally devouring monster.

—GOETHE, The Sorrows of the Young Werther

GOETHE'S THOUGHT OF AN INELIMINABLE violence plaguing life, a violence intrinsic to the human condition, haunts political theory after the Second World War. It invites reflection on the possibility that genocide may be the raison d'être of violence organized by states which, as dupes of generic human drives, act to destroy the "other" as they organize those drives to serve systemic ends. Following this reflection is unavoidably another. Perhaps all "ordinary" and everyday constructions and punishments of difference as otherness also may be driven by what is human, all too human. Political theorists drawn to this pessimism by the horror of holocaust could be drawn to theoretical schools under the spell of such thought as Goethe's and prone to the despair that it would induce. Thus was I drawn to the work of Max Horkheimer and of Theodor Adorno, whose *Dialectic of Enlightenment* seemed to support Goethe's claim.

Seeking antidotes to the disease of reason diagnosed in this great work, I have found several, though they do not abound. Two in particular offer relief, in different ways, from the violence toward difference that Hork-heimer and Adorno relentlessly track through their dark, genealogical history of reason. Both antidotes recognize violence that is not less embedded in modernity and not less ubiquitous than the violence that Goethe fears. Yet because neither antidote agrees with his premise that violence is the nature of human and nonhuman being, they both avoid the impotency attached to a trajectory of endless violence that is, according to Horkheimer and Adorno, aided and abetted by global capital without opposition. One antidote, an approach to the problem of violence toward difference that is thoroughly historical and political, is the politics and vision of a democracy of "agonistic respect" theorized by William Con-nolly. Agonistic respect promises an end to violence, though Connolly makes no such claim explicitly. A second approach to the problem of violence toward difference is developed in my own work, in which I turn to aesthetic theory to conceptualize a form of democratic individuality resis-tant to pressures to convert difference to otherness.[1] Having been influ-enced by George Kateb, my approach to violence perhaps is less political than Connolly's, indebted as it is to an ensemble of different democratic workings whose formative impact on the private sphere has been concep-tualized in Kateb's *The Inner Ocean: Individualism and Democratic Culture*,[2] a work whose contributions to my efforts I have gratefully recorded.[3]

As my engagement with this problem has been influenced by both theorists, I want to inquire now into Connolly's attack on the "second problem of evil," his apt formulation of what I refer to as the problem of violence toward difference. My inquiry can mark no more than a begin-ning, as few of Connolly's writings fail to bear on this problem. Neverthe-less, by considering three works appearing over somewhat more than two decades, *The Terms of Political Discourse*, *Identity \ Difference: Democratic Nego-tiations of Political Paradox*, and *The Ethos of Pluralization*,[4] we can arrive at an understanding of Connolly's distinctive approach to the problem of vio-lence toward difference and of his thought of how democracy can erect barriers to this evil. Of the three works considered, I will devote special attention to the earliest, *The Terms of Political Discourse*. While it is not less well known than the others, its relationship to Connolly's subsequent work is often underappreciated.

As I proceed, I want to illuminate what I believe will be one of Connolly's most important, intensely disputed contributions to modern political theory. At the center of his concept of agonistic respect lie, I will propose, two normative commitments difficult to reconcile. An ethical commitment running throughout his work, the abolition of violence toward difference, is the value for which agonistic respect appears largely to have been conceived. At the same time, we find a normative commitment of another kind, an "allegiance" to the liberal democratic subject, which Connolly esteems for its modern achievements but also knows to be responsible for the violence to which he is opposed. To honor both commitments, Connolly does not discard but revises the liberal agent. These two tasks require theoretical approaches that resist the alliance he must forge among them. "Contestation," the approach that Connolly develops continuously throughout his work, seems to have been brought into a delicate balance with his later attention to genealogy and deconstruction. For the latter two approaches that he adopts to attack the subject's violence toward difference also threaten his qualified allegiance to the liberal agent for which the first approach provides justification. Through his concept of agonistic respect and the twin normative commitments that it entails, Connolly crystallizes a dilemma in various forms confronting radical liberal democratic theorists. To act in good faith and rid themselves of the violence toward difference perpetrated by its agent, must political theorists reject the subject who is liberalism's founding condition and so retire liberalism as well? Or, to pose Connolly's dilemma in a different form for political theorists who already have parted with modern liberalism and its subject, can the achievements of liberalism be preserved once its subject is discarded? Connolly's work answers both questions.

In the argument that follows, I hope that precious connections will emerge between cultivating a sensibility to violence toward difference, a liberal democratic ethos, and a pluralist form of thinking from which both are inseparable. As I hope to show, Connolly's pluralism is a model of how these connections are formed and become the measure of a pluralist mind, which surmounts Goethe's despair.

PLURALIST THINKING: CONTESTATION

Pluralism and pluralist theory have been at the forefront of Connolly's critical attentions since his first book in 1967, *Political Science and Ideology*, which just two years later was followed by a collection of essays entitled

The Bias of Pluralism.[5] Both works remain important for their close critical examination of the ideological dimensions of political science, specifically the methodological assumptions and practices of its logical empiricism, intensely debated during the first three decades of political science after the Second World War. They remain equally noteworthy for his effort to politicize political science by pushing it to expand its concept of what counts as politics. So little in mainstream political science has changed since then that neither work has aged.

Despite the continuing relevance of these early works,[6] the appropriate place to launch a discussion about Connolly's pluralist theory, the pluralistic character of his political thought, and indeed the pluralism of his thinking generally, is with *The Terms of Political Discourse*, an influential and award-winning book that remains in print more than thirty years after its publication in 1974.[7] Importantly, it introduces the concept at the nucleus of Connolly's work in every successor publication. "Contestation"—or its original formulations, "contestability" and "essentially contested concepts"—is the concept through which Connolly develops pluralist theory. It is also the distinguishing feature of his thinking, his *quality of mind*. If we find a model of pluralist theory in Connolly's work, it is because contestation first models how to think pluralistically. Hence my distinction and the pertinence of the relation between pluralist theory and a pluralist mind.

Language and the Concept

The Terms of Political Discourse was written in the wake of developments in linguistic philosophy that had begun to influence political theorists. Connolly's approach to language bore very little of the trademark rationalism that later would complicate some linguistically informed political thought, such as Habermas's theory of communicative action. Connolly's interest lay, for example, not in universal properties attributed to language and linguistic performance but in culturally configured linguistic meaning, the ways that meaning comes to fill out our concepts and is shaped by the politics that constitute the rules governing conceptual application.

Further developing an argument made by the philosopher W. B. Gallie, Connolly argues that conceptual meaning inhabits "several dimensions," is expressed as a "broad range of criteria," and exhibits "multiple tendencies" and "heterogeneous elements." In a word, for Connolly the meanings embodied in our language are "plural." Connolly adopts a precise term to describe conceptual meaning. Concepts, all concepts, are formed as "clusters" of other concepts, which is to say that concepts are "relational." No concept can be clarified without reference to other concepts, other meanings, of which it is composed. Cluster concepts group concepts in ways that define our actions and practices. "Politics," to cite one of Connolly's examples, can refer to

1 Policies backed by the *legally binding authority* of government.

2 Actions that involve a *decision* or *choice* among *viable options*. . .

3 The sort of *considerations* or *motives* participants invoke in selecting one available option over others . . .

4 The extent to which decision outcomes affect the *interests, wishes,* or *values* of particular segments of the population . . .

5 The extent to which the outcomes of decisions are *intended* or at least *known* by the decision makers . . .

6 The *number* of people affected by the decision outcome and the *length of time* for which they are affected . . .

7 The extent to which *traditions* and *consensual expectations* of a people acknowledge the matter at hand to be one in which a public voice is legitimately involved . . .

8 The extent to which a policy or act becomes an *issue* as groups with different views about it range themselves on opposing sides to influence outcomes.[8]

Certainly this concept of politics is *complex* owing to the collection of concepts of which it is composed, though as these criteria are hardly exhaustive of how the meaning of politics is defined in the modern western world Connolly's point is that politics is more complex still. Moreover, he further complicates such concepts by showing how each is rooted in more basic ideas belonging to culture and society. Along with the concepts that it groups, every concept of politics would also suppose some concept of agency, for instance, and of responsibility. And as the meanings of the concepts grouped in the cluster are also composites of yet other concepts, the meaning of politics is *open*. Complexity and openness, Connolly explains, are two of three essential characteristics of concepts that concern him, since they imply that for every dominant meaning and application of a concept, multiple—including radical—perspectives also are available to us. Even before taking up the third and decisive feature of concepts, we see that for Connolly concepts are wonderfully complex, composed as they are of internally related multiple layers and multiple channels of meaning traveling the length of a language formed by the breadths and depths of a culture and, as we shall see, its politics.

Complexity and openness convey the richness of the concepts at our disposal. As everything we say must be more meaningful than we know and intend, we must ask why the concepts that we use appear to us to mean less than their myriad dimensions and internal connections allow. Over the course of his works Connolly offers a series of answers to this question. For the moment we are interested in the one he proposes in *The Terms of Political Discourse*, the "appraisive" feature of concepts, the value we attach to the state of affairs that our concepts describe. "Concepts are typically *appraisive*," he explains, "in that to call something a 'work of art' or a 'democracy' is both to describe it, and to ascribe a value to it or express a commitment with respect to it."[9] While complexity and openness partially account for the interpretive possibilities that concepts possess, the appraisive feature of language explains why we use concepts in certain ways rather than others. More to the point and most importantly for Connolly's argument, how each of us values what concepts describe explains why we often employ concepts *differently*.

Complexity, openness, and the values we attach to what concepts refer to enable us to take our different meanings from concepts and apply them differently, to disagree about what concepts mean and how they ought to be applied, and to turn our disagreements into serious disputes about just such matters. In Connolly's words, to introduce the basic idea that he adopts from Gallie and develops in future works, when concepts are complex, open, and appraisive they can become "essentially contested."[10] As such, they can precipitate interminable conflict over their meaning and application. Contestation governs the terms of political discourse because they are structured in all the ways noted and hence conflict-ridden to their cores. To analyze the discourse of politics, now paraphrasing Connolly's argument and to get ahead of myself somewhat, is to engage the *politics* of discourse.

The Concept and the Norm

Why contests over the application of concepts arise, and why the discourse of politics is inescapably political, has to do with the work performed by value, the appraisive aspect of concepts. When states of affairs, institutions, behavior, beliefs, and practices are described conceptually, Connolly argues, they are being characterized "from one or more possible points of view," from the vantage points of "certain interests, purposes, or standards," from "moral" or, more generally, "normative" points of view. An intrinsic part of the skeletal structure of concepts is the normative commitments and rationales of those who use them, which influence how the concepts will be used. What does it mean to say that normative considerations influence how concepts are used? It means there is a formative connection between the criteria that make up a concept and the normative points of view from which the concept is used. Our normative perspectives help to shape the criteria that we fold into our concepts and consequently the meaning of that to which our concepts are applied. As Connolly explains, if we were to "subtract" or "exorcise" the evaluative point from our concepts, we would lose our underlying reasons for *describing* things as we do, we could not determine if concepts correspond to situations that are new and unforeseen, and our concepts would fall into disuse. In effect, if we were deprived of the normative reasons for "grouping" criteria together we could neither conceptualize nor make judgments.

Once the normative point of view and the role that it plays in conceptualization are foregrounded, the implications of Connolly's argument come into view. If the beliefs and values that we hold guide how we define and apply complex and open concepts, then we have only to consider how different our norms may be to grasp how differently we can use the same concepts. Our normative perspectives may move us to adopt or reject the dominant meaning of political terms, and the prevailing meaning can be revised if, upon reflection, sufficient numbers alter their values, commitments, or rationales. Accordingly, conceptual debates are at bottom normative conflicts and often, as we shall see, political conflicts. To this point, the resolution of conceptual disputes appears intimately related to whether such disputes can be resolved at the normative and political level, and to what would be involved for normative and political agreement to be reached.

Through this argument we gain insight into Connolly's *form* of thinking. To speak of how our normative points of view influence the ways we "group" conceptual criteria for the purpose of applying concepts is to say that norms shape how potentially inclusive and exclusive our thinking is. By insisting on the *contestability* of concepts at the normative level at which thinking itself is organized, by insisting on the contestability of norms as the heart of the contestability of thought, Connolly *pluralizes* thinking to the extent that it is possible to pluralize—posit and contest—values. With the thesis of essentially contested concepts we glimpse a contingent world governed by an ethic considerate of *the pluralization of life in all its normative forms*, the ontological starting point from which Connolly never wavers. "Essentially contested concepts" is an early expression of the ethical sensibility animating the later idea of a democracy of "agonistic respect" for which it helps to prepare the foundation.

Not all concepts are contested, though all are potentially contestable and may be contested as circumstances and normative points of view allow. Connolly adopts the term "imperfectly shared" to distinguish between concepts that are more or less likely to be contested. Concepts circulating through our ordinary and political discourse are shared, albeit partly or "imperfectly," in that their underlying normative points of view and thus the criteria grouped with these concepts vary among users. Concepts that appear settled and uncontroversial—conventions, for example—possess criteria nearly all of which are shared widely—less imperfectly—by a large number who agree on how they are to be applied. This is to say that with regard to such conventions normative points of view are shared as well. Unlike sedimented conventions, many of the concepts that we use are shared more imperfectly. Greater differences in normative perspectives and conceptual criteria characterize these concepts. With the notion of "imperfect sharing" we move to the center of what Connolly understands politics to be. As he puts it, "Central to politics . . . is the ambiguous and relatively open-ended interaction of persons and groups who share a range of concepts . . . imperfectly and incompletely. Politics involves a form of interaction in which agents adjust, extend, resolve, accommodate, and transcend initial differences within a context of partly shared assumptions, concepts, and commitments. On this reading, conceptual contests are central to politics; they provide the space for political interaction."[11]

It is easy to see why Connolly is not content to entertain contests over the terms of political discourse as that which precedes politics. Since normative differences are already inscribed in the concepts we use, contestation of the values that are entailed by concepts, and that precipitate struggles over the terms of political discourse, is a first battleground without which there would be no further political battles; for it is the terms of political discourse that set the parameters for politics. How could political reform proceed without terms to allow their users to articulate the need and pressure for political reform? How could such terms emerge without a struggle over what is meant by the term democratic, or constitutional, or just, or racism, or reform, or a struggle over the meaning of politics itself? If the terms of political discourse are defined by narrow conceptions of what counts as political, by a conception that fails to recognize corporations or religious groups as political actors, for example, would the political influence of corporations and religious organizations not operate beyond the reach of political checks and challenges? Politics itself would be constrained by the concepts that govern us.

If the *politics* of contesting *concepts* or *terms* appears somewhat obscure, it would be helpful to recall the earlier mentioned point that political discourse is rooted in a society's cultural beliefs and understandings. This relationship between politics and culture is axiomatic in Connolly's argument, as evidenced by claims of the following sort that he often reiterates. "The web of concepts a populace shares *expresses* in its network of differentiations their most fundamental ideals, standards, and conflicts."[12] Here Connolly lines up with Charles Taylor, Peter Winch, Alasdair MacIntyre, and others who agree that concepts held by the members of a society partially constitute their actions and practices. Yet Connolly's claim is not only that concepts constitute actions and practices. Concepts, in part, constitute *a form of life*. What could be more clearly political than the concepts around which our forms of life are constructed? Where the concepts that constitute a form of life are contested, as occurs in every challenge to the dominant terms of political discourse, dimensions of the form of life itself are disturbed. The range of a concept's criteria and the normative points of view that organize its criteria into the dominant political discourse allow for political perspectives more and less imperfectly shared, more and less radical. And these political perspectives are all the more radical the more the challenges to the dominant terms of political discourse contest those concepts that constitute a form of life.

The Norm and Its Repression

Connolly engages in contestation at two levels. Importantly, he understands both levels of contestation to have the same "foundation," though I do not mean this in the "foundationalist" sense, as will become evident.

At the level of academic discourse, he pursues a critique of the epistemological claims and methodological approaches of empirical political science. Informed by his views on language, such critiques become staples of
his future works that in part are designed to unmask the anti-pluralist
tendencies of the social sciences. "Operationalism," one of the cardinal
methodological approaches developed by the social sciences and relied
upon in empirical investigations, is among the examples discussed in *The
Terms of Political Discourse* of how political science prescribes epistemic
practices that artificially delimit political discourse, depoliticize debate,
and restrain political change.

Political scientists' effort to rid operationalism of bias by assuming a
distinction between normative and descriptive statements is blind to the
normative points of view inherent in concepts underpinning the actions
that they analyze. Once the normative points of view belonging to concepts are explicated, as Connolly does in *The Terms of Political Discourse* with
"interest," "power," "responsibility," and "freedom," so-called descriptive
concepts are proven to be "evaluative" as well, and the distinction collapses between normative and descriptive statements, operational and
nonoperational concepts. If political scientists' claims to value-free research were to be honored, only concepts defined by operational criteria
that foregrounded empirically manageable definitions would be included.
Not only would the ineliminable normative orientations of those concepts be rendered irrelevant to debate, but concepts falling beyond the
narrows of empirical measurement would also be excluded from contestation, along with the contrary normative position that each housed. If
contestation is reduced to what is neutral, the contestation between normative points of view is defused and the forms of political action that
their alternative conceptualizations make possible remain buried. In addition to the fallacious dichotomy of normative versus descriptive, Connolly
contests a range of other key assumptions instrumental to maintaining
the positivist fiction of a value-neutral political science. To mention one
other, he shows how the multiple criteria associated with cluster concepts
belie the formulation of pure analytic concepts or, what amounts to the
same thing, limit concepts to agreed-upon operational criteria. Criteria,
Connolly concludes, have neither a purely analytic nor a purely synthetic
relationship to their concepts.[13]

Connolly also calls attention to the dependency of political science on its repression of normative perspectives. Since the application of concepts can be revised continually in relation to revisions in normative points of view and the organization of conceptual criteria with which these revisions can be accompanied, the periodic revision of concepts illuminated by the thesis of essentially contested concepts requires political science to revise the theories in which those concepts are embedded. If for political science the opening to revision at the theoretical level were not less undesirable than the opening to reform in the political arena, then the practices that ensure theoretical closure help to ensure closure in politics as well, which in turn legitimizes the theoretical claims of political "science."

Connolly's critique of operationalism moves us closer to appreciating the deepest significance of the "normative point of view." As the vantage point from which concepts are applied, the normative point of view is nothing less than the point of view from which actions spring. As Connolly summarizes the connection between concepts and actions, "To understand the political life of a community one must understand the conceptual system within which that life moves; and therefore *those concepts that help to shape the fabric of our political practices necessarily enter into any rational account of them.*"[14] By way of the normative point of view embedded in concepts, we discover that his critique of positivist political science and its repression of normative points of view necessarily leads us to actors and their actions, the *second level* on which contestation occurs for Connolly. Like the contestation of concepts constructed by social scientists, the contestation of concepts belonging to everyday actors rests on the foundation of ordinary language, the foundation for both levels of contestation. This common foundation blurs the empirical distinction, which it shows to be artificial, between the technical terms constructed by social scientists to measure, explain, and predict action and the concepts that inform the everyday actions of ordinary political actors.

Thus insofar as the contestation of concepts is directed to the normative point of view from which conceptual criteria are organized and applied, the contestation of social science concepts is not fundamentally dissimilar to the contestation of ordinary conceptual understandings from which the actions of a community and its actors flow. Put differently, Connolly's critique of the social sciences leads to political engagement with actors at the level of their norms, at the level of their concepts as they are formed and applied by means of their norms, or at the level of their terms of political discourse. This engagement is relevant not only to social science but to everyday politics and the possibilities that it offers for political action. Contestation and politics are inseparable, and contestation measures the possibilities for political engagement as the expanse of the concepts through which we determine the meaning of our world. Politics could not be deeper or broader than the parameters outlined by contestation, a characteristic of Connolly's concept of politics that will remain throughout his work and is indebted to the pluralistic character of contestation. Contestation and its politics will become our evidence that Connolly's thinking is shamelessly hospitable to opposing schools of thought, which will be proved by his later engagement with Nietzsche and Foucault. "Contestation" derives from the analytic philosophical tradition but is not reducible to that tradition. If it is reducible at all, it is to normative points of view and their contingencies, which exceed every tradition.

Social Scientist \ Citizen Provocateur

Unlike critiques of the conceptual practices developed by the social science community, Connolly's do not intend only the reform of its epistemological assumptions and methodological approaches. By modifying the distinctions between descriptive and normative vocabularies, analytic and synthetic statements, operational and nonoperational concepts, technical terms and the terms of ordinary discourse, Connolly positions himself to revise a final distinction, arguably the most important of all.

With the former modifications Connolly has also demonstrated that the distinction between the social scientist and other participants in the political process who serve as objects of investigation is never sharp. Once he has shown that concepts through which actions are *understood* are connected to concepts and norms that the authors of those actions *already accept*, Connolly has shown that social scientists who understand actions at a theoretical level have made *contact* with the authors of those actions on a practical level, if only tacitly. Reestablishing contact between the social scientist who studies action and the participant who engages in action, between theory and practice, is entailed by analyses that make explicit the normative perspectives implicit in the concepts underlying actions. Another way to express this is to say that explanations of actions that reveal the norms in which actions are rooted are not so much propositions *about* participants as accounts of actions warranted somehow by participants' normative points of view. Explanations offer accounts for action that "touch" those that would be offered by the participants themselves. What this means is that aside from the technical cast of explanations, conceptualizations of action are not *essentially* different for social scientists and participants.

Overcoming the divide—revising the distinction—between the social scientist and the participant, between theory and practice, is not completed by illuminating the point of view held by each. To make explicit the normative standpoint implicit in the concepts underlying participants' actions is potentially to offer us a virtual awareness to which we can accede by making our own norms more explicit. For Connolly, explanation of action is intended to make us more reflective about how and why participants are implicated in an array of actions, practices, and institutions—or, in a phrase, in a way of life. Indeed social scientists cannot make action-relevant claims about the normative points of view of others, Connolly insists, without also becoming reflective about *their own* normative standpoint in relation to those whose actions are being interpreted. According to Connolly's argument, it is no wonder that conflicts among social scientists over which concepts offer valid explanations for action become so intense. *For to take a position on the validity of a concept is to take a position on the norm embedded in it.* It is to become implicated in the politics in which the norm is set. As debates over normative points of view, conceptual debates are necessarily political.

It now is clear why Connolly's elucidation of the similarities between social scientists and the participants whose actions they conceptualize abridges the difference between their roles. As the normative point of view is not less essential to conceptual accounts of action and the conceptual contests to which they give rise than to those engaged in actions, the performative roles of social scientists and actors are defined by the same normative concerns that define their roles as citizens. What sometimes distinguishes the social scientist from the ordinary citizen is the theoretical self-consciousness about norms embedded in actions that concerted attention to these theoretical matters *can* afford. And, to be sure, privileged insights into actions can be shared with those with whom the social scientist imperfectly shares the norms themselves.

Connolly goes so far as to argue that it is the responsibility of the social scientist to share such insights and publicly stake out a position on the concepts proposed to account for the political actions of a community or its participants. "If the understanding of conceptual contests in politics elaborated here is at all correct, then the social scientist has an obligation to *endorse* those ideas that he thinks would help to nourish a politics of responsibility were they to be incorporated into the practices of our polity. One can and must debate just what interpretations of key social and political concepts are worthy of such endorsement, but to deny any intellectual responsibility in this area is to falsify the connection between such contests and the constitution of social and political life."[15] If Connolly's claim is still controversial, it is precisely because it contests the norms embedded in the performative stance of social scientists and because it presses a norm of responsibility upon them. By its mere articulation, in other words, Connolly's claim is proved, for the controversy it would provoke among social scientists would surround *which* values inform their work, not whether values do. And to flush out the normative points of view belonging to theoretical practitioners is to invite the participation of an audience that includes citizens affected by norms endorsed by others. Connolly does not mean to exaggerate the influence of the social scientist, whose conceptual contests, he acknowledges, do not necessarily influence politics. Neither, however, does he allow the social scientist's limited influence to "justify lack of attention to the political import of the conceptual contours commonly accepted within his profession and society."[16]

Indeed, in Connolly's estimation this limited influence demands reassessment in light of these connections between conceptual revision and political change, thought and action in politics. Recognition that accepted revisions in the terms of our political discourse can influence changes in political life, and that proposals for such revisions provoke reflections on political actions, practices, and institutions leading to political change, focus attention on those who study politics. It focuses attention on the relation between theory and practice, the social scientist as theorist and the theorist as citizen.

Connolly considers two types of relationships that social scientists can forge with the community at large.[17] Social scientists can immerse themselves in political phenomena of interest, conscientiously adhering to a passive-receptive, "indicative" mode of interaction geared to interpreting and describing the prevailing definitions of political action and the rules governing their application. Or the social scientist might pursue a more deliberate, "transactional" mode of interaction, again becoming immersed in the fabric of social life to learn which conceptual meanings, rules, and applications hold sway, though with the intent of contesting some of these understandings to alter the behavior that they enable. Beneath the surface, however, there is less difference between the indicative and transactional modes than there appears. Merely through explanatory claims interpreting actions in certain ways rather than others, Connolly points out, the indicative mode would inadvertently support the political orientations of some participants over others. If the analysis only were to be heard, even the passivity of the indicative mode would not be immune to changing the understandings and possibly the behavior of those under study. Such is the power of conceptualization to provoke reflection.

In light of this connection between conceptual revision and political change, what is true for the social scientist is not less true for anyone who, as Connolly expresses it, "seeks to comprehend the depth grammar of concepts" that enter into political life. Anyone interested in the normative perspectives according to which our concepts are sculpted and applied, and is not shy about engaging the terms of our political discourse, will provoke reflections and perhaps influence the actions that shape political life. Actually, in Connolly's view it is misleading to distinguish cleanly between reflection on political life and actions that reconstitute it. Any claims about the terms of political discourse that find their way into the mainstream of political life or into any of its minor tributaries will foster new perspectives by thematizing norms and their conceptual terms from which action can spring. By enabling actions that were not yet possible before new perspectives on old terms were provoked, interpretations of the ordinary and everyday as well as theoretical variety anticipate and to an extent already constitute changes in political life and the contests from which they evolve. What I mean to stress is that each step in the evolution of conceptualization is a step in the evolution of political life.

This is not to say that for Connolly conceptual revision is sufficient to produce political change. It is to insist that conceptual revision is a precondition for political change that prefigures it by alleging its necessity, suggesting its possibility, and opening opportunities and inferring strategies for change. Connolly's many examples from the political life of the modern democratic world bear out this plurality of ways in which conceptual revision and political change are connected. To cite one, his consideration of "institutional racism" highlights the connection between revisions in the terms of our political discourse and the prefigured political changes that ensue. The claim that private and public institutions systematically discriminated against racial minorities was an interpretation of racism contesting established understandings that had underscored *individual* responsibility for racism. No sooner did the new concept of institutional racism enter into political life than members of the polity could not avoid considering the charge, even as they resisted it, that institutions in which they were implicated and that they believed to be legitimate unwittingly promoted inequality and lagged behind democratic progress achieved in other quarters of society. They were compelled to entertain the possibility that reform should be introduced through political strategies that solicited their support. If they were to abstain from involvement they *now* ran the risk of being implicated in racist beliefs from which they thought they were free. "Institutional racism" exemplifies how reflection on established concepts can call into question long-standing practices in which everyone is implicated, where reform supposes political action that depends upon antecedent conceptual revision. Politics—in this instance political struggle surrounding claims about discriminatory policies for which institutions are responsible—is bound up with struggles over the application and revision of familiar concepts.

Politics and the Limits of Reason

Why politics takes the forms that it does is better understood in light of the connections between contestation and political change. Since political change flows in part from competing interpretations of imperfectly shared concepts rooted in differences among normative points of view, we understand Connolly's argument that "ambiguous and relatively open-ended" interaction is "central to politics." Without this conceptually ambiguous and open-ended character, it would be difficult to grasp why politics entails, as he explained, "a form of interaction in which agents adjust, extend, resolve, accommodate, and transcend initial differences within a context of partly shared assumptions."[18] So long as concepts are contestable—so long as there persist variations in the conceptual under-

standings held by actors—politics is the "sphere of the unsettled."[19] Political closure, as the conclusion to political struggle that gives birth to or
prevents political change, will often be temporary and its terms again
eligible for future contestation. No terms of political discourse are potentially exempt from contestation and the politics that follow. The positive
results of change that end contest for some are often accompanied by
negative results that reignite contest for others. Only sedimented habits,
the exercise of power, or the negotiations of a public ethos foreclose
contest.

My reconstruction of Connolly's argument has stressed the ways its
major components define politics. Politics is as pervasive as the imperfectly shared concepts constituting a way of life. Essentially contested
concepts are the essence of the political. Narrowing attention to politics
and the political, however, favors the imperfect character of imperfectly
shared concepts, specifically the differences between normative points of
view and how normative differences work to group and apply conceptual
criteria differently. But what of the shared element of imperfectly shared
concepts? Politics and the actors engaged in political contest—citizens,
associations, elected officials, challengers for political office, the courts,
media, activists, and so forth—do not interact only from the standpoint
of what separates them. With regard to how political actors apply norms
of responsibility to institutional policies and processes, for example, Connolly contends that it "is partly because we share the pertinent norms of
responsibility *imperfectly* that contests arise with respect to such political concepts, and it is because we *share* these norms imperfectly that we
are provided with some common leverage for limiting the range within
which these contests can rationally proceed."[20]

Whatever else divides them, the conceptual dimensions of a political
dispute also offer its contestants shared criteria that provide "common
leverage" for settling disputes. Political disputes can be deferred to "a
common court of appeal"[21] that subjects the disagreement to "a measure
of rational control."[22] *Imperfectly* shared, essentially contestable concepts
are the soil for political contests. *Shared* imperfectly, partly, essentially
contestable concepts offer shared, rational grounds for resolving political
disputes. Why, then, are not all political disputes settled rationally by the
common courts of appeal that the partly shared conceptual features of
their contests make available? Depending on the concepts from which

political disputes arise, politics and reason will trade more or less dominant roles in determining how contests are played out and concluded. Yet
this does not mean that reason can be the *final* court of appeal (my term),
even though in political conflict it may regularly be a *common* court of
appeal. This distinction can be appreciated by allowing Connolly to elaborate on his earlier example of institutional racism.

Connolly asks us to suppose that a militant group of black activists
charges the leaders of public and private organizations with institutional
racism, intending that they be held culpable for policies with discriminatory consequences.[23] Responsibility is assigned not to individuals primarily, but to organizations, and to individuals in the roles that they are
mandated to assume by the bureaucratic logic of their organizations.
Insisting that they themselves are not implicated in institutional racism,
elites contest the militants' application of the term "racism," responding
that "it is inappropriate to hold an organization responsible for policy
consequences unintended by its members and only marginally subject to
their control."[24] The proposed conceptual revision is explosive politically
and precipitates political conflict. Disputes to this day persist over the
racial implications of organizational behavior. With every instance of
institutional racism tried in the courts and the press, the "introduction of
the idea into public discourse has shifted the burden of evidence away
from the blacks and toward the elites, and thus the balance of political
pressures has shifted too."[25]

In this context what is pertinent about the connection that Connolly
draws between conceptual revision and political change is not only how
the new concept of institutional racism leads through political victory to
an environment more sensitive to a form of discrimination that becomes
less defensible. In addition, political conflict could be waged with those
terms of political discourse that also were rationally constrained by the
power of the underlying ideas of agency and responsibility, ideas about
which there was already tacit agreement throughout society. Widespread
agreement that it is *agents* that are *responsible* for treating all equally limited the dispute to the question: In what sense can institutions be held responsible as agents for their actions? Agency and responsibility establish
the partly shared grounds without which this particular dispute could
neither erupt nor unfold within certain limited parameters.

To return full circle: although *shared*, agency and responsibility do not admit of one interpretation, for they are *imperfectly* shared, and so the resources that they offer for initiating and limiting contest can support more than one position to bring closure to the dispute they made possible. Partly shared concepts constitute a common court of appeal. Imperfectly shared concepts make politics the *final* court of appeal; in politics this is rare enough and always provisional, as political closures do not issue in perfectly shared concepts, which would be the condition for permanent resolution of contests over the terms of political discourse. As Connolly would say, "that's politics."[26]

IDENTITY AND THE DIFFERENCE IT MAKES

My concluding remarks on *The Terms of Political Discourse* appropriately belong to the opening considerations of Connolly's *Identity\Difference: Democratic Negotiations of Political Paradox*. To close the discussion of *The Terms of Political Discourse* before taking up *Identity\Difference* may convey the false impression that it represents a stage of Connolly's thought abandoned in future work. As I indicated at the outset, however, "contestation," first introduced in *The Terms of Political Discourse*, becomes Connolly's central theoretical concept and the primary support for a pluralist way of thinking and pluralist politics developed in all subsequent arguments.

Beyond introducing contestation, *The Terms of Political Discourse* anticipates *Identity\Difference* in other ways that establish continuity between them. In the new, sixth chapter of *The Terms of Political Discourse*, published in its revised 1983 (Princeton) edition, Connolly reflects on theoretical approaches that will help form the infrastructure of *Identity\Difference*, first published in 1991.[27] In the new preface to this second edition he describes its new chapter as a consideration of "affinities" with as well as "differences between the thesis of contestability and the *more relentless theory of deconstruction*" (my italics).[28] In *Identity\Difference* deconstruction will join contestation as the second of three approaches—genealogy is the third—that further pluralize Connolly's thinking. It is an approach that he subordinates to the others, a position whose hierarchical status I shall maintain is nevertheless controversial in his work. So although when *The Terms of Political Discourse* was first published in 1974 Connolly had not yet assimilated two thinkers who would later supplement the groundwork that its concept of contestation had prepared for *Identity \ Difference*, as his new preface makes clear in the second edition *The Terms of Political Discourse* contains "affinities" as well as "differences" with ideas that he later develops with the assistance of Nietzsche and Foucault.

What I am proposing is that a deeper appreciation of *The Terms of Political Discourse* will clarify the direction and implications of the work to come. With Connolly's assimilation of Nietzsche and Foucault in *Identity \ Difference*, its central ideas—the construction of identity through its relation to difference; the pressures to convert difference to otherness to ensure the certainty of identity; and the violence visited upon difference by its conversion to otherness—enable Connolly to think differently from the way he had in *The Terms of Political Discourse*. Although the difference between these works pushes Connolly's thought beyond the point reached in *The Terms of Political Discourse*, this difference is developed through a plurality of productive tensions already present in *The Terms of Political Discourse* to which Connolly explicitly drew attention in its new final chapter and preface.

"Core Ideas" and the "As Such"

Evidence for these tensions first appears in the original final chapter (chapter 5) of *The Terms of Political Discourse*. In the context of his analysis of institutional racism, Connolly works with a concept of reason having an ambiguous relationship to the deconstruction of transcendental claims to rationality. The legality of the concept of institutional racism and its widespread acceptance rested on a shift in meaning from individual to collective agency, and from individual to collective responsibility. Among the political consequences of contestation over institutional racism are these revisions of the concepts of agency and responsibility, forcing both to conform more closely to the ways institutions and organizations should operate in democratic societies. To avoid being implicated in discriminatory practices, individuals and organizations must meet new standards of responsibility. Yet contestation accomplishes more than this. By revising the imperfectly shared norms of agency and responsibility belonging to one era so that they become serviceable in the next, contestation will "infuse the norms of responsibility themselves more deeply into the political practices of modern society."[29] Now consider this idea against the backdrop of another. "Though the standards of responsibility vary within society and across societies, there is a *central core* to this idea, which seems to be embodied to some degree and in some spheres *in the life of every society*."[30] If we had separated this last claim from the one immediately preceding it, Connolly might be construed to endorse some version of rationalism or transcendentalism, which a societally ubiquitous central core to an idea suggests.

Taken as a whole, however, his argument does not support such an interpretation. Core ideas belonging to responsibility, agency, and other imperfectly shared concepts undergo revision and transformation through contestation, either from pressures brought to bear directly on these concepts or indirectly as unintended consequences of revising concepts with which they are related, such as power, freedom, and interest. By virtue of their political evolution, no concept stands in judgment of political practices as a *universal criterion*. What core there is to responsibility or agency embodied in all societies possesses *no normative power unmitigated by the plurality of forms that such concepts assume over time*. Contestation, as the periodic political revision of core ideas, works similarly to deconstructive critiques of the transcendental bases of conceptual frameworks. In safeguarding the *openness* of concepts' criteria of application, contestation is consistent with deconstruction's insistence on the *contingency* of concepts in which social understanding is embedded. This affinity between contestation and deconstruction implies that Connolly might part company altogether with the notion of a "central core to [an] idea found in the life of every society," which can be mistaken for rationalism or transcendentalism, as could his variations of this argument that there are normative "commitments to social life *as such*" and "conventions relative to social life *as such*."[31]

As we shall now see, Connolly does part company with the "central cores" and the "as such." When he does so, it is with qualifications that sustain the tensions in his relation to deconstruction. This development represents one of the most fertile properties of a pluralist mind: namely, how understanding politics in a democratic society that affirms pluralism requires contradictory theoretical orientations that cannot be reconciled completely.

Our Achievements, Our Allegiances, and the Internal to . . .

Unfashionable as they are in the wake of poststructuralism, the "core ideas" and the "as such" belonging to the original concluding chapter (chapter 5) of *The Terms of Political Discourse* performed important work.

Agency and responsibility, as the conceptual bases for contestations that raise, address, battle, negotiate, resolve, or fail to resolve political issues, are also the bases for revised social understandings and the evolving ground of democratic progress.

With Nietzsche and Foucault in mind in the new concluding chapter (chapter 6) of *The Terms of Political Discourse* (1983), Connolly agrees with his new interlocutors that agency, responsibility, and the subject that they in part constitute cannot be vested with epistemic privilege guaranteeing their necessity, rationality, or truth, their status as core ideas universally present in the life of every society. Not only are core concepts belonging to forms of social life refused such entitlements, but so are the forms of life themselves in which these core concepts are installed, the universality of which deconstruction and genealogy invalidate by revealing their constructed character. Without core concepts and the work they perform, what becomes of contestation and its politics? Although in *The Terms of Political Discourse* Connolly originally adopts but then discards the idea of universal core concepts because as social constructions they represent contingent forms of authority, he still retains agency, responsibility, and subjectivity on the grounds that they are our modern "achievements" and the preconditions for a far greater modern achievement, democratic life itself. Regarding the concept of the subject, he reminds us, "We take it to be an achievement because we know that those who have experienced the affirmative side of modern freedom, self-consciousness and citizenship (the subject at the level of political life), invariably seek to retain and extend this experience. Even Foucault's genealogies become exercises in self-consciousness particularly available to the modern self as subject. The subject is arguably an achievement in a second sense as well. Every way of life imposes some sort of order on the chaos and multiplicity which would otherwise prevail, and every way of life must therefore develop some means of setting and enforcing limits. The development of a subject-centered morality may turn out, when compared to other conceivable alternatives, to be the most salutary way to foster order through the consent and endorsement of participants."[32]

We see that Connolly values the subject and its morality, agents who consent to exercise power and take responsibility, because they value a modern world that rests, however precariously and problematically, upon these very achievements. Now here is what is decisive. Although they are relinquished as core ideas circulating as universals through every form of society, Connolly retains agency and responsibility out of his allegiance to the subject they presuppose, which also earns his allegiance for the values that this subject constructs and translates into an imperfectly shared, democratic way of life. Connolly *values* subjectivity, agency, and responsibility, for the *value*—the *rationality*—that they constitute *internal* to modern democracy. Agency and responsibility, subjectivity and modernity, are his allegiances because they are allegiances necessary to democracy, and democracy is an allegiance valued by those who have experienced it.

By replacing the universal rationality of core ideas with normative commitments internal to a democratic way of life, Connolly safeguards the politics of contestation. Internal to a way of life, achievements and allegiances, and the concepts that they represent around which democratic life revolves, are not a form of rationality insulated from the openness of conflicting interpretations. This openness is indispensable if these conflicts over normative points of view and the conceptual criteria that they organize and apply are to fuel the contestation through which our concepts and practices are revised and continue to be valued for the democratic form of life secured by them.

So it is Connolly's own normative point of view, his allegiance to democracy and the concepts anchoring it, concepts imperfectly shared and thus essentially contestable, that supposes an equally powerful allegiance to contestation as the means to foster social change. To be committed to democracy and its constellation of supporting concepts is to be committed to contestation, and vice versa. Because these allegiances entail and justify one another, none can be retired without retiring the others. It is but a short step to see that the reciprocal entailments and justifications belonging to the thesis of essentially contested concepts would set limits to deconstruction, for if contestation and democracy require one another, they require subjectivity.[33] Connolly arrives at this point precisely with his closing sentence of the new final chapter to *The Terms of Political Discourse*: "To show the subject to be a construction is not to render its deconstruction imperative."[34]

The Ambiguity of Our Achievements

Setting limits to deconstruction by normatively affirming the achievement of democracy and its requisite other achievements, Connolly's thesis of essentially contested concepts does not also encourage him to be sanguine about these achievements, even though they justify his allegiances. Contestation is inseparable from the idea that democratic life is critically self-reflexive. Tacitly, democracy understands itself to be a life lived essentially by way of deficits in citizens' underlying agreements—by way of imperfectly shared concepts—that precipitate its political conflicts. Democracy's intrinsic self-understanding is that it essentially involves contestation. From the perspective of *Identity \ Difference* in 1991, however, and perhaps even at the time of the revised edition of *The Terms of Political Discourse* in 1983, Connolly is not satisfied with how he developed contestation in the new chapter and preface of *The Terms of Political Discourse*. As of *The Terms of Political Discourse* (1983), contestation is not adequate as a thesis or as the source of democracy's critical self-reflection—that is, as a conceptual critique and revision at the philosophical level or as political critique and social change at the level of everyday, ordinary discourse.

With *The Terms of Political Discourse* (1983) we have seen that Connolly's thesis of essentially contestable concepts accomplishes three tasks. It justifies his commitment to democracy, frames the openness of critique as the rationality internal to democracy, and within this framework exempts from deconstruction, though not from contestation, certain conditions for modern democratic life, specifically subjectivity, agency, and responsibility, which contestation opens to revision. At the same time, the conditions for modern democracy set limits to deconstruction *only insofar* as they are achievements. When Connolly problematizes these achievements, will the conditions for democracy then *exceed* the limits of his framework within which contestation and its revisions regulate critique? Do subjectivity, agency, responsibility, and democratic life as a whole, for which they are requirements, become open to critical approaches that put these achievements at risk? How does Connolly problematize these achievements so that contestation can be allied with approaches that critically engage the inadequacies of modernity while affirming, as contestation and its revisions require, modernity's achievements?

Democracy and its requirements are achievements, Connolly contends in *The Terms of Political Discourse* (1983), but they are also *ambiguous* achievements. From the very beginning, as an achievement the modern democratic subject has been deeply implicated in the conversion of difference to otherness because of the ways it has been organized and ordered through the modern normative standards of agency and responsibility. Serving as a vehicle for the extension of disciplines over the self, subjectivity's construction of otherness has also incurred high costs to be borne by the self in its manifold democratic forms. As a subject, each self is vulnerable to a range of imperatives that compel it to discipline itself, to parse out the multiplicity of its being according to self-other antinomies that deprive it, with every deprivation of possibility that it imposes on its other, of its own possibilities for being.

By problematizing in these ways the achievements of democracy in *The Terms of Political Discourse*, Connolly is prepared to complicate his critical apparatus. In *Identity\Difference* Connolly inquires into the origins of the subject and the subject's vulnerabilities to discipline; into the sources and types of disciplinary imperatives to which the subject is vulnerable; into the manifold ways in which these imperatives and their disciplines are maintained; into how the imperatives can be relaxed and the disciplines on the subject loosened; and into how the violence toward otherness issuing from the alliance of subject, discipline, and imperative can be ameliorated or eliminated. Democracy, democratic states, and eventually the global arena of which they are a part become his sites of analysis and interrogation. Once having engaged Nietzsche and Foucault in *The Terms of Political Discourse*, Connolly can go on to develop the possibilities for contestation, precisely because the achievements valued by contestation not only set limits to deconstruction, but contained ambiguities that *created space* for genealogy and deconstruction too! Through contestation, genealogy, and deconstruction the pluralist mind will be able to arrive at that relation to difference-without-otherness that in *Identity\Difference* becomes the highest value in Connolly's pluralist theory. At that point, what distinguishes Connolly's pluralism above all will be evident, though it has been present since the beginning of our discussion. By pressing theories and practices to become ever more inclusive, contestation *pluralizes* thought and action to affirm pluralism not simply as a mere fact of existence but as its highest ideal and aspiration and the highest ideal and aspiration of the democratic form of life that it overlaps.

A DEMOCRACY OF AGONISTIC RESPECT, POLITICS, AND VIOLENCE TOWARD DIFFERENCE

Contestation, Connolly's mode of critique, and the politics that it entails, occupy the foreground of his work following *The Terms of Political Discourse*. I repeat myself here to offset any impression that may be conveyed by Connolly's arguments since *The Terms of Political Discourse* that con-

testation is abandoned for other critical approaches and their theorists—
for genealogy and deconstruction, Nietzsche and Foucault, in *Identity\
Difference* and *The Ethos of Pluralization*; for cinema, memory, time, and
neuroscience, Bergson and Deleuze, the neuroscientists Antonio Demas-
sio and Joseph LeDoux in *Why I Am Not a Secularist* and *Neuropolitics: Thinking, Culture, Speed*, works that I cannot take up here.[35] At times Connolly's
own guidelines to his work encourage such impressions. In *Identity\
Difference*, for example, he reports that on problems that he has begun
to investigate and that will continue to receive attention, he owes his
"most salient debts to Nietzsche and Foucault."[36] Impressions of this
sort are balanced by qualifications, as when he explains that Nietzsche
and Foucault each serve "as a complement and corrective to the other," or
that even so, "a critical extrapolation from this combination" is yet required. These guidelines speak implicitly to Connolly's avoidance, peculiar to a plural style of thinking, of privileging any thinkers. And occasionally he offers self-descriptions that anticipate his interpreters' skewed
impressions on his critical approaches, as when he warns us in *Identity\
Difference* that "the strategies of deconstruction are not actively pursued
here."[37]

For certain, after the revised edition of *The Terms of Political Discourse*
(1983), and beginning with *Politics and Ambiguity* (1987),[38] contestation is
allied with genealogy, though genealogy does not reach its full theoretical
and political potential in Connolly's work until *Identity\Difference*. Contestation also keeps company with his critiques of opposed theoretical
frameworks whose key concepts, he shows, form interdependent, anti-
nomial constructions resting on shared sets of ontological assumptions
whose contingency is masked naturalistically. Against these frameworks
he proposes alternative ontological assumptions whose contingency he
highlights, and on the basis of this ontology he projects alternative social
arrangements that map a qualitative change in relations between identity
and difference. As critical methodologies, Connolly's interrogation of the
interdependent character of opposed theoretical frameworks, his exposure of the naturalization of their underlying assumptions and how it
suppresses their contingency and permits the illusion of their transcendental relation to the frameworks that they ground, and his insistence on
the contestability of such critiques all resemble strategies of deconstruction. So although deconstruction is not his theoretical *focus*, which is what

I take him to mean when he points out that he does not actively pursue deconstruction, I will describe as deconstructive certain features of Connolly's critical apparatus as it begins to evolve with *Identity \ Difference*.

I do this for three reasons. First, I want to differentiate among three approaches that circulate as pluralizing forces in Connolly's thinking. They are pluralizing with respect not only to the different modes of critical analysis that they exemplify, but with regard to competing sets of insights, conclusions, and possibilities that can be drawn from each. I will distinguish among the work performed by contestation, genealogy, and "deconstruction," all the while placing the last in quotation marks as a reminder that Connolly is not actively pursuing deconstruction, though his work and deconstruction possess commonalities.[39] Second, by fleshing out the work of each critical approach along with the insights, conclusions, and possibilities to which each leads, we can appreciate the distinctive contribution to democratic theory made by Connolly and the pluralist mind. Finally, we shall also be in a position to understand that Connolly uses contestation as a generic term of critical analysis and how it comes to include within it other critical approaches for which as a whole he uses contestation interchangeably. Contestation, in other words, is one critical approach among three, though it is also the concept for Connolly's critical enterprise as a whole. As a result, contestation itself is not less contestable than any other term of political discourse, because it is fundamental to contestation as a whole that the plural forms assumed by Connolly's thinking are always exceeded by the pluralizing nature of thinking itself.

"Deconstruction"

By taking up Connolly's critique of the opposing frameworks of individualist and collectivist theories, we begin to trace the work performed by contestation in both senses just distinguished, and to see how pluralist thinking leads to the conception of a democracy of "agonistic respect." As a starting point, Connolly focuses on the challenges that people face in a late modern world whose dominant institutions and practices tacitly revolve around the idea of the "death of God." Deeply inscribed in the recent history of western society and an operative cultural presumption, although one resisted widely and often in fundamentalist terms, the death of God threatens to deprive people of theological assurances for

which contemporary political theories, of which individualist and collectivist theories are examples, provide compensations.

Contemporary political theories' compensations exploit the secular
view pervading the modern individual's cultural subconscious of how life
is related to death, which Connolly refers to as the "serene phenomenology of life and death," or the "serene phenomenology of freedom and
mortality," or "freedom and finitude."[40] As compensations for an afterlife
that modernity renders dubious, serene phenomenology lays ever-greater
stress on the rewards to be expected in a lifetime. It does so by emphasiz-
ing a string of implicit understandings attached to an affirmation of life
that remains encumbered, however, by a foreknowledge of death: the
brevity of life and the burden that finitude imposes on each of us to
become someone in particular; the discretion that mortality requires us to
exercise in using freedom to achieve self-definition; and the labor to which
the pursuit of identity conscripts us. While serenity lies in the powerful
drives to individuality that the serene phenomenology sets free and in the
thought that secular achievements constituting identity redeem sacred
losses, nevertheless, Connolly adds, the "implicit foreknowledge of death
slips into every decision."[41] Freedom and the modern agent's striving for
identity are plagued by uncertainty and resentment against the human
condition for thwarting our efforts at self-identity.

Contemporary political theory easily colonizes the individual caught in
this vortex of discursive elements swirling about in this modern phenomenology. At one level, political theories war with one another for the individual's allegiance by offering competing ideals of social order. At a deeper
level, where conflicting ideals offer different versions of how social order
can furnish opportunities for achieving identity, competing theories
draw upon the *same* aspirations for identity released by the serene phenomenology of modern life. It is precisely at this level that the serene phenomenology has made agency vulnerable to colonization—the connections between freedom, mortality, and individual identity are sources for
normalized thought and action required by social imperatives and their
theoretical formulations. Individualist and collectivist theories, Connolly
argues, which are examples of interdependent frameworks whose key
concepts are defined through their exclusion of what belongs to their
theoretical opponent, oppose and compete with one another by empha-
sizing different elements of the serene phenomenology as they share oth-

ers. Whereas individualist and collectivist theories differently prioritize the right and the good, even though individualist theories valorize individualization and collectivist theories valorize the common good, individualization becomes the instrument to fulfill normative commitments to individual identity, while the common good weds individuals to community (collective identity) by converting their particular achievements to legacies obligating them to a future of ends outside themselves. In the final analysis, in other words, it makes less difference than imagined whether political theory gives primacy to the individual or to the whole. The different pressures for normalization that either type of theory brings to bear on the individual draw upon the same set of serene phenomenological assumptions that fuel the individual's appetite for identity and distinguish the modern liberal agent.

In addition to those relating to freedom, mortality, and identity, Connolly explicates other assumptions shared by individualist and collectivist theories. Both genres suppose a close alignment between the quests for identity, whether in individualist or collectivist form, and the opportunities for identity that each genre advertises. Both suppose, secondly, that this correspondence between the pursuit of identity and its socially available possibility will be able to build a future continuous with individuals' efforts. Yet neither of these two assumptions, Connolly objects, can be justified, as both intensify society's dependency for obtaining self-definitional opportunities on local, national, and international forces whose contingencies are too complex to master politically or technically. Extreme societal dependency of this sort in the context of obstacles to mastery posed by global contingencies, which is, Connolly proposes, the world-historical predicament that earns modernity the designation "late modernity," jeopardizes the individual's expectation of socially available opportunities and erodes implicit confidence in the future that it sustains. Contingency and the obstacles to mastery posed by it are thus bases for Connolly's objections to a pair of assumptions that he has already shown to be colonized by pressures for normalization. Connolly's critique of individualist and collectivist theories is concluded, though, when he revisits a concept first examined in *The Terms of Political Discourse* to lay bare one final assumption that accompanies the serene phenomenology of freedom and finitude upon which the late modern condition is balanced precariously.

A historical standard of self-responsibility inherited by the late modern individual is bound up with the idea of identity at the heart of the serene phenomenology. Each of us is responsible for defining his or her own identity, for achieving it or failing to achieve it. At the same time, confronted by contingencies beyond their powers of mastery, late modern societies must adjust for their diminished capacities to offer individuals opportunities for self-definition by imposing stricter disciplinary standards of normality. To earn recognition as responsible agents, those fortunate enough to pursue a "career" rather than a "job," for instance, must devise ways to meet these disciplinary measures of personal achievement, because anyone who fails to do so risks becoming an other. Many convert to normal selves, the standards for which will change unpredictably in relation to the impact of future contingencies. Pressures imposed by this "dependent uncertainty," as Connolly puts it, often create a "generalized resentment," which he believes is characteristic of a type of individual who targets those who deviate from the norm or challenge the terms of normalization. Connolly shows that what began as resentment against a human condition is amplified by late modern secular constraints on freedom and mortality, and redirected toward anyone whom the inherited measure of self-responsibility has fated to become the other.

Connolly's analysis of individualist and collectivist variants of contemporary political theory begins to trace his method of critique. Contemporary political theories, as we saw, limit the terms of political discourse by arranging their interdependent concepts into frameworks whose competition is further confined to their existing terms by assumptions held in common. Connolly assembles the interdependent conceptual scaffoldings of these opposed frameworks and then reveals the assumptions, the contingency of these assumptions, and the way they perform the transcendental operation of fending off critique that exceeds their terms. By excavating this groundwork in this manner, in effect he adopts a "deconstructive" approach to contemporary theory that illuminates both the boundaries within which theoretical debate is managed and the consequences of these well-maintained boundaries. These consequences include the suppression of how the construction of otherness follows from the relation between the identity that contemporary theories affirm as true and the differences from which this identity is distinguished. Connolly describes this last consequence as the suppression of the "paradox of difference" and argues that its suppression is spurred by the inherited concept of self-responsibility instrumental to the construction of those who become targets for generalized resentment and punishment.

By unearthing the roots of the late modern agent in its individualist and collectivist guises, Connolly's "deconstruction" brings us to a crossroads. Is the individual whose strivings for identity, which along with an apparently irremediable need to punish have been released by a serene phenomenology and colonized by competing theoretical frameworks of normalization, to be discarded, as Connolly's "deconstruction" appears to demand? Or can this agent be retained, and *gained*, in some revised form? To answer this question Connolly focuses again on what appears to turn the liberal subject toward violence—the historically inherited concept of self-responsibility and the resentment that it helps to breed. It is at this point that the work of "deconstruction" becomes subordinated to an approach designed to reduce the imperiousness of liberal agency, rather than discard the liberal agent and the liberal democratic form of life that it both animates and also threatens with violence.

Genealogy

To recapitulate, "deconstruction" moves critique beyond a framework of opposing theories whose conceptual interdependencies and commonly held assumptions limit debate to their competing ideals. It brings into view the assumptions on which rests a subject who seems naturally predesigned to think and act in ways that cannot be problematized so long as its assumptions remain subterranean and unreflected. It homes in further on particular assumptions about responsibility from which resentment, the need to punish, or, in a word, *violence* closely follows. Adopting this strategy precisely, "deconstruction" is the first parry of what Connolly conceptualizes as "agonistic respect," a democratic principle of social order in which a plurality of pursuits of identity adopt generous relations toward the differences that they require for their constitution. Genealogy, the second parry of his concept of agonistic respect to which this "deconstruction" leads us, will work further to alter the relation of identity to difference. It does so by problematizing our relation to self-responsibility to subdue the resentment and end the violence for which we saw self-responsibility serve as the womb. Genealogy incites reflection on responsibility and its consequences, which then leads to its contestation and revision, the third parry of Connolly's politics of agonistic respect.

When Connolly speaks of our inherited concept of responsibility, he means not merely the concept dominating the late modern world, the era of modernity coeval with the democratic age, or the western world that has evolved throughout modernity. He is also referring to the idea of responsibility in early Christianity, especially the thought of Augustine of Hippo, the architect of the modern notion of responsibility. Neither modernity nor democracy as we know them would be possible without the subject that responsibility helps to author. Connolly formulates the following question as his genealogical point of departure. "What, though, are the compulsions that drive a church, a state, a culture, an identity to close itself up by defining a range of differences as heretical, evil, irrational, perverse, or destructive, even when the bearers of difference pose no direct threat of conquest? ... To pose this question is to reterritorialize the problem of evil. It is to engage the problem of evil residing within human structures of personal identity and social order."[42] The first, theistic problem of evil appears with Augustine's efforts to protect the omnipotence and benevolence of his god from the doubt cast on both by the prospect that responsibility for worldly evil may reside with him. Augustine's solution to the problem is to insert a gap between evil and the Christian god by endowing humankind with free will, which invests responsibility for wrongdoing, suffering, and human defect in humans themselves. With this move Augustine authorizes the practices of laying blame for evil on human agency and searching for agents to hold responsible. Connolly poignantly describes Augustine's solution to the problem as a "fateful shift"—the site of a *second, secular version of the problem of evil*.

Whereas Augustine's solution to the first problem of evil established the deific certainty of an all-powerful and benevolent god, the second version establishes the certainty of individual and collective identity. Identity achieves certainty as those differences that identity requires to constitute itself are converted to "others" who are held responsible for whatever challenges an identity's certainty—individual or collective self-doubt, suffering, wrongdoing, and the like that can be borne only by attributing their causes to agents whose differences from the norm make them culpable. Genealogy accordingly locates the historical roots of the modern other in Augustine, who burdened modernity and democracy with a concept of responsibility that leads—by virtue of its ties to identity, difference, and otherness as the violence that difference must endure as a consequence of identity's need for certainty—to a "paradox of ethics" shadowing the human condition. Here are two of Connolly's formulations of this paradox: "The consolidation of identity through the constitution of difference. The self-reassurance of identity through the construction of otherness . . . The definition of difference is a requirement built into the logic of identity, and the construction of otherness is a temptation that readily insinuates itself into that logic . . . a temptation because it is constantly at work." And, secondly, "Now, the paradoxical element in the relation of identity to difference is that we cannot dispense with personal and collective identities, but the multiple drives to stamp truth upon those identities function to convert differences into otherness and otherness into scapegoats created and maintained to secure the appearance of a true identity. To possess a true identity is to be false to difference, while to be true to difference is to sacrifice the promise of a true identity."[43] By stressing the continuity of evil in our inherited concept of responsibility, Connolly is insisting that there is no more fundamental ethical problem to be confronted than the evil shadowing each church, state, culture, and individual claiming truth for its identity. Yet as Connolly's paradox maintains on balance, it is also the fundamental pull of identity toward certainty—set in motion by responsibility—that obstructs *recognition* of the violence inherent in the constitution of identity. It is this same motion that keeps this paradox buried and out of mind regardless of the extent to which responsibility makes the bearers of "true" identities vulnerable to discipline or consumed by resentment.

Contestation

Genealogy teaches us that we conceal within our relational orientations to difference the seeds of violence toward difference as otherness, which we construct for the purpose of serving as the objects of that violence. What response appears warranted? Though Connolly's response, his concept of "agonistic respect," has been considered only in part and in anticipation of discussing it more thoroughly, I intervene momentarily to pose this question more sharply to Connolly. Do the revelations concerning responsibility that your genealogy brings to light justify any response other than *discarding* an inheritance that has brought such shame to its benefactors and such hardship to its "others"? Is your concept of agonistic respect, with its contestation and revision of our model of responsibility, a response equal to the problem of evil that you elucidate?

We recognize this new question as a variation of the one first posed, when we took up Connolly's "deconstruction" of contemporary political theory to trace the work performed by his approaches. Then we asked whether the individual's need to punish flowing from the resentment created by the struggle for identity indicates that our liberal concept of agency is the enemy of a democratic form of life for which the individual is the ethical center. And Connolly's answer to the new question is a variation of his answer to its first iteration. Just as discarding the agent of liberal democracy would be to discard the possibility of liberal democracy, to discard our inherited concept of responsibility would be to discard the possibility of liberal agency. Connolly's response is to discard neither agency nor the concept of responsibility empowering it, nor the democracy for which they both are conditions. He again makes this clear when he reminds us, in *Identity\Difference*, that whether it is "possible to counter the second problem of evil without eliminating the functions served by identity . . . is one of the defining questions of this study."[44] Before returning to his response to the second problem of evil, I want to highlight still further what is at stake in his decision to pursue a *revision* of responsibility rather than an outright *rejection* of this key condition of modern and late modern political discourse. To do so I cite a problem that Connolly engages in *The Ethos of Pluralization*, the remaining work I shall introduce. With this we will be positioned to understand the meaning of contestation and the revisions that it entails—what I referred to as the third parry belonging to the concept of agonistic respect with which Connolly responds to the second problem of evil.

In *The Ethos of Pluralization* Connolly takes up the prosecution of Dontay Carter, a young black male in Baltimore convicted of the carjacking and murder of upper-middle-class white men, crimes for which he received sensationalized press coverage and "life in prison with no parole, plus 190 additional years for good measure." Here Connolly revisits the concept of responsibility, this time for the part it played in assessing Carter's guilt and punishment.[45] By first being judged a responsible offender, Carter becomes vulnerable to a surreptitious "call for revenge" and labeled a "dangerous monster who must be destroyed or interned permanently."[46] Paving the way for revenge, responsibility proves to be allied as effectively with a will to revenge in inflicting violence on the other as we earlier saw it allied with resentment. As Connolly summarizes this dynamic, whatever other purposes it serves, a key social function of the system of justice is to ensure that revenge flows "freely into the practices of responsibility and punishment."[47] It is at this point, when responsibility's connection to revenge is delineated by example, that it becomes eligible for revision.

Connolly now contests and revises the modern conceptualization of responsibility in several ways, two of which can be reviewed in summary fashion. Through a series of reflections on desire, he first attempts to release responsibility from the desire for revenge. As desire is a force evading our complete grasp, we must entertain the possibility that it may influence our thought and action in ways unpredictable and mysterious to us and acknowledge that desire may have an undiscerned affect on our judgments. Perhaps our judgments express a desire for revenge of which we remain unaware and that contaminates our efforts to arrive at fair punishments for criminal acts. If upon reflection we concede that desire may compromise judgments about punishment, should we not counter our tendencies toward revenge on those who commit criminal acts? This reflection, Connolly concludes, leads us toward the cultivation of generosity and forbearance in the treatment of agents of criminality.

A second reflection follows. If a desire for revenge invades our judgments about criminality, it may well be ubiquitous in those judgments free of the need to find satisfaction in punishing the violent. Not only should we act with generosity when *punishing* those whose violence enrages us, we should be wary of the deeper needs for satisfaction when we *assign responsibility* for wrongdoing. To rid *punishment* of the desire for revenge, we also must rid *responsibility* of the desire for revenge. Generosity and forbearance mean a willingness to redistribute responsibility from the individual agent to the role that social structure plays in determining the conditions that cause crime, a shift mitigating the individual's culpability. Taking Connolly's reflections together, noticeably instructed by a sensibility of generosity that seeks to purge the will to revenge, responsibility is *revised* and punishment checked through reflections that *contest* the deeper forces for which they are vehicles. Contestation and its revisions form Connolly's culminating strategy of a response to the violence that genealogy discovered hidden within our assumptions about self-responsibility, to which the "deconstruction" of theories commonly framing the quest for identity characteristic of liberal agency first led.

Twice earlier I·suggested that Connolly's allegiance to the concept of responsibility might be seen as problematic in light of the horror in which it is implicated. Surely not one of us "responsible" late moderns is exempt. If my use of the word "horror" to evaluate the consequences of responsibility seems to exaggerate, we should recall the insights that Connolly's response to responsibility produced. In the context of his "deconstructive" analysis of the serene phenomenology and the individual agent's strivings for identity, Connolly showed responsibility's connection to the formation of a generalized resentment readily turned toward the other. In the context of the genealogy of responsibility to which his "deconstruction" led, responsibility proved to lie at the heart of the conversion of difference to otherness and the source of the history of violence to which difference is subjected. Finally, in the context of his discussion of revenge, Connolly discovered how responsibility sponsors expressions of punishment filled with an abstract will to revenge. Resentment, revenge, outrageous punishment, the history of violence toward difference—all of these would be proof of horror if they were not mere placeholders for the suffering for which responsibility is responsible over time. Hence the word "horror" does not exaggerate. It is the value that captures the power of Connolly's response to the evil of responsibility and its progeny. So I problematize Connolly's loyalty to responsibility a last time. On the basis of his "deconstruction," genealogy, and contestation of responsibility, should Connolly not move for its rejection rather than revision, and how can he justify his restraint? Is this not a question implicitly raised by his own analysis in problematizing the alliance that he forges among theoretical strategies appearing to require a more radical response to the problem of violence toward difference?

My position here is a special form of devil's advocacy. Owing to the power of his analysis, Connolly could not have avoided this issue, and I suspect that he combined the resources of "deconstruction," genealogy, and contestation to learn what breadth and depth of consequences adhere to responsibility. Put simply, Connolly's response indicates that he is his own devil's advocate. With the consequences of responsibility writ large, he could not force the issue more decisively. If responsibility is to be revised rather than rejected, the reasons for choosing this more modest response to a condition appearing to *demand* the more radical reply must be overwhelming. Here are those reasons that I imagine Connolly's own devil's advocacy produced.

First, Connolly is committed to democracy normatively. He sees it as best expressing the "care for life" that provides the starting point for his thinking. Democracy is the value that for Connolly takes precedence over other values, allegiances, and commitments. As we learned from *The Terms of Political Discourse*, it underlies his normative point of view and performs the work that we found there. Second, if responsibility were rejected, modern, liberal agency would become impossible, and without liberal agency modern democratic society is not possible either. Third, theorists who reject modern agency and its practices, including its political practices, are left without alternatives for which it is the condition. In a word, they are left without the alternative of *democracy*. Or else their democratic alternatives are tacitly inclusive of the liberal agent they believe they rejected, including the responsible agent who authors the practices to which these theorists are often most hostile. For to value democracy explicitly is to value its modern, liberal agent (at least) implicitly and the concept of responsibility in which liberal agency is anchored. Finally, in engaging the consequences of the inherited concept of responsibility without dismantling democracy by discarding its agent, Connolly's principle of agonistic respect directly confronts the second problem of evil, the conversion of difference to otherness and its horrors. Agonistic respect helps democracy achieve what it would achieve at its best. Democracy would become a barrier to the evil of violence toward difference that accompanies the conversion of difference to otherness. Such a democracy, in Connolly's judgment, is, "of course, a liberalism, an alternative, militant liberalism both indebted to and competitive with other liberalisms and nonliberalisms contending for presence in late-modern life."[48] Connolly's democracy is a liberal democracy made deeply democratic by the politics of agonistic respect.

Deep Democracy: The Politics of Agonistic Respect

Contestation, I have argued, is a strategy of revision, such as the revision of agency and responsibility, which takes "deconstructive" and genealogical strategies as its allies. To be more precise, as I indicated above, contestation refers generically to the work of revision that all three strategies are crafted to perform as an ensemble. Connolly's "deconstructive" analysis of the serene phenomenology of freedom and finitude *contests* its ontological projections, the imperiousness of the individual's striving for identity. His genealogy of the inherited concept of responsibility *contests* its social ontology, the conversion of difference to otherness as the second problem of evil. *Contestation* is thus Connolly's critical approach as a whole and now will appear in italics when used in this sense. Yet it is also one of three distinct strategies I have taken in turn, whose alliance generates creative tensions productive of new theoretical possibilities for thinking about liberalism and our relation to liberalism, its failings, achievements, and preconditions. Hence it would be simplistic and would reflect a misunderstanding of its nature to search for radical discontinuities in Connolly's work. Whether taken alone as it was first conceived in *The Terms of Political Discourse*, or as one strategy then allied with a plurality of others as theoretical problems require, or as the term for his approach as a whole, from *The Terms of Political Discourse* onward *contestation* is a strategy for revision whose pluralization over time works to pluralize the ability of thinking to revise those concepts without which our modern achievements cannot be sustained or perhaps even imagined.

Contestation is likewise a political strategy; the allies of which it is composed are political allies and their politics the democratic politics of agonistic respect. "Deconstruction," genealogy, and contestation do not exhaust Connolly's arsenal of agonistic political weaponry, the others of which cannot be discussed here and include, prominently among them, his work on political economy.[49] But they are three of its most important. By considering these theoretical strategies we already have traveled a distance toward understanding important political dimensions of agonistic respect. All three are political in the ways that they illuminate and thus work to deflect, constrain, or limit the power of the problem of evil, whose own political power lies in the multiple ways it sponsors the conversions of difference to otherness to ensure the certainty of individual or collective identity. As we recall, the problem of evil itself, in both of its Augustinian variations, was first illuminated through the work of genealogy, the key approach to which led its ally, "deconstruction." Once the problem of evil was uncovered, genealogy illuminated a path of violence paved by responsibility, resentment, and revenge, whose political dimensions included systemic negotiations of local, national, and global contingencies; changing patterns of normalization to which individual aspirations for identity become vulnerable; and punishments exceeding rational justifications of jurisprudence.

The politics of agonistic respect deflect, constrain, or limit the power of the problem of evil by altering identity's relation to difference, which it does by providing identity with resources to resist its need to convert difference into otherness, resources such as the revision of responsibility through the reflections on desire provoked by contestation. In exercising this resistance, "identity"—that is, those possessing identities, such as churches, cultures, states, and individuals—spare difference the violence that it would endure in its multiple forms of otherness. In the language of the politics of agonistic respect, to spare difference from violence is to "cultivate presumptive care" for being in the diverse forms in which identities construct it. Of course, there is a supplemental source upon which Connolly draws here. He seeks to cultivate and draw upon a vitality of life from which presumptive generosity can be expressed in relations of agonistic respect. He solicits others to draw upon this source as well, even though he knows it will appear false to those who root their moralities in a law of God or categorical imperative or comparable theology. Thus here too he acknowledges the contestability of the source from which he draws, while inviting others to come to terms with how their own sources of morality are opaque to him and to all those who do not equate morality with law. He solicits a relation of agonistic respect with them at this level too. If relations of agonistic respect develop across such multiple differences, to that same extent would a democratic politics of agonistic respect become possible.

At the same time as cultivating care for being helps to create the possibility for a democratic politics of agonistic respect, it also cultivates opportunities for becoming different, which Connolly calls the "politics of becoming." To resist converting difference to otherness means that identity no longer requires difference to be the other who guarantees its certitude, so that identity can look upon difference as an image of what it too might become if it were not the image of what it should avoid becoming. Clearly the politics of cultivating care for being and becoming would first require individuals and constituencies to arrive at an understanding of either the *contingency* of their identities or the legitimate *contestability* of their sources of identity in the eyes of others. For without grasping the contingency of their identities, without understanding, in other words, that they can be other-than-they-are as readily as who-they-are and have been, individuals have no way to contest their self-certainty and to appreciate the contestability of their identities in the eyes of others, nor reason to relinquish the desire to convert difference to otherness or to entertain becoming different from who they are.

As a salient political lesson taught by the politics of agonistic respect, contingency is a vital dimension of the political pedagogy that Connolly builds into each of his critical strategies. After illuminating and contesting an infrastructure of assumptions, beliefs, and concepts contributing to identity's constructions of otherness and to defining relations between identity and the other as relations of violence, "deconstruction," genealogy, and contestation then intervened to illuminate elements of contingency in these constructions that represented points where they could be modified to mitigate the violence inhering in these constructions and their relations. "Deconstruction," for example, drew particular attention to the historical contingency of individual strivings for identity that became, by virtue of their relation to freedom and finitude, vulnerable to systemic contingencies whose social disciplines placed individuals' needs for achievement under increasing pressure at an ever greater cost to the other. Genealogy thematized the contingency of identity itself, problematizing the certainty of identity by revealing its connection to the conversion of difference to otherness that issued from the need to assign agency responsibility. Both interventions, emerging in the context of Connolly's analyses of agency, responsibility, and resentment, were followed by a third intervention into the construction of identity as his analyses moved from responsibility to resentment to revenge. As a moment of revision that redistributed responsibility from the individual agent to the underlying social structure, contestation remodels identity's relation to responsibility in a way contesting not only the desire for revenge that "flows into responsibility," as Connolly put it. Remodeling identity's relation to responsibility also attenuates the individual's striving for the one, true identity that responsibility intensifies, which is an attitude of contingency toward identity with further consequences. Resentment that some harbor toward others for their inability or reluctance to make the sacrifices believed required for the achievement of identity would be undermined by an attenuated commitment to the idea of a true identity. And with a weakened commitment to true identity, people might become receptive to the possibility that identities different from their own are equal to and as rewarding as theirs and hence eligible for their care and respect.

When we have taken account of the work performed by Connolly's critical strategies, it is evident from where the political character of his response to the second problem of evil derives. It derives both from the power of *contestation* to examine the ways by which individuals, churches, states, and cultures become who they are and from its power to interrogate the discursive structures that insulate from examination the plausibility of those identities. Identity comes into question politically when its certainty is probed, and its truth is shaken politically when its historical particularity is proved and its consequences to others demonstrated. By celebrating a politics of becoming that not only recognizes but also affirms our need for identity, and by insisting on recognizing the violence that a true identity entails, agonistic respect refuses to bury the paradox of ethics but politicizes it instead. At all times, though, the examinations, probings, problematizations, interrogations, interventions, recognitions, affirmations, and celebrations pressed by each critical, political strategy— or, in a word, by the strategies of *contestation* integral to agonistic respect— presuppose a democratic form of life. Set in democracy, agonistic respect politicizes the public space that *contestation* requires, while *contestation* forces democracy into a radical mode of critical self-reflection that makes everything practiced and presupposed by democracy the object of the politics of agonistic respect. Thus would the politics of agonistic respect constitute a deep democracy that forms a barrier to the evil of violence toward difference.

Through *contestation*, the politics of agonistic respect no less than the deep democratic life that it animates would be the object as well as the subject of *contestation*. *Contestation* denies Connolly's politics the same privilege it denies to everything else that falls within the purview of a politics whose activity is so theoretically self-conscious, which is to say that it has no guarantee of sovereignty. A politics that permits nothing sovereign could not itself be the politics of a sovereign body, but would thrive as a politics of a minority whose voice would be one among others. Such are the politics, in Connolly's words, of a "post-Nietzschean liberalism," "[which] requires only that an active minority of the population advance [such politics] in thought and action and that the culture more broadly come to recognize it as a competing response to the mysteries of existence worthy of agonistic respect."[50] If we listen carefully, we can hear the voice of an earlier Connolly in *The Terms of Political Discourse* instructing a minority composed of social scientists about their political responsibility to a majority whose norms and concepts, whose language and culture, provided the foundation for their own idiom.[51]

CONTESTATION: THE PLURALIST MIND

What is the measure of a pluralist mind? Denying sovereignty to every idea and practice, *contestation* challenges the closure of identity as such, the identity of every whole and every part of every church, state, culture, group, and individual proposing to regulate what life is and ought to include. In doing so, *contestation* ultimately establishes its claim not by opening itself and its politics to critical reflection but by its concept of life, which to be truly pluralistic must be receptive to the fundamental diversity of being. Life and its abundance over any particular organization of identity is the plurality that *contestation* and its agonistic politics respects. For this reason Connolly's relation to death is perhaps of greater importance as a measure of *contestation*, of its pluralism, than any of the critical strategies belonging to the politics of agonistic respect. To include death in life, not as its final and absolute negation but as a part of life, is to increase life's possibilities, to affirm a pluralism enabling life to be lived to its fullest. For by accepting death as a part of life we transcend the drive to limit our identity and self-definitional choices propelled by our fear of death, we take an expansive view of the possibilities for being, we become less vulnerable to forces that colonize our identities, and we are less tempted to convert difference to otherness and to commit the violence that it both entails and breeds. *Contestation* finds its measure on this plane mapped by the reconciliation of life and death, as do Connolly's pluralism and the horizon of the pluralist mind.

> The idea might be that by refiguring your own relation to death you are more likely to live without being overtaken by resentment against finitude, to live without projecting a fundamental unfairness into being and then resenting "it" for being unfair. In striving to fend off existential resentment by cultivating the power to die proudly (if the unlikely opportunity to do so should present itself), you may be more likely to cultivate an identity that can sustain itself without seeking to conquer, convert, marginalize, despise, or love to the point of suffocation every identity that differs from it. You may be more likely to see that part of the demand for a true identity for

oneself and others flows from the demand to attain a self-reassurance deep enough to fend off the vicissitudes of life. You may become less likely to demand that wherever evil exists a responsible agent equal to its gravity must be identifiable. You may become less punitive in the name of love and humility, more prepared to constitute adversaries worthy of agonistic respect.[52]

NOTES

1 *Reason and Horror: Critical Theory, Democracy, and Individuality* (New York: Routledge, 2001).

2 George Kateb, *The Inner Ocean: Individualism and Democratic Culture* (Ithaca: Cornell University Press, 1994).

3 See *Reason and Horror*, chapter 10.

4 *The Terms of Political Discourse* (Lexington, Mass.: D. C. Heath, 1974; 2nd edn Princeton: Princeton University Press, 1983; 3rd edn 1993); *Identity\Difference: Democratic Negotiations of Political Paradox* (Ithaca: Cornell University Press, 1991; enlarged with new essay, "Confessing Identity\Belonging to Difference," Minneapolis: University of Minnesota Press, 2002); *The Ethos of Pluralization* (Minneapolis: University of Minnesota Press, 1995).

5 William E. Connolly, *Political Science and Ideology* (New York: Atherton, 1967), and *The Bias of Pluralism* (New York: Atherton, 1969).

6 For a discussion of these works see the Introduction to this volume.

7 In 1999 *The Terms of Political Discourse* was recognized by the American Political Science Association with the Benjamin Lippincott Award, given to a book "of exceptional quality still considered important after a time span of at least 15 years."

8 Ibid., 12–13 (all italics in cited passages are Connolly's unless otherwise noted).

9 Ibid., 22.

10 The term comes from Gallie's article "Essentially Contested Concepts," in *Proceedings of the Aristotelian Society* 56 (London, 1955–56), cited in *The Terms of Political Discourse*, 9.

11 Connolly, *The Terms of Political Discourse*, 6.

12 Ibid., 223.

13 Ibid., 19.

14 Ibid., 39.

15 Ibid., 204.

16 Ibid.

17 On these types of relationships Connolly cites his indebtedness to Henry Kariel's "Neither Sticks nor Stones," *Politics and Society*, winter 1973, 183, 189.

18 Connolly, *The Terms of Political Discourse*, 6.

19 Ibid., 227.

20 Ibid., 198.

21 Ibid., 191.

22 Ibid., 4.

23 Ibid., 201–2.

24 Ibid., 202.

25 Ibid.

26 Ibid., 227.

27 *Identity\Difference* was published in an enlarged edition by the University of Minnesota Press in 2002 to include a new essay, "Confessing Identity\ Belonging to Difference." All citations are to the Minnesota edition.

28 *The Terms of Political Discourse*, vii. This second edition was followed in 1993 by a third edition, also published by Princeton, with a new preface. All further references to *The Terms of Political Discourse* will be to the Princeton 2nd edition.

29 *The Terms of Political Discourse*, 190.

30 Ibid., 192 (my italics).

31 Ibid., 196, 197 (my italics).

32 Ibid., 241.

33 I am not suggesting that deconstructive strategies entail the abolition of the modern conception of subjectivity, only that Connolly sees this as one implication and moves to set limits to deconstruction as the means to ensure space for the work it can perform in alliance with contestation. Connolly and I are fundamentally in agreement with the position on deconstruction set out by Derrida in "Jacques Derrida: In Discussion with Christopher Norris," *Deconstruction*, ed. A. Papadakis et al. (London: Academy, 1989), esp. 74.

34 *The Terms of Political Discourse*, 243.

35 See *Why I Am Not a Secularist* (Minneapolis: University of Minnesota Press, 1999), especially the Introduction and chapters 1–4, and *Neuropolitics: Thinking, Culture, Speed* (Minneapolis: University of Minnesota Press, 2002), throughout the text.

36 *Identity\Difference*, 9.

37 Ibid., 13.

38 William E. Connolly, *Politics and Ambiguity* (Madison: University of Wisconsin Press, 1987).

39 By arguing that Connolly's work and deconstruction possess commonalities I am not, I want to stress, claiming that he is a deconstructionist. Deconstructionists, such as Derrida and Levinas, often appeal to a mode of transcendence beneath levels of conceptual articulation to which they are responsible. Both Derrida and Levinas attempt to open themselves to this mystical experience of transcendence through deconstruction. Connolly admires this in both thinkers but does not embrace transcendence, although to the minds of some his concept of the abundance of life that exceeds any organization of identity and that draws upon a fugitive source of being may resemble a

transcendental realm. By virtue of his relation to this fugitive source from which the vitality of life springs, Connolly would consider himself a pagan at home in a pluralistic universe. This dimension of Connolly's work and the issues that it entails require exploring works not considered here that await another argument on another day.

40 *Identity\Difference*, 20, 27, for example.
41 Ibid., 18.
42 Ibid., 3.
43 Ibid., 9, 67.
44 Ibid., 8.
45 *The Ethos of Pluralization*, 43.
46 Ibid., 46.
47 Ibid., 40.
48 *Identity\Difference*, 93.
49 See Michael H. Best and William Connolly, *The Politicized Economy* (Lexington, Mass.: D. C. Heath, 1976), though Connolly's arguments about the political economy of modern democratic capitalism can be found scattered throughout nearly all his writing since *The Terms of Political Discourse*.
50 *Identity\Difference*, 91.
51 See the discussion earlier in this chapter.
52 *Identity\Difference*, 164–65.

CONNOLLY'S
VOICE

Thomas L. Dumm

THE VOICE I HEAR

WHAT IS VOICE AND HOW does it matter in the practice of political theory? I want to respond to this question by reflecting on a voice that matters to me, that of William E. Connolly. I have heard this voice for about twenty years (so far) in the context of a continued intellectual companionship. I have heard it in conversation—on the telephone, face to face, in hotel bars, at conferences in destination cities, in restaurants and homes, at colleges and universities, floating on a raft, with a stable and revolving swarm of others, lovers and wives, thoughtful and thoughtless protagonists in the academy (and out), a rich pageant of friends and enemies—richer as friends, no doubt, but all complicatedly assembled as multitudinous forces containing and projecting love and hate, abjection and pride, loneliness and gregariousness, and more. These conversations, like elements of a color-field painting blending into a coherent image, have been a crucial foreground to the background of the times we have mutually attended, a history consisting of the unfolding joys and sorrows produced by an American culture and polity that at times has seemed deranged in its adherence to various machines of destructive energies.

In other words, Connolly's voice has been an elementary particle in a friendship of rhizomatic connection, as he once put it to me. My hope is that an exploration of that voice may reveal more about the multitudes that shape its singularity, even as it reveals more about the singularity that has influenced so many others. Moreover—for me a happy thought— a practical consequence of attempting to identify this voice's sources and forms of articulation is to become a part of that voice, so much so that my departures from it may be understood as constituting my own attempt to assume a voice, one that is itself variously inflected by loss, freedom, trauma, whimsy, and reconnection and return. (We may already see a way in which the shape of pedagogical struggle between student and teacher may be described. And despite all denials, we cannot help being students and teachers of each other.)

An immediate complication arises because the voice I hear is not only spoken but written, and it is through the written that those of us who practice political theory are most likely to hear each other's voices. It is common knowledge—at least among us denizens of the modern age—that it is not possible to confine voice to the occasion of hearing it through one's ears. Questions concerning speaking and hearing—concerning the communication of meaning more generally—plague philosophical discourse these days primarily as the subject of a contest concerning how speaking and writing are to be connected to each other. The most prominent arguments of which I am aware in this contest address the question of the priority of writing over speaking and vice versa, and thus stake claims in regard to the indefinite character of the signs that constitute language. This contest about the constitution of language directly informs the articulation of voice for Connolly. In maintaining even an errant fidelity to Connolly's voice it is important to try to sustain this moment of reflexivity. Attending to voice as a matter of speech and writing means not only trying to think of the connections that exist between the two but uncovering the voice as another element of thinking. In this chapter I want to claim that thinking about how voice may actually materialize is a key element in Connolly's ethos of pluralization.

FINDING VOICE

As a preface to the expression of the claim that Connolly's ethos of pluralization is a political theory of voice, it may be useful to describe more directly the province of voice in the mediations of speaking and writing. Toward that end, a description of an element of the energetics offered by Jane Bennett in her handbook of ethics may help us begin. Focusing on Richard Flathman's critique of ethical rule making—Flathman wisely observes that the multiple and shifting meanings of words are such that stable signification is impossible to achieve, and hence that rules themselves are insufficient guides to ethical conduct and consequently must be deployed with care and gentleness—Bennett suggests that prior to and beyond words themselves, yet functioning as an undeniable element of language's porosity, there is a sonority underwriting the enunciation of words. "For language," she writes, "is not only a matter of significations and failures of significations ('indeterminacy'), it is also about sound, noise, and differential intensities and affects."[1] She goes on to endorse an idea vividly presented by Gilles Deleuze and Felix Guatarri in their study of Kafka: "Language always implies a deterritorialization of the mouth, the tongue, the teeth. The mouth, the tongue, and the teeth find their primitive territoriality in food. In giving themselves over to the articulation of sounds, the mouth, tongue and teeth deterritorialize. Thus, there is a certain disjunction between eating and speaking, and even more, despite all appearances, between eating and writing [because] . . . writing goes further in transforming words into things capable of competing with food . . . To speak, and above all to write, is to fast."[2] We trace the gaps between eating, speaking, and writing in what we may call a political economy of language. (While it may be that there is already an inclination toward speaking in the physiology of the human animal, it is important to understand that the processes of deterritorialization and reterritorialization do not presume a primordial or natural first position, but instead only articulate one position or posture in reference to another. And while Deleuze and Guatarri begin from animality and work their way to humanity—hence the direction of their deterritorializing and reterritorializing descriptions—they do not, to my understanding, presume animality to be a more natural state of human being than the human.)[3]

It may be that by the time our sonorities are economically wrapped into words we have gone a way toward an adequate understanding of voice, if not as far as we may yet go. But because that further place is reached by writing, which through its markings makes more enduring the resonance of words, for Bennett and Deleuze and Guatarri the sonority embedded in speaking must be even more deeply embedded, as well as more overtly marked, in writing. Thus the economy of speaking and writing, seen to be in opposition by others, is rendered here instead as a matter of varying intensities of fasting. How is it that writing would be more intense a fasting than speaking? We sometimes speak as we eat, if sloppily, but we could write and eat even more easily were it not for the intervention of the hand and the presence of those to whom we speak with our voice (unless of course we are only talking to ourselves, which does not count, or if it does count, is usually evidence of problems perhaps more directly addressed by recent innovations in psychopharmacology). Deleuze and Guatarri suggest that in tracing the transformation of words into things that compete with food we may better understand how the deterritorialization of the mouth is simultaneously a reterritorialization of sense.[4] For Kafka, the ability to abandon sense depends upon the function of language as a means of reterritorialization—since "Things are as they are." Deleuze and Guatarri emphasize how Kafka likes to say, "it is as it is, it is as it is," and call him a "marker of facts"—Kafka will retain "only a skeleton of sense." Kafka's great work is to slide between the letters of words in a language torn from sense, conquering sense, bringing about an active neutralization of sense in the face of the stubborn tendency of language to mask its active asserting of fact with the bland phrase, "Things are as they are."[5]

It appears as though there is a potential openness to this movement of language in its reterritorialization of words, a linking of language to sense through another tactility, though the claims that may be made in this regard do not follow exactly the same path that Deleuze, Guatarri, and Kafka take, at least not in this meditation. I would suggest that two openings to another element of the economy of writing might be discovered by following the path of deterritorialization a little bit more closely. First, there is the moment when eating and writing conjoin. In this moment the voice may drift to other places in the body, whether it be to the free hand or to regions of skin, face, stomach, brain, or alimentary canal, to name a few potential lines of flight. Second, as the voice is engaged in its silences, it may gravitate toward a sense of the ordinary that would underwrite the finding of voice as an end of philosophical writing. The first flight of voice is illuminated in a passage of Martin Heidegger's writing on thinking, and the second in some reflections by Henry David Thoreau and one of his intellectual descendants, Stanley Cavell.

Heidegger famously claims that thinking is a handicraft. He goes on to say, making a distinction between the hand and the grasping instruments of other animals (in what would be for Bennett a dubious distinction), "Only a being who can speak, that is, think, can have hands and can be

handy in achieving works of handicraft."[6] For Heidegger, hands themselves are—like the mouth—instruments of speaking, only decoupled
from sound, from sonority. Moreover, he insists, "And only when man
speaks, does he think." When hands speak they are not grasping, or doing
any of the other things that can be done by claws, paws, and other hand-
like things. They can even express silence. The expressiveness of hands is
an instance of their deterritorialization from grasping and their reterritorialization by language. But how may this process be said to embody
voice? Can we claim that voice is dependent upon or coterminous with
something we would call speaking and hence, for Heidegger, thinking?
How would this speaking be dependent upon writing as an intensification of fasting, as the sense of language overwhelms spoken words?

The claims and counterclaims of speech and writing in the emergence
of voice are approached much differently by Thoreau, as a distinction
between mother and father tongues. "The one is commonly transitory, a
sound, a tongue, a dialect merely, almost brutish, and we learn it unconsciously, like the brutes, of our mothers. The other is the maturity and
experience of that; if that is our mother tongue, this is our father tongue,
a reserved and select expression, too significant to be heard by the ear,
which we must be born again in order to speak."[7] The claims that Thoreau
is making here are deeply gendered—mother tongue is taught to brutes,
father tongue to the brutes upon a certain competence—distinguishing
between private and public, home and school. Thoreau emphasizes this
difference to recreate the experience of natality: out of a mute, brute
beginning we move forward to the experience of that muteness as the
basis for remembrance of things past. Thoreau's concern is not simply
with the import of the father tongue and the claims upon culture that
writing might make, but upon which silences as well as sounds might be
heard in such writing that are unavailable to our ears. He writes, "What
the Roman and Grecian multitude could not *hear*, after the lapse of ages a
few scholars *read*, and a few scholars only are reading it still."[8] For Thoreau this lapse between mother tongue and father tongue points to a hope
for a democracy, perhaps a democracy of futurity that is composed of a
more general literacy, so that we may all learn to read and hence hear what
we otherwise would not be able to hear.

The idea of a *lapse* between the spoken and the read word is of a more
general philosophical importance for Thoreau—his very theory of voice is

dependent upon it, because the lapse of time is also the primary expression of the general unfolding of human being. He writes, "No wonder the earth expresses itself outwardly in leaves, it so labors with the idea inwardly. The atoms have already learned this law, they are pregnant by it. The overhanging leaf sees here its prototype. *Internally*, whether in the globe or animal body, it is a moist thick *lobe*, a word especially applicable to the liver and lungs and *leaves* of fat (_____, *labor*, *lapsus*, to flow, to slip downward, a lapsing; _____, *globus*, lobe, globe; also lap, flap, and many other words); *externally*, a dry thin leaf, even as the *f* and *v* are a pressed and dried *b*. The radicals of lobe are *lb*, the soft mass of the *b* (single lobed, or B, double lobed) with the liquid *l* behind it pressing it forward. In globe, *glb*, the guttural *g* adds to the meaning the capacity of the throat . . . The whole tree is but one leaf, and rivers are still water leaves whose pulp is intervening earth, and towns and cities are the ova of insects in their axils."[9] In this passage as in others, Thoreau seeks to work the mouth, to have us read aloud the shape of the sounds of the letters that form the words. That the strange specificity of this plunge into the sounds of the words is embedded in a discussion of leaves as a fundamental structure of life reminds us of the deepest connections of words to embodiment and embodiment to world. The guttural *g* employs the throat, which amplifies the mouth's self-awareness of the sonority of speech and its preservation in the letters of the words that connect the written back to the spoken. Here Thoreau seems to be both highlighting the distance between written and spoken word and showing us a way to recompose ourselves through a bodily reenactment of the primal moment of their separation. The lips to which he refers are not only those of the mouth but of the labia, with the labor of birthing a child akin to the labor of birthing a word. This connecting of the visual to sonority through the guttural mouthing of the letters of the word will allow us to reflect upon the continuities underlying the separate moments of the mouth as an organ of birthing. This moment of reconciliation of mother and father may be thought of as Thoreau's sense of voice.

This sense of voice is a part of Thoreau's deeper ontological commitment to embodiment. In a passage that anticipates and yet supersedes Heidegger's insight, he writes, "What is man but a mass of thawing clay? The ball of the human finger is but a drop congealed. The fingers and toes flow to their extent from the thawing mass of the body. Who knows what the human body would expand and flow out to under a more genial heaven? Is not the hand a spreading *palm* leaf with its lobes and veins? The ear may be regarded, fancifully, as a lichen, *umbilicaria*, on the side of the head, with its lobe or drop. The lip—*labium*, from *labor* (?)—laps or lapses from the sides of a cavernous mouth."[10] This lapsing of the lips, or labor of the mouth, is the way Thoreau connects reading and speaking a new language to the event of rebirthing. It is a labor of the lips that occurs when we adopt the father tongue, when the language we read becomes the language we speak through the lapse between the written and the spoken word.[11] This is an employment of voice that returns words to speech, to the body, as a way of converting us to new meanings. (It may be thought to parallel Kafka's attempt, in Deleuze's and Guatarri's reading, to irrevocably deterritorialize sounds, which we may think of as another reconciliation of mother and father tongue, achieved through a suspension between the two.)[12]

In his study of *Walden*, a book about a book from which I first came to appreciate the import of this difference between mother and father tongues, Stanley Cavell, making Heidegger rhyme with Thoreau, reminds us that "Writing is a labor of the hands."[13] "In *Walden*, reading is not merely the other side of writing, its eventual fate; it is a metaphor of writing itself. The writer cannot invent words as 'perpetual suggestions and provocations'; the written word is already 'the choicest of relics' (III, 3, 5). His calling depends upon his acceptance of this fact about words, his letting them come to him from their own region, and then taking that occasion for inflecting them one way instead of another then and there, or for refraining from them then and there; as one may inflect the earth toward beans instead of grass, or let it alone, as it is before you are there."[14] Hence the extension of speaking to writing extends further to reading. This labor of the hands is a kind of thinking, as Heidegger would assert, but by way of letting words come to him Thoreau's poetics allow for the possibility of refraining from inflection in favor of a radical passivity, a kind of passion that would turn the world rather than simply let it be, or let it be instead of turning it, or recognizing that it is already turned. Cavell parenthetically expresses this intention as being constantly realized within the arc of a (grand) circularity of meaning: "A word has meaning against the context of a sentence. A sentence has meaning against the context of a language. A language has meaning against the context of a form of life. A form of life has meaning against the context of a world. A world has meaning against the context of a word."[15] This is an expression in language of Thoreau's preoccupation with creating a world out of the word, a restaging of the first expression of faith—that in the beginning was the word. This is also a prop for the aversion of conformity that Cavell learns from Emerson (and from Wittgenstein and from Nietzsche), a root of what he calls Emersonian perfectionism.[16] Aversion or conversion depends upon bringing words back to life, to speak again what has been written, so as to make that Emersonian iron string sing. Cavell says, "And the proof that a language is alive is precisely that it becomes spoken by the living, the reborn—'not only read but actually breathed from all human lips'—though whether current human beings are alive or whether their living is a rumor . . . is a recurrent enigma in *Walden*."[17]

In his most explicit series of meditations on voice, what he calls autobiographical exercises, Cavell describes the task of philosophy as that of finding a voice with which to speak. Among other things, the importance of Thoreau's thinking about language in this context is that it serves to refute Jacques Derrida's famous claims concerning the idea that writing has been universally considered but an extension of speech (which Derrida then refutes). Instead, Thoreau shows that writing is both closer to speech than that, and yet more radically different from that as well. "And if Thoreau's view is allowed to counter Derrida's description of the philosophical dispensation concerning writing, it does so in each particular: writing appears in *Walden* not as an extension but as an experience of speech; its alteration of speech is not accidental but essential; it is not different in means or medium if this means that you can tell the difference between writing and speaking by the senses as they stand, for reading with understanding requires reborn sensations, first in hearing; and writing differs from speaking not only by its more powerful technical mediation over greater distance but by a 'memorable interval,' which is to say, in Thoreau's lingo, by a discontinuous reconstitution of what has been said, a recounting of the past, autobiographizing, deriving words from yourself."[18] For Cavell the voice of the everyday is to be arrogated for philosophy to speak. He is attracted to ordinary language philosophy as enunciated by J. L. Austin and by the later Wittgenstein because of the way the ordinary speaks to the unsettlement of philosophy, its skepticism, not by denying that skepticism but by working through it. Cavell sees this project of working through skepticism as "'to help bring the human voice back into philosophy.' That is the charter Austin and the later Wittgenstein assume in confronting their reader with the arrogation of voice, in all its ungrounded and in a sense ungroundable arrogance—to establish their sense that the voice has become lost in thought."[19]

Cavell's attraction to Thoreau and Emerson seems to me very closely akin to the attraction that Bennett feels for Deleuze and Guatarri and Thoreau. Among other things, these thinkers all present similar ways of understanding the relations of speech to writing as a series of trans-formative extensions connected by bodily senses, through which we are able to comprehend freedom as being something other than simple self-assertion, as being instead embedded in the practices of the everyday. The study of voice for all of them requires extraordinary attention to the practical ways in which we can convert or turn or reform the conditions of our existence through assiduous attention to what is purported to escape more serious attention. Thus Bennett will seek to show us the enchant-ment of modernity so that we can bear to live: and Cavell will seek to show us how to live decently in the wake of the death of God by helping us find our voice. Both will enlist uncommon resources to show how voice may be both the vehicle of a common ethics and an element in an aesthetic way of being that is inclined toward goodness.

Let us call voice the shaped sound that vibrates through sonority, speech, and writing: a music that gives rebirth by inclining one way as opposed to another, or in its silence or noise letting things be as they are. Voice is thus not simply a reflection of thinking, nor is it engaged in a dialectic with writing as a reflection of thinking. Voice is a complex ele-ment of thinking and its experience. Tracing voice, we may be able to expand upon our possibilities for free being. (Amid the clamor for free-dom of speech perhaps it would be more astute of us to insist upon a freedom of voice.)

A POLITICS OF VOICE

Connolly's voice enacts an inclination toward an ethical way of being. How in the world does he do this? In the book that marks for me the beginning of my conversation with Connolly, he sets forth a new political theory "in the early stages of its development," which will, among other things, investigate how the disciplinary order that insinuates itself into the very being of modern people may still yield a modern way of being free.[20] He goes about this task at first as a matter of the genealogical pursuit of truth through a critique of rhetoric. He articulates a critical rhetoric in describing the dangers inherent in what he calls the expressivist view of language. "What genealogy cannot accept is the rhetoric governing expressivist texts; for that rhetoric insinuates a quest for attunement into the articulation of moods, ideals, identities, identifications, and legitimacy which the genealogist must view as destructive and dangerous. To put the 'claim' schematically (and I enclose 'claim' in quotes to ward off the tendency to draw this metaphor immediately into the circle of epistemology): the rules of articulation do not mesh nicely with the logic of impulse, and the attempt to treat them as if they were concordant imposes upon the self even when it realizes something in the self."[21] Connolly suggests that one of genealogy's tasks is to expose the falsifications that are necessarily lodged inside articulations. Unlike rationalists or expressivists who would go on to assert their core understanding as the true one, the genealogist does not urge a return to a pristine state of truth but instead seeks to enable us to realize, in Foucault's phrase, how discourse "is a violence which we do to things, or at any rate is a practice which we impose upon them."[22] Put another way, "The genealogist treats the world and the body as if, since they were not designed by some transcendent will, the points of affinity within and between them are partial and oblique, or, better, as if each affinity contains within it that which resists or subverts it."[23] He concludes this initial articulation of this theory by sharing an aspiration: "To endorse a social ontology of discord within concord, to open discourse to voices subdued by the pursuit of harmony and identity, and to endorse a set of ends, principles and standards worthy of admiration even when ambiguities within them have been acknowledged."[24]

We may note that in this early articulation of a new political theory Connolly is already attending to the politics of voice as a matter of embodiment. Discourse subdues voices through body work, shaping—through the repetitions of ritual, through the smoothness of logic, through the repressive force of taboo, through the appeal to wholeness and harmony, through the insistence of an identificatory power of a commonality out of difference—the discursive possibilities of a particular word, sentence, lan-

guage, form of life, world, and word. The articulation and disarticulation
of a possible word is not simply a matter of recognizing where a word
breaks off, in Heidegger's valorization of the poet's phrase, but the realization of a kind of ontological politics.[25] (If only (but not only) because
genealogy is interested in what Foucault once called the capillary flow of
power, this convergence with the interest of Cavell's philosophy of the
ordinary does not seem forced to me, but would lend to Cavell's project—
of seeking to restore voice to philosophy—a revitalized appreciation of the
insinuation of political forces that are found and lost in voice. (Perhaps
this could be called a politics of the ordinary?)) To think through this
perspective requires a particular discipline of voice. Rather than form
words, sentences, and paragraphs asserting that things are what they are,
Connolly will explore the productive tensions in his own assertions, trying
to evade the closed terms of political discourse that he recognizes result
from an anxiety about the inscrutability of being itself.

Connolly will go to great lengths to avoid closure of his voice, including
the enlistment of his enemies in the shaping of his voice. For instance, in
his sustained dialogue with Saint Augustine, he will never deny, and will
always appreciate, the power of the moraline force that both attracts
Connolly to Augustine and forces a confrontation with him. In his first
letter to Augustine he writes, "I read your theology as a strategy of earthly
power. I want you to hear a couple of the voices in it again . . . I write, then,
to accuse you, and in doing so to excavate political predispositions in
myself and others."[26] Connolly's strategy of writing an epistle is a key
element in the rhetoric of democratic negotiation. By responding to the
writings of this early Christian in the form favored by bishops, to letters
that may not have been written with the hope of so direct a reply, he
reminds us of the possibility of responding to any and all who claim
authority in their own voice. Directly addressing Augustine has the consequence of showing how Augustine remains alive as a voice, which matters
to Connolly to the extent that he needs to listen to himself. In a culture so
deeply influenced by the inheritors of Augustine's institutionalization of
Christianity, Connolly will need to interrogate him to expose the features
that have become a part of Connolly's own voice. But the interrogation is
not designed to lead simply to an internment or dismissal. Because Augustine is able to incite elements of Connolly's voice, it is important to the
modulations of his voice that Connolly recognize his inner Augustine.

Connolly speaks to Augustine of voice, and of what ears may hear from voices in terms of the power effects that voices produce. "You speak, Augustine, to an ear located in the interior of the self, an ear that muffles the sounds of death so that it can receive any murmur on behalf of an afterlife, an ear that drowns out sounds that equate death with oblivion, an ear that listens to secret appeals for revenge against a world that is cold and indifferent to the desire to escape oblivion, an ear that would rather hear the voice of the other through the code of heresy, damnation, apostasy, sacrilege, and sinfulness than sacrifice the possibility of eternity." This is why the confession is a powerful mode for Augustine, because it is a way to touch directly the interior of other mortals. "You go through yourself to the interior of other selves while constantly stirring up doubts requiring new forays into the same territory." This is done out of an impulse "to revenge against the human condition."[27]

We cannot simply reject this voice, because it is part of us. "But why should we contest the voice you tap within us even as we listen to it with new ears?," Connolly asks.[28] This may be called the political problem of voice. We are composed by the insistences of other voices, even as we may struggle against the injunctions that they contain. This tension is very close to that which Emerson describes so eloquently in "Self-Reliance," as hearing in the work of genius our own thoughts returning to us in alienated majesty. So with Augustine, a willingness to invoke a powerful god who underwrites the incorporation of the will for revenge into a system of justice will find expression through a variety of modes and voices that otherwise might not be thought of as sharing anything with him other than a powerful sense of the injustice of the world. But who would want to deny this sense in themselves? Enlisting Nietzsche's characterization of those in whom the impulse to punish is powerful, Connolly says to Augustine: "The hangman and the bloodhound are not simply those others; they haunt us because they also exist as proclivities within us. This you understand better than anyone else. It is what you seek to do with this understanding that I seek to contest. These are the voices in most of us that must be engaged and contested if the logic of existential revenge is to be combated. Or so it seems to me."[29] In all of his subsequent work to date Connolly pursues this contestation of voices with an insistence and care, seeking to identify those moments when his own solidity of voice threatens to overwhelm the voice of the other that he contests. "The idea is not to pursue a constantly receding depth where the true self resides," he writes, "but to excavate a patterns of insistence in ourselves."[30]

To be sure, the question of justice that appears to be at the center of political theoretical concern also animates Connolly's voice. But he is deeply wary of the ease with which the question of justice is answered by competing moralists: Rawlsian liberals, communitarians, Marxists, and Straussian authoritarians share a (too often cynical) willingness to succumb to the Augustinian imperative, to encode morality into a transcendent form and thus to do great harm in the name of goodness. So among other places, in his discussion of the Book of Job in his book-length study of Augustinian politics, Connolly renders a strong distinction between morals and ethics to evade what he calls the transcendental narcissism associated with views of nature that demand, one way or another, that the world be *for us*.[31] Stephen White trenchantly summarizes an important consequence of the view that unfolds toward the conclusion of Connolly's study of the Augustinian imperative, namely an affirmation of existence. "What remains is the idea of an ontological source that always exceeds any given interpretation, and this exceeding is itself interpreted as a giving of being, a generosity, to which we owe a peculiar kind of gratitude. To my mind, this source is affirmed by Connolly *wholeheartedly*, not strategically, provisionally, or at arm's length, for it is to the inspiriting force of such affirmation that we must look for motivational resources for our ethicalpolitical life."[32] Less emphatically registered in this passage is Connolly's wholehearted understanding of not only the excessive character of the ontological source but its amoral character (though White discusses this element at length elsewhere).[33] But for purposes of understanding Connolly's voice, it is pertinent to ask, as a matter of studied and purposeful blasphemy, how the voice in the whirlwind may become an element of our voice, even or especially in its excessiveness.

An answer to this question lies in the cultivation of strangeness. Connolly urges us not merely to be tolerant of strangeness but to recognize and cherish the strange as an essential element of our very being. "What if strangeness were treated by more people as indispensable to identity in a world without intrinsic moral design, and, hence, something to be prized as a precondition of identity and a source of possibilities for selective alliances and more generous negotiations with others? And what if more adherents of an intrinsic moral order were to acknowledge the deep and persistent contestability of this projection (along with those who oppose it) so as to allow this issue to become a more overt object of political negotiation and contestation?" Such an attitude will promote a refigured generosity, "a politics of generosity toward the strangeness in ourselves through attentiveness to whirlwinds within and without."[34] To oversimplify, such attentiveness may be thought of as proceeding at two levels—the *infra*, or the level of affective movements and sensations of a single and singular body, and the *inter*, or the level between constituent and emergent identities. But this characterization is deceptive, because in the matter of voice, the infra and inter are threaded together, mutually imbricated (as paradoxical as that may sound), shaping the strangeness of our lives together and apart. The call for an attitude of generosity emerges "from enhanced appreciation of dissonances within our own identities and of persistent implication in the differences through which we are consolidated."[35] An identity enunciates itself through this process, a political process.

Connolly's subsequent work may be imagined as a further appreciation of the voices he hears in the whirlwind, an attempt to bring them to bear upon the articulation of a voice that will inflect political thinking with an appreciation of the complex unfoldings of identity and difference which shape our existence together and apart. Depending on the focus of the work, he will be shouting at the cold and hard and fixed and powerful institutionalizations of rules—what he hopes we may recognize as the arboreal shaping of such entities as states, international orders, globalized economies, fundamentalist orders of morality—to provoke responses that he may then reshape and rethink and recirculate to represent alternative articulations of power, not always to whittle down the trees, but sometimes to retrain them into their rhizomatic shapes. This is an act of the use of power, hence an act to be thought through very carefully. Hence Connolly's deep concern for the relation between thoughts, proto-thoughts, and the unthought. So at other moments, he will be whispering to the fragile and inchoate impulses within the organization of identities, the repressed elements of embodied thinking, the unarticulated yearnings of uncertain hearts and minds, to elicit the words, sentences, languages, forms of life, worlds, and words that are always and everywhere at risk of loss, and that need to be cultivated for there to be the possibility of a lived democratic experience. This is a purpose of Connolly's ethos of pluralization.

The dynamics of voice in the play of speech and writing are not simply a matter of modulating volume—between a shout and a whisper. We whine, we drone, we lecture, we squeak, we squeal, we grunt, we mumble, we laugh, we cry, we cajole, we plead, we demand, we bloviate, we cry, we yearn, we grieve, we do all sorts of things with our voices as a part of doing things with words. Among the most ancient things we do with our voices—we sing. Attracted to Connolly by his songs (having only heard his singing in his written voice), I want to focus on an instance of his singing, drawn from his recent book, *Neuropolitics*.

CONNOLLY'S ARIA, THE FUGITIVE DOORWAY, POLITICAL POETICS

What is singing, anyway? We may imagine singing as a deterritorialization not only of the mouth but of the throat, diaphragm, lungs, stomach, and head, in which words are drawn forth into a sonority of pitch, rhythm, tempo, and more, so that we may remember not only the words, if any, that are enunciated but also recall the affective force of an emotion. Singing is a form of voicing—perhaps the most important form that voice takes. Giambattista Vico suggested as much in his *New Science* when he presented evidence that before humans learned how to speak they sang. And of course Nietzsche's first great insight concerned the singing quality of the enunciated language of ancient Greek, which lent itself to the birth of tragedy.[36] More recently Cavell, in a lengthy and complex meditation on opera and film and the question of voicing, suggests variously that singing, in opera especially but also in film, betokens a demand for voice to be heard (as in women's demand for a voice in the enunciation of their history), an attempt to reconcile the Kantian universal voice with the utter contingency of embodiment, an expression of a Cartesian counterintuition of an intimacy of body and spirit, and Emerson's thought of the relationship of breathing to character.[37] At the very least, we may reasonably claim that there is an intensification of the powers of affective embodiment at play when a voice begins to sing.

We may think of Connolly's singing as just this sort of intensification. Such moments seem to me tied most closely to moments of autobiography, not in the sense of a self-authorized representation of the arc of a life but in the sense that Emerson expresses in "The American Scholar," and that Cavell endorses at the beginning of his book of autobiographical exercises, that "the deeper the scholar dives into his privatest, secretest presentiment, to his wonder he finds this is the most acceptable, public, and universally true."[38] While autobiography can include a recitation of the past—and Connolly shows his intent with great care at the beginning of his book, offering us the terrifying, sad, and sweet story of the accident that befell his parents and generated his early curiosity about neuroscience—it also, and perhaps more intimately and immediately, involves those "secret presentiments" that may be discovered in the careful disinterment of the weaving play of proto-thoughts and thoughts enabling a fuller expression of the public character of an emotion and expression.[39]

One of my recent favorites of Connolly's performances is the aria that he sings in *Neuropolitics* on the experience of going to see a movie. Interested in the shape that thought takes and how it emerges both from the zone of indiscernibility between the human and animal and from experience through time, Connolly wants to explore the truth of Nietzsche's proposition, "Between two thoughts all kinds of affects play their games."[40] With Nietzsche, Connolly wants to draw our attention to the role of affect in thinking by mobilizing concepts to unsettle our thinking, "encouraging the movement of affect" toward the end of allowing an encounter between our thoughts and Nietzsche's. This is a practice of *reading* that has an earlier advocacy in Emerson's suggestion concerning how to use books. Emerson wrote that "one should learn to divine books, to *feel* those that you want without wasting much time on them." To a young student who wrote to him concerning how to read, he replied: "The glance reveals what the gaze obscures. Somewhere the author has hidden his message. Find it, and skip the paragraphs that do not talk to you . . . Reading long at any one time anything, no matter how it fascinates, destroys thought. Do not permit this. Stop if you find yourself becoming absorbed, at even the first paragraph."[41] While Emerson's discipline of distraction is perhaps not attainable by most of us, the point is clear enough and in deep accord with Connolly's pedagogy—we need to cultivate our receptiveness to the affectivity of thought.

Reading has always been more than scanning words on a printed page, but with the invention of film the possibilities for appreciating the dense interconnections between thought and affect expand tremendously. And this expansion of possibilities generates new creative capacities. "It is above all in the encounter between where you have gone and where

Nietzsche is going that creative things break out. Nietzsche's use of ellipses in his written texts is in fact remarkably close to the way some film
directors today use 'irrational cuts' between scenes to encourage us to
engage the nonlinear character of time."[42] More generally for Connolly,
writing in agreement with the film theorist Steven Shaviro, the "concentrated intersections of image, voice, sounds, rhythms, and musical scores
of film 'affirms the power of the body, and it sees the very opacity and
insubordination of the flesh as a stimulus of thought and as its necessary
condition.' "[43]

Connolly immediately puts this insight into play. "Consider the closing
scene of *Five Easy Pieces*, a film I saw for the second time in a theater in
Canberra in 2000, thirty years after its American release."[44] This sentence
introduces a narrative of Connolly's reception of the film. We may notice
how this sentence encourages the reader to think of a thirty-year interval
—to someone once young, now not, an American film of youthful alienation is shown again far from its home, far from its first audience. We
could ask: How does the film hold up? But that is only one thought
among many that we may implicitly or explicitly be encouraged to cultivate. Moreover, it is the closing scene of the film that Connolly asks us to
consider, although a compressed summary of the film is necessary to set
up our reading of this final scene. Karen Black is Rayette, the warm and
earthy waitress, Jack Nicholson the "man hopelessly divided between a
musical, upper-middle-class heritage, both 'Robert' and 'Bobby'." In this
final scene he leaves Rayette, hitching a ride with a truck driver who
is heading north even as they were planning on heading south, while
Rayette is inside a gas station. Credits roll as we watch a logging truck
crawl north and Rayette, emerging from the station, "looks every way but
north" for her Bobby. Enacted here is a decision that only retrospectively
makes sense in the terms of the film narrative, as the departure of Bobby/
Robert from Rayette is not necessary but spur-of-the-moment. Connolly writes, "It makes sense retrospectively, but lacks necessity prospec-
tively."[45] In short, Connolly's aria recreates for us in encapsulated form his
re-experience of the film's most important impressions.

But what turns this description into a song is that Connolly then describes the audience as it leaves the film, and devotes more words to
describing the experience of thinking about the film than to recreating
the experience of watching the film. This surprising move tonally demon-

strates to us what is somehow an overlooked truth of thinking about experiences: that their recreation in the thinking of them does much to form the experience itself. Interestingly, his voice, in the formal sense, shifts over the course of a few sentences from the third person to the second. "As you walk out, a variety of thoughts might be triggered, depending in part upon the virtual memories each brings to this encounter. You might recall a star-crossed relationship whose intensity you have never revealed to the companion strolling out with you. Or, as if from nowhere, you might wish with sudden intensity that your dad were alive again, realizing only hours later that his loss was made vivid by the juxtaposition in the closing scene with the one preceding it in which Robert leaves the home of his paralyzed father for the last time." On and on he goes, describing the bubbling up of series of memories and connections, showing how the movie, even if it isn't a great film (though we might say that a great movie will certainly do this for us), can "rapidly mobilize a series of affectively imbued virtual memories and, above them, a set of explicit recollections."[46] The rapidity of these connections is also ephemeral —we lose many of these proto-thoughts, even as they seem to jostle and leap up for our conscious attention.

Who is this "you" whose voice we hear? It is both self-referential and general, gesturing to the indeterminate place where we become out of me and you and them. The in-between-ness of you is an identity in the process of becoming something, drifting along. For Connolly the process of daydreaming, or drifting, may allow us to slow down enough to apprehend more explicitly the gaps between thoughts, to "make fugitive contact with those recurrent instants of apparent emptiness that set crucial conditions of possibility for new thoughts to arise. You thus slide a little closer to that doorway from which the virtual register opens onto the stage of consciousness . . . *Attention to this fugitive doorway discloses how thought is always already under way by the time you place it under the incomplete governance of intentionality and public expression.*"[47]

Here we are at that place where affect registers the feeling of thought. This is the place of language. But rather than imagine that affect interferes with the expression of thought in language—that emotions only tongue-tie us, so to speak, or that what we feel obscures and distorts what would otherwise be clear—we are able to realize something else, the complex interaction of feeling and language, how the two influence each other to shape new thoughts. Without language, affect would be more brutish than it is, and "affect is involved in that tricky process by which the outside of thought is translated into thought." Connolly presents an example: "If you forget a name, there is an absence where you want a presence. But it is not a situation of pure emptiness. Perhaps you remember vaguely the rhythm of the name—da, da, da, rather than da, da—and use that recollection to help you out. Or perhaps you recall a similar name each time you are trying to call up that one, and you see how this is blocking you. These examples show how forgetting does not involve a pure absence, for if it did you could never recognize the correct name when it surfaces. They suggest how layered and multidimensional thinking is, for if you forget a name it may be difficult to recall it, but if you forget a rhythm too, it may be lost forever."[48] The process of remembrance involves a recalling of rhythm. What of the process of membrance? That is, what of the word that is yet to be spoken?

At this juncture Connolly refers us to Heidegger's comments concerning the poet—"when the issue is to put into language something which has never yet been spoken, then everything depends on whether language gives or withholds the appropriate word." Connolly suggests that when we coin new words or phrases for what are until then inchoate, affectively imbued thoughts, we "express what has not yet found articulation and ... change the dark precursor as it is drawn into an intersubjective network of similarities and contrasts." But to introduce new words that are absorbed into the intersubjective network is also to change the network itself. "This is the double process that marks both creativity in thinking and the politics of becoming."[49]

The politics of becoming is enacted any time we seek to protect and nurture those tones and moods that will allow us to gain a more fulsome sense of voice. It is poetry in motion, saying what has not been said before, or, in the poet Ann Lauterbach's phrasing, answering questions that have not yet been asked.[50] Lauterbach has expressed the poetic concern with worldliness in an essay that uncannily echoes and amplifies Connolly's interest in this conjunction. She writes, "I think world presses on language and language on world at every point, and by world I mean material, spiritual, political, and cultural present, a continuous flux *of* is recuperated *as* is."[51] The poet's role of expressing this recuperation is in accord with the political task of enacting a politics of becoming. The ethos is inclined toward bringing back to life a dimension of thought that has been too often and in too many particulars repressed and shunned by the arbiters of truth and justice. It may enable us to make a future claim on each other that is not so tightly tied to the dualism of identity and difference. So that when Connolly evokes the phrase *non-theistic gratitude* as an alternative to such binaries as *theism/atheism* and *believer/nonbeliever*, he is engaging in a poetics of politics to advance an ethos of pluralization.[52] Such a poetics is not ancillary to the work of theory, but is essential, it turns out, to the fulfillment of its most meager claims to account for the world in which we live. It expresses the conjoining of lyric and affective tone in a song that we may sing, if we want.

CONNOLLY'S VOICES

Throughout this chapter on Connolly's voice I have attempted to illustrate its range and power by invoking various elements of its composition, including elements that I imagine help to compose my own voice. Beginning with Jane Bennett, a primary inspiration, and Deleuze and Guatarri, powerful attractors of his alienated thoughts, adding the powerful philosophical insights of Nietzsche and Foucault and Heidegger in the background, I have accounted for other voices that I know he knows directly, such as Thoreau, and pressed upon him other voices that I suspect he would acknowledge and appreciate at the level of the poetics of thinking, the voices of Emerson and Cavell and Lauterbach for instance. The blending with his voice of their voices and the voices of others who are assembled and disassembled here and in other places is the work of notes and quotation, but here appears as well more directly as a statement of the work that we do to sustain each other during what my first teacher of political theory, John Wikse, used to refer to as the long march through our dying institutions. Reading each other, speaking in whatever public places are available to us, such attempts to trace the influence of voice are of use to the extent that they enable us to keep on moving, to work through our skepticism, as Cavell would say, or to discover the enchantment of our lives in the modern world, as Bennett would say, or to understand our weariness with trees, as Deleuze and Guatarri would say, or to encourage the cultivation of an ethos of pluralization, which in other words is to love the world without necessarily knowing it, to be inclined toward enabling its deepest, wildest, and most fecund expressions of it-self, to assess the human as a limited but wonderful expression of the meaning that we may extract from the whirlwind, to concern ourselves with the delimitation of voice by those who would refuse to hear.

I declare—I swear—that I can hear all these voices singing within and without Connolly's voice. There are others, some that I can hear, others that I may, someday, others still that will always be silent to me. This is enough of a mystery for me, enough to continue trying to listen.

NOTES

I wish to acknowledge the help of Jane Bennett and Wendy Brown for comments on earlier drafts.

1 Jane Bennett, *The Enchantment of Modern Life: Attachments, Crossings, and Ethics* (Princeton: Princeton University Press, 2001), 153.

2 Ibid., quoting Gilles Deleuze and Felix Guatarri, *Kafka: Toward a Minor Literature*, trans. Dana Polan, foreword by Réda Bensmaïa (Minneapolis: University of Minnesota Press, 1986), 19–20.

3 My thanks to Wendy Brown for pointing out a possible confusion on this point.

4 Deleuze and Guatarri, *Kafka*, 20–21. Sense is reterritorialized by language in both a physical and a spiritual sense. For Deleuze and Guatarri this is an ordinary use of language. Thus for them, sound is what deterritorializes language when the words no longer make sense. I hope to connect this insight to the claims of both Cavell and Heidegger regarding the relationship of language to thinking.

5 Ibid., 21.

6 Martin Heidegger, *What Is Called Thinking*, trans. Fred D. Weick and J. Glenn Gray (San Francisco: Harper and Row, 1968 [originally pubd in German, 1954]), 16.

7 Henry David Thoreau, *Walden*, chapter 3, "Reading," *The Portable Thoreau*, ed. Carl Bode (New York: Penguin, 1947), 354. This passage is discussed at length by Stanley Cavell in *The Senses of Walden* (Chicago: University of Chicago Press, 1992 [1972]), chapter 1, "Words." I address Cavell's thoughts on speech, writing, and voice below.

8 Thoreau, *Walden*, 546 (italics in original).

9 Ibid., 546–47 (italics in original).

10 Ibid., 547–48 (italics in original).

11 Is this the scandal of language, the implied abandonment of the mother every time we write?

12 Deleuze and Guattari, *Kafka*, 21.

13 Cavell, *The Senses of Walden*, 27. I note here that Cavell returns to the passage in

Thoreau on mother and father voices in his essay on inheritance, "Philosophy and the Arrogation of Voice," *A Pitch of Philosophy: Autobiographical Exercises* (Cambridge: Harvard University Press, 1994), 39–40.

14 Cavell, *The Senses of Walden*, 28.

15 Ibid., 112.

16 See Cavell, *Conditions Handsome and Unhandsome: The Constitution of Emersonian Perfectionism* (Chicago: University of Chicago Press, 1988).

17 Cavell, *A Pitch of Philosophy*, 40.

18 Ibid., 41.

19 Ibid., 58.

20 Connolly, *Politics and Ambiguity* (Madison: University of Wisconsin Press, 1987), vii–viii.

21 Ibid., 154.

22 Ibid.; quotation from Foucault, "The Order of Discourse," in Robert Young, ed., *Untying the Text* (Boston: Routledge and Kegan Paul, 1981), 68.

23 Connolly, *Politics and Ambiguity*, 154–55.

24 Ibid., 160.

25 I note here appreciatively Stephen White's *Sustaining Affirmation: The Strengths of Weak Ontology in Political Theory* (Princeton: Princeton University Press, 2001). White's essay on Connolly's work frames his recent political theory in terms with which I find myself in deep agreement.

26 Connolly, *Identity\Difference: Democratic Negotiations of Political Paradox* (Ithaca: Cornell University Press, 1991), 124. This is the chapter entitled "A Letter to Augustine."

27 Ibid., 138–39.

28 Ibid., 139.

29 Ibid., 140.

30 Ibid., 155.

31 Connolly, *The Augustinian Imperative: A Reflection on the Politics of Morality* (Thousand Oaks, Calif.: Sage, 1993), 11.

32 White, *Sustaining Affirmation*, 114.

33 Ibid., 108–11.

34 Connolly, *The Augustinian Imperative*, 28.

35 Ibid.

36 For a fascinating discussion of the songlike quality of ancient Greek and its influence on Nietzsche's argument in *The Birth of Tragedy: Out of the Spirit of Music*, see Tracy Strong, "The Tragic Ethos and the Spirit of Music," *International Studies in Philosophy*, forthcoming.

37 Cavell, "Opera and the Lease of Voice," 134 (on women), 148 (on Kant), 138 (on Descartes), 150 (on Emerson).

38 Cavell, *A Pitch of Philosophy*, vii.

39 Connolly, *Neuropolitics: Thinking, Culture, Speed* (Minneapolis: University of Minnesota Press, 2002), xi–xiii.

40 Ibid., 67, citing Nietzsche, *The Will to Power*, aphorism no. 477.

41 Quotations taken from Robert Richardson Jr., *Emerson: The Mind on Fire* (Berkeley: University of California Press, 1995), 173, 174. The work cited by Richardson, by the student at Williams College who wrote to Emerson, Charles Woodbury, is *Talks with Emerson* (New York: Baker and Taylor, 1890), 27, 28, 29 (italics in original).

42 Connolly, *Neuropolitics*, 67.

43 Ibid., 68, quoting Steven Shaviro, *The Cinematic Body* (Minneapolis: University of Minnesota Press, 1993), 255, 256.

44 Connolly, *Neuropolitics*, 68.

45 Ibid., 68–69.

46 Ibid., 69–70.

47 Ibid., 71 (italics in original).

48 Ibid., 72.

49 Ibid.

50 Ann Lauterbach, "Slaves of Fashion," *Boston Review* 23, no. 3.

51 Ann Lauterbach, "On Flaws: Toward a Poetics of the Whole Fragment," *Theory and Event* 3, no. 1 (fall 1999) (italics added).

52 Connolly, *Neuropolitics*, 72–73.

THE TIME OF RIGHTS: EMERGENT THOUGHTS IN AN EMERGENCY SETTING

Bonnie Honig

Teaching which is not meant to apply to anything but the examples given is different from that which "*points beyond*" them.

—LUDWIG WITTGENSTEIN, *Philosophical Investigations* no. 208[1]

THE PARADOX OF POLITICS

Of course, it is appropriate to examine theories that insistently present themselves as exemplars of coherence to see whether they live up to the standard they impose on others and themselves. But what about those that seek to expose paradoxicality in daily life? These must be appraised, first of all, by the way they respond to the paradoxes they identify.

WILLIAM CONNOLLY, *Identity\Difference:*
Democratic Negotiations of Political Paradox[2]

IN THIS QUOTATION FROM *Identity\Difference* lie the kernels of what is the most important, in my view, of William Connolly's many significant contributions to political theory. For Connolly, paradoxes are salient clues to political life's secrets; they are challenges to be negotiated, not puzzles to be solved or overcome. Life, abundant and perpetually becoming, overflows and resists human-all-too-human demands for coherence and consistency. But it is available for understanding and crafting, especially when approached with agonistic respect and care.

The term "paradox" comes from the Greek, meaning beside or different from common opinion—para doxy. Common opinion is said to seek out consistency—clear, straight roads. Often, however, politics offers vicious circles or winding paths. For those who seek a clear and straight road, the circularity of political paradox may be enervating. But for democratic theorists who take up Connolly's invitation to rework desire and resist the force of the desiring machines (Deleuze and Guattari)[3] that produce straightness as a moral and political norm, political paradox can be illuminating. And common opinion can be responsive to its illuminations.

There are connections between (1) the promising circularity of paradox analyzed at length by Connolly in *Identity\Difference* and *The Ethos of Pluralization*,[4] (2) his later move in *Neuropolitics: Thinking, Culture, Speed*[5] to theorize an alternative to a linear conception of time, and (3) his analysis of the nonlinear composition of mind-body and brain-body relations through the materiality and affectivity of thought (also in *Neuropolitics*, in which he studies somatic affects and work on the self). Connolly does not pause to analyze these connections in detail, but as I will suggest here, focusing in particular on the first two connections, a politics committed to the affirmation and exploration of paradox must perforce be committed to a nonlinear conception of time (and a nonlinear conception of mind-body and brain-body relations).

One paradox to which Connolly has returned again and again is the paradox of politics (which he also refers to as the paradox of sovereignty, the paradox of political founding, and the paradox of politics-sovereignty in *Political Theory and Modernity, Identity\Difference*, and *The Ethos of Pluralization*).[6] Here is Connolly's parsing of the paradox, which he finds well expressed in Rousseau's *Social Contract*, book II, chapter 7:[7] "For a general will to be brought into being, effect (social spirit) would have to become cause, and cause (good laws) would have to become effect. The problem is how to establish either condition without the previous attainment of the other upon which it depends."[8] Rousseau raises the issue in the context of *founding* the ideal social contract, but Connolly insists that the problem attaches to politics more generally. If the paradox is real, then wherever good law is said to have come from the free and good willing of citizens, it will likely turn out that something else is (also) the case. Thus, where Rousseau posits "pure general will (which must be common and singular)," readers sensitive to the paradox of politics will, if they look hard enough, find "the concealment of impurities."[9] For example: "Rousseau's artful efforts to legitimize the subordination of women can be seen, first, to express the necessity of subordination (of either men or women) within the family so that the will of a unified family can contribute a single [undifferentiated] will to the public quest for a general will, and, second, to conceal the violence lodged within the practices of male authority in the family by treating subordination as suitable for women as such." Connolly concludes: "So Rousseau both exposes the paradox in the founding of the general will and conceals it in his presentations of that will once it has been founded."[10]

Rousseau's aim is to launch the ideal regime of the social contract and secure its legitimation by insulating it from implication in violence, unfreedom, or partiality. The result, however, is rather different—a politics and a citizenry potentially ill equipped to respond to the daily, ongoing exercise of government powers unleashed by their social contract, yet unharnessed by real general willing and uninterrupted by agonistic democratic engagements. If the paradox of politics is real and enduring, then a democratic politics would do well to replace its faith in a pure general will with an acceptance of its impurity and an embrace of the perpetuity of political contestation that the impurity makes necessary. In such a setting, democracy's necessary conditions (e.g. the reproduction of a supposed general will) may be found to offend some of its own commitments (to freedom and self-rule) in ways that call for (a certain model of) democracy's self-overcoming (i.e. in quest of a different democracy). This self-overcoming may take the form of civic commitments to practices of agonistic respect and to an ethos of pluralization that acknowledges the remainders of all forms of life by actively but not uncritically supporting the efforts of new identities to come into being without prior guarantees about the rightness or justice of their claims.

Many scholars have written about Rousseau's efforts to get out from under the paradox of politics. Some, including Connolly himself in *Political Theory and Modernity*, have noted in particular Rousseau's turn to a lawgiver (said to represent divine wisdom, or the objectivity of a foreigner, or idealized rationality, among other things), whose somewhat awkward role vis-à-vis Rousseau's supposedly free, self-governing, and self-initiating subjects requires a fair amount of explanation.[11] But in *The Ethos of Pluralization* Connolly notes parenthetically another solution, or another element of it: "Rousseau understood the founding of a general will to be paradoxical. He located the paradox in time (*perhaps to imagine another time when it could be resolved*)."[12] In this book Connolly has not yet turned his attention to the concept of time (one might say he is interested here more in the workings of space, but that would be misleading since territoriality, his topic in *The Ethos of Pluralization*, is a function of both space and time—national space, place, and boundaries are defined by national time, history, pace, and cultural teleology), but here, in *The Ethos*, in this allusion to the work of time or temporalization, is the promissory note upon which *Neuropolitics* later begins to deliver. Rousseau, Connolly suggests, alleviates the paradox of politics by casting it as a paradox of *founding*—a quandary, yes, but one faced at a regime's beginning, and therefore one that can be resolved or surmounted in or by time. Recast as a paradox of founding, the paradox of politics is *thereby* resolved; that is to say it is rendered in principle soluble or at least escapable by way of its location in linear time.

But the problem named by Rousseau is not one confined to the founding period.[13] Every day—through birth, immigration, and maturation to adulthood—new citizens are received by established regimes and every day established citizens are reinterpellated into the laws, norms, and expectations of their regimes such that the paradox of politics is replayed rather than overcome in time. Indeed the first thing to go, when we face the chicken-and-egg paradox of politics, is our confidence in linear time, its normativity and its form of causality. What is linear time's normativity? Belief in a linear time sequence is invariably attended by belief that that sequence is either regressive (a Fall narrative) or progressive. In both regressive and progressive time, the time sequence itself is seen to be structured by causal forces that establish meaningful, orderly connections between what comes before and what comes after (Decline or Rise), such that one thing *leads* to another rather than forming, as plural temporalities and tempos do, a random assemblage or jumble of events. *All* these elements—linearity, its normativity, causality—are thrown off balance by the paradox of politics in which what is presupposed as coming before (virtue, the people, the law) invariably comes after (if at all), and what comes after invariably replays the paradox of politics that time was supposed to surmount.

It might seem that acknowledging the vicious circularity of the paradox of politics must be costly to a democracy: If the people (or virtue, or the law) do not exist as a prior—or even as a post hoc—unifying force, then what will authorize or legitimate their exercises of power? But there is, as we shall see, also promise in such an acknowledgment, and moreover denial is costly too, for we can deny or disguise the paradox of politics only by suppressing or naturalizing the exclusion of those (elements of the) people whose residual, remaindered, minoritized existence might call the pure general will into question. From the perspective of the paradox of politics, unchosen, unarticulated, or minoritized alternatives—different forms of life, identities, solidarities, sexes or genders, alternative categories of justice, unfamiliar tempos—re-present themselves to us daily, in one form or another, sometimes inchoate. The paradox of politics provides a lens through which to re-enliven those alternatives. It helps us see the lengths to which we go or are driven to insulate ourselves from the remainders of our settled paths. Are there other, nonlinear temporalities to which we might look to avoid or interrupt this pattern? Might they open up a democratic politics sensitive to remainders and open to political paradox?[14]

Connolly has his insight about paradox and linear temporality in relation to Rousseau, but the insight exceeds Rousseau and invites a new line of critical reflection on contemporary deliberative democrats who stage their reflections on democracy and rights by taking up a political paradox and rendering it manageable by embedding it in a linear time sequence. Unlike Rousseau (as Connolly reads him), Jürgen Habermas and Seyla Benhabib do not confine the paradox of politics to a distant past. They locate the paradox in the present and look to a future in which the paradox can be worked out by way of present political practices—which Habermas calls "tapping" and Benhabib calls "iterations"—and futural orientations. While Rousseau, on Connolly's account, thought to escape the paradox of politics by confining it to a distant past, and Habermas and Benhabib seek to escape it by reference to a hoped-for future, both would-be solutions depend upon their location in linear time. We may not know the future the way we know the past (although even the past exceeds our efforts to know it, given its availability in perpetuity for reinterpretation and appropriation), but that matters less than the fact that the linear temporality in which both past and future are lodged is itself what irons out the circularity of paradox and gives us hope that present conflicts can be surmounted in ways that will not generate new remainders.

The assumption in Habermas and Benhabib of linear time secures what I call a chrono-logic in relation to which they assess new rights: new rights-claims are judged in terms of the rights' amenability to being subsumed under existing constitutional or universal categories. I look in detail at how Connolly's focus on new rights-claims in the moments of their unstable and insecure emergence points to an orientation toward rights and a register of temporality different from those operative in deliberative democratic theory. Connolly's account presses us to see how new rights-claims do not necessarily demand mere inclusion in a previously stabilized order. They may. But they may also demand a new world. They may unsettle previously existing categories of right. That capacity to unsettle (and its usual eventual loss, which is the price of inclusion by way of rights in liberal democracies) is for Connolly a fecund political resource that can be exploited only if we give up judging new rights-claims solely in terms of their fit to existing schedules of rights. Rather than pose a problem to be solved, the paradox of politics makes visible a different alternative.

I develop the argument about rights and temporality with reference to two rights-claims to which Connolly repeatedly returns in his work: gay rights and the right to doctor-assisted suicide. I focus not on the rights per se, nor on the claimants, but on the worlds potentially opened or closed by these rights. I worry about how a focus on rights is encouraged by a law-centered view of the world, and distracts our attention from common goods, the generation of which is the glue and the goal of democratic life. And I suggest that rights tend to privilege or postulate the linear temporality that Connolly wants to get away from. In short, Connolly's strong focus on rights is a bit of a weakness but is also a great strength if he can, as I believe he does, show that even rights presuppose and require the plural and uneven tempos that he prefers to the linear temporality that normally supports them and is supported by them.

I highlight some of the larger issues surrounding doctor-assisted suicide, noting its possible implication in the biopolitics in which Giorgio Agamben says we are mired. And I find in Wittgenstein a critique of something like a chrono-logic of meaning, which usefully deepens my critique of the chrono-logic of rights. Finally, I turn to a relatively new movement, Slow Food, to illustrate the sort of political actions that might arise out of an alternative to established chrono-logical understandings of rights. Slow Food's success thus far has been due in no small measure, first, to its embrace of plural tempos: it combines the slow seasonality of nature (by contrast with the fast tempo and repetitive productivity of industrial agriculture) with the fast pace of global communications and markets (by contrast with the slow-paced, face-to-face encounters preferred by some democratic theorists); and second, to its use of a rights-claim to center its agenda and challenge the larger apparatus of the chrono-logic of rights. Slow Food claims the *right to taste*. In so doing, the movement acknowledges (by embracing while accenting) the apparent ridiculousness of new rights-claims from the perspective of the established schedule of rights; and Slow Food sutures rights to goods, convivial eating, healthy food, more human and humane food production processes, as well as the local autonomies and transnational connections that these require, while affirming pleasure as the center of its politics and pointing to the capacity that Arendt, borrowing from Kant, thought was absolutely central to democratic politics: *taste*.

Slow Food, I argue, also gently presses upon us an awareness in particular of one of the remainders of the rights-centered human universe: animal life, whose existence under current food production conditions rises surely to the level of emergency and which cannot be best remedied by a further expansion of rights. The needed encounter with animality points beyond the chrono-logic of rights and calls for a different orientation, lodged in the paradox of politics and pitched on the plural tempos theorized by Connolly and inhabited by Slow Food at its best.

THE BACKWARD-LOOKING GAZE OF A STILL FUTURE CONSTITUTIONALISM AND COSMOPOLITANISM

In "Constitutional Democracy: A Paradoxical Union of Contradictory Principles?"[15] Jürgen Habermas confronts a domesticated version of Rousseau's paradox of politics. The problem of law's production as an effect of the cause by which law is supposed to have been generated in the first place is replaced by a problem less knotty though also important: the problem of how to rank or reconcile the rule of law and popular sovereignty, constitutionalism and democracy. In this version of the paradox the mystery of law's origins and legitimation is abated: we have no vicious circle of chicken and egg but rather two established principles or norms that may be incompatible—law and democracy.

Habermas argues that the so-called paradox of constitutional democracy is illusory. Law and democracy are fully compatible. Neither is conceptually or chronologically prior to the other, neither can legitimately be made subservient to the other. Habermas has only praise for the constitutional events that he names synecdochically "Paris" and "Philadelphia," or at least for what he calls their reasonable trace. But if we experience law as alien to our authorship, he explains, the solution is not to look backward to those conventions (which, though Habermas does not say this, might increase our sense of law's alienness), nor to justify law's dominance over democratic will or vice versa. Instead, we ought to look forward to a future in which law and democracy are realigned in their fundamental compatibility, their conceptual co-originality fulfilled. In the fullness of time the felt conflict between law and democracy is worked out, Habermas says, or at least we have a duty to work it out. What is important to Habermas is that the so-called paradox is not seen to be insoluble lest we fail in our obligation to do this work: "The *allegedly* paradoxical relation between democracy and the rule of law resolves itself *in the dimension of historical time, provided one conceives of the constitution as a project that makes a founding act into an ongoing process of constitution-making that continues across generations*" (my italics). Constitutions do not constrain democratic peoples in a way that calls for justification or intervention, because any sense of constraint can be overcome by the agency of the present generation whose responsibility it is to "tap the system of rights ever more fully" and realize further its constitutional inheritance in time.

For time to work as an effective solution to the paradox of constitutional democracy, time itself must be nonparadoxical in structure. It cannot, for example, send us in more than one direction at once, nor circle and fork unexpectedly. In Habermas's text, time is linear and singular. The future is modeled on and is in some ways confined to the past; the past seems to know or presage the future. The past offers a system that needs only to be tapped, not overcome, transformed, or reinterpreted in light of new events, remnants, or ideas, and the future does not escape or transform the past—it merely fulfils the past or at worst forestalls its fulfillment. In short, tapping embeds the practice of rights in a chrono-logic in which the future of rights is contained (at least in potential form) in its past. Hannah Arendt protested such narratives of progress just as she rejected narratives of doom. "Neither," Susan Neiman says, "leaves room for the forces of fortune, contingency and accident on which Arendt insists."[16] Without these forces we lose the freedom on behalf of which Arendt wrote incessantly. As Arendt put the point in *Thinking*: "either we say with Hegel: Die Weltgeschichte ist das Weltgericht, leaving the ultimate judgment to success, [or leaving it, as Habermas does, to the forecast of success], or we can maintain with Kant the autonomy of the minds of men and their possible independence of the things as they are or have come into being [or are declared likely to come into being]."[17]

Arendt was no fonder of familial metaphors in politics than she was of progress and regress narratives; for her both close down the contingency upon which politics depends. Habermas combines these, rendering time itself inalien by casting it in familial terms. He portrays the relation between past and present as a generational passing, it occurs in generational time, and his familial metaphor inoculates later generations against the trauma of norm-transmission.[18] In the passage of power from one set of persons to another, from founding fathers to today's citizens, there is little hint of imposition. Present-day citizens exercise self-rule by tapping the promise of a law-rule that need not be incompatible with democratic self-governance, if we take up our political responsibilities.

A similar temporalization is evident in *Another Cosmopolitanism*, when Seyla Benhabib addresses the paradox of democratic legitimation; this, like Habermas' paradox of constitutional democracy, lacks the vicious circularity of the paradox of politics explored here.[19] The paradox of democratic legitimation names the following difficulty: "The democratic sovereign draws its legitimacy not merely from its act of constitution [we, the people] but equally significantly, from the conformity of this act to universal principles of human rights . . . [Thus] 'We, the people' refers to a particular human community, circumscribed in space and time, sharing a particular culture, history, and legacy; yet this people establishes itself as a democratic body by acting in the name of the 'universal.' The tension between universal human rights-claims, and particularistic cultural and national identities is constitutive of democratic legitimacy," Benhabib writes.[20] In place of Rousseau's well-meaning but potentially errant people whose willings both legitimate the regime as such and might also threaten to delegitimate it if they will the wrong, undemocratic thing,

here the people's legitimacy depends upon their achievement of a particularistic democratic popular sovereignty and also upon the universality
or universalizability of their law.[21] But in Benhabib's text, the constitutive
tension central to her argument is a bit more past than present, with
universality positioned toward a (cosmopolitan) future and particularity
toward a (Westphalian) past.[22] The time of democracy moves more slowly
and less inexorably, one might say, than the time of cosmopolitanism.

One might say that. But only one linear temporality imbues the paradox here. That temporality is most evident when Benhabib turns to questions of rights. Discussing the French veiling controversy, Benhabib says
of the girls who stood up for their "cultural rights" that having learned to
"talk back to the state," they will likely one day learn as well to "talk back
to Islam."[23] Benhabib's cosmopolitanism, like the paradox of politics, *both
presupposes and promises* citizens who do not yet exist. These citizens negotiate state and cultural powers on behalf of universal human rights which
are themselves (again) *both the condition and the goal* of liberal democratic
statehood in a cosmopolitan setting. But Benhabib breaks the vicious
circle, first by staging it as a conflict between universality and particularity rather than between or within democratic freedom and democratic
(self-) sovereignty, and then by inserting the amended paradox into a time
sequence—when she wagers that these young women will likely talk back
to Islam too one day, and thereby show they have learned democratic and
cosmopolitan citizenship in the course of historical time. The prediction
of eventual Islamic cultural self-overcoming confines the paradox of politics to a particular historical moment—not to the moment of founding
perhaps, à la Connolly on Rousseau, but to a pre-cosmopolitan moment
whose eventual, promised, overcoming is what licenses *our* affirmation of
their culturalism now.[24]

Whether or not this wager is right (a great deal depends upon domestic
and international developments in France, Europe, and the Middle East,
not simply on the trajectory of rights) is less important than the work that
the wager does. The wager puts in place the backward-looking gaze of a
(still) future cosmopolitanism perched on a normative, linear temporality. We assess the present from the perspective of a posited future in which
the partialities of the present are overcome. That temporality anchors the
chrono-logic of rights, the quasi-logical unfolding of rights in accordance
with the sequencing demands of linear, normative progress—(*Das Weltgeschichte ist das Weltgerichte*)—and it also occludes from view impositional

and violent processes that help secure such developments when they do occur. Benhabib is aware of current xenophobic policies, but she does not worry that any coming cosmopolitanism may be not just obstructed by them but itself partly produced by them and carrying their traces (i.e. she does not ask whether such policies might both violate and also help to produce the projected coming of a (post-)cultural cosmopolitanism).

The power of this backward-looking gaze of a still-future cosmopolitanism is evident when Benhabib writes that the second-class status of colonial Jews in British America "can be described as one of transition from being [in Kant's terms] 'a mere auxiliary to the commonwealth' to being a full-fledged citizen."[25] This is a tempting and familiar narration, in which supposed *systems* of rights are "tapped" as liberal democracies take the protections and privileges that they first limited to propertied white males and spread them outward to include all classes, races, and genders. From this perspective the status of colonial Jews looks *transitional*. But the speaker here—unlike those in the moment—speaks as if she already knows that the human rights side of the democratic legitimation paradox will in the end win, even though we are not yet at the end of the story nor could we ever be, and so cannot ever know who or what wins in the end.[26]

Other emergent rights are assessed in a similar "transitional" fashion. Newly porous borders in the EU and beyond, Benhabib believes, promise welcome developments like alien suffrage for member-state nationals and now even for third-country nationals. These are part of a fulfillment of earlier promises, another set of "tappings," which she calls "iterations." For Benhabib these new rights fit under an umbrella of an evolutionarily developing disaggregation of citizenship of which she approves. But there is another way to think about some of these emergent rights, in relation to different contexts, not against the backdrop of the increasing universalization of rights as such but rather in relation to a politics of rights and a politics of foreignness that might (yet) go lots of different ways. For example, alien suffrage is arguably not an extension of an old commitment to universal suffrage, but a historically contested practice. Once accepted in the United States, local voting rights came with residency for many aliens until they were abolished during the xenophobia of the First World War, and these rights have barely reemerged since. In addition, expansions of formal rights for some may be accompanied by contractions of social welfare for everyone. And this may be no coincidence. In the last thirty years, as Europeans have undergone an incredible down-sizing of social welfare, Étienne Balibar points out that debates about whether "we" should share our social welfare with "them" have occurred at a moment when social welfare rights amount to less than ever. Indeed, one might add, the discourse of the foreigner purveyed by western Euro-peans in which "they" want to come "here" to take "our" welfare is not only xenophobic; it is also productive insofar as it gives the impression to Europeans that they still have social welfare worth taking (which they may by comparison with others, but not by comparison with themselves thirty years ago). The downsizing of welfare and diminished citizen ex-pectations are some of the things obscured by the emplotment of the paradox of democratic legitimation in evolutionary, linear time (and also by the symbolic politics of foreignness as they have played out in the last few years in Europe).

It is always possible to recognize departures from progress while re-cuperating progressive, linear time. Linear time runs two ways: "one step forwards, two steps back." Nonlinear time houses plural flows and multi-vocal possibilities, and several simultaneous pasts and futures. It houses directionalities but does not give or secure direction. It is full of what if's, might have been's, and might yet be's. It does not point forward or back-ward; it does not run in a single sequence, belief in which Arendt termed "Kant's embarrassment." It loops, it circles, and it forks. It is full of the multiplicities and hiatuses that mark the treasured gap between Arendt's "no more" and her "not yet."[27] In nonlinear time, new rights cast by Benhabib as transnational and by Balibar as symptomatic of a lingering, nationalist politics in Europe should themselves open new possibilities or worlds that might exceed this binary division. To do so they would have to be seen not as part of an expanding universalism or a contracting na-tionalism but rather as part of what Connolly, in *Why I Am Not a Secular-ist*[28] and elsewhere, calls the politics of becoming (and in *The Ethos of Pluralization* had referred to as the "politics of enactment"), of which nonlinear time is a postulate.

TIME AND THE POLITICS OF BECOMING

Connolly's politics of becoming brings together critical responsiveness and an ethos of pluralization on behalf of those subjects, impulses, and forms of life remaindered by any current constellation of identity\

difference. It is crucial to such a politics to shake off the perspective of the backward-looking gaze (the perspective of the dialectic) and the chrono-logic of rights from which developments in time appear necessary, chronologically if not logically; this is why the will rages against time's it was, as Nietzsche and Arendt knew—because the will seeks freedom, not the necessity, that the past seems to offer. Instead a politics of becoming postulates the perspective of the present moment, that of the actor and not the spectator, situated between past(s) and future(s) and always infiltrated by their rumblings, in which practitioners of critical responsiveness, faced with new claims from emergent identities or discourses, lose their bearings, find they have no sense of direction, and are confounded.

In potentially originary moments it is difficult to know what properly belongs to the future and what to the past, or to which future and which past. At such moments, which are continual, "Justice now trembles in its constitutive uncertainty, dependence and ambiguity."[29] At such moments, we lose our grasp of the reassuring structured time of Kant's first *Critique* (which Arendt saw as underpinning necessitarian thought) and experience instead the abyssal time(lessness) of the third *Critique*'s aesthetic of the sublime. In such a politics there may well be what we later come to call progress, and new identities may be allowed or ushered onto the threshold of justice, but progress does not come with its own guarantee, nor is it a meaningful criterion to guide us. In the moment we do not know in what progress might consist, and new claims may seem laughable. Looking backward, we can say with satisfaction that the chrono-logic of rights required and therefore delivered the eventual inclusion of women, Africans, and native peoples into the schedule of formal rights. But what actually did the work? The impulsion of rights, their chrono-logic, or the political actors who won the battles they were variously motivated to fight and whose contingent victories were later credited not to the actors but to the independent trajectory of rights as such?

Our moral clarity regarding identities or forms of life that were once but are no longer excluded is a product of political victories whereby some succeeded in their effort to migrate "from an abject abnormal subordinate or obscure Other *subsisting* in a nether world under the register of justice to a positive identity now *existing* on the register of justice/injustice."[30] Those victorious political actors *created* post hoc the clarity that we now credit with having spurred them on to victory ex ante. They may have had clarity in their minds or been motivated by a commitment that they shared with others. But that clarity and those commitments did not in the moment have the necessitarian quality that the past lends to them post hoc. On the contrary, in the moment emergent rights-claims are experienced as fragile, contingent, and paradoxical. They presuppose and claim already to inhabit a world not yet built.[31] In short, they replay, they do not govern, the Rousseauvian paradox of politics, and they launch us into their nonlinear temporality, or can do so if we see them for what they are.

Of course new worlds are built not just by way of rights-claims and new identities but also by way of new visions of political goods and goals. Seeing movements for political change in terms of rights-claims, or centering them on the politics of rights or identity politics, threatens to limit our apprehension of new political events and narrow our political aspirations.[32] Connolly's focus on rights and identity as central goals of progressive political action in place of, say, goods, especially in *The Ethos of Pluralization* and *Identity\Difference*, seems to me to point to a potential limit in his approach.[33] It may make him unmindful of the role of law in producing the unilinear temporality that he seeks to decenter. It is in the discourse of law that innovative actors are invariably depicted as having "anticipated" the law (rather than having made, countermanded, or hijacked it) when they call for the recognition or entrenchment of new rights.[34] Connolly tends, following Nietzsche, to see such future orientations as remnants of religious, redemptive thinking, whether in Kantian or Hegelian form, which they are too. Niklaus Luhmann, by contrast, notes (and *celebrates*) law's success in producing a future-oriented linear temporality that can resolve the paradox of politics.

According to Luhmann, the development of modern constitutionalism has effected (in Christodoulidis's parsing) "a displacement of temporal perspectives. The overwhelming orientation to the past that characterized pre-modern society is displaced by *a new openness to the future made possible in the new constitutional order*. Openness to the future means that law foresees its own changeability and regulates it by positioning itself before political influx and placing all law under constitutional scrutiny. What is remarkable in these new developments is that the past is relieved of its function as a horizon of legitimation; the social imaginary, more generally, is re-oriented toward the future" (my italics).[35] But the past and future may not be so easily uncoupled. Some futures function a lot like the past that they supposedly replace; other futures remain haunted by pasts that they supposedly left behind or by other supposedly parallel (e.g. colonial) pasts that they claim not to know.

Those who see rights-claims as claims to membership in the universal will judge rights-claims in relation to a past (an already established universal as ground), or future (a universal whose promise is in place but whose realization has yet to be brought about), or both. But as Connolly points out, although agitators for rights do often claim membership in a, but not *the*, universal (we are human too, or we are citizens too), they also claim membership in particulars, and in so doing they claim a present-orientation that established universals with their focus on past or future do not privilege. The success of homosexuals in rescripting themselves as gays and heterosexuals as straights (thus replacing a medicalized binary—homo- or heterosexual—with a more egalitarian difference—gay or straight) was partly achieved by their insistence "we are everywhere": as members of straight families, brothers, sisters, sons and daughters, mothers and fathers. The particularity of membership and exposure, coming out, played a very big part in the move from one identity to the other because it claimed solidarity. Success was not preordained by nor contained in nor subsumed by previous victories, which took the protection of the universal for themselves and (re-)defined others—including homosexuals—as their constitutive outside, beneath the radar of the universal. Nor was success promised by already existing declarations of right, which may or may not have been found to "encompass" these new claims. Things could have gone another way. They may yet do so.

Connolly's politics of becoming rejects mere inclusion or subsumption; it is committed to the sort of mutual and unpredictable unsettlement that follows from real, risky engagement with otherness. Here we have another departure from the usual politics of rights and identity, an element of his more expansive approach. To stay with one of Connolly's favorite examples: Homosexuals could not reach real equality as homosexuals; they had to rescript themselves as gay. In so doing they also unsettled their former partner identity, heterosexuality. There was no alternative. The demedicalization of homosexuality entailed the denaturalization and deprivileging of heterosexuality. That is why so many heterosexuals fought it and continue to fight it. And they were, they *are* right, right about the costs to their own form of life, that is. In the politics of

becoming, gays and straights inhabit their desires and experience them
with more of a sense of contingency and relation to the other than homosexuals and heterosexuals do.[36] By contrast, mere chrono-logical inclusion under the sign of the universal does not come at that high a price. It
requires tolerance, but it itself tolerates and may even, on moral grounds,
demand stasis in the identities that it already harbors. Perhaps that is
why mere inclusion almost always disappoints and sometimes enrages
the newly included. As any informed observer of the civil rights movement in the United States can see, so much changes and yet so little
changes at the same time. A politics of becoming, by contrast, recognizes
that each new inclusion comes with disturbance and possibly transformation for those already in, as well as for the antecedent rules that aspire to
govern or subsume all new cases and events. That is why time never
stands still in politics, a point noted not only by Connolly but also by a
range of thinkers from J. G. A. Pocock to Luhmann. It is, however, a risk of
real dedication to a democratic politics such as that envisioned by Connolly that one might feel as if one were living from one emergency to the
next. Each new emergent claim can be experienced as an emergency by the
existing order, by the identities challenged yet again to undergo revision
or re-experience the contingency at their heart. Hence the need for arts of
the self and the other ethico-political virtues of respect and generosity
outlined by Connolly in a series of books published over the last ten years
or more.

Hence too the need to recraft time itself. It is to this effort that Connolly turns his attention in detail in *Neuropolitics*. Perhaps having fun with
his readers or possibly at their expense, he associates linear temporality
with a past time (implying that linear temporality is therefore dead and
gone)—or he notes that Nietzsche does so, anyway. Like Nietzsche, Connolly uses that pastness to open up a new space for a new time, not a
cyclical one (the cyclical conception of time is also identified with a dead
past, even older than its linear alternative) but rather a looping, unpredictable sort of time, multiple and various, that runs and ruptures all over
the place. It forks. In response to democratic theorists like Sheldon Wolin
who insist on democracy's need for a slower and less plural tempo than
that characteristic of our cacophonous, late modern world, Connolly proceeds carefully. He is not Tocqueville; he is not merely resigned and he
does not promote one temporality in place of another. *He does not just*

embrace speed. He commits himself and invites us as well to seek out the
promise borne in our new conditions for democracy's possible futures.

"The challenge is how to support the positive connections among democracy, uneven zones of tempo, and the rift in time without legitimating a pace of life so fast that the promise of democracy becomes translated
into fascist becoming machines."[37] Connolly does not finally reject linear
time and its normative punctuality. He puts them in their place, demotes
them from the sole regnant form of time and thrusts them into a plural
and pluralizing play of temporalities. Linear, punctual time (and its normativity of progress or regress) is one temporal register on which we live
but from which we are also sometimes driven by events (and must allow
ourselves to be driven). Plural and uneven temporalities such as those
envisioned by Connolly simply cannot provide the sort of security that
comes with the backward-looking gaze of a future constitutionalism or
cosmopolitanism.

With new developments come new dangers but also new possibilities.
We lose the guarantees of a single time sequence in which what comes
later is unambiguously better or worse than what came before, but on the
other hand we don't have to work so hard to maintain those guarantees
either. And on the positive side, Connolly writes, a fast pace and plural
tempos unsettle hierarchy, one of democracy's oldest bêtes noires. He
does not worry enough, perhaps, about how a fast pace also consolidates
new hierarchies (notwithstanding his stated concern about democracy
sliding into fascist becoming machines). Where speed, in Tocqueville's
time, favored democratic upheavals, in our time speed seems to favor
instead a force not obviously democratic: that of hardly visible capital
over workers hopelessly rooted in increasingly rootless economies.

On the positive side, the pluralization of time closes down distance
and permits new coalitions and partnerships to develop transnationally.
These are opportunities, not guarantees: "my wager is that it is more
possible to negotiate a democratic ethos congruent with the accelerated
tempo of modern life than it is either to slow the world down or insulate
the majority of people from the effects of speed."[38] For the wager to work,
we democratic theorists and actors have to attenuate our allegiances to
the chrono-logic of rights. We have to open democratic theory and practice to the vicissitudes of plural timelines and emergent life forms. Without preparatory work, the pluralization of time will open huge distances

between those who affirm the multiplicity and those who respond to it by uncritically embracing familiar certainties (sexism, homophobia, nationalism, racism, natural rights, liberalism, or theocracy).

Another example to which Connolly repeatedly returns is that of the still-emerging right to doctor-assisted suicide. As he puts it in *Pluralism*, "Forty years ago that claim was not even simmering as a minority report among moralists who defined themselves to be defenders of the definitive list of human rights. The new demand is not *derived* from a thick set of principles containing it implicitly all along. [Italics in original: this, I would add, is how it is made to look from the perspective of the backward-looking gaze of a still-future universal human rights regime.] If it eventually acquires a sedimented place in the order of things, it will be *pressed* and *negotiated* into being by an assemblage consisting of insurgents who demand it, respondents who combine attention to new medical technologies and sensitivity to human suffering, and the fatigue [and, I would add in more agonistic spirit, *as well as the active discrediting*] of erstwhile opponents."³⁹

In relation to this emergent right, many feel that sense of emergency I noted above. Regarding this particular emergent right, a connection to emergency qua state of exception is invited by Giorgio Agamben, who notes that "the fundamental biopolitical structure of modernity—the decision on the value (or nonvalue) of life as such . . . finds its first juridical articulation in a well-intentioned pamphlet in favor of euthanasia" published in Germany in the 1920s.⁴⁰ Agamben himself takes no position on euthanasia—"It is not our intention here to take a position on the difficult ethical problem of euthanasia."⁴¹ But he has nothing good to say about it. He links it to the forms of sovereignty that he criticizes and to which he offers no particular alternative. Would he treat doctor-assisted suicide differently? It is admittedly somewhat different from euthanasia per se: Although we do speak of a right to doctor-assisted suicide, it would be odd to speak of a right to euthanasia.

For me, the idea of a right to doctor-assisted suicide induces a sense of panic. The right is not settled. There is no reliable apparatus for its adjudication. And the country in which I live while contemplating it offers such low levels of medical care to so many that the idea of a right to suicide seems ridiculously inapt. In the United States, as the case of Terry Schiavo reminded us in 2005, huge medical and political resources could be marshaled on behalf of sustaining life when the political will to do so exists. At the same time, innumerable lives are treated daily as unworthy of being lived, their bearers incapable of commanding the resources of medical care and compassion that they require.[42] In this ambiguous context, the possibility of a right to doctor-assisted suicide is unsettling.[43] The possibility of this right's entrenchment is frightening. As with many emergent claims, a line is being crossed. Places supposedly committed to the preservation of life—hospitals—may become arbiters and administrators of death—more like hospices, or worse yet, death houses.

Of course that line is already thoroughly attenuated (as Agamben himself points out), but as things stand or have stood until now, we do not have to acknowledge its attenuation so forcefully and consciously. Until now we could feign ignorance of the myriad, complex negotiations and relocations of life-death boundaries that occur in hospitals daily. A right to physician-assisted suicide might change that. It might change our sense of the meaning and function of medical care, of aging, of disease, of time. It might even change our understandings of life and death themselves and how we relate to them. The possible change may turn out to be for the good, it may be progress, but confronted with the possibility of such an altered world, how can we tell? Is it biopolitics turned thanatopolitics, as Agamben claims—part of a new and destructive form of sovereignty, dispersed and dangerous? Or is it a restoration to, or taking by, individuals of a decision that ought never to have been usurped by the state in its guise as religious ethical watchdog? Or is it a sovereign nonsovereignty, a moment at which individuals give up sovereignty-serving practices that seek to control or prolong life and yield instead to the sense that their time has come? Note how different these questions, wagers, and worries are from Benhabib's wager that her claimers of rights will "learn" citizenship in the future, how differently these two sets of wagers function: one disquiets, the other reassures. Reassurance may at times provide a more powerful impetus to political action and affirmation than disquiet does. But surely disquiet is the more apt mood and goal of political reflection and critique?

When I note the changes that might occur in the wake of this new right's entrenchment, I emphasize the word *might*, because how things unfold depends very much on how a new right is received, defended, and practiced even after its entrenchment, politically engaged and contested after that. In short, the right opens some possible doors, but all by itself (if we can say that) it means very little. The *practice* of the right, as Richard Flathman might say, means everything.

To those who have been in a position where it was needed, beside a loved one suffering without hope of improvement, the right to physician-assisted suicide may seem especially appealing. Personal acquaintance with such suffering may move us past our hesitations. But it may not. It depends upon how attached we are to the boundaries by which we separate life and death, daily. It depends upon our sense of how our relation to life, as a species, as a culture, may be altered by endorsing this new right to death at one's chosen time. It depends upon whether we think of death as something that we might negotiate or as something otherworldly before which we must lie, to which we must yield. It depends upon how we think about doctors and other professionals and what we make of the rather thin resources for accountability that now exist in modern American society. It depends on whether we think suffering is redemptive or meaningless, on an individual's own pain threshold (mine is low), and on how we assess the social situatedness of the pain: Could it be alleviated by access to better medical resources, community supports, ontologies of health and illness different from those that are current? It may also depend on whether we think, with Agamben, that our current commitments to preserving life are part of a sovereignty-enhancing biopolitics of bare life that is hegemonic and ultimately quite dangerous.[44] It depends on all these things and more because, as Connolly points out, rights are not just new options to be exercised, like having more money in one's wallet. Each new right inaugurates a new world. It transforms the entire economy of rights and identities, and establishes new relations and new realities, new promises and potentially new cruelties. Cora Diamond knows this. It is the central point of her critique of animal rights theorists for their misguided assumption that once animals are included in the universe of rights-bearing creatures, human rights will go on as they were.[45]

Where liberals, deliberative democrats, and universalists invite us to assess new rights-claims as judges would—in terms of their analogical fit to previous ones, of the appositeness of the claim to legitimate subsumption under existing higher law (whether constitutional or universal) in a gradually unfolding linear time, of whether the new rights were in nascent form always already somehow part of a rights machine—Connolly urges us to assess emergent claims as democratic theorists and activists should: by imagining and assessing a world, the world that might be opened by this new right, and the plural timelines, circles, and forks that might be ushered in with it. Here, rights and goods meet.

These reflections on a possible new right to physician-assisted suicide reflect the deep sense of disturbance created in me by my contemplation of it. I am glad I am not in charge of this decision, though in my gut I tend to side with proponents of this new right because I believe that its *un*-availability represents a greater and unwarranted (and perhaps even, contra Agamben, biopolitical) exercise of state and professional power than is implied by its availability to us. But something else also surfaces: a sense that the chrono-logic of rights may offer fewer resources than Connolly's politics of becoming for *resisting* the entrenchment of new rights like this one. For the chrono-logic of rights puts us into its temporality: "We are rationalizing and extending the system of rights," its proponents say. "This right is like the others that came before it. If you supported equal suffrage for women and blacks, how can you get off the bus here? This is the next stage of the same project." (The same argument can be used for *ex*clusion: "When we fought for civil rights, we did not have suicide in mind.")

In the chrono-logic of rights, the honest contemplation of the unsettling ramifications of a new right forces one into conservatism ("no, we had better not support that one; it is not like the others we fought for") or submission (to the march of progress or the chrono-logic force of rights: "I don't feel good about the likely ramifications of this new right, but I have to support it because not to do so is to cast in doubt the legitimacy of all the rights we supported until now"). In Connolly's politics of becoming, however, and this is one of the things about it that most appeals, neither conservatism nor submission is sought. Instead a certain reluctance and panic are expected, even hoped for. Reluctance and panic are markers of a disquieting awareness that we are in this moment partitioning a new time, creating a new world. New and unexpected things are occurring. Some may turn out to fulfill what we think of as the promise of rights; others may betray that promise in ways that we will regret and want to resist. Still others may take us in unanticipated new directions that may yet win from us approval and support. In such contexts reluctance and panic in the face of emergent rights may bespeak a lack of moral bearings. But they may also signal our awareness that we have received an invitation to reenter the paradox of politics and open ourselves to the work (of agonistic respect, nontheistic reverence for being) on the self that a politics of becoming periodically demands.

THE CHRONO-LOGIC OF RIGHTS

The chrono-logic of rights treats constitutional or cosmopolitan rights like Wittgenstein's "machine-as-symbol" in which "the action of the machine seems to be there in it from the start." But the machine-as-symbol misleads us, Wittgenstein explains in *Philosophical Investigations*, insofar as it suggests that

> if we know the machine, everything else, that is its movement, seems to be already completely determined. We talk as if these parts could only move in this way, as if they could not do anything else. How is this—do we forget the possibility of their bending, breaking off, melting, and so on?[46] Yes; in many cases we don't think of that at all . . . we are inclined to think of the future movements of a machine in their definiteness to objects which are already lying in a drawer and which we then take out [somewhat like "tapping" a system of rights?].—But we do not say this kind of thing when we are concerned with predicting the actual behavior of a machine [or of rights]. Then we do not forget the possibility of a distortion of the parts and so on . . . But when we reflect that the machine could also have moved differently it may look as if the way it moves must be contained in the machine-as-symbol far more determinately than in the actual machine. As if it were not enough for the movements in question to be empirically determined in advance, but they had to be really, in a mysterious sense— already present . . . *When does one have the thought that the possible movements of a machine are already there in some mysterious way?—Well, when one is doing philosophy.*[47]

Recall that philosophy, on Wittgenstein's account, makes us like "savages, primitive people, who hear the expressions of civilized men, put a false interpretation on them, and then draw the queerest conclusions from it."[48] The machine-as-symbol bewitches us in ways that the actual machine with its plural actions does not. " 'But,' " objects Wittgenstein's erstwhile interlocutor, uncannily channeling Habermas and Benhabib, " 'I don't mean that what I do now (in grasping a sense [of the machine-as-symbol]) determines the future use causally and as a matter of experience, but that in a queer way, the use itself is in some sense present.'" Wittgenstein responds in his inimitable and commonsensical fashion: "But of course it is, 'in some sense!'"

What sense of *"in some sense"* is Wittgenstein endorsing here? He is mysterious. But he has just completed a discussion of rule-following in which he resists the idea that instances of rule-following are best understood as contained in, or determined or prescribed by, the rule in question. Human agency and judgment have a role to play even in following the simplest order. As Wittgenstein says of someone instructed to continue a simple series like "add by two's,"— *"A new decision [is] needed at every stage."*[49]

Following Wittgenstein, we might distinguish between the right-as-symbol and the actual behavior of a right. The right-as-symbol is the right as it is seen by those who privilege as its meaning its capacity to be extended and tapped in certain ways that fulfill what they see as its true function or promise, regardless of its operations. The right as symbol governs the imagination of David de Grazia when he says of animal rights, "This last frontier of bigotry will be hard to cross." The behavior of a right, however, may go in many different ways and along many different temporalities. These differences may be labeled malfunctions or perversions only from the perspective of the right-as-symbol.[50] Indeed, this is where I part ways with Wittgenstein's example: departures from the machine as symbol are depicted by him as *"breaking," "bending," "distortion"*— but these are pejorative terms, like the *infelicities* that Austin attributes to speech acts[51] but that Jacques Derrida insists are part of the productive working of performatives.[52] Similarly here, the departure of actual rights from the blueprint of the right as symbol need not mean that something is broken. It may signal iteration, the birth of something new, and is in any case not something to be cast into an "external ditch of perdition" because those iterations are in fact, as Derrida points out, positive conditions of possibility. More pointedly, from the plural perspectives generated and testified to by the myriad operations of the actual right, we can see how the more essentialist notion of the right-as-symbol harbors residues of transcendentalist thinking (something that its proponents would deny).[53]

With Wittgenstein's help we see that the entrenchment of a new right can generate events unpredicted and unpredictable from within the normative framework that supposedly acted as the guarantor for the right in the first instance (the guarantor in terms of both securing the right's merits analogically and guaranteeing that the effects of entrenching the right would not spin out of control in ways that might upset old gains as well as the guaranteeing system that harbored them). These new events can occur in all their novelty because the right-as-symbol is an ideological commitment (or a philosophical one, as Wittgenstein points out), not an accurate representation of a machine's (or right's) behavior. Away from the bewitchment of philosophy, the play of rights as undecidable contenders among other forces in plural time is more discernable, and for the politics of becoming herein lies the promise of rights—actual rights and rights-as-symbols, both—for democracy.

Plural timelines, circles, and forks make it difficult to identify any single event or norm as the *origin* of a practice.[54] The paradox of politics and the absence of linear temporality put pressure on those, like Habermas and Benhabib, who want to assess new claims in terms of their fit in relation to that now unidentifiable origin, the right-as-symbol: Does the emergent right fit under the umbrella of existing understandings of rights, or is it amenable to being understood analogically as an extension or fulfillment of earlier rights declarations? Democratic theorists, especially those attracted to the various elements of a politics of becoming, should yield to the pressure exerted on them by the paradox of politics and seek out the promise that inheres in the alternative developed by Connolly (or something like it).

ONE STEP FORWARD, TWO STEPS BACK? SLOW FOOD'S FORK IN TIME

Hannah Arendt closes *Willing*, volume 2 of *Life of the Mind*, expressing the "frustrating" futility of turning to the will to seek freedom. She finds more promise in Augustine, who argued that time and man "were created together." For Arendt, this means that the purpose of man's creation was to make possible a beginning. Time and man are co-original, but not in Habermas's sense of co-originality. On Arendt's account the two are agonistically related: man as natal interrupts the would-be time sequence.

But Augustine is "opaque" on the details. He "seems to tell us no more than that we are doomed to be free by virtue of being born, no matter whether we like freedom or abhor its arbitrariness, are 'pleased' with it or prefer to escape its awesome responsibility" (through fatalism, for example). So Arendt goes Augustine one better. Although her readers have rightly noted repeatedly that she ends *Willing* with a declaration of the need to turn to "another mental faculty" instead, that of judgment, *Willing* really ends with a more direct counter to Augustine. What Arendt says she hopes to find in judgment is the very thing that Augustine could not muster for freedom: "our pleasures and displeasures."[55] Pleasure and displeasure (not hope per se, nor judgment) are for Arendt the best counter to what she sees as Augustinian doom.

I conclude with a brief discussion of an emergent movement one of whose most attractive features is its unabashed pursuit of pleasure, a movement that illustrates some of the best aspects of a politics of becoming, while also providing an opportunity to assess the stakes of interpreting new movements as expressions of the right-as-symbol or as permutations of actual rights that run along plural axes of time—or both.[56] Slow Food, whose icon is a snail, began as a protest against the first McDonald's in Italy in 1986. Slow Food called people to resist the bland homogeneity of fast food on behalf of diversity in taste—local flavors, crops, and species. Intending to defend the masses from the hegemony of fast food by making the diversity and nuance of haute cuisine accessible to them, the leaders of Slow Food soon realized that this one sybaritic and possibly élitist goal implied others that were less so. Having begun with a declaration of a right—the movement called for "the protection of the right to taste"—Slow Food soon understood correctly that the right to taste implied a form of life, in which animals are raised slowly, locally rather than industrially, and meals are prepared and eaten slowly, perhaps even punctuated by conversation. "At the table," Alice Waters notes, "we learn moderation, conversation, tolerance, generosity, conviviality: these are civic virtues."[57] The tables at which I have eaten have been somewhat more agonistic, perhaps, often featuring immoderation, interruption, and the fraught unresolved feelings of everyday life, but Waters is right—the table, in particular the slow food table, is one site at which the virtues she names are learned and practiced. Indeed, a commitment to slow food means living at least some of one's life at a pace slower than is presupposed by fast food chains, with other members of the food community (no solitary eating of anonymous mass food in the car), and in closer coordination with the slow, non-industrialized tempo of regional and local food production. A commitment to slow food means intervening in the infrastructure and the ethics and politics of consumption.

An international movement, Slow Food is made up of convivia, grassroots offices responsible for putting on events and educational programs for people in their regions. They understand the paradox of politics—that the people for whom they work and to whom they want to appeal may not yet (or ever) exist. Their Taste Education Project offers events and classes to reeducate palates and sensitize people anew to diverse, complex, and subtle flavors to which they have been made indifferent by postwar mass food production. Slow Food's "Ark Project" parodies Darwin, seeking to intervene in and reverse rather than merely catalogue evolutionary trends, by supporting with prize money those who preserve vanishing fruits, vegetables, and animal species, most of which are too delicate, quirky, or unpredictable for commercial growers. Slow Food draws attention to fruits and vegetables at risk, like the Gravenstein apple, ramps, and the Southern field pea. (The Gravenstein, one of the earliest-ripening apples, is not popular with commercial growers because it bruises easily and is difficult to ship.) And through its Ark of Taste, Slow Food "aims to rediscover, catalog, describe and publicize forgotten flavors . . . that are threatened by industrial standardization, hygiene laws, the regulations of large-scale distribution and environmental damage."[58] Slow Food's founder, Carlo Petrini, likes to note, "A hundred years ago, people ate between one hundred and a hundred and twenty different species of food. Now our diet is made up of at most ten or twelve species."[59] "In Europe, half the breeds of domestic livestock became extinct during the course of the Twentieth Century. One species of plant disappears every six hours. In the seven years between editions of Slow Food's anthology of Italian cheeses—Fromaggi d'Italia—a hundred cheese varieties became unavailable on the market. Less than 30 varieties of plant feed 95% of the world's population."[60]

Although preservation, authenticity, and tradition are valued highly by Slow Food, this is not a nostalgic movement. On the contrary, the movement represents nothing other than a fork in time: it refuses to move forward on the temporality of supposedly inexorable agribusiness, but it also refuses to move backward: "the secret to Slow Food's appeal is not that it offers a nostalgic backward glance at a world of vanishing pleasures. Globalization, in Slow Food's view, has the potential to help as well as harm the small food producer. On the one hand, globalization has the homogenizing effect of allowing multinational corporations to extend their reach to virtually every corner of the world. But at the same time, by making it easier for members of small minorities (beekeepers or Gaelic speakers) to communicate at a distance, it creates openings for niche cultures to thrive."[61] That is to say, "commercial viability," to which Slow Food is very much attuned, is expanded along with the communications reach of the local producer. This international network, which Slow Food is helping to build, is named by Petrini "virtuous globalization." Slow Food's straddle of slow and fast temporalities becomes more evident when compared to another, also attractive new movement, that of the localvores, whose Vermont chapter challenged Vermonters to eat for the month of September 2006 only food grown within one hundred miles' distance. To mark their difference from a merely nostalgic position, the localvores adopted the slogan "Eat Locally, Spice Globally."[62] Nonetheless, with their emphasis on localism, they are some distance from Slow Food's virtuous globalization.

Gastronomic pleasure entails education, biodiversification, localism, and transnationalism. It also entails political action. Beyond funding and supporting farmers, environmentalists, scientists, and others who advance the goals of the movement, and beyond creating local networks across the world (though still mostly in Europe), Slow Food has also lobbied the EU to prevent such measures as the imposition of standardized food safety requirements (developed by NASA and Kraft Foods) that would put small food producers out of business. Recently Slow Food has also turned its attention to another effect of postwar food production—obesity, which it calls *globesity*—to call attention to the connection between the expansion and export of fast food and growing rates of obesity worldwide.

The Second World War is the emergency that lurks in the background of all that Slow Food opposes. That war provided the opportunity for new, mass-oriented industrialization, and its devastation also created the hunger, especially in Europe, that made possible and even welcome the postwar degradation of taste by cheap, industrial food. When starvation seems to be the only alternative, the right to taste does not stand out as a pressing concern; it seems like a luxury. The genius of Slow Food has been its capacity (admittedly against a background of plenty in Europe by contrast with the continent's immediate postwar condition) to rescript that supposed luxury as a necessity for human health and well-being, and to orient our gaze toward a different emergency: the contemporary infrastructure of consumption. Slow Food highlights a new emergency, one *caused* rather than *solved* by standardization and mass production. This is the setting for the emergence of a new right—the right to taste—and although it is a human right, it implies (unlike many other human rights, which tend to remainder rather than imply) a set of animal rights as well (the right to be preserved from careless extinction, to be treated well and in accordance with natural health requirements, etc.).[63]

Slow Food understands the politics of procedure and standardization. For example, it exposes how neutrally imposed new health standards in food production have asymmetrical effects, exacting unaffordable costs from small local food purveyors while giving market advantages to large industrial food manufacturers.[64] It notes that local food purveyors have not been found responsible for outbreaks of illness, and that one of the largest food health scares in recent years, over mad cow disease, came not from the unmonitored local food producer but rather as a direct offshoot of industrialized agriculture, specifically the feeding of processed meat to cattle. That practice in turn was the result of a combination of pressures and incentives, ranging from the introduction to Europe of supermarkets over the last fifty years (replacing European capitalism's own "commercial ethic that still sought trust in the longevity of contacts and the solidarity of face to face contacts") to the relentless pressure for cheap food and the quest for ever greater economies of scale.[65] In response, Slow Food champions what Petrini calls "the good, the clean and the just." The good "means paying attention to the taste and smell of food, because pleasure and happiness in food are a universal right." The clean means making food "sustainably, so that it does not consume more resources than it produces." And the just means making food so that it "creates no inequities and respects every person involved in its production."[66] Thus when Slow Food supports coffee growers in Guatemala, training them to heighten and control the quality of their product while helping to bring the product to the global market (the "good and the clean"), the organization writes in to the contract that children may not pick coffee during school hours, and that women must go to the doctor at least once a year (part of the "just"). Unschooled children and poor health care violate the quality control, broadly understood, of the local coffee-growing community.[67]

How shall we interpret the Slow Food movement? We might embed it into some nonparadoxical precedent, as the American founders, on Hannah Arendt's account, sought to do when they set about researching prior constitutions rather than embracing the radical novelty of their own event.[68] Would Slow Food acquire greater legitimation if it were cast as the heir of prior declarations of human rights, as an anticipatory fulfillment of later ones? Or might it be better for democratic actors to note the boundary-breaking qualities of a new movement? It is not easy to position this new movement under existing liberal or cosmopolitan rights, because those rights presuppose the very standardizations to which Slow Foods is, as a matter of principle and practice, opposed. Nor is it easy to subsume Slow Food's activities under a schedule of formal constitutional or universal human rights, because it would be difficult to say, as with Wittgenstein's machine-as symbol, that the action—the right to taste— was "there in it from the start." From a human rights perspective, a right to taste seems laughable. It makes a mockery of serious rights won heretofore and now entrenched as universal human rights. But is a pleasure-based radical critique of the infrastructure of consumption really so far-fetched? *The new is always laughable.*[69] This is one effect of the operation in practice of the right-as-symbol: its marginalization of anything that does not analogically fit its expectations or rubric, its sense that anything not already in the drawer violates the spirit of the machine.

Universal human rights offer few resources for mounting the kind of critique carried out by the Slow Food movement. Those rights do *enable* those who want to make such efforts by providing juridical guarantees of free speech that can make a difference to free thought and critique; and for that and much else human rights are to be valued, defended, and expanded. But they are neither a substitute for, nor do they in and of themselves guarantee, the sort of scorching insights into the effects of industrialization and globalization that Slow Food names (along with many other critics and organizations). Nor do universal human rights secure movement along the trajectory that Slows Food maps and names "virtuous globalization."

And human rights do have remainders. In our rights-centered world, the capacity to make a claim has become an overly prized signifier of value

and has secured the very distinction between human and animal that
Slow Food is trying to attenuate by stressing lines of dependence and
connection across species. Others have written about the costs of universal human rights to local cultural and symbolic (rather than bio-) diversity. Another remainder of human rights is surely animal rights or welfare. Pressing the cause of animal rights seems out of step with the times,
especially when human misery is so abundant. But in the spirit of Connolly's plural tempos (which make it harder to be "out of step with the
times"), and in the spirit of Slow Food's commitment to its own fork in
time, and in the spirit of Arendt's intuition that the intimate if antagonistic connection noted by Augustine between man and time requires the
suturing powers of pleasure, it may be time to step out of one time and
broach another, in which we attend to the pleasures forgone in the name
of food production, and ruminate on the massive cruelties daily committed by humans upon animal species' in the name of human well-
being.[70] Perhaps for this to happen, something in the current chrono-
logic rights machine will have to break or bend or malfunction. It has
happened before. But how will we tell the story, once it has occurred? Will
we fold it into a narrative of law's progress and tell it as a tale of legal
triumphalism featuring self-sacrificing individuals devoted to a cause? Or
will we tell it as the outcome of a politics of pleasure that somehow, in
the process of becoming, reoriented the rights machine in unanticipated
ways and, laughingly, inaugurated a new time?[71]

NOTES

1   Ludwig Wittgenstein, *Philosophical Investigations* (Oxford: Blackwell, 2001).
2   William Connolly, *Identity\Difference: Democratic Negotiations of Political Para-
    dox*, enlarged edn (Minneapolis: University of Minnesota Press, 2002), 119.
3   Gilles Deleuze and Felix Guattari, *Anti-Oedipus: Capitalism and Schizophrenia*
    (Minneapolis: University of Minnesota Press, 1983).
4   William Connolly, *The Ethos of Pluralization* (Minneapolis: University of Min-
    nesota Press, 1995).
5   William Connolly, *Neuropolitics: Thinking, Culture, Speed* (Minneapolis: Univer-
    sity of Minnesota Press, 2002).
6   William Connolly, *Political Theory and Modernity* (Ithaca: Cornell University
    Press, 1993), 41–67; *Identity\Difference*, 193; *The Ethos of Pluralization*, 139.
7   Jean-Jacques Rousseau, *On the Social Contract: With Geneva Manuscript and Politi-
    cal Economy* (New York: St. Martin's, 1978).

8   Connolly, *The Ethos of Pluralization*, 137.

9   Or, as I myself would put the point, they may find that the general will is always inhabited by the will of all, each undecidedly implicated in the other, notwithstanding Rousseau's several efforts to secure the distinction between the two. (See my "Between Decision and Deliberation: Political Paradox in Democratic Theory," *American Political Science Review* 101, no. 1 (2007), 1–17.)

10 Connolly, *The Ethos of Pluralization*, 138.

11 Connolly, *Political Theory and Modernity*; Bonnie Honig, *Democracy and the Foreigner* (Princeton: Princeton University Press, 2001); Alan Keenan, *Democracy in Question: Democratic Openness in a Time of Political Closure* (Stanford: Stanford University Press, 2003); Seyla Benhabib, "Deliberative Rationality and Legitimacy," *Constellations* 1 (1994), 26–52.

12 Connolly, *The Ethos of Pluralization*, 137 (italics added).

13 As, I argue ("Between Decision and Deliberation: Political Paradox in Democratic Theory"), Rousseau himself shows that he knows in book II, chapter 7, of the *Social Contract* (Indianapolis: Hackett, 1988).

14 I borrow the term "remainder" from Jacques Derrida, and give a more detailed account of it in *Political Theory and the Displacement of Politics* (Ithaca: Cornell University Press, 1993).

15 Habermas's essay appeared in *Political Theory* 29, no. 6 (December 2001). A preliminary version of my reading of Habermas appeared in an essay published alongside Habermas's essay in the same issue of *Political Theory* under the title "Dead Rights, Live Futures." I later developed my views further and amended them somewhat in "Between Decision and Deliberation: Political Paradox in Democratic Theory." See the latter essay for a full discussion of the themes in Habermas, summarized briefly here.

16 Susan Neiman, "Theodicy in Jerusalem," *Hannah Arendt in Jerusalem* (Berkeley: University of California Press, 2001), 75.

17 Ibid., 216.

18 For Habermas a great deal depends upon how democratic citizens relate to their role as ongoing constitution makers. They must "recognize the project [of constitutionalism] as *the same* throughout history and to judge it from *the same* perspective" as their forebears. I comment on this requirement at length in "Dead Rights, Live Futures" and subject it to further but also more appreciative critique in "Between Decision and Deliberation: Political Paradox in Democratic Theory." Here I note simply that there is a peculiar combination of atemporality and historicity.

19 These paragraphs recraft material that appeared in my response to Benhabib's Berkeley Tanner Lectures on Human Values, March 2004, "The Philosophical Foundations of Cosmopolitan Norms" and "Democratic Iterations: the Local, the National and the Global," both in *Another Cosmopolitanism*, ed. R. Post (Oxford: Oxford University Press, 2006), 13–44, 45–82.

20 Benhabib, "The Philosophical Foundations of Cosmopolitan Norms," 25.

The same claim is made in *The Claims of Culture* (Princeton: Princeton University Press, 2002). But note: although universality and particularity are here both identified with democracy, the possibility that universality itself might be particular is rendered unthinkable by the terms of this new paradox, in which the particular and the universal are, as such, at odds.

21 This same issue arose regarding Benhabib's position when, as in her earlier work, she referred not to a tension nor to a paradox but to a "contradiction" which inaugurated and called for "a dialectic of momentous historical proportions." "Democracy and Difference: Reflections on the Metapolitics of Lyotard and Derrida," *Journal of Political Philosophy* 2 (1994).

22 This is clear in her essay "Democracy and Difference."

23 Seeing the girls as "rights" claimers already does a certain amount of conceptual work. Not all cases of political action are necessarily best captured as rights-claiming activities. This is a point that is crucial not just vis-à-vis Benhabib and Habermas, but also vis-à-vis Connolly, who knows better (I want to say), but who nonetheless has a tendency in *The Ethos of Pluralization* and *Identity\Difference* to read political action centrally in terms of emergent *rights* rather than, say, "goods."

24 This argument echoes Julia Kristeva's treatment of veils as transitional objects en route to French Enlightenment values. Kristeva, *Nations without Nationalism* (New York: Columbia University Press, 1993), and Honig, *Democracy and the Foreigner*, chapter 3.

25 Benhabib, "The Philosophical Foundations of Cosmopolitan Norms," 28.

26 Another effect of this perspective is that it obscures the question of how rights themselves change significantly over time. Benhabib knows that rights in the United States used to be limited to white, propertied males and are so no longer. But she assumes that with the expansion of rights over time, the rights are basically the same while the conditions for having them have changed. Why assume this, however? With their increased universality, rights have also been increasingly formalized. The benefit is their heightened universality. But once rights are no longer tied to those forms of material or property ownership that bespeak a relative substantive equality for rights bearers, it becomes increasingly difficult to address issues of substantive inequality in relation to rights.

27 Hannah Arendt, *The Life of the Mind* (New York: Harcourt, 1978), 204–5.

28 William Connolly, *Why I Am Not a Secularist* (Minneapolis: University of Minnesota Press, 1999).

29 Connolly, *The Ethos of Pluralization*, 187.

30 Connolly, *The Ethos of Pluralization*, 184 (italics in original).

31 I discuss this point in the context of battles for alien rights throughout the twentieth century in "Bound by Law? Alien Rights, Administrative Discretion, and the Politics of Technicality." *The Limits of Law*, ed. A. Sarat et al. (Stanford: Stanford University Press, 2005), 209–45.

32 On this point Sandel's *Liberalism and the Limits of Justice* (New York: Cambridge University Press, 1998) is still very useful.

33 On the other hand, his way of thinking about rights and identity is particularly expansive, so the risk is less here than it is with others—liberal and liberal democratic theorists—who put rights at the center of things.

34 On this point see the last section of my "Bound by Law? Alien Rights, Administrative Discretion, and the Politics of Technicality."

35 N. Luhmann, "Verfassung als evolutionäre Errungenschaft," *Rechtshistorisches Journal* 9 (1990), cited in E. Christodoulidis, "The Aporia of Sovereignty: On the Representation of the People in Constitutional Discourse," *King's College Law Journal* 12, no. 1 (2001), 126.

36 The mutuality of transformation makes new political coalitions possible, as Connolly points out: "It is often more feasible, say, for gays and straights to enter into alliances . . . than it is for heterosexuals and homosexuals to do so. This is because neither constituency, in the first set, is constituted as intrinsically unnatural, abnormal or immoral by the other." Connolly, *The Ethos of Pluralization*, 197.

37 Connolly, *Neuropolitics*, 148.

38 Ibid., 161.

39 William Connolly, *Pluralism* (Durham: Duke University Press, 2005), 121.

40 Giorgio Agamben, *Homo Sacer: Sovereign Power and Bare Life* (Stanford: Stanford University Press, 1988), 137.

41 Ibid., 139.

42 Such lives are also treated as "ungrievable," as Judith Butler points out in *Precarious Life: The Powers of Mourning and Violence* (London: Verso).

43 The ambiguity may not be deep. Eric Santner brilliantly reads the Schiavo case in a way that shows the commitment of Bush and his supporters not to life per se but to innocent, bare life. See his "Terry Schiavo and the State of Exception," http://www.press.uchicago.edu/Misc/Chicago/05april_santner .html (2005).

44 Agamben, *Homo Sacer*, esp. the last chapter.

45 Cora Diamond, "The Difficulty of Reality and the Difficulty of Philosophy," *Reading Cavell*, ed. Alice Crary and Sanford Shieh (London: Routledge, 2006), 98–118.

46 Here Wittgenstein anticipates Derrida's critique of Austin, regarding the role of infelicities in speech acts, but Wittgenstein stops short of Derrida's insight regarding the function of those infelicities and their relationship to ordinary language, as I note below.

47 Wittgenstein, *Philosophical Investigations*, nos. 193–94 (italics added).

48 Ibid., no. 194.

49 Ibid., no. 186 (italics added).

50 There is here in Wittgenstein, as elsewhere, a stubborn empiricism, captured by his repeated admonition to his readers to "Look, don't think!" Nietzsche

gives his readers similar instructions. For a discussion of nonlinear time as the product of a hyper-empiricism see M. De Landa, *A Thousand Years of Nonlinear History* (New York: Zone, 1997).

51 J. L. Austin, *How to Do Things with Words* (Cambridge: Harvard University Press, 1962).

52 Jacques Derrida, "Signature, Event, Context," *Limited Inc.* (Evanston, Ill.: Northwestern University Press, 1988), 1–23.

53 It may even be causing some of the paradoxes to which it claims to respond, a point that I develop in "Another Cosmopolitanism? Law and Politics in the New Europe," *Another Cosmopolitanism*, 102–27.

54 Indeed those who stipulate such origins, calling something out of the melee of time to stand as a beginning, often find themselves facing paradoxes that are, I argue, generated by that very insistence. On this point see my "Between Decision and Deliberation: Political Paradox in Democratic Theory."

55 Arendt, *The Life of the Mind*, 217.

56 In short, Wittgenstein is interested in the errors that we make in philosophy of language as a result of taking too seriously our notion of the machine-as-symbol. I am interested in the political errors that follow from taking too seriously the notion of right-as-symbol, especially as sole and regnant perspective.

57 E. Schlosser, M. Nestle, M. Pollan, W. Berry, T. Duster, E. Ransom, W. La-Duke, P. Singer, Dr. V. Shiva, C. Petrini, E. Coleman, and J. Hightower, *The Nation: The Food Issue* (2006), 13.

58 "Ark products range from the Italian Valchiavenna goat to the American Navajo-Churro sheep, from the last indigenous Irish cattle breed, the Kerry, to a unique variety of Greek fava beans grown only on the island of Santorini. All are endangered products that have real economic viability and commercial potential," http://www.slowfoodforum.org/archive/index.php/t-265.html.

59 A. Stilles, "Slow Food," *Nation*, 20 August 2001.

60 Andrew Finkel, "Food for Thought," CNN.com, 30 November 2000.

61 Ibid.

62 Mad River Valley, Localvore Project, "Eat Locally—Spice Globally," www.vermontlocalvore.org.

63 At the convention of the American Political Science Association in 2006, objections were raised about the classist nature of this movement. One participant objected that poor people needed fast food, both as a source of employment and as a source of cheap food. There was also a certain discomfort in the audience with the notion of taste and pleasure as sources of progressive politics or contributors to progressive politics, notwithstanding that this paper tracked the evolution of Slow Food from what may originally have been an élitist set of goals to more democratic ones. Some audience members and the panelists, myself included, responded to these objections by noting that time was not in such short supply as people think, given the number of hours spent by most Americans watching television (Jane Bennett), that slow

food need not entail any great expense (Honig), and that defending the right of the masses to fast food is itself hugely problematic because of the health effects of fast food, ranging from heart disease to diabetes (William Connolly). Just a couple of weeks later, the "Food Issue" of the *Nation* hit the stands on 11 September 2006 (the date itself marking a connection between emergency and food). Several of its articles reiterated responses to the unease expressed by some audience members at the panel, none better than Alice Waters's contribution: "We get hammered with the message that everything in our lives should be fast, cheap and easy—especially food. So conditioned are we to believe that food should be almost free that even the rich, who pay a tinier fraction of their income for food than has ever been paid before in human history, grumble at the price of an organic peach—a peach grown for flavour and picked, perfectly ripe, by a local farmer who is taking care of the land and paying his workers a fair wage! [Maybe: another article in the food issue, "Organic Farms: Hard Labor," questions the identification of organic farming with job fairness, though that article does look at large corporations, not at the small farmers whom Waters has in mind here.] And yet, as the writer and farmer David Mas Masumoto recently pointed out, pound for pound, peaches that good still cost less than Twinkies. *When we claim that eating well is an elitist preoccupation, we create a smokescreen that obscures the fundamental role our food decisions have in shaping the world.* Organic foods seem elitist only because industrial food is artificially cheap, with its real costs being charged through the public purse [through subsidies], the public health, and the environment [i.e. shipping, and its environmental impact]" (13, italics added). See also, below, Carlo Petrini on the good, the clean, and the just.

64 See for example Vandana Shiva's discussion of Indian women's noncooperation with the ban in 1998 on mustard oil, one of India's indigenous edible oils, on grounds of "food safety," which she calls "an excuse," noting that the "restrictions on import of soya oil were simultaneously removed. Ten million farmers' livelihoods were threatened." *The Nation: The Food Issue.*

65 De Grazia, quoted in Joanne Hari, "McEurope," *New York Times*, 8 May 2005, 8.

66 *The Nation: The Food Issue*, 20.

67 Again, when this paper was presented publicly, this time at the American Bar Foundation, it was objected that the Guatemalan coffee growers themselves drink Nescafe. Their right to taste is not protected, it was said. They cannot afford to drink the high-quality coffee that they produce. And there is truth in the claim. But it seems a weak charge against the Slow Food project that the organization has succeeded in enabling a community to develop a product whose sale benefits them more than its consumption would. At bottom, it is true, Slow Food works with—but also against—the capitalist economy that now dominates our lives. Were the movement more radically anticapitalist, it would fail or have less salient effects. Were it less so, it would be less interesting and important.

68 Hannah Arendt, *On Revolution* (Westport: Greenwood, 1983).

69 Stephen Holmes, "Precommitment and the Paradox of Democracy," *Constitu-tionalism and Democracy* (Cambridge: Cambridge University Press, 1998), 223 n. 89, illustrates my point about the connection between innovation and laugh-ter: "Present decisions set in motion irreversible processes which, in turn, necessarily box in future generations. This is true whether we embody our decisions in 'irrevocable' charters or not. We must adjust to this fact about historical continuity even if it violates Paine's and Jefferson's curious belief that each generation has an inviolable right to start from scratch, ex nihilo, with no inheritances from the past." Then, playing Burke to their Paine, he says, "In retrospect, nothing could appear more laughable than the French Revolutionary attempt to restart the calendar at year I" (223). Laughable, yes, but this is what new claims and new orders do: elicit laughter, especially at the moment of their still contested emergence or, as with the revolutionary calendar, after they have failed (hence Holmes's honest "in retrospect"). What Holmes does not note is that this incident is an apt metaphor for revolution-ary politics generally, since what revolutionary politics aim to do is restart time. Without defending this particular effort to restart time, I note that the distinction between the serious and the nonserious is one to which others have properly drawn critical attention (rather than simply redeploy it). See for example Jacques Derrida's "Signature, Event Context," *Limited Inc.*, 1–23.

70 I say "larger numbers" because others of course have done so, though not all with the intent of contributing to democratic theory per se. Of those in-volved in thinking critically about the human-animal divide and its repercus-sions, I would name Jane Bennett, Bill Chaloupka, Donna Haraway, Peter Singer, and John Coetzee.

71 For an interesting critique of the quest for the new see N. Kompridis, "The Idea of a New Beginning: A Romantic Source of Normativity and Freedom," *Philosophical Romanticism* (New York: Routledge, 2006), 32–59.

VISUALIZING
POST-NATIONAL DEMOCRACY

Roland Bleiker

Those strips of no-man's land between the checkpoints always seem such zones
of promise, rich with the possibilities of new lives, new scents and affections.

—J. G. BALLARD, *Cocaine Nights*

DEMOCRACY HAS UNIVERSAL APPEAL. The principle that people should
have a say about how they are being governed is one of the few stable
features in a rapidly changing world. But even democracy is swept up in a
whirlwind of modern transformations.

One of the most difficult political challenges ahead is to retain democratic ideals at a time when their traditional sphere of application, the
nation-state, has become increasingly undermined by processes of globalization. While these processes have engendered an unprecedented trans-
nationalization of governance, much is done to prevent the emergence of
a corresponding transnational realm of participation and contestation.[1]
Many of the institutions that shape global politics, from international
organizations to multinational companies, are neither transparent nor
accountable to a democratic constituency. Countless other aspects of life
today also transgress the boundaries of the state, from the flow of capital and labor to media transmissions, intelligence gathering, military interventions, criminal activities, climate change, and infectious diseases.
"Only democratic citizens," William Connolly notes, "remain locked behind the bars of the state."[2]

Scholars and practitioners who engage these challenges to democracy have come up with suggestions that are located between two opposing poles. On one end of the spectrum are communitarian approaches. They aim at slowing down or even undoing globalization, hoping to reestablish state sovereignty in a way that preserves the autonomy and power of the traditional realm of democratic participation. The assumption here is that a viable democratic system presupposes, as Michael Walzer once put it, "a bounded world."[3] At the other end of the spectrum are approaches influenced by cosmopolitan ideas. They seek to extend democracy beyond the state, hoping to articulate decision-making procedures that can be applied at the global level.[4] Connolly finds fault with both approaches, at least when articulated in the extreme. The communitarian strategy, he fears, is based on nostalgia for a time when a politics of place could still be imagined as a realistic possibility.[5] Although he embraces the inevitable forces of globalization, as cosmopolitans do, Connolly is suspicious of their global aspirations, particularly if they involve a set of principles and a desire to implement them in an institutional setting. He believes that such endeavors are unrealistic and problematic, for any rule-based governing structure that lacks a corresponding sphere of contestation risks jeopardizing the very democratic principles that it seeks to uphold.

Connolly proposes an alternative approach, one that diverges from both communitarian and cosmopolitan solutions. He stresses that democracy should be seen not only as a set of institutional arrangements but also, and perhaps even primarily, as an attitude, a cultural disposition. That in itself is not necessarily new or radical, for many commentators meanwhile suggest that conceptions of democracy, contested and contestable as they are, should be extended beyond models and institutions into a procedural realm.[6] But Connolly goes further. The democratic ethos that he wants to foster is based not on a set of fundamental principles, even if they are merely of a procedural nature, but on the need to disturb these principles. Connolly goes as far as identifying foundational norms and "final markers" as key obstacles to establishing and implementing a transnational democratic disposition.[7] He seeks to counter this danger by advocating a form of ethics that promotes respect for "multiple constituencies honoring different moral sources."[8]

The objective of this chapter is to scrutinize the potential and limits of Connolly's pluralist approach to post-national democracy. I do so by engaging what is alternatively known as the anti-globalization or global justice movement. Much like democracy as Connolly understands it, the anti-globalization movement does not aspire to establish an uncontested global consensus. It comprises many different and sometimes incompatible segments, such as feminists, environmentalists, steelworkers, anarchists, farmers, and students. The activities that these individuals and groups pursue are often spontaneous, chaotic, and disruptive. Their goals are far too diverse to ever produce agreement on a common program or even strategy. Connolly has drawn attention to the democratic potential entailed in transnational social movements. He has done so on numerous occasions, and over several years, but only through brief and largely allusive remarks.[9] Insightful and promising as these contemplations are, they leave the reader—at least this one—thirsty for more. This is why I would like to extend Connolly's line of inquiry, using his own body of work to do so. I proceed in two steps.

The first part of this chapter focuses on the protest element of the anti-globalization movement. My ambition here is to determine how transnational activism may contribute to the dissemination of a "democratic politics of disturbance" advocated by Connolly.[10] The evidence, I suggest, is largely positive. If we follow Connolly's logic of inquiry, then anti-globalization protests, anarchical and disruptive as they are, can make an important contribution to the struggle for fairness, transparency, and democracy. The significance of dissident engagements is located precisely in their refusal to be controlled by a central regulatory force. By constantly challenging institutionalized relations of power, protest actions generate public debate and scrutiny of the "final makers" that Connolly sees as one of the key obstacles to the cultivation of a democratic ethos. Without periodic political challenges, existing forms of governance tend to establish, uphold, and mask practices of domination and exclusion. Transnational protests can thus be seen as part of a cultural democratization that "embodies a productive ambiguity at its very centre, always resisting attempts to allow one side or the other to achieve final victory."[11]

The second part of the chapter engages issues that pose more difficult challenges to Connolly's vision of post-national democracy. I ask whether the anti-globalization movement itself embodies the type of approach to democracy that Connolly advocates: a form of pluralism that revolves around multiple minorities coexisting and co-governing in a safe and

mutually respectful environment. Focusing on the global justice movement, and particularly on the World Social Forum, I find mixed evidence.
On some level the decentralized decision-making procedures that are applied in this context do indeed embody a genuine attempt to implement
pluralism and participatory democracy. But at the same time it is clear
that democratic negotiations never take place outside relations of power
and domination—a feature that is particularly evident when it comes to
gender and race. Connolly would undoubtedly agree with these observations, not least because his work is shaped by a reading of Nietzsche that
views power as insinuating itself into all aspects of life.[12] But the very
same reading also brings Connolly face to face with another difficult
problem: the recognition that a transnational democratic ethos requires
more than a promotion of pluralism and a multilayered politics of disturbance. We do not necessarily need the final markers that Connolly es-
chews; but some foundations, even if they are only contingent, may be
required to articulate the type of commitment necessary to address and
solve important political challenges. Connolly has been relatively silent
on what exactly the transnational democratic ethos requires, a point that
has earned him criticism, even by otherwise admiring authors.[13] But his
work also offers suggestions, though only implicit at times, about how to
ground democratically based commitments in a perpetually contested
transnational realm.

Visualizing a new, post-national version of democracy is a daunting
task. Connolly readily admits that "it is probably impossible even to imagine a form of democratic politics today that breaks entirely with [the
model of the territorial state]."[14] I do not pretend that my brief and
selective reading of the anti-globalization and global justice movements
can possibly address this challenge. I do not even claim to provide a
remotely comprehensive overview of the issues at stake. The ambition of a
brief essay has to be, and indeed is, much more modest: to engage Connolly's work by extending one of his most promising but relatively un-
developed lines of thought. I do so with the hope, and the conviction, that
Connolly's innovative theorizing can help us to address some of the most
difficult challenges in world politics.

DEMOCRACY AND GLOBALIZATION

Let us start with the most prominent and also most controversial feature of the anti-globalization movement: street protests. At first sight they highlight not the solutions but the problems that rapid globalization poses to democracy.

Consider the first and perhaps most symbolic protest event: the four days of massive street demonstrations against the meeting of the World Trade Organization (WTO) in Seattle in December 1999. Some forty thousand demonstrators of all backgrounds and political orientations turned the city into a battleground—literally and metaphorically. Worldwide media attention was guaranteed. Some commentators speak of a "turning point," of an event that symbolized the world's discontent with the spread of globalization, with policies that promoted free trade and corporate greed over the interests of average people and the environment.[15] Others stress that Seattle "was the first time that the political presence of a range of new actors was taken seriously."[16] Similar and similarly prominent protests followed in the months and years to come: thousands of demonstrators interfered, for instance, with gatherings of the World Economic Forum in Melbourne and Davos, with meetings of the International Monetary Fund (IMF) and the World Bank in Washington and Prague, and with a G8 summit in Genoa. Perhaps the biggest simultaneous demonstrations occurred on 15 February 2003, when millions of people took to the streets in cities worldwide to demonstrate against what was then a looming war in Iraq.

The protest component of the anti-globalization movement has recently lost some of its momentum, but the issues that it brought to the forefront are here to stay. That countless people around the globe see street protests as the only chance to voice their opinions symbolizes an alarming crisis of legitimacy, one that has to do with the lack of democratic accountability of the major state and multilateral institutions that shape global politics. In some sense the events of Seattle highlight what Joan Bondurant already identified decades ago as a key weakness of liberal thought, namely "the failure to provide techniques of action for those critical occasions when the machinery of democratic government no longer functions to resolve large-scale, overt conflict."[17]

The main target of the anti-globalization critique are the three most influential institutions of the liberal world economy: the World Bank, the IMF, and the WTO. One of the key concerns expressed by protesters is the lack of democratic accountability that characterizes these influential transnational organizations. Kelly Quirk, head of the Rainforest Action Network, stresses that that "the WTO has the right to completely rescind any law passed by the citizenry to protect the environment, health and labor rights."[18] Vandana Shiva is likewise convinced that the WTO is enforcing an "anti-people, anti-nature decision to enable corporations to steal the world's harvests through secretive, undemocratic structures and processes."[19] Expressed in other words, transnational governance has not been accompanied by a corresponding development of transnational democratic accountability. We hear of a neoliberal world order that is increasingly run by a few powerful multilateral institutions and multinational corporations—big, unaccountable structures whose decision-making principles reflect the imperatives of short-term material objectives rather than the interests of the population at large. We are caught in a world that resembles J. G. Ballard's fictional Eden-Olympia: a financially thriving but highly unequal high-technology information society, seemingly run by a few successful élites but in reality spinning out of control and spiraling into an ever-deeper moral void, fed by the very need for progress and economic expansion that the multilateral institutions were supposed to deliver.[20]

Many scholars and commentators disagree with such pessimistic perspectives on globalization. The main story that we hear is much more benign: it is the story of western democracy and free-market principles bringing progress and economic benefits to an increasing part of the world.[21] Connolly too holds a more optimistic view of globalization, although for completely different reasons. He finds ground for optimism not in the prevailing free-market vision of globalization but in some of the seemingly doom-and-gloom scenarios above: in the multiplying multitudes of actors and actions that express frustration about the disempowering nature of globalization. Connolly fully accepts that globalization has accelerated the speed of politics and life in general. He embraces what he calls the politics of becoming, "that uncertain process by which the new flows or surges into being."[22] But he refuses to see the implications of these dynamics solely in negative terms. Such interpretations,

Connolly believes, are "insufficiently attuned to the *positive* role of speed in intrastate democracy and cross-state cosmopolitanism."[23] Globalization has not only disempowered citizens around the globe. It has also magnified the possibilities for average people to interfere with the conduct of global politics. Their interference is of course different from traditional forms of institutionalized democratic participation. It is linked to the changing nature and impact of dissent.

The presence of global media networks has fundamentally transformed the dynamics and terrains of citizen activism. Protest actions no longer take place solely in the streets and back allies of disaffected cities. The "Battle for Seattle," for instance, was above all a media spectacle, a battle for the hearts and minds of global television audiences. Any protest action drawing sufficient media attention has the potential to engender a political process that transcends its immediate environment. It competes for the attention of global television audiences and thus interferes with the struggle over values that ultimately shapes the world we live in.

Globalization has also provided anti-globalization activists with new tools to organize and coordinate their actions. Many of the protesters that went to Seattle, Melbourne, and Prague, for instance, were brought together by e-mail correspondences and a variety of web sites that organized resistance strategies. On-the-ground actions were coordinated with mobile phones. The increased ability to exchange information across large geographic distances has had a tremendous influence on the mobilization of dissent within civil society. The internet gives activist ready access to global knowledge and new tools to recruit like-minded individuals for actions. Social movements and NGOs that had hitherto existed in isolation can now easily communicate with each other. They can share data and insights about similar concerns and organize common actions in ways that was not possible before.[24] A study of citizen activism against the Multilateral Agreement on Investment (MAI), for instance, suggests that the internet played a vital role in the relative success of the movement—the MAI was at least temporarily pushed off the OECD agenda. The internet was central to the campaign insofar as it facilitated communication among activists, permitted publication of related information, and helped to put pressure on politicians and policymakers in member states.[25] Or consider how global networks of communication have enabled indigenous peoples in the United States, Canada, Australia, and

New Zealand to engage in forms of activism that ensured them an audience beyond their immediate surroundings. Some commentators stress
that new communication technologies favor loosely organized networks.
International organizations and government departments, by contrast,
tend to be less effective users of these technologies, for their hierarchical
structure revolves around the control of information flows.[26]

DEMOCRACY AS A POLITICS
OF DISTURBANCE

Protest actions, if carried out and communicated effectively, may well be
able to influence political dynamics. They may even constitute a new way
of yielding power. But are they also a form of democracy? Many commentators would undoubtedly suggest not, particularly those who view democracy primarily in institutional terms. But the situation looks more
complex if we follow Connolly's trajectory and push beyond institutional
boundaries. We may then be able to view anti-globalization protests as an
important aspect of transnational democratic processes.

When an existing political practice becomes too entrenched and oppressive, then hope for chance often comes not from an internal and
institutionalized effort at renewal but an externally induced politics of
disturbance. Connolly goes as far as suggesting that there are moments
when "it takes a militant, experimental, and persistent political movement to open up a line of flight from culturally induced suffering."[27] This
is why Connolly insists that some aspects of democratic participation can
never be institutionalized. Any political system, no matter how just and
refined, rests on a structure of exclusion. To remain legitimate the respective political foundations need to be submitted to periodic scrutiny.
They require constant readjustments to remain adequate and fair. The
anti-globalization movement represents an important aspect of this continuous probing process, for it constantly problematizes foundational
norms, Connolly's "final markers."

The anti-globalization movement has made globalization a topic of discussion. Repeated protest actions around the world have guaranteed that
a number of key issues, from environmental protection to indigenous
rights and minimal labor standards, will remain debated in the public
sphere. The anti-globalization movement has challenged what Manfred

Steger calls globalism: "a political ideology that endows the concept of globalization with market-oriented norms, values and meanings."[28] According to Steger's insightful analysis, this neoliberal approach to globalization became so dominant during the 1990s that some of its key values were largely accepted as factual necessities. Promoting free trade and opening new markets were not seen as political approaches to promoting economic growth but as logical and inevitable elements of globalization. This neoliberal story of globalization was so dominant, Steger stresses, that all alternative models of development could easily be presented as illegitimate, irrational, or even illusory: they were dismissed as protectionist, socialist, utopian.[29]

The persistent activities of the anti-globalization movement, and the presence of these activities in the world media, have called into question the idea that globalization naturally and inevitably leads to unrestricted free-market economics. Instead neoliberalism has become a contested and contestable ideology. Other stories about globalization are thinkable again, perhaps even possible. At a minimum, proponents of neoliberalism now need to justify more actively the political foundations of their approach to globalization.

IS A MULTIDIMENSIONAL PLURALISM POSSIBLE?

Important as it may well be, a politics of disturbance is not enough to establish a new, post-national form of democracy. One of the most pressing questions remains unanswered: How is it possible to define norms, set policy priorities, and advance justice in a world lacking both a broad political consensus and an institutional framework that can generate, legitimize, and uphold any possible compromise among clashing interests? Expressed in other words: Is Connolly's approach able to do more than make us aware that challenging practices of domination is an important aspect of democracy? Engaging this question is far more difficult, and so is the search for evidence that could sustain possible answers.

I begin the task by asking if the anti-globalization movement itself actually embodies the type of "deep, multidimensional pluralism" that Connolly foresees as playing a central role in a truly democratic setting.[30] Although he has never done so explicitly himself, one can apply Connolly's understanding of pluralism to the search for a post-national form of democracy. One would then need, once more, to follow his move away from prevailing institutionalized settings.

Two civic virtues are necessary, Connolly believes, to render a journey toward a pluralist notion of democracy feasible in practice. The first is agonistic respect among multiple groups or individuals. This respect is necessary even when—indeed precisely when—these groups or individuals passionately disagree. Whereas the liberal notion of tolerance assumes a majority that occupies an authoritative center and bestows tolerance upon minorities, agonistic respect is operating when numerous inter-dependent minorities coexist and interact in a safe and respectful en-vironment, thus generating and sustaining a form of common gover-nance.[31] These interacting units share a number of rights and duties, chief among them a willingness to respect each other's different faith or value system. Accepting difference, Connolly believes, should even in-clude the recognition that each such value system, including one's own, is and should in principle be contestable.[32]

The second of Connolly's virtues in a world of deep pluralism is critical responsiveness: the willingness to listen carefully to others, particularly those who have not yet achieved sufficient recognition in the prevailing political and social setting. Not all demands by a new constituency should necessarily be accepted, but—and Connolly admits this is the difficult part—existing norms or laws cannot necessarily serve as a base for judg-ment. A critical response must go beyond these foundations because they are often part of the problem itself. Whatever form it takes, the new, more critical attitude should involve cultivating a private disposition and the courage to express and defend this disposition in public.[33]

How well do these two seemingly idealistic principles hold up in prac-tice? Can they be applied to the search for democracy in an inherently contested transnational context?

From a structural perspective the anti-globalization movement does indeed represent the type of interaction between different minorities that Connolly sees as an alternative to majority-centered democracy. The movement can perhaps best be described by what Gilles Deleuze and Félix Guattari call a rhizome: a form of thinking and political practice that has no central regulatory core, no bounded whole, no beginning and end, but instead operates at various interconnected levels, each moving and expanding simultaneously in different directions.[34] The anti-globalization movement is a constantly shifting multiplicity with various entry and exit points. Its participants range from radical anarchists who seek to abolish the WTO to more moderate reformers who argue for a world economic system that is fairer and more democratic. The movement pops up here and there, gains and loses strength. Its actions and impact can be neither predicted nor controlled.

But does the decentered and anarchical nature of the movement also lead to agonistic respect? There is some evidence to suggest so, particularly if one views the anti-globalization movement beyond its protest element and considers efforts to establish an alternative approach to globalization. The so-called global justice movement, most notably the World Social Forum, is symbolically significant. The forum was first held in Porto Alegre in 2001 to unite and coordinate the anti-globalization movement, and has since become an annual event. Pitched as an alternative to the World Economic Forum in Davos and attracting more than 100,000 participants in certain years, the forum has returned to Porto Alegre but has also been held in other cities around the world, including Mumbai, Caracas, Bamako, Karachi, and Nairobi. Numerous regional forums emerged as well. Most adhere to the forum's Charter of Principle, which bears striking similarities to Connolly's understanding of deep pluralism.

The charter explicitly states that the World Social Forum is a "movement of ideas that prompts reflection" and that this reflection is carried out in the spirit of pluralism. Although the forum has become quasi-institutionalized, the type of post-national democracy that it envisages explicitly rejects the notion of a central locus of power, even of the idea that somebody could speak authoritatively on behalf of the forum itself. Instead, emphasis is placed on bringing together and interlinking civil society movements in a way that encourages debate and facilitates the search for viable alternatives to the prevailing neoliberal mode of globalization. All this is done in the context of facilitating a continuing process of reflection and engagement, rather than by trying to establish a fixed and permanent structure of governance.[35]

The same commitment to pluralism and critical reflection is evident in many groups that participate in the World Social Forum and the global justice movement in general. Catherine Eschle, one of the most insightful commentators, draws attention to an alternative strand of feminist engagements with democracy, a strand that does not confine itself to the institutionalized machineries of the state but searches for ways to empower vulnerable women around the world to shape the processes of globalization. Besides obvious initiatives, such as providing minority groups with veto rights to increase their chance of influencing politics, this continuing process includes, as advocated by Connolly, efforts to see democracy as a practice of contesting hierarchical and coercive power relations.[36] Eschle demonstrates the practical relevance of such ideas by showing how feminist groups involved in the anti-globalization movement tend to organize in small, non-hierarchical units. This way of structuring activities and reaching decisions, Eschle stresses, is particularly prevalent among feminists from the Third World. Decentralization plays a key role because of a strong belief that women around the globe do not share enough experiences to make a common, global position possible or even desirable.[37]

While pluralist notions of democracy seem well represented in the global justice movement, the task of implementing them is far more difficult. Here too, feminist movements are representative. And here too Eschle provides important insight. She is well aware that alternative, non-hierarchical, and unstructured processes may be inefficient or may even mask power relations.[38] She points out the long history of women being marginalized even by movements designed to oppose domination and embrace inclusion. Eschle finds ample evidence of this tendency within the anti-globalization movement. The marginalization process is accentuated, she believes, because most scholars and political commentators do not sufficiently recognize those instances when women did in fact play a central role in the movement.[39] Similar forms of exclusion and marginalization are also evident in other aspects of the anti-globalization movement. For decades, sustained popular protests against the key multilateral economic institutions have taken place in many parts of the Third World. Countless structural adjustment programs sponsored by the IMF, for instance, have triggered local protests. Widespread and vehement as these protests have been, they have received relatively little coverage in the global print and television media. A single molotov cocktail in Seattle, Washington, or Prague is worth far more media capital than an entire protest march in, say, Cochabamba, Lagos, or Port-au-Prince. This is why protest movements in the Third World operate not only in a different local environment but also according to very different rules of power.[40] The same can be said of the World Social Forum itself, where the perennial underrepresentation of participants from poor counties is a regularly discussed problem.[41]

Pluralist approaches to post-national democracy are not necessarily discredited just because they are compromised by relations of power and domination. Connolly, shaped by a close reading of Nietzsche and Foucault, fully recognizes that power inevitably insinuates itself into all aspects of life. He knows that politics cannot be taken out of ethics and that the process of becoming does not always generate positive results.[42] The Charter of the World Social Forum recognizes this limit too: it acknowledges that building alternatives is a continuing process which can never be reduced to the events supporting it.[43] This is precisely why Connolly insists on adding an element of contestation to conceptions of democracy. The ensuing pluralist approach to decision making may well be and may always remain incomplete, but it is more democratic in spirit than institutionalized and often rigid versions, which run the risk of underestimating or even ignoring the inevitable interplay of domination and resistance, inclusion and exclusion.

PLURALISM AND THE SEARCH
FOR COMMON GROUND

Connolly's reading of Nietzsche, useful as it is to recognize relations of power and domination, also bring him face to face with another difficult problem: the need to find ways of grounding post-national democracy so that it becomes possible to reach and defend particular decisions. Connolly is aware that doing so is not easy for someone who embraces pluralist values. He knows that the democratic ethos he advocates lacks "a stable set of electoral procedures through which accountability could be organized."[44] He also recognizes that "the institutions of electoral accountability do form a key condition of democracy."[45] Other scholars who push the boundaries of democracy admit as well that rules of some form are necessary to keep democratic ideas viable in practice.[46] Even the anti-globalization movement cannot quite do without at least some of the conventional components of democracy. Eschle points out, for instance, that many feminist groups also adopt formal, institutionalized procedures as a way of exchanging views and deciding how to proceed.[47] There are strong voices within the World Social Forum that lament its lack of centralized and institutionalized decision making. Rather than merely provide an open and nondeliberative space for exchanging views among multiple movements and centers, these voices stress the need to establish clear political procedures and positions. The calls for action have been particularly vocal from the left, which is part of a long tradition of understanding social struggles in terms of providing a coherent, unified, and organized opposition to the forces of capitalism.[48]

Connolly leaves behind the comfort of institutional certainty but nevertheless recognizes that not all aspects of pluralism can be defended, that there has to be some common basis upon which citizens can unite and take decisions.[49] When trying to figure out how to reach a point of convergence, Connolly gives pivotal importance to what he calls the "mobilization of a majority assemblage": a loose decision-making process that emerges when people with multiple ideas and motivations come together through a series of resonances.[50] The ensuing political perspectives are reached in a more ethical way, Connolly believes, than a forcefully established unitary position would be. But is such a view of decision making also applicable in practice, particularly in a transnational context that lacks agreement on common rules or even norms?

Judging from the experience of the global justice movement, there is evidence that a loose, pluralist notion of democratic decision making can indeed produce common ground. Points of convergence have emerged from the type of resonances that Connolly advocates: from building coalitions among decentralized and largely independent segments of the movement. At times such coalitions formed even between unlikely allies, such as the labor and environmental movements, or anarchists and church groups, which decided to present a common front in Seattle.[51]

The Charter of Principles of the World Social Forum sets out a surprisingly unambiguous set of common values and political objectives, including opposition to an unrestrainedly neoliberal, market-driven approach to globalization and the rejection of violence as a means of exerting social control or implementing political and economic projects.[52] Yet the agenda of the World Social Forum, inspired by pacificism and socialism, is far from uncontested, even among members of the loose anti-globalization movement. By contrast, the forum's critique of free-market capitalism also resonates at the opposing end of the political spectrum. Strong hostility toward neoliberal approaches to globalization equally characterizes protectionist and often xenophobic populist movements that have gained strong support in many western democracies. Even al Qaeda, which in itself can be seen as an arrangement of decentralized sets of resonances, thrives on an explicit opposition to neoliberalism and alleged imperialism by the United States.[53]

An assemblage of like-minded movements and organizations may well be able to come up with common values and political positions. But a consensus is unlikely to occur among passionately disagreeing constituencies, as between the extreme left and the extreme right of the antiglobalization movement, or between ardent proponents and opponents of neoliberal approaches to globalization. One may well ask, however, whether a broad consensus not be necessary to face the increasingly global nature of problems today, from terrorism and poverty to environmental degradation and the spread of infectious diseases. These problems have transnational causes and require transnational solutions. Is Connolly's notion of pluralism really well suited to generating enough agreement to face these challenges effectively?

PLURALISM AND THE PROBLEM
OF RELATIVISM

The most commonly leveled charge against pluralism, as Connolly knows well, is that of relativism: the accusation that a version of democracy which wholeheartedly embraces difference, which abandons the certainty of fixed standards and institutionalized procedures in favor of a more open-ended set of values, is unable to come up with the type of firm and tough decisions needed to address the most difficult problems.

Connolly has at least two answers to this charge. First, he stresses that his cultivation of a critical democratic spirit and his celebration of pluralism are advanced in addition to existing, more conventional notions of institutionalized democracy. He writes of the need to "supplement and challenge the structures of territorial democracy with a politics of nonterritorial democratization of global issues."[54] But this answer is incomplete. It leaves unaddressed the question of how to actually institutionalize democracy in a contested post-national realm. Unaddressed as

well is Connolly's own recognition that facing the challenge of globalization requires far more than a slight extension of democracy's geographic
parameters.

The second response to the charge of relativism has to be found in the
extensive scholarly debates about the issues at stake. A growing number of
authors meanwhile refuse to be associated with the either/or extremes of
objectivism and relativism. They recognize that we must take political
decisions, but that we do not need to choose between an ultimate faith in
stable foundations and a relentless fall into a nihilist abyss.[55] A short
essay cannot possibly engage these complex debates. But I briefly address
at least some aspects now in the spirit of offering concluding remarks
about the search for a post-national form of democracy.

Connolly tries to sidestep the highly polemical nature of discussions
around relativism by employing a less charged vocabulary. He speaks of
the difference between the politics of being and the politics of becoming.
The politics of being refer to existing configurations of power and politics,
to the values and institutions that have emerged over time and have become generally accepted as good and desirable. Such stable standards of
reference, Connolly recognizes, are indispensable for determining judgments and action.[56] But they are not enough. The politics of becoming are
always already lurking behind and accumulating underneath the politics
of being. Nothing ever stands still, particularly in the present age of rapid
globalization: unforeseen things happen, new beliefs surface, old ones
change, standards shift, identities and values are being challenged and
reshaped. At some stage these subterranean forces break into the open and
transform the politics of being. This constant process of renewal, Connolly reminds us, lies at the heart of finding an understanding of democracy that is sufficiently attuned to the rapidly changing challenges of
our time.

Most modern philosophers and politicians have emphasized the politics of being over the politics of becoming. Existing orders tend to be
accepted as good and desirable, simply because they exist. But even opponents of the status quo often present their arguments in terms of justifying alternative orders. Consider how Alain Joxe, one of the most ardent
critics of exiting international regimes of power, stresses that "the most
formidable enemy one must face in politics is disorder." Order, he believes,
"is always necessary because it provides protection."[57] Few if any com-

mentators would question that order is desirable, even essential. Without
order there can be no democracy, no rule of law, no protection of human
rights, no civilized life in general. But both order and disorder are far more
complex than it appears at first sight. Many if not most injustices, from
domestic abuse to torture and genocide, are not the product of disorder,
but of unjust orders. The horrors of Nazi Germany, which emerged out of
democratic processes, do not stem from the absence of order but from an
obsession with order.

Disorder can occasionally be required to promote orders that are more
just. Or perhaps most importantly, disorder can be both the only reality
we have and a valuable source of democratic politics itself. This is why
Connolly worries that theorists and politicians place too much emphasis
on state-based institutional politics, thereby failing to understand "the
positive role played by a democratic politics of disturbance."[58] He is, in
short, far more concerned about the effects of a forced consensus or an
unproblematized application of dogmatic principles than about the difficulty of grounding decisions in a contested transnational realm.

Connolly passionately believes that the biggest dangers to democracy
stem not from relativism or the lack or rules but from approaches that
uphold and defend a single point of view. He reminds us that there is no
lack of standards to judge and deal with political challenges. Quite the
contrary: the problem is often the standards themselves.[59] Consider how
well-worked-out notions of nationalism, which equate ethnic identity
with territorial boundaries, can offer us clear standards for evaluating the
sources of ethnic conflict. But they do not necessarily provide us with
innovative suggestions about how to solve the conflict. Indeed, all too
often these standards, firm, stable, and democratically sanctioned as they
are, actually accentuate the problem. David Campbell, for instance, believes that the inability of the international community to break with
territorial notions of identity and accommodate multicultural values was
one of the features that prevented a timely resolution of the ethnic conflict in Bosnia.[60]

To deal with new political challenges, particular if they are of a transnational nature, we need not only firm standards but also a certain democratic disposition that can critically evaluate these standards. Ambivalent
and open-ended as the cultivation of such a democratic disposition may
always be, it is our main point of reference when it comes to deciding

which standards require rethinking and which criteria are to guide our evaluation.[61] This difficult rethinking process can never be entirely codified or institutionalized. Its success or failure depends largely on the values that democratic citizens espouse. Martin Leet convincingly shows that Connolly's preference for "existential" over "deliberative" approaches to democracy does not necessarily lead to a relativist void. The foundations of democratic practice can be constituted not by a fixed set of rules but by the citizens and their democratic spirit, even if that spirit reflects an emphatic and empathetic acceptance of pluralism.[62] Connolly's position is not even as far-fetched and radical as it appears at first sight. Consider how some aspects of early modern thought, contrary to many subsequent interpretations, viewed abstract universal reason as a threat rather than an appropriate foundation for articulating issues such as religious toleration. Concerned more with security and peace than with remote notions of justice, positions were grounded and justified with reference to particular social challenges and through specific political and legal regimes.[63]

While opposing the long tradition of favoring the politics of being over the politics of becoming, Connolly's passion may have pushed him too far to the other extreme. If one examines his extensive scholarly engagements it becomes clear that Connolly's priorities lie with challenging rather than supplementing the institutional and territorial base of democracy. Although Connolly insists that a pluralist ethos contains all the features necessary to ground and defend political actions, he has provided few details about what exactly these features might entail. Connolly's silence is noticeable, not least because he himself underlines the significance of silences. How exactly does a majority assemblage emerge? How loose or how firm do resonances between various minorities have to be to generate a common position? How can this position be implemented in a post-national realm that lacks a central regulatory institution? And what happens when significant segments of a constituency strongly disagree, or when a seemingly legitimate majority decides, as it often does, to suppress the rights of minorities? These questions cannot be met with clear answers, except perhaps when it comes to applying one of the few irrevocable and even global principles that Connolly invokes—his gold standard, so to speak: the need to "support pluralism against counterdrives to unitarianism."[64]

Connolly's relative neglect of democratic institutions and decision-making standards is a small price to pay for the innovative dimensions that he adds to our search for an ethos that could ground post-national democracy. This search has only just begun. It is far too early to imagine how we could possibly articulate and implement democracy in a context that lacks institutionalized procedures of debate, decision making, and accountability. At this stage it is more important to ask the right questions than to jump to firm but premature conclusions. Connolly's work is of immense importance in this process, for he validates a form of insight that emerges from rethinking, from unthinking, even from respecting the very notion of the "unthought."[65] Precisely such an open-ended democratic spirit, based on critical reflection and a cultivation of pluralist sensibilities, can serve as a guiding light on a path where no one signpost can show us the right way. The climb may be steep and treacherous, the light dim and flickering. But this is democracy, Connolly would say.

NOTES

Thanks to Morgan Brigg, Bec Duffy, Emma Hutchison, Martin Leet, Oliver Richmond and two anonymous referees for insightful comments on an earlier draft. Thanks also to Catherine Eschle and Bice Maiguashca. They not only led the way with innovative research on the anti-globalization movement but also gave me the chance to first explore the respective challenges in their edited volume *Critical Theories, World Politics and the Anti-Globalisation Movement* (London: Routledge, 2005). I would also like to acknowledge a generous fellowship from the Center for Research in the Arts, Social Sciences and Humanities at Cambridge University, where part of this essay was researched and written.

1   Didier Bigo and Elspeth Guild, "De Tampere à Seville, vers une ultra gouvernementalisation de la domination transnationale?," *Cultures et Conflits: Sociologie politique de l'international* 45 (autumn 2002).

2   William E. Connolly, *The Ethos of Pluralization* (Minneapolis: University of Minnesota Press, 1995), 157; *Identity \ Difference: Democratic Negotiations of Political Paradox*, enlarged edn (Minneapolis: University of Minnesota Press, 2002), 215–17.

3   Michael Waltzer, "The Distribution of Membership," *Boundaries: National Autonomy and its Limits*, ed. Peter G. Brown and Henry Shue (Totowa, N.Y.: Rowman and Littlefield, 1981), 1.

4   Jürgen Habermas, *Die postnationale Konstellation: Politische Essays* (Frankfurt: Suhrkamp, 1998); David Held, *Democracy and the Global Order: From the Modern State to Cosmopolitan Governance* (Cambridge: Polity, 1995).

5   Connolly, *The Ethos of Pluralization*, 135. See also *Neuropolitics: Thinking, Culture, Speed* (Minneapolis: University of Minnesota Press, 2002), esp. 141–43, 162.

6   John S. Dryzek, *Deliberative Democracy and Beyond: Liberals, Critics, Contestations* (Oxford: Oxford University Press, 2000); Jürgen Habermas, *Theorie des kommunikativen Handelns* (Frankfurt: Suhrkamp, 1988).

7   Connolly, *The Ethos of Pluralization*, 154.

8   William E. Connolly, *Why I Am Not a Secularist* (Minneapolis: University of Minnesota Press, 1999), 51, 155. See also *The Ethos of Pluralization*, esp. xv–xix; *Neuropolitics*, 195–96.

9   Connolly, *Identity\Difference*, 218–20; *The Ethos of Pluralization*, 155–57; *Neuropolitics*, 158–59; and *Why I Am Not a Secularist*, 154.

10 Connolly, *The Ethos of Pluralization*, 149.

11 Ibid., 154–55.

12 Most explicitly articulated in William E. Connolly, *Political Theory and Modernity* (Ithaca: Cornell University Press, 1993).

13 J. Peter Euben, "The Polis, Globlization and the Politics of Place," *Democracy and Vision: Sheldon Wolin and The Vicissitudes of the Political*, ed. A. Botwinick and W. E. Connolly (Princeton: Princeton University Press, 2001), 280.

14 Connolly, *The Ethos of Pluralization*, 136.

15 Margaret Levi and David Olson, "The Battles for Seattle," *Politics and Society* 28, no. 3 (September 2000), 325.

16 Mary Kaldor, " 'Civilising' Globalisation: The Implications of the 'Battle' for Seattle," *Millennium: Journal of International Studies* 29, no. 1 (2000), 106.

17 Joan V. Bondurant, *Conquest of Violence: The Gandhian Philosophy of Conflict* (Berkeley: University of California Press, 1967), x.

18 Cited in Andy Rowell, "Faceless in Seattle," *Guardian*, 10 June 1999.

19 Vandana Shiva, "This Round to the Citizens," *Guardian*, 12 August 1999.

20 J. G. Ballard, *Super-Cannes* (London: Flamingo, 2000).

21 Most prominently expressed by Thomas Friedman in *The Lexus and the Olive Tree* (New York: Farrar, Straus and Giroux, 2000) and *The World Is Flat: A Brief History of the Twenty-first Century* (New York: Farrar, Straus and Giroux, 2006).

22 Connolly, *Neuropolitics*, 145; William E. Connolly, "Debate: Reworking the Democratic Imagination," *Journal of Political Philosophy* 5, no 2 (1997), 194–95.

23 Connolly, *Neuropolitics*, 178.

24 Robert O'Brien, Anne Marie Goetz, Jan Aart Scholte, and Marc Williams, *Contesting Global Governance: Multilateral Economic Institutions and Global Social Movements* (Cambridge: Cambridge University Press, 2000), 7; Manfred B. Steger, *Globalism: Market Ideology Meets Terrorism* (Lanhan, Md.: Rowman and Littlefield, 2005), 131–32; Mark Rupert, "In the belly of the beast: resisting globalisation and war in a neo-imperial moment," *Critical Theories, International Relations and the Anti-Globalization Movement*, ed. Eschle and Maiguashca, 46–47.

25 Ronald J. Deibert, "International Plug 'n Play? Citizen Activism, the Internet

and Global Public Policy," *International Studies Perspectives* 1, issue 3 (2000), 255–72.

26 Wendy Varney and Brian Martin, "Net Resistance, Net Benefits: Opposing MAI," *Social Alternatives* 19, no. 1 (January 2000), 48–51.

27 Connolly, *Why I Am Not a Secularist*, 51.

28 Steger, *Globalism*, ix.

29 Ibid., 8–9.

30 William E. Connolly, *Pluralism* (Durham: Duke University Press, 2005), 8, 169.

31 Ibid., 66, 94.

32 Ibid., 123–25.

33 Ibid., 126–27.

34 Gilles Deleuze and Félix Guattari, *A Thousand Plateaus: Capitalism and Schizophrenia*, trans. Brian Massumi (London: Athlone, 1996), 3–25. See also their *Kafka: Pour une littérature mineure* (Paris: Minuit, 1975).

35 "World Social Forum Charter of Principles," www.forumsocialmundial.org .br/main.php?id_menu=4&cd_languge=2, visited October 2006.

36 Catherine Eschle, "Engendering Global Democracy," *International Feminist Journal of Politics* 4, no. 3 (December 2002), 316, 323, 328.

37 Ibid., 329. See also Bice Maiguashca, "Making Feminist Sense of the 'Antiglobalization Movement,'" *Global Society* 20, no 2 (April 2006), 122–23.

38 Eschle, "Engendering Global Democracy," 328.

39 Eschle, "'Skeleton Women': Feminism and the Antigloblization Movement," *Signs* 30, no 3 (spring 2005), 1759–60.

40 See Ponna Wignaraja, ed., *New Social Movements in the South: Empowering the People* (London: Zed, 1993).

41 Ahmed Allahwala and Roger Keil, "Introduction to a Debate on the World Social Forum," *International Journal of Urban and Regional Research* 29, no. 2 (June 2005), 409.

42 Connolly, *Pluralism*, 121.

43 "World Social Forum Charter of Principles."

44 Connolly, *Identity\Difference*, 219.

45 Connolly, *The Ethos of Pluralization*, 153.

46 Francesca Polletta, *Freedom Is an Endless Meeting: Democracy in American Social Movements* (Chicago: University of Chicago Press, 2004).

47 Eschle, "'Skeleton Women,'" 1755.

48 Janet Conway, "Social Forums, Social Movements and Social Change," *International Journal of Urban and Regional Research* 29, no 2 (June 2005), 425–28.

49 Connolly, *Pluralism*, 8, 43.

50 Ibid., 9.

51 Steger, *Globalism*, 132; Michael Hardt, "Today's Bandung?," *New Left Review*, no. 14 (March–April 2002), 117.

52 "World Social Forum Charter of Principles."

53 See Steger, *Globalism*, 91–126.

54 Connolly, *Identity\Difference*, 218.

55 See for instance Richard Bernstein, *Beyond Objectivism and Relativism: Science, Hermeneutics, and Praxis* (Oxford: Basil Blackwell, 1983); Pierre Bourdieu, *The Logic of Practice*, trans. R. Nice (Stanford: Stanford University Press, 1980); Judith Butler, "Contingent Foundations: Feminism and the Question of 'Postmodernism,'" *Feminists Theorize the Political*, ed. J. Butler and J. W. Scott (New York: Routledge, 1992), 3–7; Axel Honneth, *Das Andere der Gerechtigkeit: Aufsätze zur praktischen Philosophie* (Frankfurt: Suhrkamp, 2000); Stephen K. White, *Sustaining Affirmation: The Strengths of Weak Ontology in Political Theory* (Princeton: Princeton University Press, 2000).

56 Connolly, *Pluralism*, 121.

57 Alain Joxe, *Empire of Disorder*, trans. A. Hodges (New York: Semiotext(e), 2002), 118, 122.

58 Connolly, *The Ethos of Pluralization*, 149.

59 Connolly, *Pluralism*, 126; Connolly, *The Ethos of Pluralization*, xxi.

60 David Campbell, *National Deconstruction: Violence, Identity and Justice in Bosnia* (Minneapolis: University of Minnesota Press, 1998), 109, 166.

61 Connolly, *Pluralism*, 126.

62 Martin Leet, *Aftereffects of Knowledge in Modernity: Politics, Aesthetics and Individuality* (Albany: State University of New York Press, 2004), 97–118.

63 Ian Hunter, "Reading Thomasius on Heresy," *Eighteenth-Century Thought* 2 (2004), 39–55.

64 Connolly, *Pluralism*, 41.

65 Connolly, *Identity\Difference*, 220.

UNCERTAIN CONSTELLATIONS: DIGNITY, EQUALITY, RESPECT AND . . . ?

Stephen K. White

AT THE CORE OF MODERN WESTERN political thought is a commitment to a constellation of three concepts: dignity, equality, and respect. Each person possesses a basic human dignity, and because of that each is owed equal respect. As we look forward into a new century in which the topics of human rights and global justice take on ever-increasing salience, this constellation is destined to bear ever more weight. But as that burden becomes increasingly heavy, it also becomes increasingly obvious that there is an unsettling lack of clarity and contention surrounding the core of dignity, equality, and respect.[1] Thus we find ourselves in a situation of asymmetry between our heavy dependence on this constellation and our uncertain ability to give a persuasive account of it.

Within the broad tradition of liberal thought, the constellation of dignity, equality, and respect has often been arrayed around a figuration of the human being as autonomous agent: a being with the capacity to shape and revise a plan of life.[2] A being possessing this unique capacity or power carries with it a unique dignity.[3] And because of that dignity, each individual human is equally owed a basic respect. We make good on this obligation by according rights to individuals and granting them space within which to live their chosen plans of life. Within liberal democratic states, we see these commitments made good in the specific form of legal and constitutional rights. In short, our ideals are roughly operationalized in concrete practices.

But as our philosophical attention is pushed more toward questions of global justice and human rights for those who live at great distances—

geographical and cultural—the structure of liberal justification becomes more uncertain. Two lines of critique are especially prominent in raising questions about this liberal structure. First, there is a culturalist argument that what liberals take to be universal, moral imperatives such as respect for human rights are in fact merely the artifacts of a specific western way of thinking. Second, there is a theistic argument that the modern, liberal constellation of dignity, equality, and respect, arrayed around the value of autonomous agency, implicitly rests upon unacknowledged religious commitments. It is the second argument that I am concerned with in this chapter.[4] First, I elucidate in more detail the character of the theistic critique.[5] Second, I sketch some ways in which nontheistic liberals have tried to blunt the force of that critique. Each of these strategies is shown to be relatively ineffective. Finally, I introduce a kind of response to the theist that both admits some of the force of that critique and yet remains nontheistic. This response involves a refiguration of the human being that makes it less "unbalanced"—that is, less exclusively focused on the powers and capacities of agency and more attentive to our subjection to mortality.

THE THEISTIC CRITIQUE

Quite often in the past, the nontheistic liberal has treated the religious critique as simply not very challenging. A fully adequate answer to that critique, it is assumed, can be found in a variety of philosophical sources. In fact, the real problem should be seen as lying with the theist for her failure to admit the cogency of the nontheistic position. The difficulty comes down to the failure of the theist to be tolerant. As David Hollinger writes: "If the religious are to be granted their Yahweh and their Christ, their Ten Commandments and their Sermon on the Mount, then we secularists should be allowed our Locke and our Rousseau, our Dewey and our Habermas, our Thomas Jefferson and our Elizabeth Cady Stanton."[6]

That Locke stands at the front of this line of philosophical sources of contemporary liberalism is not surprising. His powerful case for individual rights and freedom makes him one of the most eminent of liberalism's founding fathers. Of course Locke himself believed that these rights were rooted in God's moral order. But this fact has not daunted secular liberals. They have found it relatively easy to assume that the ideas of freedom and rights can be pried loose from their theistic foundation. The operative assumption is that freedom and rights are necessary for the protection and flourishing of human agency. The capacity for this agency —that is, the capacity to frame and potentially revise a life plan—is what raises us up over the rest of nature, and thus what gives to human life its unique dignity. And it is on the basis of the respect that is owed equally to such creatures that one accords them rights.[7] In short, the pivotal moment of sublimity that brings the self up short before the other has an adequate secular substitute. It is the grandeur of agency per se that is substituted for the elevated stature of a creature who is God's agent, who is, as Locke puts it, "sent into the World by His order and about His business."[8] But does this substitution in fact work as successfully as the nontheist imagines? Recently Jeremy Waldron has argued that in fact it does not work.[9] His position results not from his having suddenly become a believer but rather from his reexamination of the strength of the non-theist's argument. Waldron focuses upon the equality part of the constellation of dignity, equality, and respect. Within the nontheist's argument, equality is often taken to be the easiest value to establish. Consider how quickly this whole issue is laid to rest by Jack Donnelly, a prominent theorist of human rights: "Human rights are *equal* rights: one either is or is not a human being, and therefore has the same rights as everyone else (or none at all)."[10] What Waldron shows is that this kind of quick conclusion is not really persuasive. It has to establish not only the threshold for what counts as human being, but also why differences in humans *above* that threshold are really not of much significance compared to simply being *over* the threshold.[11] In short, one has to be able, first, to identify some property that establishes that being's initial claim to equal treatment; and second, to be able to show that differences in the possession of that property *above* the threshold do not warrant claims to inequality.

For Locke, humans are morally equal by virtue of possessing reason in the sense of a minimal capacity for abstraction. This threshold simply delineates the capacity to reason from the fact of one's existence back to three necessary conclusions: first, that God created the world; second, that each individual is thus his subject or servant "about His business"; and third, that each accordingly is bound to respect the right of all to go about that business unharmed. For Locke all adult humans are capable of *this* sort of reason; and thus they are morally equal. Differences *beyond* this basic competence are morally irrelevant. So in Locke, each individual who reflects on the meaning of her existence discovers God and her status as his subject bound to respect his order. By contrast, the individual as imagined by the nontheistic liberal finds through reflection only himself as a being who can in fact reflect upon himself and his choices—that is, who has the power or capacity to frame and revise his plan of life. In Locke's case the moral significance of reason is that it allows you to understand your obligation as a subject; in the liberal's case, the significance of reason is that it allows you to comprehend that you have the power to direct your life. The problem for the liberal is that this power or capacity of practical reasoning can vary rather dramatically between individuals. And if this is so, shouldn't our assessment of the dignity and moral worth of individuals vary accordingly? Here the nontheistic liberal has no argument against the basic inequality of human beings.

Waldron's specific challenge to the nontheist concerning basic equality is perhaps best understood as contributing to a more general challenge that has received its most effective formulation from Charles Taylor, at the end of his *Sources of the Self*.[12] The standard liberal constellation of dignity, equality, respect, and agency is typically connected to very high, universal moral standards. But Taylor doubts whether these values can adequately sustain such exacting standards. As he writes, "high standards need strong sources."[13] When our sources reduce simply to an affirmation of agency, we don't get the same sort of cognitive and affective power in our sense of obligation that Christianity provides through its notion of our duty to participate in a divinely rooted *agape* as we engage the other. The standard liberal position condenses the dignity of human being into the figure of the agent without the "positive underpinning" of a persisting "affirmation of being."[14] We nontheists do owe the other agent respect, but this way of imagining the initial connectedness of human beings collapses merely into an imperative to back off from the other and her projects.[15] This by itself is not an effective enough source of connectedness. It embodies nothing that enlivens the sort of ethos of attentiveness and concern for the other that can coax our moral imagination across cultural and geographic borders. Without this sort of underlying affirmation, our respect for the other's dignity or worth is deeply susceptible to disappointment, frustration, and resentment, dispositions that can easily slide toward feelings of hostility.[16]

LIBERAL RESPONSE

What sort of responses to the foregoing theistic arguments can the liberal offer? I will consider two types. First, there are those who tell us that we should not take the theist's bait, but rather simply change the subject. Second, there are those who take up the challenge more or less directly.

The theistic critique rests on some sort of appeal to ultimate or beyond-human foundations. One way that liberals deal with such claims is by effectively changing the subject at issue. A popular variant of this strategy is to turn the charge of foundational deficit back onto the theist by asserting that theistic foundations have promoted substantial violations of human rights in the past.[17] Now the issue becomes a choice between being ontologically unclear but tolerant and tending to dress up horrible abuses in the mantle of transcendent truth. The theist now will have something to worry about that weighs more heavily upon her than the mere problem of uncertain foundations that the liberal must bear.

This argument can be paired with another that also increases the relative attractiveness of the nontheistic liberal's position. Worries about unclear foundations can simply be bracketed off, and we can focus instead on the rather large areas of agreement that already exist (about torture, for example) around the globe among peoples with very different foundational commitments.[18] The agenda of global justice is best advanced by not worrying too much about which foundation is ultimately more adequate, but rather by seeking out areas of "overlapping consensus" around which a more robust human rights regime can be slowly constructed.[19]

How effective are these strategies for shifting attention away from the work of articulating foundations? It seems to me that they are both partially effective. Proponents of religiously based foundations should be reminded that their favored mode of justification has been used, and still is used, to warrant human rights violations. Similarly, it is indeed unwise to press questions that expose foundational disputes when real cooperation can be achieved regarding concrete measures to reduce specific assaults on human rights. However, even if one admits the good sense of these strategies, that does not by itself deny the importance of articulating the character of one's foundations. It merely tells us we need to think in a variety of ways about how and when we should reflect on our foundations, and how we should always be open to pragmatic options that effectively restrain clear rights violations. Nevertheless, even after we have admitted that there are multiple possible foundations for thinking about human rights, and we have become sensitized to the value of not always highlighting the points at which different foundations conflict, we are still faced with persistent questions about the clarity and coherence of the most basic affirmations that animate our moral and political reflections, judgments, and actions.

The exchange that takes place in Michael Ignatieff's volume *Human Rights as Politics and Idolatry* is instructive in this regard. In his lectures Ignatieff initially tries to work out an approach that avoids all foundational claims, and rather appeals straightforwardly and exclusively to the value of human agency and the crucial but instrumental role that human rights play in protecting it. This minimal, pragmatic appeal renounces any foundational talk about "the dignity of each human being" or "ultimate respect."[20] Ignatieff's intention is to develop a justification of human rights that continually directs us to look at every violation of rights in terms of specific remedies to be developed and implemented on the basis of political savvy about what is doable at any given time and place.

Again, there is much to admire in an effort such as this that seeks to avoid the "idolatry" of human rights, whether religious or secular. But in his response to critics, Ignatieff finds himself forced to revise his position, now admitting that rights talk still depends in one way or another upon "deeper vocabularies" of ontological figuration and moral orientation that circulate around concepts like human dignity and equality.[21] Thus Ignatieff ultimately grants that even his commonsense, pragmatic approach to human rights ends up entangled in the need for more sustained reflection upon foundations than he at first thought. He concludes by affirming what might be called the liberal's default position: one acknowledges the need to engage the idea of dignity, but one reduces it simply to the figure of agency. And yet does this affirmation of "dignity as agency" not put Ignatieff right back in the sort of position that Waldron and Taylor have effectively criticized?[22] The general moral of this story, the theist would argue, is that once one gets pushed to this foundational level, one's arguments look quite strong compared to those of the nontheistic liberal.[23]

So far I have tried to give some sense of the propensity of nontheistic liberals to meet the theist's challenge by simply avoiding it through one means or another; and I have tried to indicate that this strategy does not work quite so easily as its proponents sometimes think. I now want to examine another liberal strategy. This one employs the notion of "overlapping consensus" to some degree, but it also frankly recognizes the limits of such efforts at avoidance and thus the necessity of directly engaging the theist's challenge regarding foundations.

The strategy of seeking an overlapping consensus is of course associated with the work of John Rawls and the structure of his argument for "political liberalism." Rawls asserts that we can arrive at appropriate principles of justice if we simply agree to be "reasonable" in our deliberations and seek an agreement that each party can affirm without having his or her comprehensive, foundational commitments brought into the discussions.[24] Although Rawls's recourse to overlapping consensus emerged first in his theory of justice within nation-states rather than in the global context of human rights claims, he and others—as we have seen—deploy the notion of overlapping consensus in this context as well.[25]

One of the most prominent advocates of political liberalism, Charles Larmore, is particularly interesting because although he affirms the notion of overlapping consensus in general, he does not think that it is quite as successful as most political liberals do in thoroughly insulating reflections on justice (domestic or global) from entanglement with moral foundations. Although Rawls and his followers claim that they can justify an account of justice that is "free-standing" in regard to foundations, Larmore contends that this account nevertheless implicitly relies on a stronger and more specific moral ontology than they think. One foundational commitment that needs to be affirmed straightforwardly, Larmore argues, is basic respect for persons.[26] It is simply incorrect, as Rawls's concept would have it, that all that is needed to reach an adequate decision about basic principles is for the parties deliberating about justice to be "reasonable." The only thing that allows Rawls to make this claim is his overly expansive way of defining "reasonableness": namely, a commitment to seek and abide by fair principles of cooperation rather than a more commonsense definition such as "exercising the basic capacities of reason and conversing with others in good faith."[27]

For present purposes, what is most relevant about this line of revision in political liberalism is that it opens further questions about which other foundational commitments this perspective might implicitly affirm. Particularly interesting here is what Larmore says about the grounds for according basic respect to each person. This respect, he concludes, "cannot be easily separated from the religious traditions which gave it birth." In short, he shares Taylor's "suspicion" that the moral sources of the modern liberal self may be essentially religious in nature.[28] Larmore's surprising admission is followed, however, by the claim that the apparent victory of the theist here is in fact only that—apparent. The reason is that if we modern secular liberals are acknowledged to have a fundamental belief in human dignity and respect, then just because this belief is founded upon theistic commitments no longer seen as valid does not in itself throw the belief into doubt. This is because, Larmore argues, we do not stand under any obligation to justify a belief unless "some positive reason has arisen for us to doubt its truth." Thus if we have no such reason to doubt our belief in human dignity and basic respect, then we need have no worry about the justifiability of its foundations. "Justification is required, not so much for belief itself, as for a change in belief."[29]

In sum, Larmore admits that the theist may be pointing out something significant about political liberalism, namely that what authorizes its most basic beliefs in dignity and equal respect is a set of even more basic, religious beliefs not nearly as widely shared as they were in Locke's time. But this situation does not require political liberals to admit defeat, because there is today no pressing reason for them to doubt their standing commitment to dignity and equal respect. Larmore does admit, however, that in our "apparently biogenetic future," practices may emerge that will open this commitment to doubt.[30]

I want to suggest that Larmore's distinctive strategy for insulating political liberalism from the theistic challenge is more vulnerable than he thinks. Consider here the scandal in 2004 surrounding the abuse, torture, and murder of Iraqi prisoners held in their country by American occupation forces.[31] How should one interpret the significance of these occurrences for the self-understanding of America? It is hardly surprising that the administration of George W. Bush and some military leaders should have immediately looked for ways to downplay the implications of the whole matter. Bush contended that the problems were isolated actions for which a "few people," "a few bad apples," were responsible.[32] But this explanation was belied by mounting evidence that a substantial number of military and civilian personnel both high and low were involved, and that the mistreatment of prisoners was not confined to one prison facility or even one country, but rather seemed to be a more general problem in this era of a continual "war on terror."[33]

My suspicion is that if you asked those involved in this mistreatment, most if not all would say that they believe in human rights and subscribe to the underlying notions of dignity and equal respect. But somehow, in specific circumstances, they engaged in and justified practices that violated those commitments. If this is so, then the questions about prisoner abuse begin to take on a different and more disturbing color. Would a randomly selected U.S. citizen have likely behaved in the same way as those involved in the abuse? If so, does that perhaps say something unsettling about the relation between our general, abstract moral beliefs and the behavior that is supposed to instantiate them? Public opinion research in the United States over many decades has found substantial gaps between support for principles in the abstract and support for those same principles in specific circumstances—for example, between almost unanimous support for a basic right like freedom of speech and substantially less support for affording the right of free speech to a group toward which there is a good deal of hostility.[34] All I wish to suggest is that quite probing questions about basic values like human dignity and equal respect, and about the sources of their authority for us, may be much more in order today than Larmore thinks.

Now Larmore might object that I have misconstrued what is at issue in the allegations of torture. We don't need to ask basic, justificatory questions here; we need only condemn the individual soldiers for their blatant hypocrisy. They believe in human rights, but they fail to act in accordance with that belief. This objection, however, makes things too simple and tidy. Surely there is a question of ongoing political education that has to be broached. And if it is, I cannot see how the ensuing discourse will be able to avoid examining why the protection of human rights is so fundamental to us. Once we are on this terrain, then the theist's challenge for secular liberals remains very much within the bounds of reasonable discussion.

It is important to be precise about what I mean. I am not saying that the theist has an unassailable position in this discussion. For example, my suspicion is that President Bush's religious views, which seem to warrant his continual talk about our "struggle against evil," have helped create the sort of dehumanized perception of our enemy that has tacitly encouraged other Americans not to see their actions as being in conflict with their abstract, general commitment to dignity and respect.[35] Again, my point is simply that reflection on the deepest level of our moral sources would seem warranted to a far greater degree than Larmore thinks.

A NONTHEISTIC ONTOLOGICAL FIGURATION

If what I have said so far is correct, then arguments that place God in the constellation of dignity, equality, and respect are not so easy to ignore or knock down as nontheists have tended to imagine. The challenge is simply more fundamental and less easily answered than the liberals I surveyed above will admit. If this is so, which general standards would nontheists have to meet to respond more effectively to this challenge than they have done until now?

There seem to be two. First, one needs an ontological portrait of human being, the beyond human and the core constellation of dignity, equality, and respect that does not involve God and yet can figure persuasively a sense of *limits upon agents* functioning comparably to the theistically based one shown by Waldron to be operating within Locke. This portrait must provide some way of figuring the *connectedness of agents* that functions comparably to the connectedness shown by Taylor to spring from the Christian's belief that she should participate in the divine affirmation of human beings by loving humanity.

In what follows I will attempt to provide a sense of how the nontheist might meet these challenges. Toward that end I will first elaborate the notion of being "in subjection to mortality" and what it means to conceptualize this condition in what I call "weak" ontological terms. Then I will assess how well this notion allows us to figure limits upon agents and the character of their connectedness.

When God is in the constellation, it gives one a distinctive way of seeing how each agent, because of her equal reasoning capacity, can comprehend natural-law limitations on behavior. The dignity of each agent as a creature of God must be respected equally. And natural law sets out the specific limits that ought to constrain each agent.

The task for the nontheist is to find a way of figuring something comparable to this construction of equality and authoritative will so that each
agent can see that he ought to constrain his behavior toward others. The
difficulty of this task is pretty evident: without the authority of God, you
merely have agency and, as Waldron has shown, it is not clear how you
could delineate a sense of the basic equality of individuals around which
you might construct a sense of moral limitation. What one needs, in brief,
is something comparable to the equal capacity to reason from mere existence to the idea of a God who created human beings for a purpose. The
specific problem for the nontheist is that when you try to settle on some
central human capacity or power in terms of which you wish to frame
basic equality and limitation, it is difficult to find a candidate that can fill
this role. As I indicated above, Waldron shows us that without God in the
constellation, it is not at all evident how we could isolate a particular
characteristic of human beings and point to it as precisely the one that
anchors our equality. The nontheist may think he can root equality in,
say, the human capacity of reason, "but he will be at a loss to explain why
we should ignore the evident differences in people's rationality. He will be
at a loss to defend any particular line or threshold, [that could determine
the bounds of equality] in a non-question-begging way."[36] In sum, there
seems to be no characteristic of agency that can authoritatively frame the
individual as "subject to" in a way analogous to how the individual is
framed as subject to God within the theistic perspective.

In wrestling with this problem, the nontheist might consider Thomas
Hobbes's strategy. Just as in Locke's thought, in Hobbes's there is a "range
property" in relation to which each individual is "in subjection to." In the
state of nature, we are not in equal subjection to God's order but rather in
equal subjection to the threat of violent death from one another.[37] In
effect, each is nearly equal enough in bodily strength that each is, through
one means or another, a potentially deadly threat to any other. But if
Hobbes provides us with a "range property" of human agency comparable in one sense to Locke's, in another sense Hobbes's property illustrates precisely the difficulty to which I wish to call attention. Hobbes
wants individuals to comprehend how equal liability to violent death
should cause each to constrain his reasoning in such a way that a political
order of a certain sort is instituted. But of course equal subjection to the
threat of violent death by itself engenders no moral limit on an individ-

ual, only a *prudential* limit that the individual can suspend whenever he finds it in his interest to do so. It makes perfect sense—as rational choice theorists discovered many years ago—to free-ride on any restraints that individuals might have agreed to. Thus the Hobbesian "subjection to" engenders neither the kind of *limit upon agency* nor the *connectedness of agents* that we need.

Nevertheless, Hobbes guides our attention in a promising direction: toward mortality. Perhaps the desired range value can be got from reflecting upon mortality, but in a somewhat different way: not by contemplating the violent death with which we can equally threaten each other, but rather the death to which we are all inescapably subject. Each of us is equal by virtue of our shared consciousness or foreknowledge that we will all die.

I employ the expression "subjection to death" with the conscious intention of highlighting how alien this line of thought is to the liberal tradition today. Talk of "subjects" and "subjection" typically connotes a world of overbearing rulers and their subjects—exactly what Locke was beginning to free us from. Of course the subjection that I am referring to is not subjection to a powerful *will*, be it that of a ruler or God, but rather to a *condition*.[38] And yet even in this form it represents an unwelcome element within the modern, nontheistic liberal's ontology. For that tradition, as I noted earlier, the dignity of the human frequently coheres around the ontological figure of the capacious agent who has elevated himself above the rest of nature by choosing and pursuing a path through the world. The roots of this modern figure of dignity lie in the work of early Italian Renaissance writers who were consciously trying to overcome what they felt was a one-sided emphasis on the lowly condition of humankind in Christianity. Against the emphasis on the miserable, sinful, and mortal condition of human being, these writers saw themselves as involved in a rebalancing effort aimed at encouraging a sense of greater elevation.[39] Thus any talk today of orienting the ontological figure of human being more around its subjection to mortality is likely to be perceived by nontheistic liberals as a deeply threatening gesture.

One way of thinking about the predicament of late modernity in the West is to see ourselves as confronted with our own problem of imbalance, only in reverse. This is certainly the way some religions see the present. My intention is to take this question of imbalance seriously, but without making theism the only option. The goal is to see if one can make sense of subjection to mortality in a way that reconceives and displaces somewhat the figure of the capacious agent without thereby simply denigrating it.

Agency constituted solely in terms of its powers to frame a life plan has, as its primary orientation to the world, a disposition to encounter all entities as potentially manageable material. For my purposes, such a disposition is problematic; but it should nevertheless not be seen solely in a negative light. As Ignatieff rightly notes, when we orient the constellation of dignity, equality, and respect around the figure of the capacious agent, we enact a deeply significant shift in our categorization of others, especially those who are in dire need. This shift disposes us to see those others as "rights bearers" rather than as "the dependent beneficiaries of our moral concern." In other words, the figure of capacious agency is part of the necessary ontological infrastructure of a political world where each is to count as an "empowered" claimant.[40]

What is problematic about this otherwise admirable portrait of agency, however, emerges in the critiques that Waldron and Taylor have offered. Without a range value like Locke's which provides restraints or a disposition that connects one human to another, the default disposition of the claiming, capacious agent is one that orients it to the world as material to be managed or guarded against so as to best facilitate its plan of life. How would this change if one were to conceive of agency as taking shape from not one but two ontological sources around which we figure dignity? That is, what if one were to think in terms not only of the remarkable powers and capacities displayed by human being but also in terms of its peculiar access to the fact of its mortality?

I want to frame this question in a way that draws heavily upon Taylor's account of practical reason, according to which our engagement with new situations calls upon our skills of interpretation and judgment, and the exercise of these skills in turn progressively "articulates" our underlying "moral sources."[41] The articulation is never complete, Taylor warns, so that one is not allowed to single out some ethical principle as being uniquely derived immaculately from a source; and thus we are never in a position from which we can announce the achievement of full articulacy in regard to that source. But I am also modifying Taylor's usage in one significant way. I speak more neutrally of "ontological," rather than "moral," sources. I intend by this shift in terminology to highlight that something may function like Taylor's sources, yet be more amorphous in terms of potential moral guidance. In the present context this means that subjection to mortality may function as an ontological source, but it does not have the pronounced (if never crystal-clear) moral implications of Taylor's theistic source.

The key question now becomes this: How does one figure subjection to mortality as an ontological source that is both robust and yet in fruitful tension with that preeminent modern source, the capacious agent? It is not difficult to figure this source simply as robust; for example, one can identify it with those moments of intense dread of death, which everyone experiences from time to time. For the nontheist these moments can be thoroughly debilitating, but typically they are soon squeezed aside by more affirmative experiences of agency. For a theist these moments likely heighten the urgency with which one feels compelled to cling to and perhaps purify one's belief and its divine source.[42] But if one hopes to figure subjection to mortality in a way that more quietly and more persistently challenges the sovereign dignity of capacious agency without recourse to God, one needs to attend to mortality somewhat differently.

We might figure mortality less as that before which we stand momentarily in intense dread and more as a burden under which we continually struggle, a struggle for which we seek a mode of comprehension embedding the awareness of the struggle in our everyday life as a countervailing force to the momentum that we draw from our sense of ourselves as capacious agents. The goal we imagine is one of living in a way that balances these two sources of ourselves. My allowing the sense of myself as capacious to effectively displace the awareness of mortality now becomes an act of bad faith analogous to the one that Albert Camus famously analyzed. In his essay "The Myth of Sisyphus," Camus pondered the shape of a life continually facing the insight that we are mortals in a world with no intrinsic meaning secured by a transcendent truth.[43] Camus had relatively little to say in this essay by way of a positive prescription; rather he was at pains to show that suicide is not an adequate solution to the predicament. Suicide is an inadequate solution because it fails to honor the initial terms of the problem by simply eliminating one of them. In effect one conjures away the problem instead of meeting it. The question of how we should live with the consciousness of a world lacking

UNCERTAIN CONSTELLATIONS 157

in foundations cannot in good conscience be avoided in this fashion. It is only by grappling persistently with it that we bear witness to the terms of our existence and thereby display *the peculiar, basic dignity of which humans are capable.*

What I am suggesting is that when we orient ourselves—consciously or unconsciously—around capacious agency as our only ontological source, we are implicitly enacting an avoidance strategy analogous to the one to which Camus calls our attention. In effect, we operatively forget one of the terms of our challenge: being consciously subject to death in a world without transcendent guarantees. To grapple effectively with this challenge, we need to embrace a response that is as quietly and persistently effective in vivifying our sense of finitude as all the routines and diversions of affluent, modern life are in directing our attention away from it.

Although not formulated explicitly as a response to this specific need, William Connolly's figuration of being in a world without God is quite useful for present purposes. In a fashion that draws on Nietzsche, echoes the later Heidegger, and sometimes works parallel to Derrida, Foucault, and Deleuze, Connolly figures being as a continual, unmanageable, fugitive becoming or presencing. Within a world that corresponds to this figuration of being, my particular identity as an agent emerges from multilayered processes of isolating certain qualities from the abundance of this fugitive becoming. The construction of identity is constitutively dependent upon what is different from the continual work-in-progress that I am and that can never quite get both feet independently planted on the ground. Difference in this ontological sense means that every manifestation of my identity is enabled, disturbed, and compromised by that against which it stands out.[44] What is crucial about this ontological figuration is that it vividly portrays the finitude of all projections of identity. If identity is constitutively dependent on difference, then my agency cannot complete a portrait of itself and its projects as sovereignly free, in the sense of being beyond dependence on that which it is not.

In tension with this character of being in general is a specific propensity that Connolly accords to human being: a persistent desire to have its identity take on precisely the quality of untrammeled capaciousness. We find it too painful and unsettling to admit the full degree to which our identity is always already in debt to what is other to me. Therefore we are continually drawn to strategies of flight that deceptively promise to prove our sovereign capacity to remove ourselves from relations of dependence. We are indeed capable of fleeing any given, particular dependence. And our flight becomes increasingly easy in the conditions of an affluent, consumerist lifestyle, as I indicated above.

This sort of pain and anxiety can also be assuaged by more aggressive strategies. These include the ways in which I script that which is other to me into roles that portray it as alien, threatening, dangerous, or evil; in other words, I define the other in ways that seek to essentialize it as what must be categorically guarded against, denigrated, and combated. This underlying propensity toward a self-strengthening hostility is perhaps the most resilient and disturbing way that we attempt to shore up the seductive image of ourselves as fully capacious agents. Such a self scripts its own identity as one always on the way to some conclusive resolution or clarification of a problem, some victory, revenge, or vindication, each of which in turn promises to keep us one step ahead of the need to come to better terms with our dependence.

Given this background, how might we rescript the self in a fashion that is effective in making clear the self-deception of sovereignty? Here one can begin to appreciate the peculiar quality of our foreknowledge of mortality, and how its vivification might have distinctive effects on the character of our thought and action in this domain. Subjection to mortality engenders a pain and anxiety from which one cannot flee with the same ease as one can from the pain and anxiety arising from any given, normal relation of dependence on an other. It is far more difficult to construct a narrative for myself that denies my death than it is to construct one that portrays me as triumphing over some specific relation of dependence.

At this juncture one can better comprehend the distinctive role that the consciousness of mortality can play in persistently interrupting that smooth imaginary of a sovereign self who continually sees itself as one step ahead of the constitutive entanglement of "identity\difference." When we allow the foreknowledge of mortality to have a persistent vividness in our life, it continually highlights the deception involved in the self-image of untrammeled capaciousness. The task here is to reconfigure the pain and anxiety that we feel in the face of our dependence on the other. In this reworking, our discomfort becomes the occasion not of immediate flight or hostility but rather of a more pervasive feeling of our mortality, our non-sovereignty. In short, our everyday experiences of finitude would be felt, at least partially, as persistent reminders of our mortality.[45] The cultivation of such an ethos would aim at interrupting and slackening the momentum of the self that would be sovereign. By "ethos" I simply mean a consciously cultivated, cognitive and affective disposition that sustains a repertoire of ways of acting and reacting, continually bearing witness to or gesturing toward our mortality. This repertoire would function as a quiet, but ever-present, companion to the bold figure of capacious agency. Connolly is particularly helpful in thinking about what this ethos might involve. A core element would have to be some notion of an initial, presumptive generosity toward difference: that is, a disposition that neither automatically scripts the emergence or becoming of the other as alien and hostile nor flees from an encounter with it. Connolly calls this disposition "critical responsiveness."[46]

With the notion of this ethos in hand, let me turn back now to the two deficits that I identified in nontheistic accounts of dignity, equality, and respect: the lack of limits on the capacious agent and its ontological lack of any constitutive connectedness with other humans that is as deeply embodied as is the will to rationally pursue her plan of life. Looking first at the issue of limits, the question becomes: How might an ethos of presumptive generosity provide us with distinct limits to which we feel ourselves deeply obligated in a fashion that would parallel the dictates of Locke's natural law? To Locke, each of us has equal dignity rooted in the elevated status of being in God's service. But to the nontheist, there is no authoritative will providing that enhanced status, which is what makes me an object of a unique sort of respect.[47] My freedom as mortal agent encounters no externally grounded limits comparable to this obligation to respect all other agents who are upon God's business. All I have is the self-generated imperative to truthfully express the terms of my ontological condition. I will not to live a life that is self-deceptive, because it conjures away, through one means or another, the full force of those terms. I see this sense of bearing witness truthfully to my condition of subjection to mortality as constituting the basis for the only sort of dignity that belongs uniquely to humans. But of course the kind of elevation that warrants this construal of dignity is achieved in the same way that Baron von Munchhausen got himself out of the swamp into which he had fallen: we merely grab ourselves by the hair and pull upward. Is this a figuration of dignity?

This sort of self-elevation appears at first almost comical when contrasted with the Lockean agent whose elevation is leveraged by an omnipotent, external authority. This comical quality revolves around the
impossibility of Munchhausener maneuvers in the physical world as well
as the realm of logic. But in the figuration of entities and ethe of the
world of weak ontology, self-leveraging is a perfectly acceptable activity;
one can cultivate or work on the self to move it from one state to another.
The notion of an ethos of presumptive generosity, engaged at precisely
those moments when one feels the "natural" urge to react defensively or
with overt hostility toward that which seems to threaten the security of
one's identity and rights, enacts just this sort of maneuver.

However, the difficulty of self-leveraging or self-cultivation should not
be underestimated, especially when the self's identity is construed largely
in terms of bearing rights that protect capaciousness. What Ignatieff refers to as the "empowerment" of an agent might also be seen as a kind of
"armament." The "bearing" of rights has connotations not unlike the
"bearing" of arms. The self is heavily armored against all others. If this is
so, the weighted self is likely to be difficult to leverage by a disposition as
diffuse and "unnatural" as an ethos of finitude. In sum, one would be well
advised to retain a healthy skepticism when it comes to imagining this
ethos as a fully effective source of limits upon the momentum of the
rights-bearing, capacious self.

But perhaps the task could become more manageable if the notion of
subjection to mortality could also be comprehended in such a way that a
distinctive sense of human connectedness could be drawn out of it; in
short, something that could function in a fashion similar to that connectedness embodied in the notion of *agape*. When the sense of the basic
equality of human beings takes its shape from neither God nor pure
agency but rather from our subjection to mortality, I want to suggest
that it offers a foothold for a subtle sense of community, a connectedness arising from the awareness of our shared subjection to a condition of absolute vulnerability. An ethos of finitude here gains additional
weight because a vivification of our finitude draws from and then helps
strengthen a thread of commonality among those who equally share an
ultimate fate. This is at the core a *negative* solidarity born of the experience
of a common burden, not a positive one arising from the discovery of a
common interest among capacious agents in protecting rights. The latter

sense is the one to which a liberal nontheist like Ignatieff would direct us; all human agents can agree that the protection of human rights is crucial to the exercise of our capacities and powers. But this common interest in human rights is, as I have suggested, liable to a continual pressure of disconnection arising from the dispositional bent of the capacious agent and its hegemonic discourse of rights. The problem with this liberal, nontheistic portrait is that while it prefigures well *my* demand for protection, it does not prefigure persuasively what induces me to extend that attentiveness to rights to those who both lack them and live at a substantial geographical or cultural distance from me. When agents are positioned in close geographical and cultural proximity, and we already have a political order in which human rights are relatively secure, then a sense of connectedness in the form of an expectation of reciprocity among us can plausibly be imagined as having a reasonable amount of traction. Each of us is armed to some degree as a rights bearer and has—or at least is close to having—a chair at the common bargaining table.

But of course the real challenge to our imagination today is precisely the need to project a sense of connectedness beyond cultural borders and across large geographical spaces, onto settings where we have little or no experience of chairs at tables in common. In these settings those most in need of human rights protection are at a peculiar disadvantage, because of the recurrent difficulty that capacious agents have in vividly imagining these distant others as being in effective possession of capacities and powers. Moreover, if their efficacy is robustly imagined, the image is always liable to that persistent tendency to being interpreted as hostile and threatening to our identity.

For a capacious self that is susceptible to these sorts of pressures, it is important for it to feel a counterpressure or resistance that arises from some experience of distant others as connected through a feeling of common humanity. For the theist, such a bond is made palpable through the belief that we all mutually participate in God's love for his creation. For the nontheist who operates with agency as her only ontological source, the sense of bondedness is figured as being formed among possessors of capacities who enjoy the dignity of their self-elevation over the rest of nature.[48] Humanity is constituted by the free joining of capacious hands. For the nontheist who operates with both agency and subjection to mortality as her sources of the self, however, the rudiments of connectedness come to life quite differently. They are vivified through a cultivation of the *experience of* common *subjection*, rather than through a recognition that we *possess* the same *capacities or powers*. An effective sense of common humanity, of solidarity, seems to me likely to stand a better chance of thriving in the former experiential context than in the latter. In other words, the vivification of a *shared constitutive burden* has greater promise than the vivification of a *shared possession of powers* does, when it comes to leveraging myself into feeling that most slender, initial bond of commonality across large geographical and cultural distances.[49]

NOTES

Versions of this chapter were presented at the University of Stockholm, University of North Carolina, Yale University, University of Pennsylvania, University of Virginia, and City University of New York Graduate Center, and at the Philosophy and Social Sciences Conference in Prague. I thank the participants in those meetings for their comments. Special thanks are due to those who read the essay and offered detailed, critical insight: C. Edwin Baker, Sonu Bedi, Eva Erman, Sharon Krause, John McGowan, Sofia Nässtrom, Andrew Norris, Magnus Reitberger, Morton Schoolmon, George Shulman, and an anonymous reviewer for Duke University Press.

1 See for example J. E. Coons and P. M. Brennan, *By Nature Equal: The Anatomy of a Western Insight* (Princeton: Princeton University Press, 1999); Bernard Williams, "The Idea of Equality," *Problems of the Self* (Cambridge: Cambridge University Press, 1973); Michael Ignatieff, "Human Rights as Idolatry," *Human Rights as Politics and Idolatry*, ed. Amy Gutmann (Princeton: Princeton University Press, 2001), 77; Colin Bird, "Status, Identity and Respect," *Political Theory*, April 2004, 207–32; and Oliver Sensen, "How Human Dignity Grounds Human Rights: Two Paradigms," paper delivered at the Midwest Political Science Convention, April 2004.

2 J. S. Mill expresses the core sense of what I am referring to as the autonomous or capacious agent: "He who chooses his plan [of life] for himself employs all his faculties. He must use observation to see, reasoning and judgment to foresee, activity to gather materials for decision, discrimination to decide, and when he has decided, firmness and self-control to hold to his deliberate decision." *"On Liberty" and Other Writings*, ed. Stefan Collini (Cambridge, Cambridge University Press, 1989), 59.

3 See for example Will Kymlicka, *Multicultural Citizenship: A Liberal Theory of Minority Rights* (Oxford: Clarendon, 1993), 80–81. Quite often the sense of dignity that is attached to this notion of agency is left implicit; cf. Ignatieff, "Response to Commentators: Dignity as Agency," *Human Rights as Politics and Idolatry*, ed. Gutmann, 165–66.

4   The culturalist and theistic critiques are of course frequently entwined with each other.

5   In this chapter I am confining myself to theism in the Christian tradition.

6   David Hollinger, "Debates with the PTA and Others," *Human Rights as Politics and Idolatry*, ed. Gutmann, 125–26.

7   Jeremy Waldron, *God, Locke and Equality: Christian Foundations in Locke's Political Thought* (Cambridge: Cambridge University Press, 2003), 12–14, 44–45, 81–82.

8   John Locke, *Second Treatise of Government*, chapter 2, paragraph 6.

9   See note 5, above.

10 Jack Donnelly, *Universal Human Rights in Theory and Practice*, 2nd edn (Ithaca: Cornell University Press, 2003), 10. Cf. Ignatieff, "Human Rights as Politics," *Human Rights as Politics and Idolatry*, ed. Gutmann, 3–4.

11 Waldron, *God, Locke and Equality*, 71–72, 75–81.

12 Charles Taylor, *Sources of the Self: The Making of Modern Identity* (Cambridge: Harvard University Press, 1989).

13 Ibid., 515–17.

14 Taylor, *Sources of the Self*, 516.

15 *Sustaining Affirmation: The Strengths of Weak Ontology in Contemporary Political Theory* (Princeton: Princeton University Press, 2000), 147–48; and "After Critique: Affirming Subjectivity in Contemporary Political Theory," *European Journal of Political Theory* 2 (April 2003), 217–25.

16 Taylor, *Sources of the Self*, 316–17.

17 See for example Quentin Skinner, "Modernity and Disenchantment: Some Historical Reflections," *Philosophy in an Age of Pluralism*, ed. James Tully (Cambridge: Cambridge University Press, 1994), 46–47; and Ignatieff, "Human Rights as Idolatry," 86–87.

18 Donnelly, *Universal Human Rights*, 17–21. The idea of a consensus on such things as torture has of course been clouded by the policy of the Bush administration toward detainees in the "war on terror." I will return to this topic later in the paper.

19 Amy Gutmann, Introduction, *Human Rights as Politics and Idolatry*, xix. It is important to see that appeals to "overlapping consensus" can in fact be quite varied in terms of their philosophical content. For example, both Gutmann and Charles Taylor make such an appeal, but they have in mind different overall notions as to what is the subject of consensus. Cf. Taylor, "Conditions of an Unforced Consensus on Human Rights," *The East Asian Challenge for Human Rights*, ed. J. R. Bauer and D. Bell (Cambridge: Cambridge University Press, 1999), 124–44; and Taylor, *Sources of the Self*, 515–16. A variation of this strategy is recommended by Richard Rorty. However, his suggestion that we should ignore foundational issues is joined to the idea that we should focus instead on "sentimental education." Although I think he is onto something with the latter recommendation, I would argue that it can be combined with the notion of weak ontological reflection; Rorty, "Human Rights, Rationality

and Sentimentality," *Philosophical Papers*, vol. 3, *Truth and Progress* (Cambridge: Cambridge University Press, 1998), 180–81.

20 Ignatieff, "Human Rights as Idolatry," 82–85. Ignatieff's argument is one variation on the strategy of "overlapping consensus." He asks us not to delve into foundations but rather to stick to the simple idea of agency plus the historical lesson that human rights are necessary to protect the autonomy of the agent (55–57, 83–34). In her introduction to this book, Amy Gutmann finds fault with such an approach to "overlapping consensus" (xvi–xix).

21 Ignatieff, "Response to Commentators," 163–65.

22 Ibid., 164–65, 169, 171.

23 See for example Max Stackhouse, "Human Rights and Public Theology: The Basic Validation of Human Rights," *Religion and Human Rights: Competing Claims?*, ed. C. Gustafson and P. Juviler (Armonk, N.Y.: M.E. Sharpe, 1999), 12–27; and Michael J. Perry, *The Idea of Human Rights: Four Inquiries* (Oxford: Oxford University Press, 1998), chapter 1.

24 John Rawls, *Political Liberalism* (New York: Columbia University Press, 1993).

25 Rawls considers issues of global justice and human rights in *The Law of Peoples* (Cambridge: Harvard University Press, 1999).

26 Charles Larmore, "The Moral Basis of Liberalism," *Journal of Philosophy* 12 (December 1999), 40, 61.

27 Larmore, "Respect for Persons," *Hedgehog Review* 7, no. 2 (summer 2005), 13 [special issue, *Commitments in a Post-Foundationalist World: Exploring the Possibilities of "Weak Ontology"*].

28 Larmore, "Respect for Persons," 8, 14–15.

29 Ibid., 3, 14–15.

30 Ibid., 14.

31 See Mark Danner, *Torture and the Truth: America, Abu Ghraib, and the War on Terror* (New York: New York Review of Books, 2004).

32 This was the way the problem was characterized by President Bush in an interview with the Al Arabiya television network on 5 May 2004.

33 See note 31, above.

34 For a summary of research in this area see J. L. Sullivan and J. C. Transue, "The Psychological Underpinnings of Democracy: A Selective Review of Research on Political Tolerance, Interpersonal Trust, and Social Capital," *Annual Review of Psychology* 50 (February 1999).

35 For Bush's persistent use of the language of evil, see for example his speeches on 11 September, 12 September ("This will be a monumental struggle of good versus evil, but good will prevail."), and 13 September at http://www.americanrhetoric.com/speeches/gwbush911addresstothe nation .htm; http://www.americanrhetoric.com/speeches/gwbush911cabinet room address.htm; http://www.americanrhetoric.com/speeches/gwbush911memo nationaldayofprayerandrememberance.htm. Until February 2004 the web page for the "USA Freedom Corps," the new umbrella organization for volun-

teerism, featured a photograph of President Bush surrounded by small children; the banner next to it called citizens to "love someone, mentor a child, stand up to evil"; http://www.usafreedom corps.gov/.

36 Waldron, *God, Locke and Equality*, 81.

37 Cf. ibid., 77.

38 The *Oxford English Dictionary* illustrates this sense of subjection with a quotation from T. Spencer in 1628: "His subjection to death; as a quality of his being."

39 See Sensen, "How Human Dignity Grounds Human Rights," 14–16.

40 Ignatieff, "Response to Commentators: Dignity and Agency," *Human Rights as Politics and Idolatry*, ed. Gutmann, 163.

41 Taylor, *Sources of the Self*, part I.

42 See the interesting discussion of this in Richard Marius, *Martin Luther: The Christian between God and Death* (Cambridge: Harvard University Press, 1999), 59ff.

43 Albert Camus, "The Myth of Sisyphus," *The Myth of Sisyphus and Other Essays*, trans. J. O'Brien (New York: Random House, 1955), 88–91.

44 William Connolly, *Identity\Difference: Democratic Negotiations of Political Paradox* (Ithaca: Cornell University Press, 1991), esp. Introduction and chapter 1.

45 There is a rough parallel here between my sense of how we might configure the relation between pain and mortality and Edmond Burke's understanding of "pain . . . as an emissary of this king of terrors." See Edmund Burke, *A Philosophical Enquiry into the Origin of our Ideas of the Sublime and Beautiful* (Oxford: Oxford University Press, 1990), 36.

46 Connolly, *The Ethos of Pluralism* (Minneapolis: University of Minnesota Press, 1995), xv–xix, 178–88. See also Rom Coles's idea of "an agonistic receptive generosity" in *Rethinking Generosity: Critical Theory and the Politics of Caritas* (Ithaca: Cornell University Press, 1997), chapter 2 and Conclusion.

47 On the connection between respect and status see Bird, "Status, Identity and Respect."

48 Although Jürgen Habermas comes at agency from the intersubjective viewpoint of "communicative rationality," one can see the kind of claim I am attributing to defenders of capacious agency in his suggestion that "the sole source of solidarity among strangers" is constituted by their possible "communicative mastery" of conflicts; see Habermas, *Between Facts and Norms: Contributions to a Discourse Theory of Law and Democracy*. trans. William Rehg (Cambridge: MIT Press, 1989), 308.

49 This commonality is too slender by itself to generate a sense of connectedness strong enough to sustain a continuing sense of ethico-political obligation. For that to occur one needs as well some understanding of the minimal criteria of practical reason that is neither theistically informed, such as Locke's, nor stripped down, such as Hobbes's. Obviously I cannot appeal to the former in the sort of nontheistic project that I am undertaking; and an appeal to

the latter actually pulls us away from connectedness, as I indicated in my earlier criticism of Hobbes. I have tried elsewhere to construct a portrait of a minimal, late modern "reasonableness" that would be capable of overcoming this philosophical deficit. See "Reason and the Ethos of a Late-Modern Citizen," *Contemporary Debates in Political Philosophy*, ed. Thomas Christiano and John Christman (Oxford: Blackwell, forthcoming).

PROHIBITION
AND TRANSGRESSION

George Kateb

IN HIS "A LETTER TO AUGUSTINE," William Connolly writes that "you peer more deeply into this abyss than anyone before and most after." The abyss is "the depths of the human condition" (*Identity \ Difference: Democratic Negotiations of Political Paradox*, 126).[1] Connolly's tremendous praise for Augustine's power as a moral psychologist is all the more telling because Connolly himself is a subtle and resourceful practitioner of this mode of inquiry. (Assume with me that a principal part of reflection on the human condition is reflection on human nature.) I have no doubt that he was drawn to Augustine because of an affinity between their interests, but also because he thinks that Augustine, though god-intoxicated, will always have much to teach even the most nontheistic student of moral psychology. Even if Connolly's own tendency, which is neither religious nor secular, "subverts Augustinianism and neo-Augustinianisms," it "remains close to Augustine in certain ways" (*The Augustinian Imperative: A Reflection on the Politics of Morality*, xxxi).[2]

In this chapter I wish to explore aspects of Augustinian moral psychology that Connolly himself explores. My perspective is friendly to Nietzsche and indebted to him, as Connolly's is. I hope to make some distinctions that are not foreign to Connolly's undertaking, but that may strike a somewhat different note. I think that Augustine's fervent Christianity may reduce some of his power to instruct nontheistic and anti-theistic readers in moral psychology. I will be guided throughout by the conviction that Augustine both enlarges our conception of human nature and misrepresents human nature. He enlarges our conception of human nature by enlarging our awareness of human capacities, for good and bad, especially when these capacities in society at large are unexpressed, unadmitted, or unnoticed; and he simultaneously misrepresents human nature in his pursuit of composing a theological picture of existence—a picture more inclusive than Connolly's "Augustinian imperative," which is "the insistence that there is an intrinsic moral order" (*The Augustinian Imperative*, xxvii). There is more than morality in the Augustinian world-picture.

Augustine contributes profoundly to the truth about human nature, and some of the truth that he introspects, intuits, or discovers is a hard-earned pessimism. But not all of Augustine's pessimism is true; some of it is necessitated by the effort to fill out his theological system. Augustine works with great theological fervor, and some of the time he imposes on a generally valid and generally available pessimism a theological interpretation of existence that provides a false depth to his pessimism. To be sure, Augustine (like others) can express truth about human nature theologically; but then we must "demythologize" the writing and translate it into secular terms. If there is some rhetorical or imaginative loss, there is gain in truth. However, when vice is transformed into sin, and when sin is traced to the original sin in the garden, the needs of a theological interpretation of existence may displace the search for truth. Even more, when offense to God rather than intentional harm to others is seen as the highest sin, Augustine's pessimism loses a fair amount of its secular relevance. I do not say that his religiousness invariably leads him astray; it may rather sharpen his initial insight or even prompt it. In any case, I will try to point out some of what I think remains of permanent validity, unhurt by theological commitment, and sometimes reliant on it.

Now, it is not only a matter of damage done to moral psychology through the distortions effected by theological commitment. The mere fact of decisive difference between the Christian worldview and all others, but especially the pre-Christian outlooks of Greece and Rome, makes it difficult to assess the comparative merits or depth of their moral psychologies. It is likely that Augustine is the deepest of all Christian moral psychologists, but is Connolly right to see him as peering into the abyss more deeply than "anyone before and most after"? (*Identity\Difference*, 126). The possibly superior claims of Plato to universal validity—not to mention the Greek dramatists and historians—are not the whole issue. The fact is that every moral psychology pays attention, whether consciously or not, to the numerous ways in which human beings are and must be affected by the particularities of their culture. If, for example, a culture is polytheistic or does not assert that God or the gods made the world from nothing, much of the mental atmosphere of that culture will be significantly affected and take on features absent in a culture devoted to an idea of God as one and omnipotent.

Human beings are capable of conforming to an indefinitely large number of world-outlooks, with the result that their psyches are in some main respects, though not all, different from place to place and time to time. To some extent, therefore, it is not possible for us to adjudicate the rival claims of Plato and Augustine to have the greater depth. Perhaps Plato in the common judgment of posterity probes most deeply of all into the psychic recesses of classical humanity, while Augustine does the same for devoutly Christian humanity. But is Plato a more adequate moral psychologist for the classical world than Augustine is for the Christian world (say, through the middle ages)? Do we know enough to say? And is there a moral psychologist yet more adequate for his or her different world than Plato or Augustine is for his?

Yet there is after all a common humanity—common instincts, capacities, and traits—across cultures and through time. In certain respects moral psychologists through the ages can be measured by the same standard, as if they constituted one species. Plato's impact survives the loss of the classical world, and Augustine's survives the heterogeneity or attenuation of the Christian world. With a common humanity, the claims of Plato and Augustine become commensurable, though their ranking will always remain open to dispute. At the same time, analysis of what is particular to a culture may some of the time be more instructive to the student than analysis of commonality. On many occasions we may learn more about the common human condition by a deep analysis of particularity than by a deep analysis of commonality. The simple fact of indefinite plurality instructs us in the vastness of human nature, a truth that helps to protect us against the flattening effects of any theoretical reduction. Even more important, deep analyses of particular cultures make life altogether more interesting, more gratifying to contemplate in the extended range of its diversity.

Who am I to be lecturing Connolly about cultural difference?

A distinctive contribution that Christian theology has made to moral psychology is inquiry into how norms of various sorts are violated, or appear to be violated, on account of drives that do *not* come only or primarily from the appetites, desires, or fantasies of the body or the senses; or from worldly motives such as wealth, prestige, glory, office, influence, and domination; or from ideological motives that impel people to any degree of excess or wickedness with little or no sense of transgression (in my discussion I will exclude ideological motives). There are transgressions that are, or seem to be, impelled to a great extent by drives that signify resistance to a given prohibition for the sake of resistance, or that find in a given prohibition an incitement or invitation to resist it (my formulations are tentative). In the considerations that I examine, bodily or worldly gains, when they exist, are not the philosophically most interesting point of transgression. Relatedly, moral transgression may be of secondary importance or nonexistent. Prohibition is experienced as an impediment, but not merely to familiar desires, even the grandest or cruelest. On the other hand, transgression may be experienced not simply as transgression but also as something necessary for one's dignity or for pursuit of a purpose that raises no moral questions. The stakes are those of self-conception, and how one's self-conception depends on the nature of the relationship that one has to supernatural (or other superior) authority. How one appears in one's own eyes matters at least as much as how one appears to others—a sentiment more Christian perhaps than classical. Through a certain self-consciousness, the Christian self doubles itself and haunts itself. Yet how one appears in one's own eyes is closely bound up with a more than human authority that one posits or accepts on faith. The transgression also has relevance, however, for secular readers.

I wish to look at two all-too-famous analyses made by Augustine where transgression is the theme and where the role of prohibition is not felt solely as a barrier to familiar private or public desires. What is the general validity of Augustine's analyses? Outside his theology, what value do these analyses have for the nonbeliever? Augustine intimates that he touches bottom, that he has seen the sources of the greatest evils in human life. Has he?

Before I turn to Augustine's analyses of two acts of transgression—stealing pears, and eating forbidden fruit in Eden—allow me to offer a classification of kinds of transgression in order to place Augustine's two cases in a larger scheme. I want to emphasize that transgression of moral rules plays a variable role in this scheme; transgression may sometimes be only an offense to the majesty of the lawgiver and inflict no intentional harm on others, and therefore have no immoral content. I distinguish as follows.

Ordinary transgression occurs when a norm or rule gets in the way of a specific appetite or desire or passion. Often there is an act of will or determination or resolve that strengthens and concentrates the appetite or desire or passion, often to the point of ruthlessness, just as there is likely to be a flash of the imagination that inflames any of these three. Bodily reflexes are not paradigmatic. Ordinariness is Kant's radical evil: self-preferment overriding the rules that protect everyone. Typically the transgression harms others through injustice or offense, directly or indirectly, but occasionally it does not.

Measured transgression occurs when a person or a group adheres imperfectly or selectively to a prohibition or set of prohibitions. It may think that authority makes or issues some excessively difficult or even unnecessary demands or commands, but there is no basic questioning of authority. The transgression is not likely to harm others.

Spiritually vainglorious transgression occurs when a person or group feels resentment over not being recognized as an equal or as a superior to the authority that prohibits, even though a skeptical or hostile observer may plausibly doubt the merits of the claim to being so recognized. What is involved is not vainglorious worldly ambition, which I categorize as ordinary transgression. A friendly observer would regard spiritually vainglorious transgression as a legitimate claim to dignity in one's own eyes. When such dignity is involved, the transgression is not likely to harm others, unlike transgression involving worldly ambition, which is sometimes meant to harm others and often does.

Deliberately guilty transgression occurs when a person violates a prohibition for the sake of violating it and thus acts perversely. A person turns away from the prohibition for no reason, for a twisted reason, or for a reason that is not at all transparent. Here the arbitrariness or seeming arbitrariness inheres in the transgression rather than in the prohibition. The transgression may or may not harm others.

"Innocent" transgression occurs when a person or group feels righteous indignation or some kindred emotion. The prohibition is thought arbi-

trary or not quite comprehensible or even pointless, and hence insulting or manipulative or sadistic. The transgression is not the same as civil disobedience or conscientious noncompliance, both of which protest (directly or by proxy) the substantive injustice of a command to do something or cooperate with it, though there is kinship between the two sorts of lawbreaking. By definition, the transgression does not harm others.

This list is by no means complete. Furthermore, it is not always obvious or indisputable in which category to place a given act of transgression; the act may perhaps fit in more than one; the categories may blend into or anticipate one another. We may even feel that ultimately one or more categories have no real existence. Interpretation of the transgressive act is indispensable but sometimes afflicted by the elusiveness of the phenomenon. But at the risk of oversimplification, I suggest these distinctions. To repeat, my main interest is in two particular acts: the theft of pears by a sixteen-year-old Augustine and his friends; and the eating of forbidden fruit in Eden by the first couple. A secular observer may come to interpret the first act as an instance of deliberately guilty (or perverse) transgression, the second as an instance of "innocent" transgression. Augustine agrees with that interpretation of the first act. But since he can never see any act of transgression as innocent, even if the word is put in quotation marks, he ultimately interprets the fall of Adam and Eve as spiritually vainglorious transgression. We must add, however, that as his analysis of stolen (forbidden) pears and the eating of forbidden fruit proceeds—both are strange fruit—he supplies qualifications that are important enough to make us wonder whether he thinks that both cases involve only ordinary transgression after all, and indeed transgression arising from the passions of companionship, which wring from him a measure of sympathy. Yet despite his sympathy, Augustine's rhetoric is powerfully enlisted in the cause of condemning transgression when he preponderantly interprets it as either deliberately guilty or spiritually vainglorious—not to mention his constant eagerness to condemn every kind of transgression and find for it a suitable punishment, which is always harsh and sometimes infinitely merciless.

Let us begin with the theft of pears in the year 370. The account appears in the second chapter of the *Confessions* (written in 397–98) and takes up six pages or so (sections 4–10). Augustine's writing is always dense and quest-ing, but these pages are also restless, and perhaps inconclusive. Born in 354, he had experienced conversion to Christianity in 386. Thus when he wrote the *Confessions*, he was a mature man looking back at his youth, and he was looking back at his non-Christian years from the vantage point of one who was reborn or profoundly converted. He has every interest in making the before-and-after dramatic. This is not to say that he invents episodes; only that conversion guarantees a significant discontinuity be-tween the mentality of the person before his conversion and his mentality now. The memory of the deed may be accurate, but the later construal of it need not be the construal that Augustine would have given at the time of the deed or at any time before the conversion. The person's past will be a source of distasteful amazement, not of accepted continuity with the present. It will be described in a spirit of condemnation. How could one have been as bad or stupid as that? Still, if the conversion is to count as profound, the person must have been either bad or stupid before he underwent conversion.

Augustine does not spare even his preadolescent childhood (recounted in book I) from condemnation. He refuses to see it as in any sense inno-cent. He refers to lying and to cheating at games as a boy. He writes, "I even stole from my parents' larder and from their table, either from greed or to get something to give to other boys in exchange for their favorite toys" (*Confessions* I:19, p. 39).[3] He not only denies that children are inno-cent, he also likens the activities of adults—"grown-up games known as 'business'"—to the games children play; he subsumes all human action, when not transfigured by grace, under the same condemnation. That the adult games are "less creditable" than those of children barely matters (*Confessions* I:9, p. 30). Children are as inwardly guilty as adults; guilty adults are only stronger children. To think of adults as children is not to extenuate adult crimes, but only to incriminate children as fathers to these crimes. To grow up truly can only mean conversion—a leap, a rup-ture with all that one has been, and certainly not a recovery of innocence, which one never had. It is not clear, however, whether Augustine holds that children sin because of their will, as adults and presumably adoles-cents do. In any case, Augustine does not say that children should be spared from punishment, even though he often writes in *On Free Choice of the Will* (begun c. 387, finished c. 395) that the presence of the faculty of will in human beings alone makes their punishment justifiable. Will is the "power to accept or reject" one's inclinations towards what one sees or touches (*On Free Choice of the Will* III:25, p. 146).[4]

Augustine's childhood is a preparation for a sinful adolescence in which some of the sins are those of lust, where transgression is what I have called ordinary. But the famous sin that he analyzes is the theft of pears that he as a "boy of sixteen" carried out with a gang of friends. For the most part Augustine presents the theft as a deliberately guilty transgression, to use the phrase from our scheme. This is anything but ordinary transgression, though it is surely common enough in various forms of mischief and purposeless adventure; human beings of any age engage in this kind of transgression every day. To highlight the nature of the deed Augustine compares it to the crimes (or alleged crimes) of Catiline (c. 108–62 B.C.) and presents it in a worse light than all of Catiline's reputed deeds. The theft of pears was, we could say following Augustine's lead, perverse (*Confessions* II:6, p. 50), while Catiline was (in Sallust's probably tendentious phrase) "a man of insane ferocity" (*Confessions* II:5, p. 48). Augustine finds it much easier to understand this man whom he takes to be a ferocious political and personal criminal and who he believes committed numerous serious crimes than to understand himself as a petty but un-needy thief.

Is it odd or not to find systematic ruthlessness easier to understand than one minor act of perversity? I cannot say. Augustine insists, however, that at least "Catiline did not love crime for crime's sake" (*Confessions* II:5, p.49). Augustine does quote Sallust as saying that Catiline "chose to be cruel and vicious without apparent reason," but Augustine disagrees. He finds un-perverse reasons for Catiline's actions and therefore saves Catiline from the imputation of transgressing for the sake of transgressing. Catiline wanted "honor, power, and wealth" and to further these ends "committed his crimes" (*Confessions* II:5, p. 49). The greatest crimes, the crimes of political policy, do not arise from perversity but from the ruthless attempt to secure certain worldly ends that everyone dreams of. Augustine asserts that the motives of crimes are typically "either the desire of gaining, or the fear of losing" some worldly object or other (*Confessions* II:5, p. 48). These motives impel human beings to what I have called ordinary transgression.

Does Augustine explain ruthlessness? In the *City of God* (begun 413, finished 426), he does distinguish the ruthlessness that comes from a love of country interwoven with a sense of honor or glory from the ruthlessness that pursues domination for the sake of domination irrespective of glory. There are varieties of worldly vainglory. At least concern for glory "makes a man fear the disapprobation of sound judges," and thus supposedly excludes "barefaced crimes" (*City of God* V:19, p. 212).[5] But ruthlessness of method and means, whatever the ends in view, is to be expected. It is not as if Augustine ranks in the scale of crimes the perverse but petty theft of pears as more grave than the great crimes of political policy or personal ambition and hence as deserving greater secular punishment. Rather it seems as if perversity reveals a darker truth about humanity than murderous or unscrupulous ruthlessness does, especially when ruthlessness occurs as a matter of policy. Policy is often either impersonal or not merely self-regarding. In contrast, perversity is more than merely playing "grown-up games," whereas war and conquest are only that. Perversity is precisely doing, indeed loving, transgression for the sake of transgression and therefore holding the prohibition in a special sort of contempt. In this light the offenses against God's will that perversity produces are much more serious than the vast injustices that ruthless human beings inflict on other human beings in (as it were, incidental) defiance of God's law.

What does it mean to love being perverse, to love transgression for the sake of transgression? Augustine spends several pages trying to get to the bottom of the matter. He tries to recall his feelings at the time (*Confessions* II:8, p. 51); he is thus straining not to let his converted self totally misrepresent the person he was before the conversion, despite the inescapable influence of that conversion on his memory. For one thing, he is certain that he did not join others because they were all "compelled by any lack" (*Confessions* II:4, p. 47). He had plenty of his own pears, and they were much better to eat than the ones he stole, which he did not eat. Then too, Augustine allows that he might have committed the crime by himself if he had really desired someone else's more excellent pears (*Confessions* II:8, p. 52). Nevertheless there is a puzzle; a refrain of the *Confessions* is that Augustine is a puzzle or problem to himself. Stealing inferior pears with a gang of friends is, however, an emblematic puzzle. "Can anyone unravel this twisted tangle of knots?" (*Confessions* II:10, p. 52). Of course God can, he writes. But God has not spoken directly. Augustine's explanation will go as deeply as it can, but perhaps never really can get to the bottom of the matter.

Augustine asks what pleasure he had in the theft (*Confessions* II:6, p. 49). He thus works with the assumption that pleasure (or happiness) or the avoidance of pain is the constant human aim (this hedonism extends to concern for salvation itself). When an act is deliberate and done with full awareness that it is a transgression, its aim must be pleasure or the avoidance of pain. The deliberately guilty transgressor is seeking pleasure or trying to avoid pain. What is the pleasure, what is the pain avoided, in such transgression? Clearly it is not a question of the appetites, as Augustine makes clear. Indeed, in the *City of God* Augustine insists that "we must not attribute to the flesh all the faults of a wicked life"; the Devil has no flesh (*City of God* XIV:3, p. 551). It is not even a question of sensory or aesthetic gratification. Augustine found then and finds now no beauty in the theft, "not even . . . the shadowy, deceptive beauty which makes vice attractive." The theft also lacked the elevation of great ambition and of the great vices that accompany great ambition (*Confessions* II:6, pp. 49–50). If not the appetites or worldly ambitions or sense of beauty, what then?

In much of his analysis Augustine can only repeat the assertion that he simply loved to do the wrong thing; that "he had a greedy love of doing wrong" (*Confessions* II:4, p. 47); that he enjoyed the theft; that he loved mischief: "I loved my own perdition and my own faults, not the things for which I committed wrong, but the wrong itself" (*Confessions* II:4, p. 47). Yet these formulations only redescribe the problem; they do not solve it. The problem is to explain, if possible, why the adolescent Augustine (or anyone at any time) loved or loves doing the wrong thing when the appetites are not the driving force, and neither is the attraction of sensory beauty. What is in Augustine's nature, what in ours? What is the pleasure in view, or the pain avoided? Is there a decipherable motive to perversity, to transgress for the sake of transgression? Or does perversity precisely lack motivation, and is it thereby arbitrary or gratuitous? Augustine writes that he did wrong "for no purpose" (*Confessions* II:4, p. 47): "I loved evil even if it served no purpose" (*Confessions* II:7, p. 51). If so, then the theft of pears threatens to become inexplicable. Yet transgressing for the sake of transgression means transgressing for the sake of the pleasure that one gets from transgressing. "I loved nothing in it except the thieving" (*Confessions* II:8, p. 51). Pleasure is the motive. But isn't pleasure (or the avoidance of pain) always the motive for any act, when one accepts the hedonist psychology as truthful? To invoke pleasure takes us a step closer to a solution, perhaps. But what is the pleasure, if not an appetitive or aesthetic one? What is the pleasure in thieving for no purpose?

I think that Augustine comes closest to solving the problem—at least for a devout monotheistic culture—when he takes back his earlier rejection of the idea that the theft of pears lacked any resemblance to the dignity of great ambition and the (worldly) vainglory or pride that lies behind it, and in the next page posits that it did. Of course the dignity is spurious to religious eyes. Without mentioning pride, Augustine nevertheless attributes to his adolescent self the ambition of imitating "in a perverse and wicked way" the powers of God (*Confessions* II:6, p. 50). Is the attribution fair, or simply the only way out of the philosophical puzzle, at whatever cost in accuracy to rendering the mentality of the adolescent boy? Augustine will eventually elaborate the project of the deluded imitation of God in the *City of God*. But the hidden will to the imitation of God is here sketched.

Transgressing for the sake of transgression turns out to mean transgressing for the sake of the particular pleasure of thinking that one is acting like God, the god of power. This would be extreme spiritual vainglory. Augustine compares himself, however, to a powerless prisoner "who creates for himself the illusion of liberty by doing something wrong, when he has no fear of [secular] punishment, under a feeble hallucination of power" (*Confessions* II:6, p. 50). In Augustine's interpretation deliberately guilty transgression therefore is not so much a source of pleasure as an attempt to mitigate the pain of humiliated inferiority. Surely such a possibility is not confined to devout monotheistic cultures. At any time or place, people can see life as dominated by symbols of prohibition; revenge against authority takes the form of a symbolic rejoinder; an act of theft is actually an act of defacement or vandalism. The imitation of God (or some more-than-human power) cannot be creation, only de-creation. Perhaps we can say that at least some acts that appear to belong only to the category of deliberately guilty transgression belong also to the category of spiritually vainglorious transgression, which is often rebellious in nature. Or, the act appears at first to fit in one category and then slides into another.

Augustine's analysis of the theft of pears contains a second motivation besides the one we have been discussing, however the first one is to be categorized. He is quite sure, he writes, that he would not have committed the theft on his own (*Confessions* II:8, p. 51). As the analysis unfolds, Augustine refers repeatedly to the influence that comradeship had on his decision to join the gang that stole a neighbor's pears. On the one hand, he would have been ashamed to be less dissolute than his companions; he did not wish them to despise him (*Confessions* II:3, p. 46). He writes, "I used to pretend that I had done things I had not done at all, because I was afraid that innocence would be taken for cowardice and chastity for weakness" (ibid.). Augustine adds, "we are ashamed to hold back when others say 'Come on! Let's do it!'" (*Confessions* II:9, p. 52). On the other hand, he loved the company of his friends; he stoked his glowing desire "by rubbing shoulders with a gang of accomplices" (*Confessions* II:8, p. 52). He loved the applause of his friends for his bad deeds. His grim conclusion is that "this was friendship of a most unfriendly sort," but he cannot resist restoring mystery when he adds that he was bewitched by it "in an inexplicable way" (*Confessions* II:9, p. 52). But it does not seem inexplicable, certainly not as hard to explain as loving to transgress against a prohibition just because it is a prohibition.

The question persists. Why should companionship, and not only in adolescence, often define itself as transgressive? What is "the thrill of having partners in sin" (*Confessions* II:8, p. 52)? Is there a mystery here too? If companionship makes all the companions feel stronger than any of them would feel alone, is the typical tendency of enhanced strength an increased proclivity to act transgressively? Does power exist to be misused? Is the mind of power disposed to believe that prohibitions exist to be transgressed? In a renowned formulation in the *City of God*, Augustine asks rhetorically, "Remove justice, and what are kingdoms but gangs of criminals on a large scale? What are criminal gangs but petty kingdoms?" (*City of God* IV:4, p. 139). If Augustine's gang of adolescents is not a habitually criminal association, there is nonetheless some continuity between criminal adolescence and criminal adulthood, while the predatory character of all adult associations, official or irregular, is highlighted. Yet enhanced strength is not all that Augustine mentions. There is also loyalty to comrades; it is enclosed within transgression but is not in itself transgressive. Some part of comradely loyalty exists supposedly untouched by the mischief and the vandalism; it is not exclusively a wish to impress comrades or avoid earning their ridicule. There may be not only honor among thieves; there may also be love, if not the best love. If so, the deliberately guilty act of transgression may also appear to be only ordinary transgression, in which the felt superiority of human ties obscures the criminality of the act and hence facilitates transgression, even if it does not necessitate it.

Augustine gives central place to the interpretation of the theft of pears as a perverse act, a deliberately or willfully guilty act of transgression. But the richness of his restlessness pushes his analysis in two other directions. First, he opens up the incriminating possibility that pride or spiritual vainglory, arising from a certain sort of humiliation, may actually supply the energy for the act of transgression; second, he opens up the extenuating possibility that loyalty to one's fellows may have the side effect of enlisting one's energy in criminal exploits, even though no one by himself may have a particular liking for transgression. Comradeship is impersonally corrupting. Of course loyalty to one's fellows can, even unintentionally or indifferently, help to sustain the worst policies of atrocity. That leaders can count on it in advance also emboldens the initiation of those policies. The extenuation therefore can never be other than small; it is always cruelty to victims. Who can unravel this tangle?

My sense is that when we deduct what a secular outlook might have to deduct from Augustine's analysis, his complex and unselfconfident analysis of the theft of pears contains powerful instruction in the nature of transgression. Much of the analysis is independent of theology; its worth is even independent of the redescription of vice as sin, if sin means not any offense to any authority but only offense to God's authority. Even if a pure example of deliberately guilty transgression may be found mostly in literature or theology, and even if actual examples tend to resist being placed in only one category of transgression, the phenomenon of perversity mixed with or resulting from other psychological elements commonly exists. Perhaps perversity must always be explained as the result of other psychological elements, even if it is something in itself. In any case, the effort to explain perversity as a human, not satanic, phenomenon, and to resist seeing it as nonhuman "motiveless malignity" or gratuitous bad will, is exemplary. It is exemplary because Augustine moves uneasily back and forth between claimed knowledge and admitted uncertainty. On the theme of perversity and apparent perversity, we should feel greatly indebted to Augustine.

The second act that Augustine discusses memorably, and that I want to take up, is the disobedience of Adam and Eve in Eden: their fall, their sin.

Augustine also takes up the rebellion of some of the angels and tries, oddly, to impute human motives to bodiless creatures who are supposed to be nonhuman. Indeed the psychology of Adam and Eve—minus the rancor of defeat and with it, the perverse will to vandalize God's felicitous creation—turns out to be almost indistinguishable from that of rebellious angels. (I am fascinated by the thought that one who believes in angels sees in them, when they are rebellious, only human passions. There are no limits to a gullible believer's epistemological presumptuousness.)

The story of man's fall has been endlessly written about, especially by Christians. It is a sketchy story yet so suggestive that it gives itself over to indefinite interpretation. It may appear shallow in its psychology, its imputed motivations, but correspondingly it has a bottomless depth once one's literary imagination has been captured. It certainly provides Augustine with the opportunity to interpret the human condition. Like Connolly, who sustains a continuously incisive reading, I am absorbed by Augustine's analysis (*The Augustinian Imperative*, 94–127). Perhaps everyone should be allowed, at least once in a lifetime, to interpret the original sin. My interpretation is mostly a study and critique of Augustine's and not freestanding. I mean to proceed by using the scheme, already introduced, of kinds of transgression.

The story of the fall—what tradition calls the original sin—has helped to organize western civilization. It is no mere story, but a world-opening and world-sustaining myth. Its brevity is part of its greatness: it is only one chapter long (Genesis 3:1–24).[6] It has engendered much of Christian theology, especially that of Augustine and the Protestant reformers. It has, in demythologized forms, influenced secular pessimism to various degrees. It proposes to answer such questions as why there is death, why there is a preponderance of pain in human life, and why human beings hasten death and inflict pain on themselves in a world that already has so much natural pain. The short form of the explanation is that human beings refuse to do what God tells them to do; for whatever reasons they disobey God, not only parents, superiors, and political authorities, all of whom are assumed to be worthy of full obedience. But of course the psychology of disobedience turns out to be in Augustine's analysis another tangle. If Augustine is intermittently candid about his uncertainty in the story of the pears, however, and leaves the reader not quite decided as to what his emphasis is and how therefore one should explain the theft, he is less willing to admit uncertainty in his construal of the fall. The more abstract and less personal the story, the greater Augustine's confidence in his analysis. Yet it is not possible to say where Augustine places his strongest emphasis. If he professes no uncertainty, a well-intentioned reader will still find it in him.

One secular difficulty with the story is that Adam and Eve were created by human imagination. They are characters, not people. Furthermore, they were born or came into being as adults without a past, without parents and relatives, and especially without infancy and childhood. Their psyches have no layers. They also have no fellows. They can speak and understand without having slowly acquired language over the years. When they do the forbidden deed, they have no history of activity; the only prior deed is verbal: before the fall, Adam names the living creatures at God's request (Genesis 2:19–20). Thus at the time of the fall, Adam and Eve are inexperienced to the point of blankness—call it innocence. Yet adult readers of Genesis are supposed to see themselves in Adam and Eve; indeed, they are supposed to see in the couple the original parents of all humanity. Above all, they are supposed to see in the original sin their own innate—that is, inherited—proclivity to violate prohibitions; to be creatures disposed to disobedience and transgression. Nevertheless, we must let all these mythical difficulties evaporate if we want to see how Augustine interprets the story and, as secular readers, learn from him what we can about the subject of prohibition and transgression.

Genesis is spare in its description of the disobedience of Eve and then of Adam. God tells Adam (before the account of the creation of Eve from Adam's rib, the second account of the creation of the female), "You may eat from every tree in the garden, but not from the tree of the knowledge of good and evil; for on the day that you eat from it, you will certainly die" (Genesis 2:16–17). There is, however, no indication that Adam could possibly have had the experience to know the meaning of the terms "good" and "evil," even though readers of the book will know and may just assume that Adam and Eve must have known what they themselves know. But at a minimum we have to allow that Adam and Eve must know the difference between obedience and disobedience.

The tempter promises that eating the forbidden fruit will open Eve's eyes and give her the godlike capacity to know good and evil. Again, it is hard to see that Eve knows the meaning of the promise. Why does she succumb to temptation? In the translations that I follow, her motives do not include the desire to grow wise (by knowing the difference between good and evil); rather, she eats because she "saw that the fruit of the tree was good to eat, and that it was pleasing to the eye and tempting to contemplate" (Genesis 3:6). Not only the appetite but also the aesthetic sense is attracted.

According to the King James Bible and two modern revisions of it Eve saw that the fruit was "to be desired to make one wise"; so say some other translations as well. But I rely on the unrevised *New English Bible* throughout. Of course, my analysis would have to change somewhat if this translation were incomplete. But I see no reason to abandon the unrevised *New English Bible*, which is superior in style to the revised edition, and no reason to accept instead the revised reading that Eve found the fruit desirable "for the knowledge it could give." The Latin Vulgate, known to Augustine, does not attribute to Eve the thought that eating the fruit could make the eater wise; neither does the Douay Rheims translation of the Vulgate or Robert Alter's recent translation, *The Five Books of Moses* (24–25).[7] *The Interpreter's Bible*, in its original edition, reports the suggestion that the words attributing to Eve a desire to become wise are the interpretive addition of a glossator (vol. 1, 505–6).[8] Perhaps most important, Augustine only describes man as "delighted" with the serpent's statement that if he ate the fruit he would "be like gods," as if amoral powers of authority and command, rather than "knowing both good and evil," were the essence of being like gods (*City of God* XIV:13, 573).

Why did Adam eat? Nothing is said except: "She also gave her husband some and he ate it" (Genesis 3:6). How do he and Eve try to exonerate themselves when they are accused by God of transgression? Eve simply says, "The serpent tricked me, and I ate" (Genesis 3:13). Adam with apparent simplicity says, "The woman you gave me for a companion, she gave me fruit from the tree and I ate it" (Genesis 3:12). From the couple's awareness of their nakedness, God recognizes that they have eaten the forbidden fruit (Genesis 3:11). Although God created humanity in "our own image and likeness" (Genesis 1:26–27), he now says that eating the forbidden fruit, not being created in God's image, has made "the man become like one of us, knowing good and evil" (Genesis 3:22). To prevent Adam from gaining immortality by eating the unforbidden fruit of the tree of life, God expels Adam and Eve from Eden. The story in Genesis, until interpreted (as it should and will be), tells of ordinary transgression, nothing more complex. The transgression is the more fascinating because it is not an act of immorality: there is no injustice in it; the fruit does not belong to another human being. The (only) offense is to the majesty of the prohibiter. The words of the tempter direct the attention of Eve to the forbidden fruit, but once he has her attention, her act is on its face only an instance of ordinary transgression: the pleasure of the senses and a sense of beauty together cause the transgression of eating what she is not supposed to eat. There is no uncontestable textual indication of impious curiosity or a thirst for knowledge for the pleasure of knowledge. Adam chooses to disobey God for no reason other than to do what his wife does. From these simple elements, theology and philosophy have erected an enormous structure of imputed meaning. There is nothing inherently wrong with that; the trouble is that for skewed theological reasons, the imputed meaning soaks life in imputed human sinfulness. I certainly do not question the urge to interpret the bare story of Adam and Eve and take it beyond the category of ordinary transgression; but I do question the necessity of always interpreting disobedience as incriminating and hence as the principal basis for pessimism concerning human nature.

In Augustine's analysis in the *City of God*, which is spread out in parts of books XII to XV (and mentioned elsewhere), I find four of the five kinds of transgression that I have schematically isolated. I find ordinary transgression, spiritually vainglorious transgression, deliberately guilty transgression (perversity), and even innocent transgression (so to speak). The last of these is barely present, but it is present, if only so that Augustine may discredit it. He makes the most of the three other kinds. In attributing a psyche to Adam and Eve, he presents one explanation after another for the original transgression; but if a reader is asked whether Augustine ranks these three, I do not know what the sure answer should be. Perhaps a plausible answer is that he appears to give more or less equal weight to spiritually vainglorious transgression and deliberately guilty transgression; and as in the story of the pears, ordinary transgression enters as an extenuation. Innocent transgression is mentioned only to be turned into further incrimination.

I will begin with the kind of transgression that Augustine begins with, and end my reading with the kind that Augustine ends with. The first is deliberately guilty transgression and the last ordinary transgression. But I will take up second his third kind, and take up third his second kind. Thus I will move from deliberately guilty transgression to spiritually vain-glorious transgression and then to "innocent" transgression before ending with ordinary transgression.

The first kind is deliberately guilty transgression or perversity. Augustine's account of perversity seems a bit different from the one he gave in the *Confessions* but close to that in *On Free Choice of the Will*. He proposes that among creatures, only angels and human beings possess will. Let us recall that Augustine defines will as the "power to accept or reject" one's inclinations (*On Free Choice of the Will* III:25, p. 146). Having a will makes possessors of it responsible for their actions; all other creatures, lacking will, cannot be held responsible. As creatures of will, human beings are created capable of freedom. Perhaps for Augustine having a will and being capable of freedom are exactly synonymous. Original sin came out of a condition of undamaged will, out of the first or lesser freedom, which contained the ability to sin or abstain from sin. The freedom of the saved in heaven is the greater freedom, which lacks the ability to sin (*City of God* XXII:30, p. 1089). It is not clear in Augustine's analysis how in the absence of the ability to choose to sin, it would be appropriate to speak of freedom, even greater freedom; but he does so anyway. (Even if it does not belong, freedom is too good to leave out of heaven.) What is more, Augustine eventually distinguishes the condition of will after the fall from both the original condition and the condition to come: the damaged will of fallen humanity is marked by ignorance of truth and the weakness of will incurred by bondage to the flesh (*On Free Choice of the Will* III:18, p. 128). He makes this apparent concession to radical frailty very late in the book on will; if he had made it sooner, I do not see how he could have consistently gone on to express his opinion about everyone's responsibility for being a sinner and making sinful choices.

It is not univocally clear therefore to what extent Augustine attributes to humanity after the fall free choice of will—that is, the freedom to abstain from sin, if human beings have a will to do so, if they are determined to do so. In fact, he affirms against the Pelagians that only by the grace of God are people capable of abstaining from sin in this life. How can people born with damaged wills still be responsible for sinning as Adam and Eve, born with undamaged wills, originally were? Yet Augustine also insists that only where there is free choice of will can punishment (not merely pain or penalty) be rightfully inflicted. Certainly Augustine is always justifying punishment, including eternal punishment for temporal sins. Throughout his writings he speaks as if people always get what they deserve, which is usually punishment. His position seems, however, to come to this: able to abstain from sin or not, people deserve punishment. Such a position is untenable; it seems a lapse from Augustine's intellectual integrity. The problem of sin and responsibility cannot be solved on Augustine's own conflicting terms. So let us disregard his remark about the altered condition of will owing to the original sin, and proceed on the assumption that after the fall, people have strength of will sufficient to abstain from sin if they choose to do so. I do not see how his argument could get started otherwise.

As if there were not enough trouble already, Augustine is not of one mind on the question of what the will to sin means. At times he speaks as if the will to sin were driven by the pressures of familiar desires, by the wish to find pleasure and avoid pain by satisfying those desires. When he speaks in this way, the story he tells is unremarkable: people disobey because they are tempted by un-obscure desires. Their whole story is ordinary transgression. But Augustine is not at all consistent on this score. We have already seen that in the *Confessions* he renders transgression for the sake of transgression as transgression for the perverse (obscure) pleasure of transgression, and then tries to say in what the pleasure consists. In the *On Free Choice of the Will* and the *City of God*, he alternates between the pleasure of transgression (apart from its anticipated benefits) and what Connolly nicely calls the idea of "pure will" (*The Augustinian Imperative*, 44, 115, and passim). I incline to the view that perverse pleasure (the satisfaction of obscure desires) rather than pure will is what is involved preponderantly, even though Augustine produces sentences that appear to enunciate a doctrine of pure will.

Let us look for a moment at the notion of pure will as a contrast to perversity. As presented in the *City of God* (which recapitulates many of the teachings of *On Free Choice of the Will*), it would seem to mean a will unaffected by any consideration or end or purpose and unconditioned by innate temperament or experience. Pure will is thus a gratuitous will, a will that its bearer probably cannot explain to himself. It partakes of the random, even the uncaused. A pure will is an uncaused will—uncaused by either conscious pressures (internal or external) or a course of rational deliberation; an uncaused will is not moved by the pursuit of pleasure or the avoidance of pain. Augustine struggles with the idea of uncaused will, but not as a godlike attribute. Perhaps he is drawn to pure will because, as we have said, Adam and Eve have no past and no experience before they fall. But Augustine also seems to attribute pure will to human beings after the fall.

Augustine asserts that "nothing causes an evil will," even though "it is the evil will which causes the evil act" (*City of God* XII:6, p. 477). When Augustine writes that nothing causes an evil will, he really means *nothing*. That is, "one should not try to find an efficient cause for a wrong choice. It is not a matter of efficiency, but of deficiency; the evil will itself is not effective but defective." To be defective is to defect from God to something of "less reality" (*City of God* XII:7, p. 479). Trying "to discover the causes of such defection—deficient, not efficient causes—is like trying to see darkness or to hear silence" (*City of God* XII:9, p. 480). Deficiency or defection occurs because creatures of will, like all other creatures, are created out of nothing (*City of God* XII:1, p. 472; XII:6, p. 479). What does that mean? Its meaning is not, I think, that desire stems from lack, as in Plato. Rather, Augustine intends to repudiate the belief that nature, which is God's creation, suffers from inherent deficiency. He wishes to attribute all deficiency, including that which derives from will, to nothing, from which God created everything. Only the uncreated—God alone—is fully real and hence incapable of defection. The greater the deficiency in the degree of reality, the greater will be the departure from the goodness of created nature. Human beings transgress from pure willfulness in pursuit of unreality. Their freedom, wrongly used, makes them the least real of all creatures. This explanation, I am afraid, does not explain. We are left with a view of uncaused will that dissolves into nothingness before our eyes.

The conclusion is that Augustine employs an idea of perversity (or deliberately guilty transgressive will), rather than an idea of pure will. He is intelligible only if we take him to say that pleasure, or avoidance of pain, of some special kind is moving the human being, as it moved Adam and Eve, to transgress for the sake of transgression. The pleasure that Augustine detects in Adam and Eve is not quite the same as that which he attributes to the gang of adolescents: the compensatory pleasure of spiritual vainglory or pride that covers an attempt to mitigate the pain of

humiliated inferiority. I do not think that Augustine attributes an ab-
original dejection to Adam and Eve. For him, their wish for exaltation
appears to come not from impotence but from an initial sense of unused
strength that knows no way of expressing itself except in transgressive
action. This orientation seems less like perversity and more like a spiritually vainglorious self-conception, though I grant that it is not always
possible to rule out dejection altogether when self-assertion is present.
Pride blends easily with the dejected emotions of envy and jealousy. In any
case, the category of deliberately guilty transgression is made to yield, if
not completely, to the category of spiritually vainglorious transgression.

At the heart of vainglory or pride is the will. (The will is intrinsic to both
spiritual and worldly vainglory, but the subject here is spiritual vainglory.) There is no pride without will and hence no evil without will. The
evil will causes the evil act (*City of God* XII:6, p. 477; XIV:11, p. 568). But at
the heart of the will is pride. This statement and its converse are both
true. Pride is the essential manifestation of the will. Pure will is actually
will that is inflamed by spiritually vainglorious passion. Augustine asks
rhetorically, "Could anything but pride have been the start of the evil
will?" (*City of God* XIV:13, p. 571). If that is so, there is never such a thing as a
pure will, an uncaused will without purposive content that is capable of
authoring deeds that do have content. What holds for Adam and Eve
holds for all human beings, even if Adam and Eve were not abject and the
rest of us are. Transgression for the sake of transgression is not pure
willfulness, but an act that satisfies the desire for a certain kind of pleasure (of self-conception) independent of ordinary or worldly appetites
and passions (no matter how vain and ambitious) and of an attraction to
sensory beauty.

Augustine tries to indicate the beginnings of the fall. What helps to
prepare the way for the pleasure that is perhaps most agreeable to a sense
of spiritual pride, or even definitive of it, is an unnoticed inner movement
in the mind and heart of both Adam and Eve that inclines them to defiance or disobedience. "It was in secret that the first human beings began
to be evil; and the result was that they slipped into open disobedience"
(*City of God* XIV:13, p. 571). In modern language we could say perhaps that
the cause of the supposedly uncaused will is found in unconscious prom-
ptings, undetectable stirrings of creativity and initiative, for good and
evil. Should we add that they come from we know not what where? They

are not repressed longings—Adam and Eve had no childhood; but in human beings after Adam and Eve, these longings take their time to mature,
and might never become conscious, or quite conscious. Augustine writes,
"The fall that happens in secret inevitably precedes the fall that occurs in
broad daylight, though the former is not recognized as a fall" (*City of God*
XIV:13, p. 573). There is a fall before the fall. Spiritual pride is its source. Is
it injured pride?

As I have said, the pride of Augustine's Adam and Eve does not seem to
begin in a certain sort of dejection, like that of the transgressive adoles-
cents in the *Confessions*. Perhaps he thinks that the pride of Adam and
Eve is closer to that of the rebellious angels than to that of human beings
after Adam and Eve: some envy or jealousy rooted in an ache of unused
strength, not humiliation. He defines pride as "a longing for a perverse
kind of exaltation" (*City of God* XIV:13, p. 571). "The exaltation itself is in
fact already an overthrow" (573). What is involved here is a self-conception
associated by Augustine with all acts of transgression that resent subordination and the obedience enjoined on the subordinate. Submission is
not only to the commands of a superior but also to the status of being
subordinate. The tempter could not have succeeded "had not man already
started to please himself." Indeed, man became "too pleased with himself" (571). By speaking of man, Augustine is attributing these dispositions of Adam and Eve to all humanity. Since Adam and Eve fell before
the fall, they were never innocent: such is Augustine's radical suggestion.

Was unfallen man proud of his incipient powers because they were so
remarkable? And did his pride grow out of an initial secret chagrin that
stemmed from being blocked in rightfully exercising powers awaiting
expression? From chagrin, did he begin to feel that the command to
abstain from self-expression was insulting, and that obedience was dis-
honorable? Why accept everything passively as a gift from God and not
strive instead to seize or realize possibilities? Augustine writes that Adam
and Eve wished "to abandon the basis on which the mind should be firmly
fixed, and to become, as it were, based on oneself and so remain"; the
"original evil" is that "man regards himself as his own light" (*City of God*
XIV:13, p. 571). Adam and Eve wished to make themselves "their own
ground" (573). The forbidden fruit is not a special substance that mag-
ically transforms them into self-exalting creatures. Their very transgression shows that they wish to depose God and take his place, not only to
imitate him. Augustine demands subjection, which is a perfect obedience

to the will of God. This subjection is the highest human condition. Perfect (pure) obedience to God's will is a complete guide to conduct and makes unnecessary the difficult and often futile work of knowing the difference between good and evil. (Augustine's political theory and ecclesiastical theory show a similar advocacy of nearly unqualified obedience.)

Abraham, a model of subjection, was willing to kill his own son in obedience to God's extraordinarily difficult command, but Adam and Eve could not obey the one easy command they were given. To be fair, Augustine does not go the length of Kierkegaard in *Fear and Trembling* in vindicating to an only nominally Christian society Abraham's decision by redescribing it as a "teleological suspension of the ethical"; Kierkegaard is admiring of Abraham, though also appalled by him.[9] But Augustine is ruthless in another direction. He believes that eternal death will appear as an excessive punishment only to those who do not know "how to measure the immensity of the wickedness in sinning when it was so immensely easy to avoid the sin" (*City of God* XIV:15, p. 575). In *Totem and Taboo* Freud writes that there is "no need to prohibit something that no one desires to do, and a thing that is forbidden with the greatest emphasis must be a thing that is desired."[10] By making so much of how easy it was for Adam and Eve to obey the supercharged taboo, Augustine is turning Freud inside out. (Alas, Freud does not reckon with the possibility that a prohibition itself may be perverse.) Of course the command is easy to obey only if one is disposed to humility. Yet without experience of defeat where would humility come from? God never asks Adam and Eve to love him or be grateful. Are they supposed to have these feelings without being coached?

Augustine wants to pull down human spiritual pride in the face of God. Yet secular thinkers too can find instruction in his wariness of the hubris of rebellious angels and disobedient human beings. Although Adam and Eve are scarcely hubristic to those who do not accept Augustine's reading, his indictment of them can be redirected toward the pervasive desire of civilized humanity to be its own base or ground, to resent what is merely given, to endeavor to remake and reshape, to alter or abolish nature, to depose nature as it is and replace it as much as possible with nature as humanly remade. Secular people can learn from Augustine's indictment of vainglorious self-conception as destructive, not merely creative. Humanity destroys as it creates. How is the balance to be struck?

Thus deliberately guilty or perverse transgression gives way in large part to spiritually vainglorious transgression in Augustine's analysis of the original sin. There is, however, a moment in the *City of God* when he entertains the thought that the transgression of Adam and Eve was innocent, so to speak. Augustine quotes Paul (1 Corinthians 15:56):[11] "sin gains its power from the law" (*City of God* XIII:5, p. 514). But then Augustine goes on to trample over the subtleties of Paul's teaching and render the law's strange effect on the sinner as simply a further indication of the sinner's evil proclivities. The law encourages transgression, does the work of entrapment, but bears no blame for doing so. By itself, the tendency of the prohibition to increase the desire to transgress should not only extenuate the transgressor but incriminate the prohibition. The transgression becomes innocent, in a manner of speaking. Instead, in Augustine's analysis the fact of increased desire to transgress is only further incrimination of the transgressor. Augustine writes that "the prohibition increases the desire to commit the unlawful act," but the next words are: "when the love of righteousness is not strong enough to overcome the sinful desire by the delight it affords" (*City of God* XIII:5, p. 514).

Interestingly, Augustine acknowledges that prohibition may encourage transgression. I suppose that he did not have to insert this point into his analysis. But because he is, despite his theological need, a true philosopher after all, he will often make trouble for himself by speculating beyond the boundaries of safety. Nevertheless the only response he can offer to a troubling thought is to invoke a rare emotion: a love of righteousness so strong as to overcome the strengthened temptation that God, as author of the prohibition, places in the way of a creature already weak just by being human. There is finally no innocent transgression in Augustine's system, not even in a manner of speaking, unless we cite a passing remark by Augustine that Adam "was unacquainted with the strictness of God," and perhaps mistakenly thought that his offense was "pardonable" (*City of God* XIV:12, p. 570). But to be uncomprehending of punishment and of death as the supreme punishment, not to mention eternal death after earthly death, is for Augustine not sufficient to establish innocence or even mitigate the punishment of guilt. "Need I say more?," he asks with satisfaction (*City of God* XIV:12, p. 570).

More than one kind of transgression is present in Augustine's analysis of the original sin. The last kind that he considers is what I have called ordinary transgression. It has a sympathetic quality, but may lack the gravitas of the other kinds. Adam transgressed, Augustine writes, not because he was seduced into thinking that the serpent spoke the truth, as Eve was; rather, Adam fell in with Eve because the two were "so closely bound in partnership"; Adam "refused to be separated from his only companion, even if it involved sharing her sin" (*City of God* XIV:11, p. 570). Adam's fault was loyalty, a trait that led him to commit an unforgivable sin deliberately. Perhaps this loyalty was not romantic love (as in *Paradise Lost*, in which Adam and Eve had sex before the fall; in Augustine they could have had non-concupiscent sex, but did not, perhaps because the fall took place too soon for them to find their parts), but something closer to the comradeship in stealing pears that so engrossed Augustine in the *Confessions*.

From a democratic perspective, the stakes are greatest when the possibility of innocent transgression (as right in itself, not as the lesser evil) is theoretically allowable. Two religious thinkers, Paul before Augustine and Kierkegaard after him, open up that possibility for both religious and secular adherents, rather than striving to close it off. A brief comparison between Augustine and them could be instructive, especially because Paul and Augustine are often joined in one tradition, while Kierkegaard, a Lutheran heretic who lived centuries after them, belongs by temperament in their company.

In a delicate passage in his letter to the Romans, Paul approaches the idea that some transgressions are oddly innocent. Paul makes the claim of innocence, though the claim is hesitant or ambiguous. When he retracts it, the retraction is rather willed. He asks, "Is the law identical with sin?" (Romans 7:7).[12] The meaning of "the law" is not stable in Paul's discourse. Most obviously, it refers to the prohibitions against covetousness in the great commandments of Moses. At his most antinomian, Paul is therefore quarreling with some of the great commandments and in the name of innocent transgression. But sometimes the law is not described explicitly: it can refer to the numerous prescriptions of the Mosaic law. Paul is championing faith above laws and works, love above the conformity that comes from ritualism or fear of God's punishment. He verges on separating goodness from obedience. He answers, "Of course not": law is not identical with sin. Yet then he writes, "But except through law I should not have become acquainted with sin. For example, I should never have known what it was to covet, if the law had not said, 'Thou shalt not covet.' Through that commandment sin found its opportunity and produced in me all kinds of wrong desires" (Romans 7:7–8). At most there is a slight or tentative inclination to do a deed; but prohibition intensifies such an inclination by defining the deed as a transgression and therefore invests the inclination with a force and hence an importance that it would otherwise lack.

Whatever his retractions or his efforts to climb above his initial assertions, Paul leaves us thinking that prohibition induces or excites the will to transgress: the commandment "produced in me all kinds of wrong desires." It is only when a human being is uncommanded and filled with a sense of liberation that he may do the right thing in the right spirit. But under the regime of command, where every prohibition is charged with the surplus significance of sin, which is offense to the majesty of the divine lawgiver, transgression is inevitable. Transgression is a response to what is felt as a taunt: I dare you to disobey. The law "seduced me" (Romans 7:11). Paul continues: "There was a time when, in the absence of the law, I was fully alive; but when the commandment came, sin sprang to life and I died" (Romans 7:9). The spirit of Paul's words is hostile to the all-too-human craving for the mystery that adheres to nonmoral prohibitions when they are charged with dread. Of course all that Paul says about the law assumes the redemption offered by faith in Christ. Yet it seems to me that with some adaptation, his words about the demoralizing effects of prohibition, and not only when there are numerous laws, might be applicable to Adam and Eve (and all their children). The aim need not be complete exoneration, but only extenuation within a Christian framework, and a democratic leniency outside it. There is something innocent in the original transgression and recurrently in ours.

To bring the point home, we must psychologize with the help of Paul, while remembering that the Lord's Prayer implores Him not to lead us into temptation. Let us attribute the following anachronistic thoughts to Adam or Eve.

It had not occurred to me to break the law until I was told not to do so. I did not even know that it was possible to disobey until there was a prohibition. Once there was a prohibition my whole mentality changed. The prohibition was invested with an inscrutable importance and supported by equally inscrutable warnings of the dangers of transgression. I sought the reason for the prohibition and was told none and could find none. The prohibition struck me as an act of pure will by the prohibiter, arbitrary or gratuitous. It is less comprehensible than a reverse equivalent of perverse transgression would be. A needless prohibition is like a false accusation. Why was the tree of knowledge planted in the first place? If as a permanent test or temptation, then its mere existence enslaves. Is God the tempter? Why should eating be so charged with importance? Why should there be a taboo when there is no strong desire to do the tabooed thing? Why should Eden contain any prohibition? The prohibition's meaning was like a secret kept from me. Who can resist trying to find out what the secret is? (There turned out to be no secret, only punishment for wanting to know it.) The prohibition opened up an otherwise unimagined and undesired opportunity. But if I refused the challenge and unquestioningly obeyed an inscrutable command, my whole self-conception would have been radically changed. I would have remained forever in perpetual uncertainty and impure docility. I was never a child. I would have been less than human if I had complied, even though it turns out that I am not more than human for having disobeyed.

The line of psychology suggested by Paul has application beyond monotheism or any religious outlook. A noteworthy and partly contrasting picture is offered by Kierkegaard in *The Concept of Anxiety*.[13] It is still religious, but Kierkegaard is willing to propose what he calls a psychological analysis that is secular for as long as it can be, and only after that point does he become religious in his interpretation. The psychological analysis portends Heidegger's ontology and Sartre's existentialism. Kierkegaard holds that every man is like Adam, not because he has inherited sinfulness from Adam but because like Adam every man must lose his innocence in a certain kind of transgression, which Kierkegaard recurrently calls a leap (*The Concept of Anxiety*, 31). A leap has the "suddenness of the enigmatic" (30). A temptation, but not the sensual kind, is a spiritual test or trial, which is not to be wanted but is not to be shunned (174). Prohibition (of some spiritual endeavor) induces anxiety in a person hitherto innocent of a determinate endeavor. Anxiety is the "qualification of the dreaming spirit" (41). In children, anxiety is intimated as a seeking for the adventurous, monstrous, and enigmatic (41). In adults, there is undeniably a desire for the forbidden (40); but Kierkegaard's interest is in the spiritually forbidden, symbolized physically by forbidden fruit. The prohibition of spiritual endeavor necessitates a leap, not a series of easy steps. Once awakened by the prohibition into anxiety, one is also awakened to "freedom's possibility" (44). Adam did not need the Devil: "one need merely assume that Adam talked to himself" (45). We cannot expect Adam to have been able to understand all that was involved in the prohibition or in the guile of the Devil. But once anxiety is awake, the condition is comparable to "the dizziness of freedom, which emerges when ... freedom looks down into its own possibility" (61).

I take Kierkegaard to be saying that freedom is shown in the dash across the boundary line, the transgression that is a spiritual leap into guilt, the spiritual guilt incurred in committing the absolutely indispensable sin of rejecting complete and unquestioning obedience. No science can understand the spiritual leap that is inherent in moving in a moment from the anxiety of innocence to the ambiguous anxiety of spiritual guilt (*The Concept of Anxiety*, 61). Adam became an adult, and we become adults when we dare to awaken to anxiety and then transgress; that is, to put it in secular terms, we try to possess our life by entering unafraid into a direct relation with the highest principles of freedom. I think that Kierkegaard sees Adam and Eve as the inventors of freedom through disobedience, a disobedience that is not sensual but spiritual. This may not be a reassuring innocence; it is an innocence of transgression. Paul also hints at it, but Augustine cannot bear to countenance it. (He feared his own wildness.)

One last word. "Innocent" transgression is a serious questioning of prohibitions and their source. I think that there are several versions of innocent transgression; the attitudes and feelings that animate them are congenial to the democratic spirit. To finish our treatment of the theme of prohibition and transgression, I would like to suggest that the versions in Paul and Kierkegaard have relevance to democracy, which in itself is a system of questioning prohibitions and their source. I think that these two thinkers do more unintentional good to democracy than Augustine does. What then is Augustine's value to modern democracy? I have already said that he enlarges our conception of human nature. I mean above all that he did the inestimable favor of enlarging awareness of the self's inward and introspective capacities and exploring its richness, and thereby encouraging people to revere one another's human dignity, the founding sentiment of modern democracy. At the same time, his explorations of the complex and unsettled nature of the passions contribute to a realistic pessimism that is not intrinsically inimical to democracy and that can contribute to a greater sobriety of democratic expectations. (For the secular reader in general, some of his pessimism is surely applicable to cultures that are not devoutly or are only culturally Christian, whether democratic or not.) Yet when it comes to prohibition and transgression, Augustine the driven theologian, for all his exceptional acuteness, for all his wisdom, tends to harm the sentiments of democracy.

In his novella *The Tables of the Law*, which is a meditation on Moses, Thomas Mann tries to probe the mentality of the prohibiter. Mann reconstructs the reasons for the absoluteness and severity of the commandments and for the multiplication of prohibitions that not only regulate life but prescribe practically every aspect and detail of it. He writes of Moses, "His birth was irregular, hence it was he passionately loved order, the absolute, the shalt and shalt not. In his youth, in a blazing fit of rage, he had killed a man; so he knew better than the innocent, that to kill is very fine but to have killed is most horrible, and that it is forbidden to kill. His senses were hot, so he craved the spiritual, the pure, the holy; he craved the unseen, because he felt that the unseen was spiritual, holy and pure."[14] With some changes, Mann's portrait of Moses becomes a portrait of Augustine.

Mann's story reminds us that prohibitions come from only human beings, whatever the claim for more-than-human authority, and warns us that to worship the unaccountable and surround it with ferocity and unapproachability is but to worship the extremist psychology of one man or perhaps a few men. Majestic prohibitions are projections on to others of the lawgiver's own unusually strong transgressive impulses; his remorse for these impulses may have the odd result of intensifying his need to cajole others into facing restraints so majestic that they may eventually strengthen some people's desire to transgress for the sake of transgression or, more likely, to transgress out of an outraged innocence. A network of mystification and humiliation is established. By its pervasive cultural influence, a civilly rebellious democratic politics exists in part to dismantle this continuously recreated network. When the law goes beyond basic morality, while pretending to an importance higher than morality, it enslaves the spirit. Democracy is a refusal to leave authority majestic, absolute, unaccountable, and pleased to multiply prohibitions obnoxiously; authority must be transparent and reasonable. When authority is otherwise, transgression is a gesture by which to express both shock and righteous indignation, and then it is perhaps innocent.

NOTES

I wish to thank Sharon Cameron for her criticisms.

1   William E. Connolly, *Identity\Difference: Democratic Negotiations of Political Paradox* (Ithaca: Cornell University Press, 1991).

2   William E. Connolly, *The Augustinian Imperative: A Reflection on the Politics of Morality* (1993; rev. edn New York: Rowman and Littlefield, 2002).

3   Augustine, *Confessions*, trans. R. S. Pine-Coffin (New York: Penguin, 1961).

4   Augustine, *On Free Choice of the Will*, trans. Anna S. Benjamin and L. H. Hackstaff (Indianapolis: Bobbs-Merrill, 1964).

5   Augustine, *Concerning the City of God against the Pagans*, ed. David Knowles, trans. Henry Bettenson (Baltimore: Penguin, 1972).

6   Genesis, *The New English Bible* (Oxford: Oxford University Press, 1970).

7   Robert Alter, *The Five Books of Moses* (New York: W. W. Norton, 2004).

8   Genesis, *The New Interpreter's Bible* (Nashville: Abingdon, 1952).

9   Søren Kierkegaard, *Fear and Trembling: A Dialectical Lyric* (1843), trans. Walter Lowrie (Princeton: Princeton University Press, 1941), 100, 90.

10 Sigmund Freud, *Totem and Taboo* (1913) (New York: W. W. Norton, 1962), 69.

11 First Letter of Paul to the Corinthians, *The New English Bible* (Oxford: Oxford University Press, 1970).

12 Letter of Paul to the Romans, *The New English Bible* (Oxford: Oxford University Press, 1970).

13 Søren Kierkegaard, *The Concept of Anxiety* (1844), ed. and trans. Reidar Thomte and Albert B. Anderson (Princeton: Princeton University Press, 1980).

14 Thomas Mann, *The Tables of the Law* [*Das Gesetz*], trans. H. T. Lowe-Porter (New York: Alfred A. Knopf, 1945), 1.

RADICALIZING DEMOCRATIC THEORY: SOCIAL SPACE IN CONNOLLY, DELEUZE, AND RANCIÈRE

Michael J. Shapiro

RECONCEIVING DEMOCRACY: RANCIÈRE AND CONNOLLY ON CONTINGENCY

IN A RADICAL CHALLENGE to the dominant approach of traditional political theory to democracy, Jacques Rancière writes: "Democracy is not a regime or a social way of life. It is the institution of politics itself. The system of forms of subjectification through which any order of distribution of bodies into functions corresponding to their 'nature' and places corresponding to their functions is undermined, thrown back on its contingency."[1] Deploying a grammatical figure that implicates the becoming of subjects as intelligible parts of the social order, he extends his challenge to the social sciences, pointing out that they have historically assisted a "modern parapolitical enterprise,"[2] an effacement of the contingencies of political encounter in favor of "the problematization of origins of power and the terms in which it is framed—the social contract, alienation, and sovereignty."[3] Social science takes as its starting point an "individuality," according to which entitlement is simply "the *entitlement* of anyone at all to question the state or to serve as proof of its fidelity to its own principle."[4] In contrast, politics, in Rancière's sense, escapes the compass of social and political science's concern with policy. "The political" makes an appearance through a "polemicization,"[5] an action in which a part that has had no part makes itself manifest, an enactment of what Rancière calls subjectification. The political is therefore not a set of structures or a continuing process that enables disinterested knowledge to be applied to the arithmetic distribution of identical bodies, or to the reality expressed in the discourses of individuals and modes of governance.

In contrast to "the arithmetic of shopkeepers and barterers," Rancière speaks of "a magnitude that escapes ordinary measurement," a "paradoxical magnitude" that escapes a logic regarding as interchangeable "the equality of anyone at all with anyone else."[6] The logic of subjectification derives from a pluralism of *disparity*. Resisting metaphysical foundations, Rancière sees the social order as sheer contingency. There are no political parties with an existence prior to "the declaration of a wrong."[7]

But what is "society" for Rancière? How are democratic subjects situated? Referring only indirectly to the social frame within which democratic encounters emerge, he writes: "Real democracy would presuppose that the *demos* be constituted as a subject present to itself across the whole surface of the social body."[8] Apart from implying that the democratic subject must be socially pervasive, Rancière does not elaborate a structural model of segments composing the social body. Instead of mapping a static social space, he implies that social segments are episodic; insofar as they have political significance, they arise during encounters. While canonical political thinkers since the eighteenth century have constructed society as a regulative ideal and the legitimating basis or substitute for "the political," Rancière reverses the order of significance.[9] Politics is Rancière's regulative ideal. It is to be judged on the basis of a steadfast commitment to the equality of everyone and is understood as the proper regulator of social bonds. Critical of all sociological conceits, Rancière indicts political theory, sociology, and the administrative agencies of a hierarchical order, which invent "the social" and then distribute "justice" as a logical outgrowth of naturalized social arrangements.[10] Rancière's social order is contingent on events of subjectification. To take one of his examples: "Before the wrong that its name exposes, the proletariat [which designates any politically excluded other, not merely workers] has no existence as a real part of society."[11]

Here Rancière is caught in a dilemma of intelligibility. Despite the absence of a stable referent called "society," it emerges nevertheless as one of his discursive objects. This is necessarily so not only because ordinary grammar is recalcitrant to the instability that Rancière wants to convey but also because however contingent and contestable social segments may be, any approach to democracy must contend with a complex history of imposed segmentation and boundary making, even if one concedes that much of what is intelligible as "the social" is epiphenomenal to a history of modes of domination. Thus any radical democratic politics must necessarily challenge the reigning order of intelligibility, which is always an ambiguous achievement. On the one hand, it creates the conditions of possibility for communication, but on the other, it achieves a unified grammar of subjectivity and objectness at the expense of the subjunctive; it pushes alternative possibilities to the margin or erases them altogether. Accordingly, before assessing the implications of Rancière's protean and historically malleable social order, I want to summon William Connolly's meditation on the ambiguous achievement of social and symbolic boundaries, for he provides a threshold for critically treating foundational commitments underlying America's democratic social space.

In a chapter on Alexis de Tocqueville's conception of American democracy, Connolly begins with some general observations on boundaries: "Boundaries abound. Between humanity and the gods. Between human and animal. Between culture and nature. Between life and death. Between genders, nations, peoples, times, races, classes, and territories."[12] The historical establishments of boundaries are power-invested, collective acts that affirm and legitimate some practices and interests while discrediting others. It is through such enactments that at an abstract level peoples become coherent collectives, giving their worlds meaning and value and, at a more concrete level, organizing their social and political spaces. But foundational acts, however contingent and conflictual they have been, are lent transcendent necessity in founding documents and by much of "modern political thought" which celebrates the advantages of overcoded boundaries by suppressing the violences accompanying those codes.[13] Contemporary political theorist-apologists follow a venerable tradition of those canonical thinkers in the history of political thought, who have recognized the political ambiguities of boundary making but have been reluctant to acknowledge or, in Connolly's words, "come to terms with them."[14]

Connolly suggests that the question of ambiguous boundaries is more likely to surface now, "in a world experienced by many to be without a natural design," and goes on to explore the consequences of a hospitality to this question for democratic theory. However, it is important to recognize that the "now" has a historical legacy. For this reason, as a supplement to treating the ways that Connolly and Rancière integrate ambiguity and contingency into their democratic imaginaries and conceive democratic social space (and the bodies inhabiting those spaces), I want to introduce some of the conceptual contributions of Gilles Deleuze, who shares and historicizes many aspects of their positions, and to stage an encounter between two Thomases—Jefferson, who embraced a "natural design" and sought to displace contingency with necessity; and Pynchon, who explicitly engages a fictionalized version of Jefferson and restores contingency with a historically informed, novelistic critique of this still institutionalized Jeffersonian impulse, one that has resulted in the Euro-domination of the North American continent. The ambiguity, which Connolly conceives as essential to a pluralistic democratic ethos, can only thrive when disturbances to the regulative ideals embodied in founding episodes are allowed to flourish, and when contingencies are restored by allowing finite history (and stagings of alternative historical possibilities) to displace teleological ontologies and legendary narratives.[15]

DISTURBING UNITIES

Connolly's meditation on boundaries articulates well with significant contributions of both Rancière and Deleuze. In accord with Rancière's insistence that there are no political parties with an existence prior to "the declaration of a wrong," Connolly summons the "Indian" subject to illuminate some of the dire consequences of Tocqueville's version of American pluralism, which necessitated "the elimination of the Indian."[16] And in accord with the treatment by Deleuze and Guattari of the modern state's containment of nomadism (as a deployment of apparatuses of capture),[17] Connolly points to Tocqueville's toleration of a "modest nomadism," coupled with his pessimism about the ability of American democracy to evince "a viable response to forms of nomadism that cannot be eliminated by, nor are they very consonant with, the civi-territorial complex," which Tocqueville saw as essential to democracy's future.[18]

Nomadism (a way of being-in-the-world that cannot be captured within contemporary society's authorized model of social segments) and other modes of inhabiting "the social" have not had conceptual leverage in the dominant empiricist approach to democracy, according to which the idea of "political participation" tends to exhaust ideas about the democratic subject. Social space for empiricist social scientists and traditional theorists of democracy is constructed as a set of majorities and minorities who form around particular issues. Within this liberal individualist model, deployed on a homogeneous social space, every person is present to the political process in the same way. Each is a political participant in a "[d]emocratic social space [that is] a universal and everywhere similar medium in which rights and opportunities are identical, a space in which the right and even the ability to move from place to place is assured."[19]

Addressing the conceptual impoverishment rendered by participation enthusiasts, who homogenize and dehistoricize the social domain, Rancière asserts: "The idea of participation blends two ideas of different origins: the reformist idea of necessary mediations between the center and the periphery, and the evolutionary idea of a permanent involvement of citizen-subjects in every domain."[20] And Connolly is critical of how the standard participatory model, which deploys freely acting agents in a homogeneous space, constitutes an attempt to "resolve ambiguity" and to press individuality and commonality "to harmonize more closely."[21] Ultimately for both Rancière and Connolly, attempts at adding up preferences fail to acknowledge the forms of difference that a democratic order must recognize—"the part of those who have no part"[22] for Rancière, whose logic of subjectification derives from a pluralism of disparity, and "the claims of diversity" for Connolly, who privileges a pluralism that requires negotiations among persons separated by ambiguous boundaries.[23]

But perhaps the most thoroughgoing critique of the majority-versus-minority model of democratic social orders is that of Deleuze and Guattari. They argue that no majority has an unproblematic representational value because there is no homogeneous order from which it can be drawn as a quantitative solution. Rather, such "majorities" are a product of "state power and domination." Deleuze and Guattari offer as an example, "the average adult-white-heterosexual-male-speaking in a standard language" and note that this "man ... holds the majority, even if he is less numerous than mosquitos, children, women, blacks, homosexuals."[24] Such a character can constitute a majority by being a norm, or what Deleuze and Guattari call a "majoritarian 'fact'" that "constitutes a homogeneous system in which the minorities are sub groups."[25] A conventional political response, in which one posits a multicultural solution that extends rights to minorities, does not address Deleuze's and Guattari's critique of the majoritarian image of democracy. The issue for them is not that "minorities" are excluded. Their point is that no majority can represent because there is no definitive unity from which minorities can be drawn. All such unities, they point out, are imposed as norms.

Rancière is similarly suspicious of the "unities" deployed by apparatuses of power, of those "social groups" or "political subjects" who are put into play within the official political discourse. Their recognition as legitimate participants is part of policing, a fixing of the terrain of individuals relative to public power,[26] rather than politics. "Politics," as Rancière conceives it, is carried on by "subjects that are not social groups."[27] And Connolly shares Rancière's resistance to a rigid model of social identity and to the familiar forms of identity politics with which it is associated. Similarly suspicious of officially imposed "unities," Connolly prescribes a moderation of the urge for "attunement" between identities and the order. Rather than adhering to the typical pluralism, which favors the inclusion of various underrepresented social groups, his model of diversity endorses "a social ontology of discord,"[28] which "would require that we acknowledge and seek to articulate the elements of discordance in the unities we establish."[29]

For all three theorists, therefore, social space is an unstable arena of discord. Rather than see society as a stable set of arrangements, Connolly, Deleuze, and Rancière constitute the social arena as a domain of evolving force and counterforce. For Connolly, the significant opposing forces are ideational. One is fundamentalism, an impulse that he has addressed often and has characterized most recently as the neoconservative platform in a culture war, "the futile drive to reinstate the old picture through force and repression,"[30] a firming up and policing of identity boundaries and the abjection of identity types that do not fit the "old picture." The counterforce, which would enable what Connolly calls "a multidimensional pluralism of democratic life,"[31] consists of all those impulses toward negotiating a commonality with difference while appreciating "the constitutive ambiguity of identity."[32]

While Connolly's social arena is in his terms "agonistic," in Rancière's it is "polemical." Critical of historians of ideas who distinguish what is thought from what is unthought, Rancière argues that the more basic issue is "the very right to think."[33] The contention within Rancière's polemical social space is a struggle between the forces of policing: the familiar social policies within which some bodies receive recognition as bona fide political subjects and others do not, versus the forces of politics— events of subjectification in which excluded parts of the social order demand to be heard. Articulated with a spatial idiom, these episodes disturb the institutionalized "distribution of bodies into functions" and also challenge the epistemic basis for the prior exclusion, the naturalization of the differences among bodies and of the appropriate "places" where those bodies belong; they disturb, in Rancière's terms (already quoted), "the order of distribution of bodies into functions corresponding to their 'nature' and places corresponding to their functions."[34]

As part of his conception of the episodic partitioning of social space, Rancière sees the political as arising from a continuous mobility within the social configuration. Because democracy rests not on specific leadership qualities but rather on "an absence of qualifications that, in turn, becomes the qualification for the exercise of a democratic *arche*,"[35] democratic challenges to the policing order arise from a non-place. While what is proffered by Rancière appears to be a structural phenomenon, a "democratic void" that is "a given constitutive of politics," it is also implicitly a temporal phenomenon. The moments of democratic enactment come from a supplement that arises as disconnected from that part of the population which, at any time, is regarded as politically qualified.

Because Rancière's rendering of the temporal aspect of the political is structurally embedded, his history of the political is necessarily predicated on a structural logic rather than a finite genealogy of power and resistance. The social base from which politics arises is constituted as a mobile set of "vanishing difference[s]."[36] On the one hand, this approach supplies a radical alternative to the classic contractual narratives of the political, which emphasize a mythic consensus, a politics "deduced from the necessity of gathering people into communities."[37] And it avoids identifying the political with the groupings produced by a state-centered discourse, the "well defined interest groups."[38] Against a politics of already politically enfranchised identities, Rancière insists that "there is politics as long as 'the people' is not identified with the race or a population … [as long as] the poor are not equated with a particular disadvantaged sector, and as long as the proletariat is not a group of industrial workers, etc." On the other hand, although Rancière provides an exemplary episode of contention in his work on the organs articulating workers' complaints in nineteenth-century France, his structural frame leaves a conceptual void, the absence of a treatment of how "dis-agreement" emerges in different historical periods.[39]

Although Deleuze also tends toward exemplification to treat historical

forces, he does treat specifically the historical shift from the epoch dynas-
ties and despotic orders to the state, and thus provides a more temporally
sensitive model, a rough history of modernity. The pre-state despotic
order is a centrally focused machine of capture, with the social body (the
"socius") symbolically captured by "the body of the despot," a "detached
object" that preempts all social coding.[40] The state is also a machine of
capture. But in contrast with despotic orders, this capture consists in a
dense coding, the production of rigid segmentation that displaces or
overcodes former modes of attachment and affiliation.

In response to state-imposed segmentation (citizens, ethnic majorities
and minorities, gender and age categories, etc.)—the creation of what
Deleuze and Guattari refer to as molarities—there are flows and movements of resistance within the social field, the pursuit of lines of flight
from state-imposed modes of segmentation and coding. As they put it,
a "social field is always animated by all kinds of movements of decoding and deterritorialization affecting 'masses' and operating at different
speeds and paces."[41] The Deleuzian modern society is therefore conflictual in that a series of micro political initiatives is always in tension with
the molar politics of the state: "From the viewpoint of micropolitics, a
society is defined by its lines of flight, which are molecular. There is always
something that flows or flees, that escapes the binary organizations, the
resonance apparatus and the overcoding machine."[42] The micro political
forces are reflected by, among other things, alternative modes of collective
assembly (effectively "subjects that are not social groups," in Rancière's
above-noted terms). For example, when confronted with the molar politics of a state's security oriented segmentation, "there is always a Palestin-
ian or Basque or Corsican to bring about a 'regional destabilization of
security.'"[43]

TOWARD A DEMOCRATIC ETHOS:
RESTORING THE SUBJUNCTIVE

Connolly, Deleuze, and Rancière all see the restoration of contingency as a
prerequisite for the institution of democratic social space. For Rancière it
involves the encounter between policing and politics, in which nongram-
matical excluded parts voice claims and thereby "undermine" the authorized "distribution of bodies into functions corresponding to their

'nature' and places corresponding to their functions."[44] Contingency for Deleuze arises in connection with his advocacy of multiplicity, by which he means not a simple politics of recognition, not the familiar promotion of "diversity," but rather the creation space for *potential* difference, for the possibilities of becoming outside the forms of segmentation that are authoritative within the state-dominated socius. Democratic social space for Deleuze therefore requires a retreat from contemporary society's "hypersegmentation,"[45] and a move toward what he calls a "flexible segmentarity," a retreat from state-imposed rigid segmentarity.

Connolly's more recent contingency-affirming formulation is his conception of a "deep plurality": "Incorporating deep plurality into existing political pluralism is consonant with democracy if and when an ethos of engagement is negotiated between numerous constituencies honoring different assumptions and moral sources."[46] Accordingly, among the threats to "democracy," as Connolly conceives it, is "the refusal to acknowledge the contingency of one's position and the violent assertion of one's right to protect this refusal." But I want to return here to an earlier formulation of contingency that Connolly achieves by staging a counterfactual historical conversation, after being inspired by one that Henry David Thoreau reports in "The Allegash and East Branch."

Resisting a homogeneous model of nineteenth-century social space, Connolly notes that the reported conversation on a canoeing trip between Thoreau and his Indian guide, Joe Polis, is one taking place "on the edges of 'American' cultural space."[47] He then supposes that "the contingencies of chance and timing had spawned an encounter between Thoreau and a Mashpee" and goes on to stage a conversation on another part of that edge, one between Thoreau and a contemporary, the Mashpee Pequot political philosopher William Apess, whose polemical writings reveal not only the particularities of the historically produced "Indian" locus of enunciation (in a Euro-American-dominated political order) but also the contradictions and hypocrisies inhabiting Euro-America's democratic conceits.[48]

Connolly's staging of this counterfactual encounter articulates well with Thomas Pynchon's privileging of the subjunctive over necessity in his novel *Mason & Dixon*,[49] for in Connolly's words, "The very identification of this unpursued space of historical *possibility* begins to crack the Tocquevillean/American code of moral/civilizational/territorial necessity . . . The hypothetical Apess/Thoreau conjunction drains the presumption of necessity from the historical options between assimilation of the Indian and exclusion of the Indian from civilized land."[50] In addition, by staging this conversation Connolly creates an instance of subjectification, adding a voice and thus widening the scene of "American political thought" as it developed during the nineteenth century. Like Rancière, Connolly summons the genre of the conversation to intervene in the reigning structure of intelligible politics and reconstitute the distribution of eligible political bodies. But such instances of political initiative arise in diverse genres. For example, both Connolly and Rancière have recourse to film (a genre that Deleuze has famously explored), which for Connolly evokes layers of subjective presence that evade ordinary consciousness, and for Rancière tends to provide critical reflection on the relations of the sensible and the sayable.[51] And both pay attention to writing genres: Connolly to a historical trajectory of political thinking and Rancière to journals that workers published in France beginning in 1839.[52] Here my focus is on the interarticulation between modes of writing and social space, which provides me with a frame to extend the radical implications of what Connolly, Deleuze, and Rancière have done to radicalize democratic thought for the contemporary "American" scene.

EXTRACTING POLITICAL PRESENCE
FROM A FRACTAL SOCIAL ORDER

In a brief but politically pregnant meditation on writing and time, the Mexican novelist Carlos Fuentes asserts that writing can "alter the spaces of presence."[53] Although he does not provide an elaborate diagram of social space, Fuentes discerns an element of politically significant difference in Mexico's social space—in a village in which the historical time of the Zapatista insurrection shapes the spatio-temporal perspective of its inhabitants. In a chance conversational encounter with a *compesino* in the Morellos district, he learns of social spaces that resist the modes of citizen presence constructed by the "linear time of the calendars of the West."[54] Certainly the critical writing performances toward which Fuentes gestures arise from a far more complicated, historically engendered set of social spaces than he was able to treat in a brief meditation. To deepen the relationship between writing and space suggested by Fuentes, I want to

summon Pierre Bourdieu (for both appreciation and criticism) because
he has concerned himself with this connection more extensively, particularly with respect to how writing has resisted the dominance of state-
oriented modes of intelligibility, or what he calls "the thought of the
state."[55]

Briefly, in his opposition to the dominance of the thought of the state,
Bourdieu creates a synthesis between speech act theory and his Heidegger-
influenced construction of social and literary fields. Because he regards
speech acts as constrained by the socially governed system of intelligibility, to speak, according to Bourdieu, is to appropriate a socially recognized style or idiom.[56] Thus Bourdieu's social field, within which the
speaking or writing subject comes to "be" (takes on a social identity),
determines the performative force of the subject's utterances. Bourdieu's
analysis of the productive effect of writing performances is elaborated in
his treatment of the writing of Gustave Flaubert. In accord with his emphasis on the way a social field determines the conditions of possibility
for a subject's actions, Bourdieu locates Flaubert's writing within the
nineteenth-century socio-literary field, a field of " relationship[s] between
the producers of culture and the dominant social groups."[57] The Flauber-
tian "creative project" must be understood as a product of what Bourdieu
terms "the genesis and structure of the social space" in which creativity is
possible.[58] Given the limitations with respect to "viable careers," and Flaubert's experience of limits for distinction within both his family and the
bourgeois social order, Flaubert's writing must reflect feelings evinced by
sociohistorical constraints; Flaubert "felt obliged to manifest a certain
distance from dominant values."[59]

While Bourdieu's analysis of the spatio-temporality of the field within
which a writer either recycles or challenges the dominant orders of intelligibility may provide a path to the resistance of state-dominated political
thinking, it fails to comprehend the diversity of thought worlds that
compose the "social field." To heed the fractionated diversity—the vestiges of the subjunctive America—that Pynchon's novel seeks to redeem,
we need to replace Bourdieu's model of the social field, which he renders
as a hierarchical system of social "fractions,"[60] with a model of a fractal
social order, a historically effected collage of diverse life worlds that have
been coercively assembled by a history of state-directed "nation building"
and its attendant forms of political economy. Among the relevant aspects

of fractal systems for treating social organization are their micro structures and indeterminacy. A fractal order consists of many micro-orders
within it, which yields a configuration that has no single focal point and is
subject to an indeterminate number of modes of measurement.[61] Analo-
gously, to treat the social order as a protean clustering of micro orders
is to recognize alternative ways in which social space, for historical reasons, is constituted as many different, interrelated spaces, whose contours speak to complex differences in historical assembly. As a result,
within such a fractal structure there emerge speaking and writing performances whose challenges stem from systems of exclusion with considerable historical depth.

More specifically, much of the politics of contemporary writing reflects
the counter memories of those groups that have been victimized by a
history of political economy associated with the formation of the Euro-
oriented model of political order, which was largely responsible for depos-
iting the diverse bodies that inhabit the system of disparate but interconnected social fields within the modern nation-state. For example, in
the United States many African American, Native American, and third
world, migrant writers do not, à la Bourdieu, select from extant idioms
within a hierarchy of available styles that have persisted within state-
dominated social orders. Rather, their writing expresses profound ambivalence toward the dominant literary field within which their work is
deployed, precisely because of the tendency of that field to be complicit
with the state's presumption (its primary mode of "thought") that it
governs a unitary and coherent national culture, a state-managed unitary
social order.

Although there are numerous examples, here I focus on three writers
with diverse and fraught relationships with the dominant American social and political American imaginaries because of their explicit ambivalence about participating in America's main, commercially controlled literary culture—Michelle Cliff, a diasporic Jamaican, Sherman Alexie, a
Native American, and Toni Morrison, an African American, all of whose
writing performances enact modes of thought that challenge the conventional nation-building narrative and the liberal democratic model of the
citizen-subject (within which every individual is an undifferentiated citizen subject, and the social order is merely an ahistorical class structure).

MICHELLE CLIFF

Cliff's observations on languages, expressed by one of her fictional characters, characterizes the agenda for writers who recognize the ideational traps lurking in the familiar systems of intelligibility created by a historical trajectory of Euro-American political thought. In her novel *Free Enterprise*, the narrator reflects on the historical role of each language's participation in the imperial domination of her homeland. "English," she says, "was the tongue of commerce . . . Spanish was the language of categories" (by which she means the creation of a biopolitical matrix of economically and politically ineligible, miscegenated blood types), and Latin was the language of Christian spiritual hegemony. "Against these tongues," she adds, "African of every stripe collided."[62]

Cliff stands with her feet in two worlds and thus writes not only in English toward which she feels ambivalent but also from disjunctive loci of enunciation. Identifying with the diasporic part of social order, which cannot be comfortably assimilated as unitary national subjects, much of her writing focuses on transnational lives. For example, in her novel *No Telephone to Heaven*, a diasporic perspective is enacted both geopolitically and linguistically—geopolitically by the back-and-forth movement of her main character, Kitty Savage, between the United States and Jamaica (as well as back and forth from England) and linguistically in the collision of idioms, standard English and Jamaican patois, and anti-narrative structure, a set of dissociated narrative fragments.

Cliff's novelistic contribution to diversifying America's thought world reflects a significant historical change in the role of that genre, which in the nineteenth century and early twentieth displaced other narrative forms in the third world. Although the novel initially was primarily a nation-building genre, subsequently Cliff, like many other third world writers, diasporic and otherwise, has made the novel a site of resistance to the global, national, and social imaginaries of the "first world."[63] Yet Cliff evinces a profound ambivalence toward writing in general because she recognizes the difficulty of extracting a thought from the outside within languages that encode a dominant Anglo-American thought world.[64] As she has noted, her primary linguistic imaginary is silence, a form of resistant aphasia, which she sees as the ultimate discursive location for one who would wholly resist the colonizing forces within language.[65]

Cliff's political inflection of silence is manifested in *No Telephone to Heaven* when her character, Kitty Savage, is described as breaking her silence after she discovers a shop with Jamaican foods in New York.[66] Ultimately, although Cliff's "attempt to bound off a space of silence via the symptom of aphasia"[67] is never consummated—Cliff continues to write—it reflects her suspicion that however hybrid and resistant the cacophony and assemblage of narrative fragments in her novels are to the dominant idioms and historical memories of the Euro-dominant state, she can never be wholly present to herself as a resisting body in her writing. Nevertheless, her struggle with the ambiguous achievement of an intelligibility that bridges thought worlds is exemplary. It plays a role in articulating a subjunctive America that the familiar Euro-American narratives (e.g. the melting pot story) overcode.

SHERMAN ALEXIE

Like Michelle Cliff, Alexie embodies the split consciousness of one with his feet in different life worlds. And he shares Cliff's expressed ambivalence toward writing. In his short story "Indian Country," Alexie treats the geographic and ethnographic ambiguity of his Indian-ness through his character Low Man Smith, a writer and doubtless his alter ego. Low Man describes himself in one of the story's conversations as one who is "not supposed to be anywhere."[68] His Indian-ness, along with that of other Native American characters, is highly diluted; a "Spokane," he speaks and understands no tribal languages, was born and raised in Seattle, and has visited his own reservation only six times.

The "Indian country" for which Alexie's story provides a fragmentary mapping has resonances with Black Elk's sentiments about how the Euro-American conquest has created an Indian country consisting of "little islands [that are] always . . . becoming smaller." But Alexie adds another, more ambiguous "Indian country," to the Indian landscape that he maps (which, if represented pictorially, would be a few color flecks on a map of the western United States); he treats the discursively muffled Indian country. Alexie's dialogic version of the precarious and obscure visibility of the country is reinforced throughout the story's conversations, which convey a dilemma of intelligibility for Native Americans existing in two alternative thought worlds, articulated in different idioms. For example, at one point Low Man asks an older Indian, Raymond, if he is an elder. Shifting to a non-Indian idiom, Raymond replies, "elder than some, not as elder as others."[69]

Reflecting Alexie's awareness of how Native American sense making is always already colonized by a Euro-American idiom, Low Man Smith manifests a profound ambivalence toward being immersed in the Euro-dominated literary field of the United States. He refers to the chain bookstores that carry his books as "colonial clipper ships,"[70] and in the process of moving about an urban venue in search of an independent bookstore he tries to divest himself of his laptop, first evoking a traditional Native American practice and trying to trade it in at a 7 Eleven convenience store and then handing it to a clerk at Barnes & Noble, pretending that he found it.

The discursive ambiguities and writer's ambivalence toward writing in Alexie's short story reflect the condition of his characters throughout his writing—novels, poetry, and screenplays—in which his Indians struggle within what M. M. Bakhtin refers to as "the framework of other people's words."[71] In several places Alexie evokes a reversal of the captivity narrative, locating the Indian instead of the white woman as victim (in his case of a Euro-American discursive hegemony). When he worked in Hollywood as a screenwriter (a writing vocation subject to studio revisions) he became blocked, he says, because he "started to hear 'their' voices, those Hollywood voices whenever [he] tried to write anything."[72] And in one of his poems, addressed to Mary Rowlandson's captivity story, he articulates his struggle against captivity by the "language of the enemy: *heavy lightness*, house insurance, *serious vanity*, safe-deposit box."[73]

Alexie's response to the perils of linguistic capture is not to retreat to a version of Indian discursive authenticity. As he puts it, he resists the "corn pollen and eagle feather school of poetry."[74] Recognizing that he writes from a colonized locus of enunciation, he articulates the dilemma of the contemporary Indian writer who stands partly within the dominant system of intelligibility (for example, he acknowledges such disparate influences as Stephen King's novels and the television show *The Brady Bunch*) but seeks at the same time to disrupt the power relations inherent in conventional sense making. John Newton describes the dilemma of Alexie (and Native American writers) well: "As the subjugated 'other' of an invader discourse synonymous with global media saturation, the Native

American subject finds himself spectacularized on a global scale . . . Alexie makes his stand in the struggle for subjective agency not in some autochthonous interiority but on the flat, open ground of the invader's own image-repertoire."[75]

To figure his dilemma Alexie invokes the concept of the treaty. Seeing the history of the United States vis-à-vis its European and Native American inhabitants as a series of broken treaties, his love poems are often allegorical; they feature Indian-white romances that must manage the historical and ethnic rift with "tiny treaties."[76] And doubtless the allegory works at another level, referring to the treaty that his participation in a white-dominated literary culture represents. In accepting the necessity of using a language that will not allow an expression of an Indian-ness free of Euro-American hegemony, Alexie's writing nevertheless restores another dimension of subjunctive America, however buried it might be within a hybridized and overcoded landscape.

TONI MORRISON

Morrison expresses the same ambivalence toward her participation in American literary culture as Cliff and Alexie do. She functions within what she calls "a singular landscape for a writer," inasmuch as she writes "in a nation of people who *decided* that their world view would combine agendas for individual freedom *and* mechanisms for devastating oppression."[77] Given that the extant American literary culture articulates the legacy of this duplicitous founding, there is a paradox inherent in her participation as a novelist in the culture of literacy. Although she "participates in the public sphere constituted by print literacy, . . . her fiction strains to constitute itself as anti-literature and to address a type of racial community that she herself recognizes to be unavailable to the novelist."[78] Morrison's audience, or constituency, takes on its coherence as a protean transnational black culture, forged as much through structures of exclusion and episodes of displacement as through practices of solidarity. And much of the cultural imaginary, which forms the implied readership of her novels, is "preliterate."[79] Yet like Cliff and Alexie, Morrison continues to write. And most significantly, her novel *Paradise*, which addresses itself to a historical episode of racial exclusion, effectively enacts the critical posture that Bourdieu has identified as the antidote to "state thinking," the necessity of creating a "rupture" that challenges the state's *"symbolic* violence," its mobilization of and control over the mental structures that make its institutions appear *"natural."*[80] For Morrison the tools for rupture are literary. They include, as a commentary on her novel *Beloved* puts it, "the creation of a narrative text that radically opens the literary canon to counter-discursive strategies of re-memory, as well as grounding of the cultural politics of difference in the language of the contingent and the provisional."[81]

Morrison's enactment of a rupture is especially evident in *Paradise*, because it involves, in Bourdieu's language, "the reconstruction of genesis," which brings "back into view the conflicts and confrontations of the early beginnings and therefore all the discarded possibilities."[82] *Paradise* recovers vestiges of a subjunctive America that are obliterated in the dominant version of Euro-America's national memory. Specifically, the "genesis" to which Morrison's novel is addressed is the ideology and story of American exceptionalism that was central to the Euro-American nationhood project. Initially the religious, patriarchal leaders of the early New England settlers strove to inculcate the presumption that American was to be a new Jerusalem, "a site specifically favored by God—perhaps the very place that he had chosen to initiate the millennial Kingdom of Christ."[83] Subsequently, since the early nineteenth century, a secularized version of American exceptionalism has held sway among many American historians: "the assumption that the United States, unlike European nations, has a covenant that makes Americans a chosen people who have escaped from the terror of historical change to live in timeless harmony with nature."[84]

The idea of the covenant and the imperatives that flow from it—the need to resist change and the need to maintain the purity of the lineage that is charged with the special mission—produce the woeful consequences described at the beginning and end of Morrison's novel. The novel suggests that at best the exceptionalist narrative stifles politics and at worst it leads to violence, as in the chilling first line of the novel: "They kill the white girl first." An understanding of this opening event requires the reader to follow a complex and shifting narrative that eventually explains a deadly attack on a women's shelter by a group of men from a small, covenanted, all-black community in western Oklahoma.

The community is Ruby, where the older members situate themselves in a self-described historical narrative that celebrates the perseverance of their ancestors in the face of rejection and their subsequent redemption through adherence to the codes of a special mission. Descended from former slaves, the town's ancestors left areas of the American South where they had endured discrimination in the years after Reconstruction only to be denied entry into both white and black communities in Oklahoma, which as Morrison learned, had twenty-six all-black towns at the beginning of the twentieth century.[85] The Rubyites' special mission, an African American version of American exceptionalism, is engendered by their rejections, to which they refer in their narrative as the "disallowing." Having walked from Mississippi to Oklahoma, attracted by an advertisement about an all-black town, they discovered that their blackness was a threat to the lighter-skinned "Negroes" who shunned them: "The sign of racial purity they had taken for granted had become a stain."[86]

Coping with the shock of a rejection (which they had expected only from whites), they founded their own all-black community of Haven in Oklahoma and subsequently moved even farther into western Oklahoma to found Ruby, which they regarded as the fulfillment of their ancestors' intention to construct an Eden, a paradise on earth run by a group of racially pure blacks. The town chronicler, Patricia, summarizes the model of the "8-rock's" (descendants from the original founders) for maintaining purity: "Unadulterated and unadultered 8-rock blood held its magic as long as it resided in Ruby. That was their recipe. That was their deal. For immortality."[87] But while "Ruby" ("who can find a virtuous woman? For her price is far above Rubies," Proverbs 41:10) contains paradisiacal signs—for example, the soil seems almost miraculously fertile, so that while Haven had only barren, muddy ground, Ruby has flourishing gardens—it also turns out to be a stiflingly conservative, patriarchal, and even misogynist community. And rather than turn inward to confront divisive issues, when the younger Ruby generation departs from the original covenant the patriarchs of Ruby displace their problems on a nearby community functioning with a different covenant. The women's shelter that is the target of the assault with which the novel begins is in a former convent outside the town (in a mansion that had once served as a "cathouse"), and its residents have had connections with some of the town's men.

Morrison's novel enacts Bourdieu's suggestion about the necessity for creating a rupture by returning to the founding myths that sustain violence, actual or symbolic. While identifying a racially fractured America, she contests at once the Puritan reading of American exceptionalism and the African American attempt to simulate that exceptionalism and treat it as a dogma by preserving or freezing the meanings generated in founding acts. A resistance to the freezing of meanings also characterizes Morrison's approach to her writing. She seeks to avoid "oppressive language . . . [w]hether it is the obscuring state language or the faux-language of mindless media . . . [or] the calcified language of the academy or the commodity driven language of science . . . or language designed for the estrangement of minorities, hiding its racist plunder in its literary cheek."[88] By inventing fresh voices and subjecting them to telling encounters, she enacts, like Connolly (in his staging of a conversation between Thoreau and Apess) a subjectification.

CONCLUSION: RESTORING THE SUBJUNCTIVE

As I noted above, Bourdieu's analysis of Flaubert's writing provides exemplary insight into his radical epistemology. He locates the significance of Flaubert's texts in "the genesis and structure of the social space" within which Flaubert's creativity was possible. However, Bourdieu's "social space" in this case is an assemblage of culture producers and dominant social groups. By preserving the critical insights in Bourdieu's notion of the genesis and structure of social spaces but rethinking the social field as a fractal space—a series of interconnected micro spaces that has been filled over time by bodies set adrift by the forces of imperial political economy—I focus on the counter-memories of writers who do not fit comfortably within state-controlled social orders. A history of political economy haunts the writings of Michelle Cliff, Sherman Alexie, and Toni Morrison. Taken together, their texts reflect, as I noted, an "amalgam of diverse life worlds that have been assembled by a history of state directed, and largely coercive 'nation building' and its attendant forms of political economy." Although they all write in English—"the tongue of commerce," as one of Cliff's characters puts it—rather than merely affirming the world that "English" (in all of its power-related manifestations) has made, they use language in a way that accords with both the critical impetus of Bourdieu's sociological work and Thomas Pynchon's novelistic restoration of contingency, his displacement of the declarative with the subjunctive. Their articulated ambivalence toward the language within which they write encourages an acknowledgment of the contention that the dominant thought world, recycled in conventional approaches to American political theory, tends to obscure.

However, there is a remaining issue: the issue of how the concept of a fractal socio-literary order can migrate into an effective notion of the political, one that affords a loosening of the hold of necessity. Even as we recognize that fractal structures—for example those realized in African architecture—have no definitive center, no "central focus," [89] an avenue of transition from the fractal and social to the political is provided in the critique by Gilles Deleuze and Felix Guattari noted above of the majoritarian emphasis in democratic theory; this critique, and the accompanying turn to "minority literature," provide lines of flight from the symbolic tyranny of a majoritarian thinking that seeks to stabilize majorities and minorities. Cliff, Alexie, and Morrison—all products of historical encounters and acts of coercion—are in effect minoritarian writers. Like Franz Kafka, Deleuze's and Guattari's exemplar of one who *becomes* minoritarian through writing, and like Connolly, in his imagined conversation between Thoreau and Apess, Cliff, Elxie, and Morrison all stage new encounters in their writing to affect both the past and present (and like Rancière, they are engaged in acts of subjectification).[90] Writing in the major language but seeking to escape its historical trajectory of domination, they write to "deterritorialize" the extant grid of biopolitical and geopolitical essences. They refigure the past, creating counter-memories that challenge the narrative of an emerging, homogenous society (a definitive declarative) and at the same time, create the imaginative conditions of possibility for a restoration of the subjunctive, a contingency-embracing order where new relations, based on de-identification with old imposed essences, can flourish. Here we should heed Rancière's version of the relationship between politics and contingency, which emerges from the equivalence that he asserts between democracy and politics: as he insists, politics takes place when a distribution of bodies (as inscribed within authoritative discourses) is thrown back on its contingency.

NOTES

1 Jacques Rancière, *Disagreement*, trans. Julie Rose (Minneapolis: University of Minnesota Press, 1998), 101.

2 Ibid., 75.

3 Ibid., 77.

4 Ibid., 79.

5 For an application of Rancière's insights under this rubric see Benjamin Arditi and Jeremy Valentine, *Polemicization* (Edinburgh: Edinburgh University Press, 1999).

6 Rancière, *Disagreement*, 15.

7 Ibid., 39.

8 Jacques Rancière, *On the Shores of Politics*, trans. Liz Heron (New York: Verso, 1995), 39.

9 Foucault's brief geneaology of the political is in his essay "Governmentality" in *The Foucault Effect*, ed. Graham Burchell, Colin Gordon, and Peter Miller (London: Harvester Wheatsheaf, 1991), 87–104.

10 See Rancière, *Disagreement*, 91–93.

11 Ibid., 39.

12 William E. Connolly, *The Ethos of Pluralization* (Minneapolis: University of Minnesota Press, 1995), 163.

13 Ibid., 167.

14 Ibid., 163. Connolly specifically mentions Rousseau as one who "recognizes the ambiguity involved in the founding of a people" (165).

15 In a critique of attempts by authorities to expunge ambiguity, Connolly refers to "a teleological ontology [which] seems to presuppose a transcendental designer"; *Politics and Ambiguity* (Madison: University of Wisconsin Press, 1987), 129. "Finite history," as Jean-Luc Nancy characterizes it, is history in the sense of events in which people share a time period that has no natural boundaries and relationships that are not governed by definitive warrants such as "reason" or "nature"; see his *The Birth to Presence*, trans. B. Holmes et al. (Stanford: Stanford University Press, 1993), 143–66.

16 Nancy, *The Birth to Presence*, 170. Rancière's characteristic examples focus on the historical wrongs visited on proletarians: "Before the wrong that its name exposes, the proletariat has no existence as a real part of society." *Disagreement*, 39.

17 See Deleuze and Guattari, *A Thousand Plateaus*, 424–73.

18 Connolly, *The Ethos of Pluralization*, 172.

19 The quotations are from Fisher, "Democratic Social Space," 64.

20 Rancière, *On the Shores of Politics*, 60.

21 Connolly, *Politics and Ambiguity*, 5–6.

22 Rancière, *Disagreement*, 11.

23 William E. Connolly, *Identity\Difference: Democratic Negotiations of Political Paradox*, enlarged edn (Minneapolis: University of Minnesota Press, 2002), 81.

24 Deleuze and Guattari, *A Thousand Plateaus*, 105. My treatment of the position benefits from Paola Marratti's treatment of Deleuze's and Guattari's politics. See his "Against the Doxa: Politics of Immanence and Becoming Minoritarian," *Micropolitics of Media Culture: Reading the Rhizomes of Deleuze and*

Guattari, ed. Patrica Pister (Amsterdam: Amsterdam University Press, 2001), 205–20.

25 Quotation from Marratti, "Against the Doxa," 207.

26 Rancière, *Disagreement*, 31.

27 Jacques Rancière, "Post-Democracy, Politics and Philosophy: An Interview with Jacques Rancière," *Angelaki* 1, no. 3 (1995), 178.

28 Connolly, *Politics and Ambiguity*, 160.

29 Ibid., 157.

30 William E. Connolly, *Neuropolitics: Thinking, Culture, Speed* (Minneapolis: University of Minnesota Press, 2002), 160.

31 Ibid., 165.

32 Connolly, *Why I Am Not a Secularist* (Minneapolis: University of Minnesota Press), 155.

33 Jacques Rancière, "Literature, Politics, Aesthetics: An Interview by Solange Guenoun and James H. Kavanagh," *SubStance* 29, no. 2 (2000), 13.

34 Rancière, *Disagreement*, 101.

35 Jacques Rancière, "Ten Theses on Politics," *Theory and Event* 5, no. 3 (2001), 5.

36 Ibid., 8.

37 Ibid.

38 Ibid.

39 For Rancière's analysis of nineteenth-century worker movements see his *The Nights of Labor: The Workers' Dream in Nineteenth-Century France*, trans. John Drury (Philadelphia: Temple University Press, 1989).

40 See Gilles Deleuze and Felix Guattari, *Anti-Oedipus: Capitalism and Schizophrenia* trans. Robert Hurley, Mark Seem, and Helen R. Lane (New York: Viking, 1977), 194.

41 Deleuze and Guattari, *A Thousand Plateaus*, 220.

42 Ibid., 216.

43 Ibid., 215.

44 Rancière, *Disagreement*, 101.

45 Gilles Deleuze, "Postscript," 33.

46 Connolly, *Why I Am Not a Secularist*, 158.

47 Connolly, *The Ethos of Pluralization*, 175.

48 Ibid., 177.

49 Thomas Pynchon, *Mason & Dixon* (New York: Henry Holt, 1997), 345, notes that Mason's and Dixon's surveying process was involved in "changing all from subjunctive to declarative, reducing Possibilities to Simplicities that serve the ends of Governments."

50 Ibid., 177–78.

51 For Connolly on film see various sections in his *Neuropolitics*. For Rancière on film see Solange Guenoun, "An Interview with Jacques Rancière: Cinematographic Image, Democracy, and the Splendor of the . . . ," *Sites* 4, no. 2 (fall 2000), 1–7.

52 See Jacques Rancière, *The Nights of Labor*.

53 Carlos Fuentes, "Writing in Time," *Democracy* 2, no. 1 (winter 1962), 63.

54 Ibid., 61.

55 See Pierre Bourdieu, "Rethinking the State: Genesis and Structure of the Bureaucratic Field," *Practical Reason: On the Theory of Action* (Stanford: Stanford University Press, 1998), 35.

56 See Pierre Bourdieu, *Language and Symbolic Power*, trans. Gina Raymond and Matthew Adamson (Cambridge: Harvard University Press, 1991), 54.

57 Pierre Bourdieu, "Flaubert's Point of View," trans. Priscilla Parkhurst Ferguson, *Literature and Social Practice*, ed. Phillipe Desan, Priscilla Parkhurst Ferguson, and Wendy Griswold (Chicago: University of Chicago Press, 1989), 215.

58 Ibid., 213.

59 Ibid., 219.

60 See for example Pierre Bourdieu, *Distinction: A Social Critique of the Judgement of Taste*, trans. Richard Nice (Cambridge: Harvard University Press, 1984).

61 On the issue of focality in fractals see Steven Mason's remarks on the fractal aesthetics of the cubist movement, with special attention to Pablo Picasso's *Les Demoiselles d'Avignon*, on the web at http://www.whatrain.com/fractal logic/page44.htm.

62 Michelle Cliff, *Free Enterprise* (New York: Dutton, 1993), 7.

63 As Mary N. Layoun puts it, the novel "quickly predominated as a privileged narrative form" in the third world, but it soon became reconfigured as a site of resistance rather than a vehicle for imposing European civilizational and cultural conceits." *Travels of a Genre: The Modern Novel and Ideology* (Princeton: Princeton University Press, 1990), xii.

64 For a treatment of the contribution that "thought from the outside" lends to critical thinking, see Michel Foucault, "The Thought from the Outside," *Foucault/Blanchot*, trans. Jeffrey Mehlman and Brian Massumi (New York: Zone, 1987).

65 See Michelle Cliff, "Notes on Speechlessness," *Sinister Wisdom*, 1978, and "A Journey into Speech," *Graywolf Annual: Multicultural Literacy*, ed. Ricki Simonson and Scott Walker (St. Paul: Graywolf, 1988), 57.

66 Michelle Cliff, *No Telephone to Heaven* (New York: Dutton, 1987).

67 Quotation from: Marian Aguiar, "Decolonizing the Tongue: Reading Speech and Aphasia in the Work of Michelle Cliff," *Literature and Psychology* 47½ (2001), 108.

68 Sherman Alexie, "Indian Country," *New Yorker*, 13 March 2000, 82.

69 Ibid., 77.

70 Ibid., 78.

71 M. M. Bakhtin, *Problems of Dostoevsky's Poetics*, trans. Caryl Emerson (Minneapolis: University of Minnesota Press, 1984), 59. The application of this Bakhtinian phrase to Alexie can also be found in Jerome Denounce, "Slow Dancing with Skeletons: Sherman Alexie's *The Lone Ranger and Tonto Fistfight in Heaven*," *Critique* 44, no. 1 (fall 2002), 86.

72 Sherman Alexie, "Death in Hollywood," *Literary Cavalcade* 53, no. 8 (May 2001), 2.

73 Sherman Alexie, *First Indian on the Moon*, 98.

74 Sherman Alexie, "Sherman Alexie, Literary Rebel," *Bloomsbury Review* 14 (1994), 15 [interview by John and Carl Belante].

75 John Newton, "Sherman Alexie's Autoethnography," *Contemporary Literature* 42, no. 2 (2001), 415.

76 See Alexie's poems "Tiny Treaties" and "Seven Love Songs Which Include the Collected History of the United States of America," in *First Indian on the Moon* (New York: Hanging Loose, 1993), 56–57, 62–65.

77 Toni Morrison, *Playing in the Dark* (Cambridge: Harvard University Press, 1990), xiii.

78 Quotation from Madhu Dubey, "The Politics of Genre in *Beloved*," *Novel: A Forum on Fiction* 32, no. 2 (1999), 188.

79 Ibid.

80 Toni Morrison, *Paradise* (New York: Plume, 1999).

81 Abdellatif Khayati, "Representation, Race and the 'Language' of The Ineffable in Toni Morrison's Narrative," *African American Review* 33, no. 2 (summer 1999), 315.

82 Bourdieu, "Rethinking the State," 40.

83 Michael Kammen, *In the Past Lane: Historical Perspectives on American Culture* (New York: Oxford University Press, 1997), 175.

84 The quotation is from David Noble, *The Eternal Adam and the New World Garden* (New York: George Braziller, 1968), ix. The exceptionalist ideology has been subject to numerous critiques, most notably in David Veysey's influential essay, where he dismisses the notion of an American distinctiveness and asserts that contrary to the presumption of a generalized, unique, and singular American character (and mission), "we are but one fractional (and internally fractionated) unit in a polyglot world, and that social history is composed of a vast number of separate and distinct pieces, like a mosaic that seldom stops at international boundary lines." Quoted in Kammen, *In the Past Lane*, 179.

85 Morrison discovered the basis for her story when, as she says, "I was looking at the book of photographs *Ghost Towns of Oklahoma*," and noticed that "it scarcely mentions any of the black ones." Christopher Hitchens, "Morrison's West," *Vanity Fair*, February 1998, 144.

86 Morrison, *Paradise*, 194.

87 Ibid., 217.

88 From Toni Morrison's Nobel lecture, 7 December 1993.

89 Ron Eglash, *African Fractals* (New Brunswick: Rutgers University Press, 1999), 31.

90 See Gilles Deleuze and Felix Guattari, *Kafka: Towards a Minor Literature*, trans. Dana Polan (Minneapolis: University of Minnesota Press, 1986).

THEORIZING DYSLEXIA
WITH CONNOLLY AND HARAWAY

Kathy E. Ferguson

IN *NEUROPOLITICS: THINKING, CULTURE, SPEED*, William Connolly sets himself two missions, which I'm calling his thinking project and his pluralism project. The first is "to explore the critical role that technique and discipline play in thinking, ethics, and politics, and to do so in a way that accentuates the creative and compositional dimensions of thinking," and the second, "to explore the new cultural pluralism, within and across territorial states, that beckons on the horizon of contemporary possibility."[1] In *The Companion Species Manifesto*, Donna Haraway explores two similar questions (although she lists them in reverse order): "1) how might an ethics and politics committed to the flourishing of significant otherness be learned from taking dog-human relations seriously; and 2) how might stories about dog-human worlds finally convince brain-damaged US Americans, and maybe other less historically challenged people, that history matters in naturecultures?"[2] I'm calling the first Haraway's otherness project and the second her history project.

Both books work against the nature-culture dyad, not simply by refuting it but by replacing it with accounts that cut through the biosocial material differently. This chapter incites a conversation between the nature-culture conversations enabled by these two texts, exploring their compatibilities and inviting each to put pressure on the other. I draw energy from this conversation to investigate an area of the relations of brain, body, and culture that particularly compels me, that of learning "disabilities." In relating these two projects to one another, a 2 × 2 table is irresistible:

HARAWAY

		Otherness	History
C O N N O L L Y	Thinking	strategies for thinking dyslexia	(shared historical and temporal analysis)
	Pluralism	(shared ethics and ontologies of difference)	strategies for changing education

Pluralism and otherness, in these authors' formulations, cover similar ground. The authors use this pair of conceptual resources to contribute to a cultural shift in thinking across given categories, a shift that enables greater exploration and appreciation of differences within and between persons, events, and ideas. Similarly, thinking and history are closely related. Connolly explores the arts of creative self-construction in opening thinking to its layers of neural and cultural histories, while Haraway articulates multiple histories for relations between dogs and humans to facilitate cross-species thinking. I have contained those more familiar shared ideas in parentheses to foreground the upper left and lower right quadrants, where unconventional resources for interrogating dyslexia can be found.

CREATING BIOCULTURES

Connolly and Haraway employ a number of common strategies and call on an array of shared resources to rethink dichotomies in prevailing thought worlds between nature and culture, minds and bodies, inside and outside, and before and after. Both books challenge dichotomous thinking by providing creative and useful resources for reframing nature and culture in a zone of indiscernibility within which potentially radical politics can be thought. Imposing my own linear organization on Connolly's richness and Haraway's wildness, I've drawn them together to create a sort of ex post facto twelve-step program for rethinking biocultures. Among the authors' shared practices:

1   They encourage their own curiosities about nature-culture relations through modest autobiographical reflections, notably their relations with their fathers. Connolly writes movingly about his father's brain injury, while Haraway incorporates her father's approach to narrative in

"Notes from a Sports Writer's Daughter." Haraway's father's professional work taught her to respect the integrity of play: he preferred covering games to writing a column because his "faith was in the game, where fact and story cohabit."[3] Connolly's father did proletarian work from which the non–brain damaged must struggle to recover: "A little brain damage goes a long way on the assembly line."[4] These authors' return to their fathers positions their current intellectual and political interests in relation to intense and meaningful family pasts, and at the same time brings critical attention to the constitutive relations of present and past, what Connolly calls virtual memory, when "the past operates on the present below the threshold of explicit memory."[5]

2   The authors' stories build on an accumulating literature of feminist and other relational analyses of subjectivity: body-brain relations for Connolly, like dog-human relations for Haraway, are always already relational: "co-constitutive relationships in which none of the partners preexist the relating, and the relating is never done once and for all."[6] While elements can usefully be pulled out for closer examination, "the relation is the smallest possible unit of analysis."[7] There is less agonistics in Connolly's book than in his earlier work, more emphasis on connection and receptivity. I take this not as a turning away from the agonistic respect that he cultivated in earlier books but as supplementing it with a greater appreciation and fuller theorizing of the webs of relations that we might cultivate to sustain the agonistic struggles we need to face. Haraway's project might be thought of, in Deleuzian terms, as "becoming-dog," a mutual modification of human-dog brain-bodies resulting from "engagement with the powers of other bodies."[8] With Deleuze, Haraway strives for alliances, not appropriations; she cultivates a moving toward the other that is not a simple merger, but an engagement with affects and powers that deterritorializes the human-centered social imaginary.

3   Both Connolly and Haraway reflect on the politics of "motor memory," the fast-working virtual memories in our bodies that organize events into perceptions working "below explicit awareness as a repository of cultural life from the past."[9] Connolly draws examples from film, such as flashbacks and close-ups, as well as from everyday events such as responding to an emergency or watching a soap opera, to "encourage reflection on fugitive features of everyday perception that could other-

wise remain in the dark."[10] Haraway brings examples from dog training, noting many points of intersection between the dog's "biosocial predilections" and human political economies of herding, hunting, and showing. Both write about what Haraway calls metaplasms, alterations in words or patterns (intentional or not) that call attention, through their stumblings, stutterings, and detours, to aspects of memory in excess of conscious recall.

4   Both writers employ temporal and spatial complexities and layerings, putting concepts into mobile relations both to recognize creativity and to enhance it. Connolly explores the "fugitive doorway" between layers of accessible and virtual memories to find the affect-invested workings of thought that precede the labor of reason or judgment. Haraway explores the interspecies "ontological choreographies" (a phrase from Charis (Cussins) Thompson) by which participants invent themselves out of their inheritances. Both are temporal thinkers, looking at the emergent processes by which thinking is framed and reframed across three contrasting temporal registers: "evolutionary time at the level of the planet earth and its naturalcultural species"; "face-to-face time at the scale of mortal bodies and individual lifetimes";[11] and historical time at the scale of "living labor, class formations, gender and sexual elaborations, racial categories, and other layers of locals and globals."[12] Both authors are ecumenical about the virtues of different times: Connolly argues for the virtues of speed (against fears that a rapidly moving world makes democracy impossible) while Haraway argues for the virtues of history (against indifference to past injustices that continue to mark canine and human bodies and to structure the commerce between them).

Both authors pull resources of temporal reflection into their thinking about language and politics. Connolly draws insight from Nietzsche's grammar and syntax to illustrate active textual practices that allow us to surprise ourselves. For example, Nietzsche's use of ellipses to unfinish the endings of sentences encourages the reader to break away from the text, to pause, to encounter the written words differently; like a film director using "irrational cuts" to interrupt linear time, Nietzsche stages an interaction with, rather than simply a reception by, his readers—"It is above all in the *encounter* between where you have gone and where Nietzsche is going that creative things break out."[13]

Haraway takes every opportunity to give dogs a history. She tells stories of dog-human relations involving global shifts in political economies that rendered herding cultures obsolete; interventions of government agencies to bring back predator species or settle livestock guardian dogs (LGDs) in place of poisoning and shooting predators; and debates among breeding clubs over population genetics. Dogs are active agents, responding to opportunities and threats in their relations with herders, tourists, hunters, ecologists, ranchers, bureaucrats, cooks, soldiers, breeders, and researchers. "Along with the whole dog," Haraway writes, "we need the whole legacy, which is, after all, what makes the whole companion species possible. Not so oddly, all those are non-Euclidean knots of partial connections. Inhabiting that legacy without the pose of innocence, we might hope for the creative grace of play."[14]

5   Both authors are radically interdisciplinary, triangulating their analyses: Haraway interdigitates evolutionary biology, feminist theory, and livestock guardian dogs (LGDs), while Connolly presses brain research, political theory, and film studies into mutual service. While Connolly mines the work of neuroscientists, Haraway draws in paleobiologists, environmental historians, and ecological developmental biologists: from these quarters comes support for their shared argument that there is no time or place where biology ends and environment begins. Both avoid closure, willing to wander in search of new connections. Their work across academic categories is not additive, nor merely allegorical, but reciprocally constitutive within the material data as well as the discursive practices of the less familiar disciplines. Dogs, Haraway cautions us, are "not an alibi for other themes; dogs are fleshly material-semiotic presences in the body of technoscience. Dogs are not surrogates for theory; they are not here just to think with. They are here to live with."[15]

6   Both Connolly and Haraway work the liminal, offering creative juxtapositions of elements that escape their previous confinements to move into new vocabularies now available for critical thinking. Both create Nietzschean "untimely concepts" which act counter to our time and thus offer us resources for acting upon our time differently. Connolly offers the resources of "nontheistic gratitude," for example, inviting us toward world-affirming sensibilities embracing the excess of "a protean set of energies" over any particular organization of those energies.[16] Connolly similarly builds "immanent naturalism" out of the combined

workings of "the idea that all human activities function without the aid of a divine or supernatural force" (naturalism), along with careful attention to the layered complexities of an infrasensible (rather than supersensible) field of biosocial practices (immanent-ness).[17] As with jumps in time or discontinuities in prose, fresh relations between familiar concepts can open opportunities for innovative thinking.

Haraway's labors in liminality often take the form of disruptive identity categories.[18] An earlier example is of course the cyborg, her human-machine hybrid figure that both emerged from the belly of the war machine and offered some critical ways out of it. In *The Companion Species Manifesto* Haraway looks back at the cyborg metaphor that she coined in the mid-1980s and finds it fatigued, so she turns happily to the tropic resources of companion species. "I have come to see cyborgs," she writes, "as junior siblings in the much bigger, queer family of companion species."[19] Her old slogan, "Cyborgs for earthly survival," has given way to one inspired by LGDs: "Run fast; bite hard!"[20]

7   Both authors face resistance from their usual fellow travelers because of their turn to science. Connolly reports that his friends inquire, with some anxiety, "Doesn't that venture drive you into the very reductionism [or some other bad ism] you have heretofore fought against?"[21] Haraway similarly faces her "political people's fears of biological reductionism."[22] Both challenge theorists who "ignore how biology is mixed into thinking and culture and how other aspects of nature are folded into both."[23] Both urge their comrades who are "haunted by determinist images of nature" to get over it and learn to explore "the corporeal layering of language, perception, and thinking in human [and other] life."[24]

8   They have similar modes of engagement. Both are generous in the ways they engage other theories, nudging and supplementing—sometimes teasing—but not trashing them. They recognize their debts and honor the intellectual currents within which they swim. Both cultivate modesty in their modes of argument, asking for open-ended experimentation rather than explanatory sufficiency, both because the logics of their arguments require it and because they are setting a good example. They look for alliances not by insisting on fully fledged agreement but by cultivating partial convergence.

9   They're both funny: Connolly in a wry and understated way, Haraway in a more polemical and flamboyant one. (Fortunately, Haraway exhausts

her dog puns early in the manifesto: "half-trained arguments," "going to the dogs," several god-dog reversals, and best of all, "the birth of the kennel.")[25] Both rely on irony to resist nostalgia, stressing the political dangers of recourse to "the good old days." Connolly argues that longing for a slower tempo of life produces the temptation to find some vulnerable constituency to blame for the dislocations of contemporary speed. Haraway maintains that respect for the labor of livestock guardian dogs should not take the form of return to a timeless past of peasants and herders but rather must be negotiated in relation to changing political economies of domestication and wildness.

10   They both theorize respectfully about affect, exploring complex relations between proto-feeling, pre-thoughts, and conscious knowing across temporal registers as well as interspecies relations. Connolly applies Nietzsche's insights—"Between two thoughts all kinds of affects play their game; but their motions are too fast, therefore we fail to recognize them"[26]—to draw in the affective charge of virtual memories as they are folded into thinking and judging. "Attention to the role of affect in thought," Connolly argues, "brings out how thinking is already under way as you strain to compose a train of thought. New thoughts bubble, flow, or surge into being from a virtual register hard at work below the threshold of feeling and intellectual attention. Since affect is not entirely under the regulation of consciousness, the flow of thinking exceeds its governance too."[27]

Haraway makes room for affect at several levels. First, she honors the emotional lives of dogs, and affection between dogs and people, outside of narcissistic human desires for "unconditional love." Haraway further calls attention to the "underground passages" connecting "sign and flesh" through partial connections that require concentrated labor to bring into articulation.[28] She assesses canine programs in terms of the multileveled practices of interspecies relations, attending to "all of the conditions of their possibility, all of what makes relating with these beings actual, all of the prehensions that constitute companion species."[29] Her contempt for animal rights discourse is based on her determination to stretch outside of human-centered concerns and to encounter dogs on something like their own terms.

Haraway's use of prehensions taps a dense and inchoate realm in a way similar to Connolly's use of affect. He does not simply mean feelings, although the affective register includes emotive elements. He is not arguing only that feeling is a form of knowing, although he would not, if I understand correctly, disagree with that feminist argument; rather, he is saying that for there to be identifiable feelings and knowings, we must tap a prior "dense interweaving of genetic endowment, image, movement, sound, rhythm, smell, touch, technique, trauma, exercise, thinking, and sensibility."[30] Haraway similarly addresses affect not simply as the feelings that already-constituted beings have, but as the prior, thick relational weave of " 'prehensions' or graspings [through which] beings constitute each other and themselves."[31]

11   Both authors are intrigued by the politics of training. Haraway reflects on how she and her dog "are training each other in acts of communication we barely understand."[32] She reflects on various approaches to dog training, including the "click and treat" school of canine behaviorism and others that stress reciprocal communication.[33] Looking at discipline in terms of what it can accomplish, Haraway endorses those techniques that enhance the freedom and accomplishment available to dogs while enabling mutual respect. Haraway also works on herself, learning not just the disciplined sport of agility but also "how to narrate this co-history and how to inherit the consequences of co-evolution in nature-culture."[34] Connolly similarly approaches technique in terms of what it can accomplish, looking at various exercises and experiments to diminish existential resentment and to labor constructively on oneself. He "makes technique the hinge that links thought (as corporeally stored thinking) to ethical sensibility."[35] Haraway's approach to the mutual training of dog and human readily coheres with Connolly's account of self-labor on "those complex mixtures of word, image, habit, feeling, touch, smell, concept, and judgment that give texture to cultural life."[36] Both thinkers derive their appreciation of self-training in part from their assessments of the ubiquity of institutions already inflicting their techniques upon people and dogs: advertising and puppy mills, education and inbreeding, churches and animal shelters, professional organizations and pet hierarchies. "In a world in which institutional discipline has become extensive and intensive," Connolly writes, "such tactics can function as countermeasures to build more independence and thoughtful responsiveness into ethico-political sensibilities."[37]

12   They both have faith and hope in the ability of their words to con-

tribute to political change, along with an awareness of the dangers that their projects entail. They cultivate a politics that opens rather than completes its missions, that insists on being open to surprise. Connolly encourages us to explore the creative and compositional politics of thinking: new concepts can reveal retrospectively an absence in available public reflections; they can express a previously underthematized sensibility, representing that sensibility in public discourse so that it can be attended by others; and they can offer practical opportunities for people to work on their self-organizations to induce modifying effects upon themselves. To take these steps shows "how thinking crisscrosses between the brains of thinkers and the public worlds in which they participate. Even more, it reveals how public expression faces in two directions: toward the world and toward those individuals and constituencies whose reiterated self-expressions induce effects upon themselves that strengthen or modify their sensibilities."[38] Connolly invites us to change ourselves by working on our proto-thoughts, convincing our bodies, writing on our surfaces to etch modest new beginnings into being.

For Haraway the possibilities of political change come from working on history in the same ways that Connolly works on thinking. *The Companion Species Manifesto* is "a political act of hope in a world on the edge of global war, and a work permanently in progress, in principle."[39] Haraway invites her communities in Great Pyrenees and Australian Shepherd dogland to politicize their historical locations, to accept the "as yet unarticulated responsibility to participate in re-imagining grasslands ecologies and ways of life that were blasted in significant part by the very ranching practices that required the work of these dogs. Through their dogs, people like me are tied to indigenous sovereignty rights, ranching economic and ecological survival, radical reform of the meat-industrial complex, racial justice, the consequences of war and migration, and the institutions of technoculture."[40] On-the-ground ethical considerations compel her: "I want to know how to live with the histories I am coming to know."[41]

In pursuing their closely related political projects, both thinkers pay attention to the dangers thus incurred. For Haraway, danger lurks in her ambivalent but thoroughly engaged relation with the organizational apparatus of doggie-human governmentalities—the world of professional dog breeding and animal shelters. She resigns herself to the limits of the

dog-breeding world to cherish its opportunities and change its more ob-
jectionable practices from the inside: "In current naturecultures, breeds
might be a necessary, if deeply flawed, means to continue the useful kinds
of dogs they come from."[42] The national and international administration of dog "adoptions" provokes concerns that she cannot resolve by
turning away: "Adopting a shelter dog takes a lot of work, a fair amount of
money (but not as much as it costs to prepare the dogs), and a willingness
to submit to a governing apparatus sufficient to activate the allergies of
any Foucauldian or garden-variety libertarian. I support that apparatus—
and many other kinds of institutionalized power—to protect classes of
subjects, including dogs. I also vigorously support adopting rescue and
shelter animals. And so my dyspepsia at recognizing where all this comes
from will have to be endured rather than relieved."[43] Haraway gives a
compelling example of such an apparatus at work in the story of Satos,
the Puerto Rican street dogs who have become the object of an international adoption apparatus. Like healthy white babies, smallish shelter
dogs are hard to come by in the domestic adoption and shelter market.
A network of individuals and institutions in the United States has created a complex transit system to transfer about ten thousand dogs from
the colonies to their "forever families" in the metropole. This "kinship-
making apparatus" produces families incorporating dogs and humans
across multiple histories of colonialism and patriarchy through the Save-
a-Sato Foundation.[44] Haraway notes that "smallish dogs, like girls in the
human scene, are the gold standard in the dog adoption market. US fear
of aggression from the Other knows few bounds, and certainly not those
of species or sex."[45] Haraway's misgivings about the colonial baggage and
domestic sentimentality embedded in the Save-the-Satos project inform
but do not derail her support for adopting stray dogs.

For Connolly, dangers emerge in the close proximity of the self-artistry
that he advocates to regimes of therapy about which he holds reservations.
Recognizing their similarities, he tries to nudge them apart by locating
therapy in the realm of professionally directed help for dealing with neu-
rosis to function in daily life, while self-artistry is "work applied by the self
to itself to render its relational proclivities more congruent with principles
it professes, or to build up resistance to oppressive institutional regimes,
or to modify a relational pattern of thought or judgment that seems
closed, or to put the self in the position of responding more generously to
newly emerging identities that call into question the self's implicit sense

to embody in its mode of being the dictates of the universal."[46] Yet this border does not always hold: our efforts to modify ourselves toward greater generosity or more effective resistance are likely to be bound up with addressing the damage that our society may have done to us and our subsequent neurotic investments. Like Haraway's unrest at her collaboration with canine disciplinary institutions, Connolly's discomfort at the proximity of self-artistry to therapy has to be endured rather than relieved—that's why, I believe, both authors call on the sustenance offered by irony. My point is not to scold either for getting too close to problematic disciplinary authorities, but rather to learn from the strategies that both employ. Most political thinkers confront similar problems when the institutions or practices that we affirm—teaching, for example—bleed into those we reject—say, colonialism. Purity is not an option in these circumstances, but irony can be useful in negotiating such problematic terrain.

Haraway calls upon us to "inhabit histories, not disown them"[47] so that we can become "answerable for what we have learned how to see."[48] Connolly invites us to cultivate the "wild element" in thinking to facilitate a "generous and responsive sensibility."[49] The very openness of these invitations suggests that there is more than one way to move toward these goals. Therefore I wonder why the animal rights people do not, in Haraway's account, seem to qualify. I can see that making dogs into rights-bearing creatures comes up short, in that it fits dogs into prevailing human models of subjectivity rather than relating more vigorously to the unique world of the dog. But given the acceptance noted above of partial opportunities and flawed organizations, why not include animal rights activists as problematic fellow travelers? Rights talk is one of the resources available to articulate claims on being; it carries a problematic history that we might contest without abandoning. Animal rights activists may be doing a version of exactly what Haraway calls for, which is inhabiting their histories and becoming responsible for what they have learned how to see.

STYLISH QUESTIONS

There are so many shared questions and compatible ways of framing inquiry between Haraway and Connolly generally, and between their two books in particular, that it is tempting to attribute remaining divergences between them to secondary issues of "style," meaning form as opposed to content. Yet the thinking practices of both authors would immediately question the trivialization of form and the too-easy separation of form and content. So, taking "style" seriously, in what ways do the two sets of authorial practices put pressure on one another?

Again, let me start with their similarities. Certainly both Connolly and Haraway have "style" in the sense of "distinction, excellence, originality, and character," the fourth meaning of style in *Webster's New Twentieth Century Dictionary*, unabridged, 2nd edition. They both engage in the act of styling, meaning to call or to name. Yet there remain significant differences in their "specific or characteristic manner of expression, execution, construction, or design."[50]

Connolly is a careful writer. His analyses are framed with qualifiers that render his generalizations modest: "some" neuroscientists make the arguments that he carries; cultural theorists "often" shun biology in an attempt to avoid determinism; democratic theorists "tend to" over-territorialize their understandings of democratic space. A characteristic gesture of his writing is to read the layers of an argument or practice to show that more than one thing is happening: Virilio's horror at the speed of the war machine, for example, leaves him sunk in a military paradigm and "insufficiently attuned to the *positive* role of speed in intrastate democracy and cross-state cosmopolitanism."[51] When Connolly introduces political theorists to the unfamiliar world of neuroscience, he lays out relevant debates and gives needed background. He takes care to bring his readers with him. What does this heedful attention to the context and limits of his analysis allow him to accomplish? He can invite a broader array of readers into his conversations because he refrains from overstating his case. He enhances his credibility: we believe him—at least, I believe him—even if we or I know little about the world of neuroscience. Most importantly, we learn more about *how* he came to his conclusions because the threads of argument are made available to the reader.[52]

Haraway, at least in *The Companion Species Manifesto*, is a more impulsive writer. Her extravagant prose can be delightfully poetic but is less informative, because she is less careful about taking her readers through the process that enabled her insights. It is as though Connolly does his thinking with us, on the page, while Haraway has done her thinking earlier and is carrying it back to us.

There are also significant differences in the "delivery vehicles" that each author uses. In reflecting on these differences I'd like to speak a word for pamphlets. Haraway writes manifestos. *The Companion Species Manifesto* is short. It has pictures. It's cheap. I'd like to see Connolly write a manifesto, working the liminal again, this time between genres. A good pamphlet—small, accessible, illustrated, compelling, and inexpensive—can contribute to a critical micropolitics. It's readily usable in high school and college courses. Impoverished local libraries can afford it. It's easy to send to city council members, state and federal representatives, churches, unions, and community organizations. It can be left in doctor's offices, hair-cutting establishments, bureaus of motor vehicles, or any place else where people need something to read while they wait. It can be an organizing tool, ready to hand out on street corners or at demonstrations. When many people are inundated with electronic communications, which begin to evince a distressing sameness, the old-fashioned appeal of a pamphlet could have refreshing tactile advantages. There is a special technique in a good pamphlet, a charm of imagery and touch. Connolly suggested in an earlier book that maybe it's time for us to do talk shows—along those same lines, but more modest and more doable, is the pamphlet. There are a few models around: the earnest feminist organizing pamphlet *Peace and Power: a Handbook of Feminist Process*; Art Spiegelman's subversive comic book *Maus*; *Addicted to War: Why the U.S. Can't Kick Militarism*, a polemic by Joel Andreas against global militarism; and the early efforts that Phyllis Turnbull and I made to publicize our local critique of militarism, *Rethinking the Military in Hawai'i*. The more fully theorized version of arguments that books facilitate could be followed by a streamlined version for broader public consumption.

A second difference between Connolly's and Haraway's authorial practices appears in their brief definitions of their respective audiences. Connolly speaks to "liberals, democrats, pluralists, and cosmopolites," urging them and us to look at the positive possibilities of technique in relation to culture, since "nationalists and dogmatists of other sorts already actively engage this register of being."[53] Haraway names her audience as "feminist, anti-racist, queer, and socialist."[54] While many of us find ourselves on both lists, they are not quite the same. Why isn't feminist on Connolly's list? This is a significant omission, since a great deal of critical work on the relations of nature and culture has taken place in feminist theory, including Haraway's pathbreaking *Primate Visions*. Why isn't liberal on Haraway's list? This too figures as a significant omission, since in contemporary American politics, if one subtracts liberals from the Left, then there is not much Left left at all.

BECOMING-DYSLEXIC

I began this paper with Connolly, Haraway, and the fathers; I now shift to a different set of family-inspired curiosities, those between mother and sons. Both my sons are dyslexic. Their struggles have taken us into an awesome, ominous world of body-brain zones of indiscernability, life-changing techniques, and struggles to cherish difference while still living successfully in the world at hand. Helping my sons learn to read and write, and subsequently tutoring other dyslexic learners, has resituated me in relation to language and politics in ways requiring interdisciplinary assistance. Connolly and Haraway both investigate political questions by immersing themselves in realms of theorizing typically outside the reach of political theory and feminist theory. Evolutionary biology and neuroscience are a stretch for many political theorists, yet their combined insights give me resources to think usefully about "learning disabilities." My contribution to these interdisciplinary adventures relies on the productive utility of political theory and feminist theory and the investments of mothering, brought to bear on the work of the early neuropsychologist Samuel Orton, the intense techniques of Orton-Gillingham instruction (OG), and current neuropsychological and educational research on dyslexia. I invite Connolly and Haraway to bring their untimely concepts to bear on this unfamiliar context, to explore the politics of becoming-literate as well as becoming-dyslexic. To structure my adventures in dyslexia, I return to the handy 2 x 2 table upon which I plotted the intersections of Haraway's and Connolly's projects. Two quadrants are particularly suggestive in relation to dyslexia: the intersection of thinking and otherness, where we can explore strategies for thinking dyslexia; and the intersection of pluralism and history, where we can explore educational and political strategies for teaching dyslexic learners and organizing education.

THINKING/OTHERNESS: STRATEGIES FOR THINKING DYSLEXIA

One irony in becoming-dyslexic is that to engage this oppositional relation to written language, one has no adequate language. Dyslexia is considered a learning disability (LD), a necessary and hard-fought term allowing access to rights and legal redress of grievances under the Americans with Disabilities Act (ADA) and other laws. Tutors, teachers, and parents often speak instead of learning differences, making a claim for equal worth against the weight of marginalization. The term dyslexia (*dys* = difficulty; *lex* = verbal language) was given its current scientific definition by the National Institute of Child Health and Human Development (NICHD) on 3 August 2002: "Dyslexia is a specific learning disability that is neurobiological in origin. It is characterized by difficulties with accurate and/or fluent word recognition and by poor spelling and decoding abilities. These difficulties typically result from a deficit in the phonological component of language that is often unexpected in relation to other cognitive abilities and the provision of effective classroom instruction. Secondary consequences may include problems in reading comprehension and reduced reading experience that can impede growth of vocabulary and background knowledge."[55] One might summarize this by saying that dyslexia entails a troubled relation with written signs.[56] Dyslexic learners, even though they are often very bright in other ways, have trouble relating sounds and symbols and thus have difficulty in decoding (reading) and encoding (writing and spelling). The relation of sound to symbol is a puzzle to them; they just don't get representation.

Dyslexic learners are, as Sartre said of Flaubert, "badly anchored in the universe of discourse."[57] They tend not to hear, unless painstakingly taught, the sounds that make up syllables or the syllables that make up words; to them the word is an undifferentiated blast of sound lacking identifiable subelements. They often have trouble rhyming or in other ways coming to terms with "the lifeless imperatives of the alphabet."[58] Confronted with a written text, a dyslexic child may cry, in frustration or mourning, "I can't find the words" or "I can't make the book talk."[59] The child may be exceptionally articulate when speaking, and may excel at mathematics (as opposed to arithmetic), music, or art, but the world of written signs is a bitter and frightening mystery.

The "down side" of dyslexia is readily apparent. In a culture that privileges literacy, in a school system that considers laziness and stupidity the only two explanations for inability to succeed, it really sucks when you can't read or write. While about 5–15 percent of the general population is dyslexic, at least twice that many boys and men in prison are dyslexic.[60] About half of children and teenagers in the United States with drug and alcohol problems also have significant reading problems.[61] A whopping 38 percent of fourth-grade students fail to learn to read well in school. The two main reasons are poverty and dyslexia (or both together).[62] Dyslexic children are more likely than nondyslexics "to drop out of school, withdraw from friends and family or attempt suicide."[63] A person with dyslexia is often viewed, as Sartre's account of Flaubert suggests, as "the idiot in the family." Because as a society we are too quick to equate thinking with representation, we tend to conclude that dyslexic people's trouble with representation makes them stupid. Unfortunately, dyslexic people often conclude this as well, producing a low self-regard that makes effective remediation more difficult.

Neurologists studying dyslexia concur with Connolly in stressing the "brain-environment dynamic." Gordon Sherman and Carolyn Cowen, following Stephen Jay Gould, suggest that "we might regard dyslexia with its concomitant reading disabilities as a spandrel, a byproduct of *cerebrodiversity*. A spandrel—an architectural term for the space between the curve of an arch and a rectangular boundary or molding—is an unintended byproduct of a structure's design, secondary in origin, which nevertheless can turn out to be pivotal to that structure's essence. Perhaps every now and then *cerebrodiversity* yields byproducts (e.g., dyslexia) that may not serve an apparent adaptive purpose; although the underlying neural design may embody wonderful even pivotal possibilities." Cerebrodiversity goes beyond the "disability model" and "[is] a step toward a more comprehensive model of brain and learning variation." Earlier neurological analyses attempted to rule out environmental contributions in order to establish "genuine" learning disabilities, and in the process underestimated the impact that appropriate teaching can have on the complex intermix of brain and culture. Sherman and Cowen, in contrast, insist that the brain-environment dynamic is both cause and effect of dyslexia: "Neural circuitry reflects both biological makeup and environmental influence (e.g., early reading instruction); neural systems develop and are deployed for specific cognitive functions through brain-environment interaction." Adopting the "wide-angle lens of evolution," Sherman and Cowen point out that "dyslexia exists as a 'disability' only in the context of today's society, a fleeting moment in geological time." They celebrate cerebrodiversity as an "evolutionary asset" reflecting our "collective neural heterogeneity." Dyslexia is a product of a writing culture; dyslexia can also be written, its neural contours rewritten with powerful techniques.[64]

Some geneticists studying dyslexia join neurologists in arguing that "the brain is always a work in progress."[65] Summarizing current research on dyslexia and genetics, Jeff Gilger, professor of child and family studies at California State University, Los Angeles, states that "gene effects only culminate in a behavior after going through a variety of intermediary steps and interactions, including responses to, and interactions with, the environment. Thus, traits with a genetic component are not immutable or predetermined. Rather, they can be modified through the environment and for this reason it is better to speak in terms of *probabilities* of outcomes and risks due to genes instead of absolutes like *genetic causes*." Gilger reports that while "dyslexia has a genetic component" there is no identifiable dyslexia gene but rather an inherited pattern of "risk."[66]

Sherman and Cowen summarize three typical differences between dyslexic and nondyslexic brains: (1) gross anatomical differences—the brains of dyslexic people are usually almost perfectly symmetrical, whereas the rest of us usually have one hemisphere larger than the other; (2) cellular differences—dyslexic brains have smaller neurons in the thalamus, which "may disrupt the precise timing required to efficiently transmit information across brain networks"; (3) connectional differences—dyslexic brains often manifest "ectopic wiring," meaning that bundles of nerve cells are found in a part of the brain where nerve cell bodies are normally absent. These differences produce a "neurological glitch," a change in the brain's wiring that makes learning to read, write, and spell extremely difficult.[67]

Once dyslexia is theorized outside the dyad of nature and environment, in an interactive relation between bodies and culture, the significance of teaching changes dramatically. "Teaching matters!," Sherman and Cowen exclaim. The "dynamic gene-brain-environment interaction" can be partially redrawn.[68] Drawing upon recent fMRI data, Guinevere Eden from the Georgetown University Medical Center concurs, stating that "the experience of reading itself changes the brain."[69] Not only do dyslexics manifest a different pattern of neuronal activity when reading than nondyslexics do, but the energy output of their brains is reduced after they are taught to read by people like me. Orton-Gillingham instruction strengthens "the brain's aptitude for linking letters to the sounds they represent." If we begin early enough, we may teach the child's brain to change by "rewir[ing] the brain so thoroughly that the neurological glitch disappears entirely."[70]

og practitioners employ multisensory, cumulative, incremental instruction with plenty of repetition and review. We learn OG in an intensive two- or three-week class that teaches us the proper pronunciation of the forty-four sound units making up the English language, the rules and generalizations for spelling and adding suffixes, an extensive array of Latin affixes and roots, the proper scope and sequence for teaching these elements to dyslexic learners, and a precise method of multisensory presentation, reinforcement, and review. While periodic refresher courses and more advanced OG instruction are sometimes available, many of us go to work on our children or the children of others armed only with our initial training and a determination that every child can, with proper instruction, learn to read. Some of us also tutor dyslexic adults, who are both highly motivated and heavily damaged by the institutional violence that's been done to them. OG instruction is most effective one on one, but can be adapted to small groups and classrooms. Tutors go through the English language step by step, beginning at the most basic level, methodically breaking language down and putting it back together. We teach our students to identify the sound units that make up the language. We explain the rules and the exceptions, building a logical edifice to capture the flows of Latin, Greek, French, Anglo-Saxon, and Middle English that mix into contemporary English. We teach to the students' intelligence, compensating for their inability to intuit the patterns among sounds and symbols by directly explaining those patterns. For example, a very satisfying rule (because there are few exceptions) taught early in OG tutoring is the Floss Rule: when you have a one-syllable word with a single short vowel ending in *f*, *l*, *s*, or *z*, you double the final consonant. This explains why cliff, doll, grass, and fuzz have two final consonants, while other short words with short vowels (e.g. pin, cat, dog, and tub) do not. Although learning this rule introduces unnecessary complexity into the language lives of nondyslexics, who can intuit the pattern after modest exposure to its elements, the Floss Rule often gives great pleasure to a dyslexic child because it cracks the code: this space of language finally makes sense; it has a graspable pattern. When my seven-year-old son first learned this rule after two years of struggling unsuccessfully to read, he gloried in his new knowledge: I overhead him in his room, lying on his bed, softly chanting to himself, "when you have a one-syllable word with a single short vowel . . ."

Employing the related skills from an OG-based program called Project

Read, we take the same methodical approach to writing sentences, paragraphs, and essays: break the task down into its component parts, organize the parts in logical sequence, reconstruct them step by step. Repeat, review, take another step. Dyslexics struggle to learn representation, while critical theorists struggle to unlearn it so as to conceive of the world outside the correspondence theory of truth. Haraway insists, and Connolly would agree, that "all language swerves and trips; there is never direct meaning; only the dogmatic think that trope-free communication is our province."[71] Connolly and Haraway celebrate the spaces of critical freedom flagged by such swerves and stumbles. Yet for dyslexics there is no prior illusion of clarity in relations between sound, symbol, and meaning; dyslexics are thrown into the swerving and tripping straight away. They fight to make and hold onto a consistent connection between sound, symbol, and meaning because that is their ticket for entering the world of written signs. OG instruction disciplines the swerving and tripping of language by regularizing and normalizing it.

The multisensory dimension of OG is one of its most potent techniques. We bring every sense to bear on the often painful, sometimes exhilarating process of cracking the code. Students see the written sign, hear the spoken sound, write or trace the letters, feel their mouths and throats make the sound, hear themselves repeat the sound. Sometimes they write with large motions in the air, or trace difficult letters in sand, or use their fingers to count off syllables. OG tutors etch the language on the bodies of our students, rewiring resistant neural pathways to be more receptive to written signs.

Metaplasms abound in dyslexialand, where motor memories are made to work overtime to rewrite themselves. The Greek prefix *meta* means "over" or "beyond"; *plasm*, from *plassein*, means to form or mold. Dyslexics are metaplastic, going beyond the form of language, needing direct instruction to be brought back into the form or else they will always exceed and confound it. The pattern of altered words and sentences, the repeated misapprehensions, tell me, as a tutor, where my dyslexic students don't "get it." I then tutor them in the form, engrave the form on their bodies, and even rewrite the patterns of their brains. I organize language for them, bring it under the rule of reason. This, as you might imagine, sometimes gives me pause. In Deleuzian terms, I make language molar for them, beating back language's intense molecular multiplicity, which in other contexts I cherish. By helping my students to make their way in a "linguistically alien world," I discipline the metaplasms that might also exemplify a creative excess.[72]

Advocates of cerebrodiversity like Sherman and Cowen encourage us to heed the "up side" of dyslexia, to celebrate the utility of different relations between brain and culture. Following Haraway, perhaps we could encourage cerebrodiversity by considering dyslexics, metaphorically at least, as a companion species. Dyslexics are not "like me," except slower to read and write; they are different from me, they come at language differently, they inhabit the dense layers and rapid feedback loops of thinking in a quite different register. What do we gain by cherishing dyslexia as a way of being? Sally Shaywitz of the Center for the Study of Learning and Attention at Yale University calls dyslexia an "encapsulated weakness surrounded by many strengths."[73] Sherman and Cowen suggest that dyslexic brains "process information more globally" and thus are better at three-dimensional thinking than at sequential, linear thinking.[74] Dyslexics tend to think in pictures rather than in words. They are often creative thinkers, innovative problem solvers, imaginative storytellers, and intuitive interpreters of patterns or people.[75] They excel at expressing humor, avoiding closure to think past commonplace conclusions, and articulating the heart of a design or scenario.[76] Several successful business executives who have been identified as dyslexic attribute their achievements to "a distinctly different way of processing information that gave them an edge in a volatile, fast-moving world."[77] Dyslexics often excel at activities that require holding complex images in their minds, including art, engineering, architecture, and computers. Massachusetts Institute of Technology is sometimes called Dyslexia U.; Silicon Valley is Dyslexia Corridor. Dyslexics frequently have talent for making things and putting objects together; many a dyslexic boy has been saved from complete failure in high school by the hands-on opportunities in shop class. Dyslexics are often skilled at oral language; a number of famous dyslexics are successful actors and political leaders. Flaubert obviously overcame his initial "linguistic malaise" to participate exquisitely in written language.[78] While Sartre characterizes Flaubert as "an idiot who becomes a genius," we might think instead that the little boy who could not read until he was nine became a master writer not despite his language differences, but because of them.[79]

Celebrating cerebrodiversity might mean not making dyslexics be like us, but developing the capacity to affect and be affected by them to re-order the world and make it more receptive to difference. If those deficits which I strive to remediate and those gifts I have just enumerated are mutually productive, then successful OG strategies and techniques may be teaching dyslexic learners to read, write, and spell while also killing something of value. When I teach, I change the brain waves of my students. What might those brain waves have accomplished had I left them alone? Of course there is no ultimate hands-off policy on the brain, since "the brain is always a work-in-progress."[80] Yet there is nonetheless a certain chutzpah at work in rewriting the neurological order of things so as to bring dyslexics into literacy.

While it may be offensive to some dyslexics or their advocates to draw a parallel to companion species, I find Haraway's playfully serious project of "becoming-dog" quite useful for exploring relations while valuing difference. The word "species" carries an unsavory history in the annals of scientific racism, yet it allows Haraway and me to struggle against both sameness and hierarchy. Haraway warns that "contrary to lots of dangerous and unethical projection in the Western world that makes domestic canines into furry children, dogs are not about oneself."[81] Neither are dyslexics, although their survival often requires them to position themselves in relation to a distant nondyslexic norm. Just as dogs communicate but don't speak "furry humanese," so dyslexics think, but not in lesser words.[82] When thinking across difference, we must recognize the other's presence, but never assume that we know what it means.

Because dyslexics are a minority, and because my kind is in charge, dyslexics don't seem to spend a lot of time figuring out how to make me more like them. They are already, in Deleuzian terms, well positioned to be minoritarian. Nondyslexics might be in a better position to make cerebrodiversity more than an empty formula if we approached dyslexics in something like the way Haraway approaches dogs: not a smaller, lesser version of me, but a thought-inviting space of difference. Becoming-dyslexic might mean moving toward the life-space of dyslexic ways of being while still retaining an anchor in nondyslexic life. Becoming-dyslexic for the nondyslexic majority could invite us to cultivate a line of flight in relation to language, enhancing creativity by challenging the orthodoxy of the written sign.

PLURALISM/HISTORY: STRATEGIES FOR
ORGANIZING EDUCATION

Dyslexialand offers fertile grounds for developing political strategies to enhance pluralism by distributing educational resources and opportunities differently and by recrafting our comprehension of thinking. Like Haraway's adventures in dogland, my move into the world of dyslexia entails engagement with an array of political movements, organizational structures, and administrative apparatuses that bring order to the world of this companion species. Politically, dyslexia is part of the larger web of disability activism, a complex and often militant international movement for equal rights. Yet dyslexia, as a "hidden disability," is not fully parallel to more overtly physical disabilities, suggesting both internal diversity and potential schisms within the disability movement. As an arena of governmentality, dyslexia is organized through and with an extensive array of legal provisions, court battles, professional organizations, training and accreditation programs, internet sites, state agencies, special education programs, research and publications, and lobbying efforts. For example, the International Dyslexia Association (IDA) is a global organization with branches in nearly every state and in many countries. We— I am a board member for the Hawai'i branch, called HIDA—raise public awareness about dyslexia, conduct public education, train teachers, provide services to dyslexic learners and their families, and lobby Congress for dyslexia-friendly legislation. Like other movements, we have our quacks: those who promise desperate parents a quick fix by selling them, for example, tinted lenses, expensive "auditory retraining," special dietary supplements, complex exercise programs, special bedsheets and shoe inserts, or "orientation counseling."[83] We also police our borders, insisting that any proposed remediation be research-based, published in peer-reviewed journals, and subject to replication.

The political and organizational web around dyslexia is not unlike that which Haraway describes around dogs—a world in which lovers of the breed labor to understand otherness and enhance its life chances. Both worlds seem to be made up largely of women. Haraway reports that the breeders and showers of livestock guardian dogs are primarily middle-class, middle-aged women, while a tour through an IDA conference will reveal a predominance of mothers and teachers. Like the world of dog breeding, dyslexia fosters a politics that cares about and pays attention to science; somewhat like the environmental movement, advocates for dyslexics need to be informed about emergent research as well as to scrutinize it for system-sustaining, anti-difference bias.

Like Haraway in dogland, I'm an insider in dyslexialand, and for the same reason—love of the whole person, and love of the breed. Like her I participate in a problematic apparatus of governmentality, which I try to influence from the inside but still support even though apparatuses like it are likely to become agents of capture. Like Connolly I employ life-changing techniques that come close to the politically alarming conventions of therapy. Like him I worry about the neighborhood and try to nudge my teaching away from psychology and toward education ("I'm a tutor," I sometimes insist, "not a therapist"). Yet the boundary remains porous; a dyslexic person struggling to become functional within the written language often has therapeutic needs that I must try to address so that OG can do its work. With both authors I acknowledge that I cannot resolve these tensions but must continually negotiate them.

Giving dyslexia a history or calibrating it through multiple temporal registers helps to pluralize the educational world so that dyslexics have a useful place within it. Dyslexia has many times. On an evolutionary scale of time dyslexia is a creation of literacy—before the invention and imposition of written language, a dyslexic formation of body, brain, and culture might have meant many things, but not a failure to learn to read. Dyslexics might be seen allegorically as "throwbacks" to oral cultures, which we call preliterate because written language is the standard for a proper culture. On an historical scale of time, "text-blindness" or "word blindness" has been identified in medical literature from the late nineteenth century. Several physicians in England and Scotland described children "who were bright and motivated, came from concerned and educated families, and had interested teachers, but who, nevertheless, could not learn to read."[84] Dyslexia has been confused with mental retardation and attributed to stupidity or laziness. The pioneering work of Dr. Samuel Orton in the 1930s established crucial distinctions between retardation and "word blindness," although today's special education programs often lump all learning difficulties back into one dysfunctional classroom. Within the pace of time folded into an individual life, the clock is ticking

for every dyslexic learner: the "down side" of dyslexia can be readily addressed at an early age, but is increasingly difficult to remediate as the
person ages. Within the brain's tempo of split-second neural relays and
instant feedback loops, a "neurological glitch" might also be a novel line
of thought, a possibility that throws doubt on the wisdom of the very
remediation that dyslexic learners and their teachers labor to produce.

What would a becoming-dyslexic school system look like? What would
schools be like if colleges of education stopped fighting about the one
best way to teach reading and instead delighted in assisting the flourishing of many ways, paces, and extents of learning to read? Why shouldn't
there be room in our society for people who can't read or spell very well?
Why can't our educational system accommodate different kinds of learners and enable them all to flourish? Educators and researchers in the
dyslexia movement have some ideas about how these changes could take
place. Their reforms often call for more extensive teacher training and
a greater role for the teacher-student relation as it develops over time.
While I'm proud of my OG tutoring abilities, I have to confess that these
techniques are not rocket science. Every teacher in the country could learn
to do this sort of teaching. Every college of education could routinely
teach these strategies and techniques to future teachers. Every student in
elementary education could be swiftly assessed for reading problems, and
every curriculum could be adjusted as needed for each student.

The standard method for identifying a dyslexic learner centers on finding a discrepancy between ability and performance: a person who scores
high on IQ tests but fails on tests of achievement is likely to be dyslexic.
While tutors and teachers as yet have no better method to use, the discrepancy model is problematic, both because it misses some students and
because it focuses on the test rather than the learner.[85] Some educators
are suggesting a different approach called a "response to intervention"
model, represented in the ubiquitous acronyms of educators as RTI. Jack
Fletcher, a professor of pediatrics and reading at the University of Texas,
Houston, urges schools to turn away from the question of who is eligible
for special education services and move toward the question of how to
provide effective instruction to every child. Fletcher's approach would
require a massive paradigm shift away from standardized testing and
toward extensive teacher training to prepare teachers to see problems;
intervene; conduct multiple, short assessments to see if the intervention

is working; and plan further interventions based on changes in the student's performance over time. Douglas Fuchs, special education professor at Vanderbilt University, elaborates on this proposal, which has support within the U.S. Department of Education as well as IDA and other educational associations dealing with learning disabilities. Effectively introducing RTI would mean strengthening teachers' capacities to respond to struggling students and focusing on students' classroom performance over time rather than their test scores.

These reforms would require radical changes in education. They would foster a pluralistic ethics and support it with concrete institutions that pluralize education and value every learner. We could hope for an educational system in which every child is taught to read in appropriate ways, taking into account the possibility that some people might not learn very well and would still have value. For dyslexics and others for whom entry into the world of the written sign is problematic, such schools could offer a strange twist on Deleuzian becomings, a becoming-literate or becoming-majoritarian. Most dyslexics, so far as I can tell, would experience this becoming-literate as liberating, enhancing their capacity to affect and be affected. And perhaps the nondyslexic majority would entertain a modest deterritorializing of society, a decentering of written language and a denormalization of its majoritarian ways.

CONCLUDING THOUGHTS

This chapter has traveled from my twelve-step program for doing theory the Connolly and Haraway way, into unfamiliar regimes of neuroscience and instructional research, and on to dyslexia as a site for theorizing linkages of brain, body, culture. This is an appropriate journey for an exploration of these two thinkers, who both eschew linear presentation in favor of the Nietzschean delights of wandering. We are now back where we started, having roved over unexpected ground in search of useful connections and ethically enhancing openings.

As a mother of dyslexic sons, as well as a political theorist looking for critical purchase to think against prevailing practices of power, thinking the Connolly and Haraway way offers relational rather than dyadic thinking and attends to connections of body, brain, and culture rather than dualisms of nature and nurture. As an academic invested in the very print culture that disqualifies many dyslexics from education, I benefit from Haraway's struggles with flawed yet needed governmentalities. Like Haraway's dogs, my sons are not here for us to think with, but to live with. Yet it is the immense political challenge of changing the world for them, and the daunting simultaneous process of changing them so that they can live well within the world at hand, that stimulates my effort to think with them, to use their minoritarian status as a site of interrogation. Connolly's investigation of the fugitive doorway to the affect-invested workings of proto-thoughts helps to explain how Orton-Gillingham tutoring works on dyslexic learners by accessing that virtual register of prehensions and rewriting it around the requirements of written language. Connolly's pluralist vision both welcomes and problematizes the project of becoming-dyslexic. Both Connolly and Haraway help move us toward a dyslexia-friendly world by contributing needed resources toward a potentially radical shift in the relations of body, brain, and culture.

NOTES

1 William E. Connolly, *Neuropolitics: Thinking, Culture, Speed* (Minneapolis: University of Minnesota, 2002), 1–2.
2 Donna Haraway, *The Companion Species Manifesto: Dogs, People, and Significant Otherness* (Chicago: Prickly Paradigm, 2003), 18.
3 Ibid., 18.
4 Connolly, *Neuropolitics*, xii.
5 Ibid., 24.
6 Haraway, *The Companion Species Manifesto*, 12.
7 Ibid., 20.
8 Paul Patton, *Deleuze and the Political* (New York: Routledge, 2000), 78.
9 Connolly, *Neuropolitics*, 26.
10 Ibid., 30.
11 Haraway, *The Companion Species Manifesto*, 63.
12 Ibid., 97.
13 Connolly, *Neuropolitics*, 67.
14 Haraway, *The Companion Species Manifesto*, 98.
15 Ibid., 5.
16 Connolly, *Neuropolitics*, 73.
17 Ibid., 85–86.
18 Between cyborgs and companion species, Haraway took a brief detour through vampires; see Ingrid Bartsch, Carolyn DiPalma, and Laura Sells, "Witnessing the Postmodern Jeremiad: (Mis)understanding Donna Haraway's Method of Inquiry," *Configurations* 8 (2000), 127–64.

19 Haraway, *The Companion Species Manifesto*, 11.

20 Ibid., 5.

21 Connolly, *Neuropolitics*, 3.

22 Haraway, *The Companion Species Manifesto*, 63.

23 Connolly, *Neuropolitics*, 3.

24 Ibid., 62.

25 Haraway, *The Companion Species Manifesto*, 3–5.

26 Nietzsche in Connolly, *Neuropolitics*, 67.

27 Ibid., 75.

28 Haraway, *The Companion Species Manifesto*, 18.

29 Ibid., 81.

30 Connolly, *Neuropolitics*, 13.

31 Haraway, *The Companion Species Manifesto*, 6.

32 Ibid., 2.

33 Ibid., 43.

34 Ibid., 12.

35 Connolly, *Neuropolitics*, 107.

36 Ibid., 133.

37 Ibid., 107.

38 Ibid., 74.

39 Haraway, *The Companion Species Manifesto*, 3.

40 Ibid., 97–98.

41 Ibid., 81.

42 Ibid., 97.

43 Ibid., 94.

44 Ibid., 89–96.

45 Ibid., 93. A stronger parallel between dog and human adoption markets, I think, rests on race rather than gender. Girls' greater presence in international adoption circuits is a "supply" rather than a "demand" factor—local patriarchies produce greater value for boys, leading to more girls in orphanages. Smallish dogs are like healthy white babies in their gold standard status.

46 Connolly, *Neuropolitics*, 132.

47 Haraway, *The Companion Species Manifesto*, 89.

48 Donna Haraway, "Situated Knowledges: The Science Question in Feminism and the Privilege of Partial Perspective," *Feminist Studies* 14, no. 3 (fall 1988), 583.

49 Connolly, *Neuropolitics*, 95, 106.

50 The third meaning of "style" in *Webster's New Twentieth Century Dictionary, Unabridged*, 2nd edn.

51 Connolly, *Neuropolitics*, 178.

52 This doesn't always work, evidently, since Connolly evinces some exasperation with critics who continue to find fault with his use of Nietzsche despite his careful qualifications, in earlier books, of his selective recruitment of Nietzsche's ideas.

53 Connolly, *Neuropolitics*, 65.

54 Haraway, *The Companion Species Manifesto*, 64.

55 G. Emerson Dickman, "The Nature of Learning Disabilities through the Lens of Reading Research," *Perspectives* 29, no. 2 (spring 2003), 1.

56 I am excluding other kinds of learning disabilities and differences, such as dyscalculia (difficulty with math), dysgraphia (difficulty with writing), etc.

57 Jean-Paul Sartre, *The Family Idiot: Gustave Flaubert, 1821–1857*, trans. Carol Cosman (Chicago: University of Chicago Press, 1981), 15–16. There are many differences among dyslexic learners, and many degrees of dyslexia. Flaubert seems to have been extreme in that he had significant difficulties with speaking as well as reading. In his five-volume biography, Sartre does not use the term "dyslexia" to characterize his subject (not surprisingly, since the term did not gain popular currency until the 1990s), but his description of Flaubert's early and intense bewilderment in relation to language strongly suggests a dyslexic learner. My thanks to Michael Shapiro for calling my attention to Sartre's analysis of Flaubert's problematic entry into language.

58 Ibid., 4.

59 Rick Lavoi, "On the Waterbed: The Impact of Learning Disabilities," Kapiolani Community College, 13 September 2003.

60 The National Council on Disability (Washington, 2003) estimates that about 30 percent of children in the juvenile court system have learning disabilities, the most common being dyslexia. See "Addressing the Needs of Youth with Disabilities in the Juvenile Justice System: The Current Status of Evidence-Based Research," cited in Marshall Raskind, "Research Trends: Is There a Link between LD and Juvenile Delinquency?," www.schwablearning.org. See also "The Incidence of Hidden Disabilities in the Prison Population," Dyslexia Institute, 10 March 2005, www.dyslexia-inst.org.uk/news45/htm.

61 G. Reid Lyons, "Reading Disabilities: Why Do Some Children Have Difficulty Learning to Read? What Can Be Done about It?," *Perspectives* 29, no. 2 (spring 2003), 17.

62 Sally Shaywitz, *Overcoming Dyslexia: A New and Complete Science-Based Program for Reading Problems at Any Level* (New York: Alfred A. Knopf, 2003), 23.

63 Christine Gorman, "The New Science of Dyslexia," *Time*, 28 July 2003, 55.

64 Gordon Sherman and Carolyn D. Cowen, "Neuroanatomy of Dyslexia through the Lens of Cerebrodiversity," *Perspectives* 29, no. 2 (spring 2003), 11–12.

65 Dickman, "The Nature of Learning Disabilities through the Lens of Reading Research," 4.

66 Jeff Gilger, "Genes and Dyslexia," *Perspectives* 29, no. 2 (spring 2003), 6–7.

67 Sherman and Cowen, "Neuroanatomy of Dyslexia through the Lens of Cerebrodiversity," 9–10.

68 Ibid., 9.

69 Gueinevere Eden, "The Role of Brain Imaging in Dyslexia Research," *Perspectives* 29, no. 2 (spring 2003), 14.

70   Gorman, "The New Science of Dyslexia," 54.

71   Haraway, *The Companion Species Manifesto*, 20.

72   Michael J. Shapiro, *The Politics of Representation* (Madison: University of Wisconsin Press, 1988), 82.

73   Shaywitz, *Overcoming Dyslexia*, 58.

74   Sherman and Cowen, "Neuroanatomy of Dyslexia through the Lens of Cerebrodiversity," 12.

75   Edith Bird La France, "The Gifted/Dyslexic Child: Characterizing and Addressing Strengths and Weaknesses," *Annals of Dyslexia* 46 (1997), 164–65.

76   Ibid., 173–74.

77   Betsy Morris, Lisa Munoz, and Patricia Neering, "Overcoming Dyslexia," *Fortune*, 13 May 2002.

78   Sartre, *The Family Idiot*, 30.

79   Ibid., 41.

80   Dickman, "The Nature of Learning Disabilities through the Lens of Reading Research," 4.

81   Haraway, *The Companion Species Manifesto*, 11.

82   Ibid., 49.

83   Larry Silver, "Controversial Therapies," *Perspectives* 27, no. 3 (summer 2001), 4; Regina Cicci, "*The Gift of Dyslexia* by Ronald D. Davis," *Perspectives* 27, no. 3 (summer 2001), 11.

84   Shaywitz, *Overcoming Dyslexia*, 13.

85   Jack Fletcher, "Operationalizing Learning Disabilities: The Importance of Treatment-Oriented Models," *Perspectives* 29, no. 2 (spring 2003), 23–24; Douglas Fuchs, "On Responsiveness-to-Intervention as a Valid Method of LD Identification: Some Things We Need to Know," *Perspectives* 29, no. 2 (spring 2003), 28–29.

SOVEREIGNTY AND THE RETURN
OF THE REPRESSED

Wendy Brown

Sovereignty means that—it's sovereign. You're a—you've been given sovereignty and you're viewed as a sovereign entity.
—GEORGE W. BUSH, on the meaning of tribal sovereignty, 4 August 2004

You have rejected the European constitution by a majority. It is your sovereign decision and I take note of it.
—JACQUES CHIRAC, speaking of the French referendum on the European
Constitution, 29 May 2005

My sovereign, my thrice-loving liege, my wedded husband . . .
—Countess, SHAKESPEARE'S *Edward III*, II:2

The project is to generalize partiality for democracy and to infuse agonistic respect between diverse constituencies into the ethos of sovereignty.
—WILLIAM CONNOLLY, *Pluralism*

WHY SOVEREIGNTY NOW?

SOVEREIGNTY IS A POLITICAL-THEORETICAL TOPIC that mostly lay dormant from the late eighteenth century until recently, when an extraordinary range of thinkers took it up. One way of reading this sudden interest would focus on the owl of Minerva's flight hour: the decline of nation-state sovereignty and individual sovereignty amid globalization and unprecedentedly dense social powers together mark the waning of sovereignty identified with Westphalia (the articulation of an international

order based on sovereign nation-states), the French Revolution (the articulation of popular sovereignty), and Kant (the articulation of the sovereign moral subject). By this account, sovereignty becomes a theoretical
preoccupation as it is literally dying. Rogue powers from Empire to Al
Qaeda; managed or bought "democratic" elections from the American
presidential election in 2000 to the first post-Hussein Iraqi elections in
2005; not to mention hyperbolic assertions of the freedom of Western
subjects—all represent traces of sovereignty's decline rather than embodi-
ments of its robustness.

But there are less Hegelian ways of understanding the theoretical concern with sovereignty against the ebbing of its modern form. What
political-theoretical anxiety might the current preoccupation with sovereignty indicate? To what extent is much left and liberal theoretical sovereignty talk today a search for a kind of Viagra for the political? That is,
how might the theoretical preoccupation with sovereignty, along with the
political assertion of it by a motley range of bellicose states, constitute an
indirect and potentially even unconscious effort to revive and reassert a
theologically contoured fiction about the autonomy of the political as it is
overwhelmed by the economic, by the materiality of global capital, and by
the political rationality of neoliberalism? And to what extent does this
effort to revive the autonomy of the political implied by the fiction of sovereignty paradoxically involve accession to the permanence of capital and
the generation of a comforting illusion in the face of that permanence?

I will argue that traces of sovereignty are appearing today in two do-
mains of power that are, not coincidentally, the very powers that the
political sovereignty of nation-states emerged to contain: capital and religiously legitimated violence. In contrast with the claim by Hardt and
Negri that nation-state sovereignty has transformed into global Empire,
and by Agamben that sovereignty has metamorphosed into a worldwide
production and sacrifice of bare life (global civil war), my argument is that
sovereignty is migrating from the nation-state to the unrelieved domination of capital on the one hand and god-sanctioned political violence on
the other. Both are indifferent to and tacticalize domestic and international law; both spurn juridical norms; both recuperate the promise of
sovereignty: *e pluribus unum*. I will further suggest that this migration of
sovereign political power is shadowed by a set of intellectual practices on
the left that while aimed at resisting these new developments, draw on

and perpetuate the specifically theological dimension of political sovereignty, in which the political is formulated as capable of subordinating
capital to its will, a subordination presumed achieved by the sovereign and
autonomous status of the political itself. This theological remainder prevents political thought that is in its grip from reckoning with the nature
of sovereignty's practical breakdown and re-located trace effects, and
above all from reckoning with capital's historically unprecedented powers
of domination.

SOVEREIGNTY, WHAT?

Like democracy, sovereignty is spoken of today as if we know what we
mean by it when discussing its achievement, its violation, its assertion, its
jurisdiction, or even its waning. Yet sovereignty is an unusually amorphous, illusive, and polysemic term of political life. The leader of the free
world is not alone in defining it tautologically ("sovereignty means . . .
you've been given sovereignty . . . and you're viewed as a sovereign entity")
and its primordial status as "the unmoved mover" is noted often in contemporary discussions.[1] Even among political theorists, usage varies significantly: sovereignty is equated for some with the rule and jurisdiction
of law and for others with legitimate extralegal action, just as some insist
on its inherently absolute and unified nature while others insist that
sovereignty can be both partial and divisible.[2]

To a degree, political sovereignty's roving and ambiguous meaning has
to do with its peculiar double place in *liberal* democracy, and the shell
game with power that this double place facilitates in liberalism. In liberal
democratic practice, that which *constitutes* sovereignty in the Schmittian
sense is precisely that which is not named as sovereign in the Lockean or
Rousseauian sense. The premise of democracy is that sovereignty lies with
the people, yet liberalism necessarily features what Locke names Preroga-
tive power—the power of the executive to abrogate or suspend law, or to
act without regard for the law—and it is the latter that theorists and
commentators have in mind in their objections to oppressive or excessive
sovereign power today.[3] To the extent that contemporary discussions of
sovereignty are centered upon the state's power to act or defend itself
rather than the power of the demos to make laws for itself, this is a
slip that either outs liberalism as tacitly conferring sovereignty to non-

representative state power while denying that it does so, or suggests the extent to which the Schmittian intellectual revival has overwhelmed contemporary discussions of sovereignty.[4]

But even apart from the distinctive problematic of popular sovereignty, there is ambiguity in the term and paradox in the phenomenon. Sovereignty is a peculiar border concept[5]—not only demarking the boundaries of an entity (as in jurisdictional sovereignty) but through this demarcation setting terms and organizing the space both inside and outside the entity. As a boundary marker that is also a form of power, sovereignty bears two different faces; these appear in two different dictionary meanings of sovereignty—supremacy and autonomy—and two equally discrepant political usages—rule and freedom from occupation by another.[6] Within the space that is its jurisdiction, sovereignty signifies supremacy of power or authority (a meaning that is also captured by the Middle English use of the term "sovereign" for a husband or master, as in "my sovereign, my lord"). Yet turned outward, or in the space beyond its jurisdiction, sovereignty conveys autonomy or self-rule, and the capacity for independence in action. Inside, sovereignty expresses power beyond accountability; outside, sovereignty expresses the capacity for autonomous agency, including aggression or defense against other sovereign entities. The two are related, of course, insofar as it is the supremacy within that enables the autonomy without; the autonomy derives from convening and mobilizing by a master power an otherwise diffuse body—whether a diverse population or the diverse inclinations of an individual subject. Thus the importance of sovereignty's attributes of unity and indivisibility (attributes that Derrida deconstructs from one direction and Connolly from another) is that they literally enable the autonomy that is its external sign. Sovereignty does not simply unify or repress but is both generated and generative. It promises to convene and mobilize the energies of a body to render that body capable of autonomous action.[7]

There are a number of ambiguities and paradoxes of sovereignty that are subsets of its Janus-faced character:

1   Sovereignty is both a name for absolute power and a name for political freedom.
2   Sovereignty generates order through subordination and freedom through autonomy.
3   Sovereignty has no internal essence but is rather fully dependent

and relational even as it stands for autonomy, self-presence, and self-sufficiency.[8]

4   Sovereignty produces internal hierarchy (sovereignty is always over something) and external anarchy (by definition there can be nothing governing a sovereign entity, so if there is more than one sovereign entity in the universe, there is necessarily anarchy among them). Both hierarchy and anarchy are at odds with democracy understood as a modestly egalitarian sharing of power. Yet with rare exceptions, political theorists take sovereignty to be a necessary feature of political life: the very possibility of political action, political order, and political protection seem to depend upon it. Perhaps the existence of this paradox is one reason why liberals tend not to examine sovereignty closely even as they assume that it rests with the people, why radicals such as Agamben, Hardt, and Negri develop a politics opposed to sovereignty, and why leftish liberals like Connolly seek to pluralize sovereignty's undemocratic core . . . thus undoing sovereignty itself.

5   Sovereignty is a sign of the rule of law and the jurisdiction of law *and* supervenes the law. Or, sovereignty is both the source of law and above the law, the origin of juridicism and that which resides outside it. It is all law and no law; its every utterance is law and it is lawless.

6   Sovereignty is both generated and generative, yet it is also ontologically a priori, presupposed, original. Even practically, as Bodin notes, sovereignty cannot be conferred.[9] The presupposed or a priori nature of political sovereignty is both drawn from theology and part of what gives sovereignty its theological character; it is a reminder that all political sovereignty is modeled on that religiously attributed to God.

7   The theological aspect of sovereignty is the internal condition of the secular notion of the autonomy of the political articulated by and through sovereignty. This paradox is particularly important to grasping what sovereignty is becoming today.[10]

SOVEREIGN AUTONOMY AND THE
AUTONOMY OF THE POLITICAL

Schmitt is of course the thinker who explicitly crafts the autonomy of the political through the concept of sovereignty. Schmitt famously identifies the political with the friend-enemy distinction "as the utmost degree of intensity of a union or disassociation."[11] This identification in turn generates the signature action of political life, decisionism—deciding who the enemy is and what to do about the enmity. And decisionism in turn is the action constituting the basis of sovereignty: "sovereign is he who *decides* the exception."

Response to the friend-enemy condition—which cannot be codified or normalized—is not merely the essence but the substance of the political; it is what breaks the equation of the political and the juridical. Decisionism, which Schmitt defines as "pure will that bows before no sovereign truth," is *the* modality of political action because the political is sovereign, subject to neither norms nor the law, accountable to nothing else and derived from nothing else.[12] The sovereignty of the political proceeds from its being concerned with the life-and-death matter of the friend-enemy relation, that is, the realities that life is at stake and that there can be no norm to decide who is friend or enemy. This decision is even outside whatever norms bind the polity.

If the decisions about who the enemy is and what to do about the enemy are *the* political decisions, and if the autonomous capacity to make these decisions is the sign of political sovereignty, then sovereignty in turn articulates the autonomy of the political. This syllogism, congealed as a thesis, is generally regarded as the heart of Schmitt's antiliberalism; it is the basis of his critique of a liberal foregrounding of law, norm, and procedure in politics. For Schmitt this foregrounding compromises the political insofar as it compromises its autonomy and hence its sovereignty.[13]

Most liberal democrats regard this thesis as shocking and unacceptable. But to the extent that a softened version of it appears in social contract theory, Schmitt may be more bold messenger than iconoclast here. In contrast with Aristotle's notion that political life is natural to man, indeed that the polis is man's distinct "life form," in social contract theory the political emerges from a nonpolitical, ontological condition and is brought into being through artifice. The birth of the political through the social contract is at the same time the birth of political sovereignty; the social contract constitutes the temporal end and spatial limit of the sovereignty of nature or God and the inauguration of a distinctly human form in the domain of the political. The contract simultaneously establishes the sovereignty and the autonomy of the political, even if the impetus for the social contract is social or economic forces, for example the desire for security in life, liberty, property, or possessions, or for a resolution to estrangement or the despotism of nature. As apparent in the harsh authoritarianism of Hobbes as it is in the soft liberalism of Mill, and made explicit by the social contract stories of Rousseau and Locke, the jurisdiction of the political is distinct from those of nature, God, and family, and is that which both facilitates and contains the economy.[14]

What are the implications of sovereignty signifying both the autonomy of a polity and the autonomy of the political? As we have already learned, the two-sided nature of sovereignty means that its external autonomy entails internal mastery or subordination of powers that would rival, disperse, or fragment it. *Thus, the autonomy of the political articulated by sovereignty entails the conceit of political dominance or containment of other powers, including the economic and the religious.* In this regard sovereignty represents both a cleansing or purification of the political and a reigning supreme of the political, a purification and a reigning, again, that is of consequence despite being aspirational or even ideological rather than actual.

Through the classic works of early modernity and their contextualization by bloody religious wars, we are attuned to the quest for mastery over transnational religious authority sought by political sovereignty attached to nation-states. Equally important, however, is political sovereignty's bid to subordinate the economic to the political. This is not to say that the modern sovereign nation-state always heavy-handedly governs or regulates the economy but that it is premised on the notion that it can, and that it *decides* whether and when to do so. Laissez-faire capitalism is as much the expression of such a decision as state socialism is.

Political sovereignty's reach for autonomy from and mastery over the economic is well captured in an anachronistic meaning of "sovereign": as the gold coin (also known as the "coin of the realm") minted in England from the time of Henry VII to that of Charles I. The identification of currency with the Crown ("crown" being another name for the coin) signifies a subtending of the economic by the political, and more specifically the Crown's assertion of political control over the economy in order to unify and consolidate the realm. This meaning suggests as well that sovereignty is never simply held and wielded but from the beginning circulates; it works as currency and through currency, and not only through law or command.[15] (Just as sovereignty takes over theological practices of power, including the practice of making its word into law, it takes over economic practices of power that include circulation, fetishism, incorporation, and more.) And the generation of a coin of the realm in early seventeenth century, like the generation of the Euro four centuries later, reminds us that the early modern preoccupation with sovereignty coincides with (1) consolidation of the nation-state out of decentralized local political and economic powers (the abolition of local currencies is equated with abolition of local sovereignties), (2) an anxious relationship between national wealth and national power in mercantilist economies, even as a force is ascending that will burst these boundaries asunder. Capital will break apart the relation between wealth and nation by internationalizing markets and production. So sovereignty here expresses the subordination of the economic to the political, paradoxically but unsurprisingly at the very moment when the economic is so clearly evincing its own power, indeed its own autonomy.[16]

My thesis about the relation of political sovereignty to the economic differs sharply from that put forth by Hardt and Negri, for whom sovereignty emerges in service to the economic. Capital, they claim, becomes the content of the political form of sovereignty.[17] By contrast, I am arguing that even if the modern state emerges and develops, inter alia, in response to capital, political sovereignty—as idea, fiction, or practice—is neither equivalent to the state nor merely in service to capital. Rather sovereignty is a *theological* political practice that aims to supervene the economic; it aims to contain and direct the economy, and to detach political life from it.

THE THEOLOGY OF SOVEREIGNTY

If the early modern emergence of political sovereignty reacts to capital's emerging power in social or political life by attempting to coopt this power, it does something similar with religion. The context of the early modern religious wars produces sovereignty as both a reaction against religious authority and an attempt to appropriate it. This reaction and appropriation is apparent in the numerous godlike characteristics of political sovereignty. Ontologically, sovereignty is the unmoved mover. Epistemologically it is a priori. As a power it is supreme, unified, unaccountable, and generative. It is the condition of life and protector of life, and it is a unique form of power insofar as it both creates and sustains control over its creation. It punishes *and* protects; it is the source of law and above the law.

The homological and isomorphic dimensions of the relation between political sovereignty and God are not merely the result of reactive imitation or appropriation. God is the original sovereign, overtly displaced by political sovereignty in the early modern accounts. But more than the origin, the theological remains a necessary supplement to political sovereignty, making sovereignty work and yet not made manifest in its workings—why?

"All significant concepts of the modern theory of the state are secularized theological concepts," Schmitt writes, because these concepts were literally borrowed from theology, because of their systematic structure, and because of the state's status as an "invisible person."[18] Again, however, this thesis is not unique to Schmitt. There is Hobbes's infamous opening of Leviathan: "Nature (the art whereby God hath made and governs the world) is by the art of man, as in many other things, so in this also imitated."[19] Leviathan, the literally terrifying monster made by God, is imitated, rivaled, and finally bested by the issue of man's own creative powers.[20] Or, in a softer reading of Hobbes, if God makes man, man makes the larger and more powerful collective subject that is the commonwealth.

Sovereignty, Hobbes writes in the Introduction to *Leviathan*, is the soul of this man-made creature; it is what "gives life and motion to the whole body."[21] Consider the implications of designating sovereignty as the soul of the commonwealth. First, it is a life principle, that which animates and governs the movements of the commonwealth, and not simply a politically repressive solution to civil strife or external danger. Second, sovereignty as soul, though made by human artifice, is linked to God; souls are the sign of God's presence in earthly bodies—they come from God and return to God. Thus Hobbes does not simply rival God but instrumentalizes him in constructing political sovereignty, an instrumentalization that is repeated in parts III and IV of *Leviathan*, in which Hobbes both establishes the consonance between Christianity and the commonwealth and mobilizes the fear of God to produce fealty to the commonwealth. Perhaps most importantly, Hobbes describes both God and sovereignty as powers that "over-awe"; sovereignty literally imitates God's awesomeness, not merely his power. Or, political sovereignty is the power-form that works by "over-awing" us, rather than through governance or rule.[22] The borrowing from God here is complex: by analogizing sovereignty to the soul of the Artificial Man generated by human artifice, Hobbes reveals one of the fundamental tricks of sovereignty: we generate and authorize that which then over-awes us and is unaccountable to us because of its divine status. Man generates political sovereignty through conferral of his own power, but since sovereignty is the divine element within the commonwealth, this process of generation or fabrication is disavowed and covered over.

Just as Hobbes's account of political sovereignty borrows explicitly from God for its power and legitimacy, has recourse to God for sanctification of its status, and as "soul" is the voice or presence of God in the commonwealth, similar links between political and divine sovereignty appear in other early modern theorists, including the Abbé Sieyès, Jean Bodin, and Jean-Jacques Rousseau. Moreover, the divine quality of political sovereignty is what articulates the fiction of its containment of economic powers. In *What Is the Third Estate?*, for example, Abbé Sieyès makes clear that while political economy is what generates the social contract, political sovereignty is its effect.[23] Thus in his brief for radical popular sovereignty, Sieyès literally theorizes the subordination of the economic by the political as the logic and the conclusion of the social contract. But this logic depends upon a theological rendering of the political will of the nation as a priori, eternal, the foundation of all law yet before the law and prior to the law.[24]

For Jean Bodin, the identification of political sovereignty with God is in part a technique for containing potential excesses or abuses of sovereignty. When Bodin says that "justice is the end of the law, law the work of the prince, and the prince the image of God. Hence, the law of the prince must be modeled on the law of God," he draws a set of links between God and sovereign political power that simultaneously produce the absolutism of sovereignty and hedge sovereign power with God's own law and beneficence. Sovereign power, supreme on earth, at once imitates God and becomes something like a mediator for God. As I shall suggest in the conclusion, if Bodin's hope was to limit abuses through the linking of political sovereignty with God, today it seems that this very link may license rather than contain sovereign power, as rogue sovereigns cast themselves as mediators for God or in the service of God—whether Allah, Jahweh, or the Christian Lord.

The persistent and lingering theological dimension of sovereignty is evident in the very modalities through which contemporary scholars conceive sovereignty. Think of Agamben's formalistic account in which sovereignty and *homo sacer* are as timeless and eternal as the Latin Mass. Or think of Connolly's (still theological) atheism, which refuses to grant omnipotence, supreme power, or totality to the concept of sovereignty as he insists on its porous, layered, oscillating, and pluralizable character. Or consider Foucault, the lapsed Catholic, for whom sovereignty is mostly a story we tell ourselves, and one which shrouds the real story. Or think of Hardt and Negri, for whom sovereignty is only and always the suppression of the multitude and must be opposed, as God must be, for the multitude to know and enact its powers. Political sovereignty is never absent theological structure and overtones, whether it is impersonating, dispelling, killing, rivaling, or serving God. But the containment and regulation of religion are also always a dimension of sovereignty's function, even in the most overtly religious or theocratic states. And because its own power derives in part from appropriating and imitating what it neuters and subtends, sovereignty is not undone by refusing to believe in God or by the death of God.

THE LATE MODERN WANING OF POLITICAL SOVEREIGNTY AND THE UNLEASHING OF GOD AND CAPITAL

If political sovereignty is structured theologically, if it is the supreme and unaccountable political power and draws on God for legitimacy, and if its theological dimensions enable the conceit of the autonomy and sovereignty of the political vis-à-vis the economic, what happens as nation-state sovereignty wanes? What becomes of the theology of the autonomy of the political in the post-Westphalian era? What kind of crisis in thought and politics is consequent to the transnational flows of capital, labor, people, cultures, religions, politics, and above all, political fealties that erode political sovereignty from both sides? And what happens when this crisis occurs at the conjuncture in which most left theory has abandoned the project of replacing capitalism, and instead tacitly cedes to its

relative permanence as a global power? Here are my provisional and spec-
ulative theses:

> As it is weakened and rivaled by other forces, nation-state sovereignty
>   becomes openly and aggressively rather than covertly and passively
>   theological.
> At the same time, as political sovereignty recedes, the theological and the
>   economic reemerge as uncontained powers, relatively independent of
>   each other but convergent in abetting the erosion of political
>   sovereignty.
> Most progressive political thought remains caught in the theology of
>   sovereignty insofar as it remains attached to fiction of the autonomy
>   and sovereignty of the political.

Theological Political Sovereignty. As nation-state sovereignty wanes, both
internal and external assertions of it are increasingly dressed in diverse
religious regalia. Countless activations of state power today rest on a
strange brew of gratifying the will of Allah, Jahweh, or a New Testament
God, and fulfilling vaguely liberal democratic principles. While, for example, President Bush yokes American imperial actions to the delivery of the
Almighty's "gift of freedom," the Iranian president elected in June 2005
declared Iranians as free as Allah intended and linked his renewed nuclear
weapons program to the service of Allah.[25] Consider too how Bush draws
on God to legitimate his use of veto powers or proposed constitutional
amendments to protect "unborn life" and the "sanctity of marriage" inside the nation, and to withdraw funds from organizations promoting
the use of condoms or abortifacients in the international sphere. Paral-
leled by state and stateless sovereigns resting their authority on other
gods in other corners of the earth, Samuel Huntington's much-derided
thesis of civilizational clash takes on a different hue: conflicting sovereign and would-be sovereign powers appear increasingly as though they
are serving warring godheads. Tentatively, I would suggest that political
sovereignty's theological supplement becomes more manifest as sovereignty itself weakens. Concretely, sovereignty needs God more as its other
sources thin and its territorial grip falters. Religion has also become a
critical vehicle for linking national and transnational fealties in the post-
Westphalian era.

The Decontainment of Theology by Sovereignty. However, if political sovereignty becomes more intensively and openly theological in its waning, this contributes to its undoing in the long run. On the one hand, the religions mobilized by it are transnational rather than national, and hence contribute to the very erosion of nation-state sovereignty that prompts its theological outing in the first place. On the other hand, interpretations and implications of these religions vary even within national settings, and religion is as likely to instrumentalize the nation-state as the other way round. From the mosque movement in Egypt to rapture Christians and AIPAC in the United States, from the scarf affair in France to the threat of civil war from Orthodox settlers in Israel, from rising Islam in secular Turkey to the militancy of the Falun Gong in China, political sovereignties are newly vulnerable to politicized religious claims, transnational religious forces, religious conflict, and the cultural and religious heterogeneity of the nations whose unification and protection they must also stand for.

Capital. While local (statist, substatist, and transnational) bursts of political sovereignty cloak themselves in god-talk and are asserted through demands for fealty and claims to paternalistic protection in an openly theological frame, capital takes shape as an emerging *global* sovereign. Capital alone appears perpetual and absolute, indivisible, unaccountable, primordial, the source of all commands yet outside the law. It is global capital that produces bare life, turning populations around the world into *homo sacer*. It is global capital that integrates if not unifies the diverse peoples and cultures of the world, and subordinates all other powers to its own. It is global capital that creates the conditions for all life while being accountable to none. It is global capital that mocks nation-state claims to control their own fate, protect borders, even decide laws and priorities; indeed, such claims look like the last gasps of feudal fiefdoms at the dawn of modernity. And neoliberal political rationality, which disseminates market rationality across the social and governmental fields, is nothing less than a prescription and endorsement of capital as global sovereign.[26]

However, although capitalist managers certainly decide things, the *sovereign force* of capital does not take the form of decisionism, and capital thus lacks the signature attribute by which Schmitt distinguished sovereignty. If global capital is perpetual, indivisible, absolute, unifying, and the site of the command outside the law, but yet does not decide, then perhaps it is something like sovereignty without the sovereign, and its ascendance represents the real and final death of God. This development would be consonant with capital's relentlessly secularizing tendencies: it would be the capital of the *Communist Manifesto* as well as of the neo-liberals who regard the market as the ultimate instrument for attenuating fundamentalist and tribal zeals and fealties. Alternatively, if global capital represents sovereignty without the sovereign, perhaps it is even more godlike than modern political sovereigns ever were, insofar as it more closely approximates God's power to make the world without deliberating about it. Decisionism, which conjures the problems of choice, knowledge, judgment, calculation, even doubt and uncertainty, may then turn out to be the distinctly human sign of sovereignty—the definition of sovereign as "he who *decides*" would pertain only when "he" is human rather than divine.

Here is how the first two theses—concerning the intensification of theology and the sovereignty of global capital—could be put together: capital is both master and coin of the realm, except that there is no realm, no global polity, governance, or society, and neither are there boundaries or territory that delimit capital's domain. Rather, today we face increasingly theological local political sovereignty on the one hand and capital as global power on the other. This makes for a strange inversion and paradox: while weakening nation-state sovereigns yoke their fate and legitimacy to God, capital, that most desacralizing of forces, becomes godlike: almighty, limitless, and uncontrollable. In what should be the final and complete triumph of secularism, there is only theology. This is how the decontainment of the theological and the economic rhetorically echo each other, even as they move along distinct trajectories.

Left Theological Politics. Finally, insofar as much left thinking sustains the fiction of the sovereignty of the political, especially over the economic, it remains problematically caught in the theology of sovereignty. The left attempt to restore the autonomy of the political is the result of the contingent convergence of a historical phenomenon—the waning of political sovereignty—and two political-intellectual ones—despair over alternatives to capital and anxiety about the play of religious powers in the political scene. The tendency I am seeking to thematize is common to post-Marxist theorists who have repudiated materialist accounts of history, who are concerned to discover routes by which the economic can be resubordinated to the political, *and* who have abandoned the possibility, perhaps even the desirability, of alternatives to a capitalist mode of production and exchange. However contingently produced, these moves converge and reinforce each other. Only a post-materialist account of history can feature the autonomy of the political and its capacity to tame capital. Conversely, the theoretical embrace of the autonomy and supremacy of the political denies capital the status of sovereignty that I am suggesting is its globalized form.

In recent works, Jürgen Habermas and Étienne Balibar have turned their attention to the development of a democratic form of political sovereignty that could replace the eroded Westphalian system and steer global capitalism. Each seeks a political form that would reestablish the dominance of the political in general and democracy in particular amid economic globalization and a post-national constellation. Habermas calls this project "cosmopolitan democracy" and pins on it his hopes for developing "a world domestic policy without a world government" that will "catch up with global markets" and achieve "a renewed political closure of an economically unmastered world society."[27] Habermas's vision entails coordination among what he takes to be progressive European forces oriented toward cosmopolitanism rather than nationalism: enlightened governing élites, uncoopted and uncorrupted political parties, an emerging cosmopolitan and solidaristic citizenry, and citizens' movements.[28] For Balibar the project of creating "a public sphere and public authority above spheres of private initiative" to reassert "the primacy of the political" involves "collectively inventing a *new* image of a people, a new image of the relation between membership in historical communities (*ethnos*) and the continued creation of citizenship (*demos*) through collective action and the acquisition of fundamental rights."[29] In contrast to Habermas's reliance on élites and parties, and the development of ethics and juridical norms, Balibar calls for "worksites of (and for) democracy."[30] These worksites focus respectively on democratization of the European courts and European legal system, labor politics, border politics, and the politics of culture, language, and literacy. In each case the aim is to produce a European program and community of citizens "that would be more advanced than [those of] the national communities themselves" and to convert what is now empty European "public space" into democratic "civic space."[31]

Both Habermas and Balibar consider the question of dissolving nation-state sovereignty primarily in terms of an emerging post-national European political and economic order. William Connolly's reflections on sovereignty are less Eurocentric and more American. For Connolly the decline of national sovereignties and the rise of global capitalist power do not call for reconstructing a unified and institutionalized public sphere but rather (1) recognizing that sovereignty contains more ambiguity, ambivalence, and porousness than stipulative definitions and tight logics imply; (2) recognizing that sovereignty is not institutionally fixed in one site within liberal democratic polities or even in a transnational or global setting, but rather "circulates" across several sites; and (3) grasping sovereignty as a practice of power that "is composed by a plurality of elements —an oscillation between irresistible power and official authority and between the official site of sovereignty and the institutionally embedded ethos flowing into it."[32] This view, Connolly notes, may discourage those who seek tight causal explanations and closed models of process, but "it points to strategic issues and sites to address by those who seek to infuse pluralism into the ethos of sovereignty."[33] In short, what Connolly describes as the porous, oscillating, ambiguous, uncertainly circulating, and ethos-contoured characteristics of sovereignty make it available to intervention by Connolly's three favorite strategies of democratic political change: micro-politics, pluralization, and ethos.

If sovereignty for Connolly is not the Leviathan that modern theory and conventional definitions have made it out to be, neither is capital: "the order of global capital conforms neatly neither to the logic of self-regulation and light state monetary policy commended by classical economists nor to that of necessary crisis elaborated by its revolutionary opponents. Therefore it might be turned in new directions by an effective combination of institutional regulation, vital citizen movements and revised state priorities . . . that which is not formed by a tight logic or design is also unlikely to succumb to a simple logic of management, revolution, or transformation."[34] The idea that capitalism might be "turned in new directions" (more specifically, that "states and corporations might be turned in directions resisted by the inertia of Empire") indicates that even as Connolly rejects a unified and autonomous figure of sovereign power, he joins Habermas and Balibar in resurrecting the mythos of sovereignty in which the economic is steered by the political. But it is the "therefore"

in the passage above that openly reveals the (atheistic) theological moment in Connolly's thinking. If capitalism doesn't conform to a tight and
predictable logic, Connolly implies, then it is available for creative redirection. But what makes the absence of tight logic equivalent to limited capacities or radically malleable trajectories on the part of organized
powers? Why doesn't this absence add up to the opposite? Conversely,
what makes ambiguity or complexity into availability for intervention of
the sort that Connolly argues for? If the tight or simple logics of power
that others have attributed to capitalism, to the nation-state, or to sovereignty misapprehend and mis-describe their objects, does this make
these objects any more available to democratization? Isn't one of the
lessons of the last fifty years of capitalism that its very flexibility, inventiveness, and adaptability are a critical part of its power and perdurance?
If capitalism is not bound by tight logics or smooth trajectories, does this
make it less ordered by anti-democratic or inegalitarian drives, or more
available to justice projects of modest economic equality, ecological reason, meaningful work, and livable organizations of the social? Is the necessary alternative to tight logic no logic? Is the absence of a smooth trajectory no trajectory? Are the complexity and flexibility of capitalism
equivalent to its malleability by any political project, any ethos? If capital is inventive in the production of conditions and possibilities for its
own survival, are there limits to this inventiveness? If there is no God,
and metaphysical conceptions of power modeled on God's omnipotence
are false, does this mean that orders of human power, especially those
quaintly known as "modes of production," are available to any direction,
any end? Connolly's rejection of such conceptions is incomplete insofar as
it sustains the metaphysical conceit that equates tight logics with absolute power or control, and the absence of such logics with availability
to intervention and significant redirection. Thus does Connolly remain
trapped in the (theological) metaphysics of power that he aims to escape.

To my knowledge, no economist or other theorist of capitalism has ever
shown that it can do the following: (1) set aside the imperative to grow, to
relentlessly search out new products, new markets, and new sites of investment to produce new venues for capital accumulation; (2) fulfill its
profit imperative without exploiting labor and without degrading the
vast majority of the human minds and bodies that perform this labor;
(3) accumulate capital without producing radically unequal distributions

of wealth; (4) make a consistent priority of care for the fragility and finitude of the earth; (5) make a consistent priority of basic human needs for food, shelter, connection with others, and meaningful work; (6) protect or nurture what it commodifies, which is everything; or (7) generate social and political institutions, and subjectivities, that are just and community-oriented, humane and uncorrupt. If capital cannot be turned in these directions, what precisely is the significance of ethos and micropolitics in relation to its sovereignty?

To be clear, Connolly does not argue that capital can be *controlled* by or through political intervention. Rather, he says that "the world exceeds any system of explanation or control brought to bear on it" and that the best we can do is *"intervene* creatively and proximately in events, not to know or master them from beginning to end or start to finish."[35] Nonetheless, Connolly sneaks the autonomy of the political back in, even as he converts it to a matter of ethos and of a nonsovereign player amid other nonsovereign powers. By conceptually dethroning all aspirants to sovereignty—from capital to the nation-state to (Hardt's and Negri's conception of) Empire—through revealing the ambivalence, porousness, and oscillation in each, they become available to redirection by citizen micropolitics and "the institutionally embedded ethos flowing into [them]." Nothing is in control of itself, nothing is supreme or autonomous and hence sovereign; therefore redirection is possible. There is no god, no controlling or final power anywhere; therefore all possibilities are open. Ethos and micropolitics matter *because and insofar as* sovereignty is revealed as the emperor who has no clothes. Connolly's theological relationship to the crisis of sovereignty lies in his atheistic rejection of sovereignty, which results in a continued conflation of power and trajectory with agency and design.

Despite important differences among these thinkers, they share the conviction—explicitly stated by Balibar and Habermas—that politics can obtain primacy over economics (again) in service to democratic aims. Aside from the complicated question of what democracy could mean at the transnational or global level, this conviction presumes: (1) that political sovereignty ever had this primacy—in other words, that the conceit of autonomy was real, a presumption contradicting even heavily reconstructed materialist premises; (2) that there are democratic forms capable of overcoming global capital's radically undemocratic thrust; (3) that global capital can be subordinated to political ends antagonistic to its interests, that it is a subduable force, capable of being dominated by the political rather than the other way round; (4) that global capital can be harnessed for socially and ecologically progressive ends and *thrive*, meaning that the imperatives of capitalist growth are not inherently tethered to its history of social and ecological plunder; (5) that such harnessing in the North, even if it were possible, would not further offload the socially deracinating, economically inegalitarian, politically de-democratizing, and ecologically devastating effects of global capital onto the South, meaning that the democratic project could be a global one rather than one limited to the European Union and other regions of the North.[36]

Certainly it is possible to imagine sovereign political decisions in the North that contain or defer the ravaging effects of globalization on the nature of work, employment levels, urban planning, social welfare, and local ecology. Indeed, a desire for this containment was a significant element in the recent French and Dutch votes against the European Constitution. But even if these kinds of political efforts can stem certain currents of globalization locally and temporarily, they cannot actually acquire control over the economy. Rather, they can resist in the short run what competitiveness will require either submitting to in the medium run or deflecting to other sites in the globe.

I do not have a solution to the political problem of the emerging global sovereignty of capital—or if one prefers, capital's supervenience of political sovereignty. My concern in this chapter has been with how and whether we confront this problem in a manner that abandons the fictional autonomy of the political sustained in and by the discourse of sovereignty in western modernity. The fiction of autonomy, resurrected in different ways by Habermas, Balibar, and Connolly, makes clear that neither secularism nor atheism provides inoculations against the theology of political sovereignty. Habermas's left Kantianism is as susceptible to it as Connolly's Deleuzian liberalism or Balibar's Spinozist post-Marxism. If the work of these critical intellectuals fails to come to terms with what I am suggesting is the supreme power of our time, a power that their work despairs of capturing or vanquishing, it is unsurprising that they share an investment in a fantasy of the resurrected potency of the political even if each etches the particulars of the fantasy differently. Their problem is our problem.

NOTES

1 See for example Jens Bartelson, *A Genealogy of Sovereignty* (Cambridge: Cambridge University Press), 16–17, 24; and Jacques Derrida, *Rogues: Two Essays on Reason*, trans. M. Brault and P. A. Naas (Stanford: Stanford University Press, 2005), 15.

2 "Partial sovereignty" was described by the U.S. Department of State as the goal for Iraq in 2005. Derrida insists that sovereignty is always already partial and disunified. See *Rogues*.

3 The extreme of this appears in Rousseau, whose placement of the people's sovereignty and the state's power in two different books of the *Social Contract* has confused novice readers for millennia.

4 Connolly works to finesse this problem by positing what he variously terms ambiguity, equivocation, and oscillation in sovereignty in general and an "uncertain circulation" in the sovereignty characteristic of democratic constitutional states. *Pluralism* (Durham: Duke University Press, 2005), 141. According to Connolly, there is an "equivocation inside the idea of sovereignty between acting with final authority and acting with irresistible effect," an "oscillation between a juridical authority that decides the exception . . . and other cultural forces that insert themselves irresistibly into the outcome," the "[uncertain circulation of sovereignty] between authoritative sites of enunciation and irresistible forces of power," and, "in democratic constitutional states, sovereignty['s] circulat[ion] between the multitude, traditions infused into it, and constitutionally sanctioned authorities" (140–41). Each of these claims is aimed at deconstructing and debunking the conceptual bid of sovereignty to represent an independent and supreme power. They are ways of saying that sovereignty as it has been defined by others does not really *exist* but is at best the conditioned site of a conditioned decision. This approach to sovereignty is part and parcel of Connolly's larger rejection of systems, logics, and absolutes in both language and politics.

5 Schmitt also calls sovereignty a "borderline concept" but means something else by this annotation: "a borderline concept is not a vague concept, but one pertaining to the outermost sphere. This definition of sovereignty [Sovereign is he who decides on the exception] must therefore be associated with a borderline case and not with routine." *Political Theology: Four Chapters on the Concept of Sovereignty*, trans. George Schwab (Cambridge: MIT Press, 1985), 5.

6 *Webster's College Dictionary* gives "supreme power especially over a political unit" as the first definition of sovereignty and "freedom from external control" as the second. *Webster's College Dictionary* (New York: Barnes and Noble, 2003), 872.

7 Liberalism seeks to split the supremacy from the autonomy, the power of the people from the action of the state. But as already suggested, in so doing liberalism disavows the nonsupremacy of the demos at the moment of sovereign state action. It disavows the inherently antidemocratic moment in the

production of state autonomy—not only the incoherence of submitting autonomy to the rule of law but the incoherence of generating autonomy from dispersion or disunity. Moreover, insofar as internal and external dangers are what activate the state, when these dangers become persistent or permanent, the outside turns inward, taking the form of lawless autonomous action directed toward the populace and subordinating to unify the populace in order to produce itself.

8 See Bartelson, *Genealogy of Sovereignty*, 28, 48.

9 Bush made a major political gaffe in discussing Native American sovereignty when he said that the federal government "gave" the Native Americans sovereignty over themselves.

10 This claim differs substantially from Hardt's and Negri's thesis that sovereignty entails the conjoining of the political and the economic, the service of the former to the latter, or economic content and political form, and that it is borne of secularism.

11 For Carl Schmitt, the friend-enemy distinction is the ultimate and singular distinction that defines the political, expressing not merely its essence but what marks its difference from other fields. See Carl Schmitt, *The Concept of the Political*, trans. George Schwab (Chicago: University of Chicago Press, 1996), 26.

12 Schmitt acknowledges that political enmity may acquire a moral, juridical, or economic character—but that this acquisition is secondary *if* the enmity is political. See *The Concept of the Political*, 38.

13 All anxieties about the "death of the political" center on the erosion of its autonomy, purity, or sovereignty. For Weber this threat came from bureaucracy and rationalization, for Arendt it came from the social, for Machiavelli it came from religion, and so on.

14 Here is John Stuart Mill in the opening of Book 4 of *On Liberty*: "What, then, is the rightful limit to the sovereignty of the individual over himself? Where does the authority of society begin? How much of human life should be assigned to individuality, and how much to society?" (New York: Hackett, 1978), 73; or consider Thomas Hobbes's argument in *Leviathan* that the individual is free where "the laws are silent," or John Locke's efforts to delineate the respective jurisdictions of religious and state authority in the *Letter on Toleration*.

15 This would seem to erode one of the crucial distinctions that Foucault uses to hold sovereignty apart from biopower, and suggests instead that sovereignty sometimes operates in the modality of biopower.

16 In his unique origin story for the social contract in *What Is the Third Estate?*, Abbé Sieyès explicitly features sovereignty as emerging to manage the political life of *homo oeconomicus* and yet detaching from its economic origins as it does so. This detachment takes an explicitly theological form. My gratitude goes to Asaf Kedar for bringing this to my attention in a first-rate graduate seminar paper.

17 *Empire* (Cambridge: Harvard University Press, 2000), 85–86. Hardt and Negri assert this without showing it, and it appears more as a Marxist reflex than anything else.

18 Schmitt, *Political Theology*, 37.

19 Hobbes, Introduction, *Leviathan*, ed. C. B. MacPherson (London: Penguin, 1981), 81.

20 See Norman Jacobson, "Behold Leviathan!," *Pride and Solace: The Functions and Limits of Political Theory* (Berkeley: University of California Press, 1977), 53–54.

21 Hobbes, *Leviathan*, 81.

22 Ibid., chapter 13, 185.

23 Asaf Kedar showed me the political-economic basis for the social contract in Sieyès's essay.

24 Consider these lines from *What Is the Third Estate?*:

> The nation exists prior to everything; it is the origin of everything. Its will is always legal. It is the law itself.
>
> A nation is all that it can be simply by virtue of being what it is.
>
> However a nation may will, it is enough for it to will. Every form is good, and its will is always the supreme law.
>
> A nation is independent of all forms and, however it may will, it is enough for its will to be made known for all positive law to fall silent in its presence, because it is the source and supreme master of all positive law.

25 In the following account of American actions abroad, note Bush's striking conflations of God and state, authorship and interpellation, sovereign utterances and holy truth: "I believe the United States is *the* beacon for freedom in the world. And I believe we have a responsibility to promote freedom. [But] freedom is not America's gift to the world. Freedom is God's gift to everybody in the world. I believe that. As a matter of fact, I was the person that wrote the line, or said it. I didn't write it, I just said it in a speech. And it became part of the jargon. And I believe that. And I believe we have a duty to free people." George W. Bush, speaking to Bob Woodward in Woodward, *Plan of Attack* (New York: Simon and Schuster, 2004), 88–89.

26 For the neoliberals, "democracy" is identified with the embrace of this sovereign. Their designation of Iraq as a democracy, amid its political and economic rebuilding conducted entirely by corporate managers, is only one of the more blatant examples. See Wendy Brown, "Neoliberalism and the End of Liberal Democracy," *Theory and Event: A Journal of Cultural and Political Theory* 5, no. 1.

27 Habermas, *Postnational Constellations: Political Essays*, trans. Max Pensky (Cambridge: MIT Press, 2001), 107, 109, 110, 111.

28 Ibid., 111–12.

29 Balibar, *We the People of Europe? Reflections on Transnational Citizenship*, trans. J. Swenson (Princeton: Princeton University Press, 2004), 147, 9.

30 Ibid., 173.
31 Ibid., 174, 178.
32 Connolly, *Pluralism*, 143.
33 Ibid., 145.
34 Ibid., 158 (italics added).
35 Ibid.
36 Pheng Cheah has written a searing indictment of the antidemocratic implica-
    tions of the literal Eurocentrism underlying Habermas's vision. See "Post-
    national Light," a chapter in *Inhuman Conditions: Cosmopolitanism and Human
    Rights in the Current Conjuncture* (Cambridge: Harvard University Press, 2006).

BECOMING CONNOLLY:
CRITIQUE, CROSSING OVER, AND CONCEPTS

James Der Derian

CONNOLLY AND CRITIQUE

ANY ACCOUNT OF William Connolly's work needs to engage the function of the author in the context of critique. Authorial intention and audience reception: it is not such a strange place to begin, given Connolly's focus on how identity is formed through difference as well as a career dogged—if not defined—by controversy. But it is not the easiest strategy: criticism is often ambiguous, not always transparent, and critics—like authors—move with the times.

For instance, criticism can take the form of neutral observation, like (and not unlike this one): "he certainly writes a lot." Having now revisited the Connolly corpus, from *The Terms of Political Discourse* (1975) to *Pluralism* (2005), as well as the welter of articles, chapters, and reviews written in the interim, I do have some sympathy for this view—but much less so when this amounts to *all* that someone might have to say about Connolly's work, leaving instead only a sentiment that when it comes to the production of knowledge, less is more.[1] As Connolly has demonstrated—as aptly as any philosopher since Nietzsche—such metaphors masquerading as truths usually express a deeper *ressentiment* that derives and sustains much of its power from the unwillingness of the target to appear as petty as his critic. That said, I imagine that if Connolly were back in his hometown of Flint, Michigan, and if there were an assembly line that had not yet gone south, and if there were still a card-carrying union member to be found, and if at the sight of Connolly he was heard to mutter, "Stakhonovite," Connolly would most likely punch him, in a playful but not necessarily metaphorical manner. Truth be told, Connolly enjoys counterpunching, and not always in kind.

Critics also take issue with Connolly's bravura epistemological leaps: just when the reader has finally got up to speed with Connolly's post-Marxist, Habermasian turn in the 1970s, they discover him off and running-at-the-mouth about Foucault in the 1980s, getting deeper into Deleuze and the grey-matter of amygdalic politics in the 1990s, and re-discovering the timelessness of Spinoza, Proust, Bergson, and James in the twenty-first century. This has prompted more than one lagging fellow traveler to throw at Connolly—not unlike the audiences' response when Bob Dylan went electric—the epithet "traitor." And very much like Dylan, Connolly has just played it faster, looser, and louder.

Then there is the sheer complexity of Connolly's thought. A tactic favored by the less sympathetic critic (not me), or by one *merely* wishing to exemplify this tactic (now me), is to excerpt out of context a dense paragraph or a less-than-limpid phrase, like "participants in the theo-teleological tradition are wise to link their reading of corporeo-cultural life to an ethic of cultivation over a morality of command."[2] As the reader's head spins, the critic proceeds to dismiss the body of work as needlessly difficult or obscurantist, and therefore not worth the effort. This was one of several strategies symptomatic of the "theory wars" in the 1980s, when continental philosophy began to infiltrate the social sciences. Although many in the field kept a safe distance by declaring it all a fad, hoping that in time it would just fade away, the critics continued to base their critique on secondary literature (rarely rising above the sloganeering of "po-mo-has-got-to-go"), rather than engaging with the primary writings, including Connolly's. In the midst of these wars Connolly never backed down; he meticulously took apart these disciplinary practices, memorably referring to them as "a strategy of condemnation by refraction."[3]

And finally, critics often have a problem with Connolly's politics, both with a small "p" and a big "P." Connolly has never run from an academic or political fight, and indeed has started a few; moreover, as an outspoken critical intellectual, he has taken on hot-button issues like abortion, gay rights, the wars in Vietnam and Iraq, and a whole host of dangerous, deceitful, and other anti-democratic practices of past and current administrations.[4] And he has done so with off-balanced questions and counter-arguments that have avoided the usual descent into ideological cant, from the left or right.[5]

I cite and address these criticisms because many scholars first (and only) came to know Connolly's work through his critics' rather than his own writings. However, Connolly's high productivity, relentless intellectual counter-punching, and restless political engagement made short work of these efforts. Moreover, his critical pedagogy yielded a second generation of scholars who, informed by continental philosophy and motivated by the most pressing political issues, were not about to duck a fight. Some called them "Connolly clones"—perhaps another sign of critical envy but also a major reason why his ideas stay forever young.

However, before anyone starts painting heroic Diego Rivera murals on the walls of the Academy, some self-criticism and disciplinary perspective are in order. A few of us did get a little drunk on theory in the 1980s. This is more understandable in International Relations (IR) theory, which has always been marked, as Martin Wight famously put it, by "paucity" as well as "intellectual and moral poverty." It also helps to explain why so many of us, having found the keys to the cabinet of continental thought, came to rely on Connolly, for his analytical punch came without the debilitating hangover of more exuberant writers like Baudrillard, Virilio, and others hyerventilating about hyperreality, hypermodernity, the *hyper-marché*. Connolly, already a veteran of the theory wars in political science, was able to outflank many of the early contretemps in IR that passed as intellectual debates. He never got bogged down in parsing what "post-modernism" is—a term that enjoys the curious utility of transparent meaning for some and utter meaninglessness for others—preferring in-stead to treat postmodernism as an event and a paradoxical symptom of a more general condition. And when a variety of temperance unions sprung up, more so in the United States than in the United Kingdom—where the classical school's preference for philosophy over methodology and the tolerance for marxoid tippling opened up a critical space—Connolly pro-vided some of the best counter-polemics of the day, mainly through his writings but also through a series of exemplary public speaking events.[6]

CONNOLLY CROSSES OVER

Connolly, more than any of his peers, created a post-Marxist brand of theory-as-practice that methodologically, critically, and aesthetically cut across the traditional disciplines, subfields, and arbitrary fact-value di-vides of the social sciences. This supra-disciplinarity is why (along with wanting to pander to a senior colleague) I first asked him to participate in a variety of international relations events, starting with a double panel at the meeting of the International Studies Association in Washington in 1987 that became the basis for the collected volume *International/ Intertextual Relations*.[7] Long before constructivism rendered continental thought safe for the discipline of international relations, Connolly was tracking the mutually constitutive link between theory and a wide range of social and political practices.

Connolly quickly established himself as a crossover scholar, opening new intellectual and political spaces as well as providing professional opportunities for those of us in international relations who did not "fit" in the conventional boxes of political science. He did this in several ways, most of which adeptly combined philosophical critique, political insights, and empirical examples to produce strategic interventions in the most important contemporary debates. Presenting international theory as the necessary enabler and supplement of global politics, Connolly put into practice Gilles Deleuze's dictum that theory should be worthy of the event.[8] In less nimble hands this can come off as a bumper-sticker slogan. But Connolly transformed the dictum into a replicable plan of theoretical intervention by creating an armory of critical concepts that disturbed the core conventions of international relations. In the process he extracted seemingly fixed states of being—most notably (as we shall see) sovereignty as a necessitous effect of anarchy—and reinterpreted and rehistoricized them as pluralist states of becoming. In his theoretical mimicry of contemporary forces of deterritorialization, Connolly provided intellectual traction for ethical and political responses to crimes—petty and felonious —against humanity.

Connolly confronted head-on the chorus of critics who maintained that there were no ethics to continental philosophy—or worse, that it advocated or contributed to relativist or nihilist positions. By his account relativism, or "the breath of empty space," as Nietzsche poetically put it, has always been with us, in spite of the diligent efforts by philosophers, priests, and politicians to keep it at bay with first principles, transcendental commands, and patriotic absolutes. From Connolly I learned the value of "deep contestability" as a method of historicizing responses to show how the metaphysical desire for the last word and highest truth had prompted similar attacks in the past.[9] In Connolly's hands, the charge of relativism was a goad for challenging the politics of stasis.

Connolly held that we cannot help being relativists if we are to under-stand—without resort to external authorities or transcendental values—why one moral or political system attains a higher status and exercises more influence than another at a particular historical moment. This is why he described in several works how the current worry of academics about relativism was "untimely"; indeed, their acts of theoretical closure and nostalgia for lost certainties revealed an anxiety about the openness of late modernity: "Nor is relativism the consummate danger in the late-modern world, where every culture intersects with most others in econo-mies of interdependence, exchange, and competition. Relativism is an invention of academics who yearn for a type of unity that probably never existed, who worry about an alienation from established culture that seldom finds sufficient opportunity to get off the ground, and who insist that ethical discourse cannot proceed unless it locates its authority in a transcendental command."[10] In contrast to the higher authorities, Con-nolly locates his ethics in and through the construction and contestabil-ity of subjectivity. Ethics does not reside outside as a set of principles to guide individual behavior, but as a prior and necessary condition for identity formation.[11] In *Identity\Difference* (and following the subtle logic of the backward-slash in the title), ethics is always already an interdepen-dent relationship that begins with the recognition of the need for the other and of the need for the other's recognition. It proceeds from an interdependency of caring and responsibility that cannot be separated from the pluralism and relativism of living with multiple identities. An ethical way of being emerges when we recognize the very necessity of heterogeneity for understanding ourselves and others through a critical responsiveness.

Connolly also made short work of the claim that he and other theorists of late modernity were seeking to reduce everything to a linguistic prac-tice, to claim that there is no truth, no values, no reality. He exposed the double game played by many of his critics, in which they confused or conflated a critique of epistemic realism with a rejection of reality. In this manner they would not need to deal with the "no-thing" at the center; instead the foundationalists relied on the "McGuffin" (to borrow from one of Connolly's favorite directors, Alfred Hitchcock) of an external be-ing, supreme epistemology, or total theory that proved, adjudicated, veri-fied an existence or truth independent of its representation. Connolly was not a proponent of "all is permitted" or "all is relative," but of "all is contestable," in recognition that the most pernicious truths are the effects of unchallenged interpretations (think no further than the fear and deceit that plagues the "Global War on Terror" and that prompted the Iraq war). Connolly proceeds from an abiding suspicion of power and knowledge that elevates one truth over another, that legitimates and subjects one identity against another, that presents social formations as natural conditions, that makes, in short, one discourse matter more than the next. His goals were radical: to de-territorialize not just such truth-claims but the politics of sovereignty as well.

But one criticism lingers. Could this not all be said more simply? At the disciplinary level, this question and others like it too often reflect the continuing domination of an epistemic realism as well as an aesthetic sensibility in the social sciences—from its logical positivist to rational choice forms—which holds that the most parsimonious statement most accurately, usefully, and artlessly expresses a thought or reflects an event. At the level of common sense, this sensibility suggests a natural preference for conceptual rigor and clarity. It also reflects in conservative quarters a longing for simpler times expressed in simpler terms; and as so often with nostalgia, those commonsensical times are often more imaginary than real. This issue dominated many of the earliest crossover gatherings among international and political theorists. I remember it surfacing at one of the earliest occasions, a meeting of the ISA in Washington in 1987, at which Connolly acted as a panel discussant.[12] I am not sure who on the panel made the remark, but one of us likened it to the conversations often overheard at an art gallery when standing in front of a cubist, abstract expressionist, or other avant-garde work of art. Someone invariably says, "I could do that," and in the same breath, "not that I would want to." Of course few can, and worse, many do not know why they cannot—nor why they would not wish to. All too often, what one lacks in capability is cloaked as a lack of will. But I suspect that more is going on here. In other words Connolly tries to get closer to the constraints of meaning, to understanding the aporia, or gap between rhetoric and rationality that invariably opens up when a critical language is applied to the various constructions of language. This "making strange" through language is therefore meant to disturb. Why its continental, rhetorical form should be more disturbing than its positivist, modeled form is for the most part a matter of acceptable styles and disciplinary practices.[13]

Enmeshed in a similar debate in the 1960s about the "dangerous language" of the "new criticism," Roland Barthes launched an attack on the ideological assumptions that were implicit in the call for clarity. His response to his critics helps us to understand why traditional social science theory seems perennially predisposed to an epistemological status quo: "When a word like dangerous is applied to ideas, language or art, it immediately signals a desire to return to the past . . . Discourse reflecting upon discourse is the object of a special vigilance on the part of institutions, which normally contain it within the limits of a strict code: in the literary State, criticism must be controlled as much as a police force is: to free the one would be quite as 'dangerous' as democratizing the other: it would be to threaten the power of power, the language of language."[14]

CONNOLLY CONCEPTUALIZES

Like Barthes, Connolly mapped the contiguities of language, power, and subjectivity through the concept of sovereignty. Indeed, his effort to decenter the sovereign positions of signs, self, and state is seamless and central to his work. He tirelessly shows how sovereignty exists as a sign of another sign, and how its real presence, if ever a historical "fact," gave way in the face of global forces to simulated appearance. Through his close readings of Ashley, Shapiro, Walker, Campbell, Weber, Constantinou, and others, he interprets IR in particular as being in a constant process of construction through discursive and performative acts of diplomacy, statecraft, and intervention. Theory is inseparable from the production of sovereignty, the state, and the subject, and as such is always already a political practice. Theorization is not a substitute for action or an excuse for quietism: without any givens, without any self-evident subjects, there is always something to decide, to do, to become.

Connolly shares with Deleuze not only an event-driven theory but also an appreciation of how relative the significance of the event is to the conceptual interventions of the theorist. But Connolly goes further, recognizing that neither theory nor sovereignty can sustain self-generated myths of autonomy and supremacy. Beset by multiple actors, international capital, transnational conflicts, and ubiquitous media, all events, from climate change to Saddam Hussein's hanging, go global in near real time. The global event is particularly, even peculiarly resistant to mono-

disciplinary theorization; and indeed, no single theory might ever quite
be worthy enough of the global event (like Wayne and Garth upon meeting Alice Cooper). This simple fact more than justifies Connolly's endorsement of critical, pluralist approaches. Nonetheless, Connolly would
be criticized—often in that ultra-leftist way of attacking most vociferously
those closest to your own view—as being insufficiently materialist: he did
not fully appreciate the power of capitalism and other, more tangible
forces of production and destruction. He was too little a realist, too much
the virtualist, but always a pluralist. Fair enough: but I did wonder what
these critics thought upon reading the remarkable story in the *New York
Times Sunday Magazine*, published shortly before the presidential elections
of 2004, in which Ron Suskind recounted his conversation with an aide to
President Bush: "The aide said that guys like me were 'in what we call the
reality-based community,' which he defined as people who 'believe that
solutions emerge from your judicious study of discernible reality.' I nod-
ded and murmured something about enlightenment principles and empiricism. He cut me off. 'That's not the way the world really works any-
more,' he continued. 'We're an empire now, and when we act, we create
our own reality. And while you're studying that reality—judiciously, as
you will—we'll act again, creating other new realities, which you can study
too, and that's how things will sort out. We're history's actors . . . and you,
all of you, will be left to just study what we do.'"[15] As an injudicious
theorist, Connolly might not feel wholly vindicated; but he does seem
more politically attuned than many of his social scientific brethren to the
virtualized nature of the beast.

   In a kind of rapid response to the morphing of supposedly sovereign truths, Connolly deployed an arsenal of critical concepts. Like Foucault's genealogical *dispositif* and Deleuze's nomadological *rhizome*, Connolly coined comparable concepts to warp—or as he might put it, to "am-
biguate"—our conventional, commonsensical views of a world that is now
lived in the logic and at the speed of cinema, video, and internet. As
Deleuze worked to make theory politically worthy of the event, so too has
Connolly turned the study and generation of concepts into new forms
that could *keep up* with the heavily mediated global event. Indeed, as
traditional theory strains to comprehend the accelerated pace of social
practices, Connolly became our premier coiner as well as connoisseur of
political concepts. Savoring the power of such concepts to constitute as

well as describe reality, he does on occasion overstate the prospects of a global politics democratized by conceptual acts of deterritorialization. But Connolly undeniably provides a way of (be)coming closer to that goal. In his later work he increasingly does so by becoming cinematic.

BECOMING CONNOLLY

Few theorists use cinema to such powerful interpretive effect as Connolly. In several of his writings he pairs the films of Welles, Hitchcock, Kubrick, Figgis, Linklater, and others to cinematic writers like Deleuze, Virilio, and Shaviro, to delve into complex issues of space-time, perception, memory, faith, and feeling—hardly the usual terrain of the political theorist. At times the mix reads like a lucid dream, in which Connolly's weaving of alternative realities come to displace the commonplace truths (and lies) of everyday life. We know we are in a dream-state, and yet, through his invocation of a cinematic, fictive presence, we begin to question the reality of the linear, factual world we have left behind, where words transparently mirror objects, facts reside apart from values, and theory is independent of the reality which it represents. Caught somewhere between Hitchcock's and Connolly's treatment of vertigo (and dare I add, U2's high-kicking musical version of it), the reader gains new insights into the relationships of memory to perception, pleasure to power, seduction to danger.

Inspired by Connolly, and as a final tribute to his style (defined by Derrida as the author's will to power in the text), I want to conclude by *becoming Connolly*. This is not the same as *being Bill*: the aim is to be neither him nor me, here nor there, but through Connolly's conceptual cosmos to become different, creative of rather than dependent upon the actual: in other, Deleuzean terms, to get (virtually) real. We know from another film, *Being John Malkovich*, just how easily the desire to *be* different through others can degenerate into celebrity worship, exoticism, and ultimately, puppetry. Our desire to control others is all-too-easily mimicked. Here Nietzsche, channeled through Connolly, is instructive. Life is a contest of wills and a desire for recognition. Under conditions of freedom, the will to power can be an active and affirmative force that pits individuals against themselves, not others, in an act of self-overcoming. But freedom comes with an attendant cost: radical contingency, indeterminacy, and all the anxieties of late modern life. We might seek security through faith, rationality, sovereignty, but the "will to a system" that once provided security now ends up corrupting life; rather than a self-becoming and mastery over oneself, the will to power deteriorates into a desire to master others. Repressed, domesticated, and bureaucratized by the dominant system of modernity, the nation-state, the will to power produces all kinds of pathologies: "madness is rare among individuals," says Nietzsche, "in entire nations it is common."[16] Take the Sovereign State (and, as I cannot help adding in the spirit of Henny Youngman, "*Please*"). To keep us safe, we place our faith in national borders and guards, bureaucracies and experts, technologies and armies. These and other instruments of national security are empowered and legitimated by the assumption that it falls upon the sovereign state to protect us from the turbulence of nature and anarchy that permanently lies in wait offshore and over the horizon for the unprepared and inadequately defended.

These parochial hopes and fears, posing as a realistic worldview, have recently taken some very hard knocks. Indeed, a catastrophe is often needed for the world to catch up to Connolly, who has over the course of his career so aptly exposed the illusory nature of the beliefs that we continue to harbor in the concepts of national (now backslash) homeland security. And at the top of this holy writ of illusion remains the concept of sovereignty itself. Before 9/11 national borders were thought necessary and sufficient to keep our enemies at bay; upon entry to Baghdad, a virtuous triumphalism and a revolution in military affairs were touted as the best means to bring peace and democracy to the Middle East; and before Hurricane Katrina, emergency preparedness and an intricate system of levees were supposed to keep New Orleans safe and dry.

The intractability of disaster, especially its unexpected, unplanned, unprecedented nature, erodes not only the very distinction of the local, national, and global but, assisted and amplified by an unblinking global media, reveals the contingent and highly interconnected character of life in general. Yet when it comes to dealing with natural and unnatural disasters, we continue to expect (and in the absence of a credible alternative, understandably so) if not certainty and total safety at least a high level of probability and competence from our national and homeland security experts. Sovereignty would appear to be indefensible; yet it remains indispensable.

Consider (this empirical signage piles up in Connolly's writing's, much like the detritus of history that drives Walter Benjamin's angel of progress backwards into the future), the words of the homeland security director Michael Chertoff on this weighty matter: "At a news conference, Mr. Chertoff called the hurricane and subsequent flooding, an 'ultra-catastrophe' that exceeded the foresight of planners. Asked what the government's response signified about the nation's preparedness for a potential terrorist attack, Mr. Chertoff said, 'If an ultra-catastrophe occurs, there's going to be some harmful fallout.'"[17] Between the mixed metaphors and behind the metaphysical concepts expressed early in the crisis by Chertoff, there lurks an uneasy recognition that this administration—and perhaps any national government—is not up to the task of managing national incidents capable of rapidly cascading into global events. Indeed, they suggest that our national plans and preparations for the "big one"—a force-five hurricane, terrorist attack, pandemic disease—have become part of the problem, not the solution. Chertoff's use of hyberbolic terms like "ultra-catastrophe" and "fallout" is telling: such events exceed not only local and national capabilities but the capacity of conventional language itself.

An easy deflection would be to lay the blame on the neoconservative faithful of Bush's first term, who in viewing through an inverted Wilsonian prism the world as they would wish it to be have now been forced by natural and unnatural disasters to face the world as it really is—and not even the most sophisticated public affairs machine of dissimulations, distortions, and lies, can close this gap. However, the discourse of Bush's second term has increasingly returned to the dominant worldview of national security: realism. And if language is, as Nietzsche claimed, a prison house, realism is its supermax penitentiary. Or as Connolly once put it while acting as a discussant for another panel of the ISA and offering his own critique of the "contemporary unrealism of territorial democracy": "There is always more in the world than any hegemonic discourse officially acknowledges and the political effects of these closures can be dangerous, destructive, and cruel to that which exceeds the terms of their constitution."[18] Based on linear notions of causality, a correspondence theory of truth, and the independence of power from discourse, how can a state-bound realism possibly account for—let alone prepare or provide remedies for—complex global catastrophes like the toppling of the World Trade Center and the attack on the Pentagon by a handful of jihadists armed with box cutters and a few months of flight training? A force-five hurricane that might well have begun with the flapping of a butterfly's wings? An electrical blackout on the East Coast that started with a falling tree limb in Ohio? A possible pandemic triggered by the mutation of an avian virus? Events of such complex, nonlinear origins have such tightly coupled, quantum effects—how, for instance, are we to measure the immaterial power of the CNN effect on the first Gulf War, the Al-Jazeera effect on the Iraq War, the Nokia effect on the terrorist bombings in London, or the "You Tube" effect on the hanging of Saddam Hussein? The national security discourse of realism is inadequate.

Worse, what if the "failure of imagination" identified by the 9/11 Commission is built into our national and homeland security systems? What if our reliance on planning for the catastrophe that never came reduced our capability to flexibly respond and improvise for the "ultracatastrophe" that did? What if worst-case scenarios, simulation training, and disaster exercises, as well as border guards, concrete barriers, and earthen levees, not only prove inadequate but act as force multipliers—organizational theorists refer to "negative synergy" and "cascading effects"—producing automated bungling (think FEMA) that transforms isolated events and singular attacks into global disasters? Just as "normal accidents" are built into new technologies—in response to disasters ranging from the sinking of the *Titanic* to the meltdown of Chernobyl to the explosion of the space shuttle *Challenger*—we must ask whether "ultracatastrophes" are no longer the exception but now part and parcel of densely networked systems that defy national management; in other words, "planned disasters." What, in other words, if Virilio, Deleuze, and Connolly are right?

Unlike many critics, Connolly does show us a way to move beyond the wheel-spinning debates that perennially keep security discourse always one step behind the global event. The power configuration of the states system may well have been uni-, bi-, or multipolar, but it is time to recognize—and time to coin a new concept and totally become Connolly—that it is rapidly being subsumed by a *heteropolar matrix*, in which a wide range of actors and technological drivers are producing profound global effects through interconnectivity. Varying in identity, interests, and strength, these new actors and drivers gain advantage through the broad bandwidth of information technology, for networked IT provides the means to traverse political, economic, religious, and cultural boundaries, not only changing how we interpret events but making it ever more difficult to maintain the very distinction of intended events from accidental ones. Cinema projects and confirms this heteropolarity better than any journal article or think-tank paper: consider *Traffic*, *The Constant Gardener*, *Syriana*, *Blood Diamonds*, and others among the rash of recently released political films.

Decrying the weakness of Weimar liberalism (and eventually becoming a member of the Nazi party), the legal philosopher Carl Schmitt defined the concept of sovereignty by the exception. When the state is unable to deliver on its traditional promissory notes of safety, security, and well-being through legal, democratic means, it will necessarily exercise the sovereign "exception": declaring a state of emergency, distinguishing friend from foe, and if necessary eradicating the threat to the state. But what now, when the state, facing the global event, cannot discern the accidental from the intentional? An external attack from an internal auto-immune response? The natural as opposed to the "planned disaster"? The enemy within from the enemy without?

Once the solution was cast as barbarism or socialism. But now—as global capitalism waxes and sovereignty wanes—what? We can, as the United States has done since 9/11, continue to treat catastrophic threats as issues of national rather than global security, and go it alone. However, national states of emergency, once declared, bureaucratically installed, and repetitively gamed, grow recalcitrant and prone to even worse disasters. As Paul Virilio, master theorist of the war machine and the integral accident, once told me: "The full-scale accident is now the prolongation of total war by other means." Every new complex technology and network produces its own form of accident, and the interconnectedness of global capitalism defies sovereign management and rational actor theory. If anything, sovereignty—in the way that organizational theorists speak of "normal accidents"—contributes to the "planned disasters" of Iraq, Katrina, Darfur, and the next global event, be it a currency failure, pandemic, or computer virus. Multilateral and not unilateral actions, coalitions of the caring and not just the willing, will be needed to get us out of current and pending predicaments.

CLOSING ON CONNOLLY

In the end, what have we—Connolly and his admirers—become? Apocalyptic doomsayers? Mimetic critics of modernity? Tenured rebels without a cause? Perhaps. Given the times as well as the allure of the courtier life, there are probably worse things to become. But as distinctions of time and distance, near and the far, fact and fiction blur and collapse in late modernity, as some strive to keep up and others to slow down, the old labels seem out of date and out of synch. Michael Shapiro, a fount of "po-mo" and other anecdotes, recounts somewhere how Michel Foucault, when asked whether he was a postmodernist, replied that he wasn't sure if he was sufficiently up to date to know. William Connolly—crossover conceptualist of becoming—similarly defies definition. But as for "Bill"—a man who lives his credo more than any scholar I know—the care that we put into our relationships with others, domestically and globally, defines us more than any other quality. And since one would not wish him an enemy, I call him my friend.

NOTES

I want to thank Joan Cocks for very useful criticisms, and the editors for their comments and support.

1 When I started my job in 1984 at the University of Massachusetts, Amherst, as an assistant professor Connolly offered me a great deal of advice, some of it solicited, much of it on the rites and taboos of the political science discipline, and all of it useful. This essay follows his early enjoinder that whatever I wrote should appear first in a journal, then as chapter in an edited volume, and eventually in my own book. This proved to be good professional advice, both in the interests of reaching the widest audience and in recognition that the first draft is rarely the best version. I also found it sympathetic to a critical perspective captured by the Situationist slogan "Plagiarism is necessary: Progress implies it"; by Walter Benjamin's endorsement of montage as "citation without quotation"; and by Roland Barthes's infamous take on the "death of the author," which holds there are no original or final texts, only iterated versions subject to multiple interpretations by the reader. In this spirit, this essay is a montage of new and old writings that draw on and attempt to take Connolly's work into new areas of inquiry, including international and media studies.

2 Connolly, *Neuropolitics: Thinking, Culture, Speed* (Minneapolis: University of Minnesota Press, 2002), 17.

3 Connolly directly addresses the application of this strategy in international relations theory by Kenneth Waltz, Robert Keohane, and others in "Global Political Discourses," *Identity\Difference: Democratic Negotiations of Political Paradox* (Ithaca: Cornell University Press, 1991), 49–63.

4 Connolly has even earned the wrath of the bloggers in this regard, having recently received the honor of "Academic of the Month" in Hatemongers

Quarterly, a blog site dedicated to outing "tenured radicals." See http://hate mongersquarterly.blogspot.com/.

5 When facing some intractable political issue or a delicate departmental matter, his was the first office I would go to (after which I would proceed directly to Jean Elshtain's for a reality check).

6 Many of us fell for the bait and spent a lot of time responding to theoretical attacks, *only* counterpunching rather than getting to the punch line. Connolly held his own in this war and continues to do so; but he was never one to let his critics *wholly* determine the path of his critical inquiry. He lived his concepts; and I suspect that his notions of "agonistic respect" and "critical responsiveness" helped keep him intellectually engaged with his interlocuters yet free of the *ressentiment* that antagonized and self-marginalized many from both sides of the debates. He actively engaged behavioralism in the 1970s, rational choice theory in the 1990s (which, as editor of *Political Theory*, he once described as the "continuation of behavorialism by other means"), and the anti-theory backlash which, by labeling young proponents of continental philosophy "relativists" or even "nihilists," effectively avoided any serious engagement with their ideas.

7 *International/Intertextual Relations: Postmodern Readings of World Politics*, ed. James Der Derian and Michael Shapiro (Lexington, Mass.: Lexington, 1989), 323–42. It should be noted that our sympathetic series editor, James Rosenau, thought that the book required the "Postmodern" tag in the subtitle, and won out over the objections of the volume editors.

8 "Philosophy's sole aim is to become worthy of the event." See Deleuze and Guattari, *What is Philosophy?*, trans. Hugh Tomlinson and Graham Burchell (New York: Columbia University Press, 1994), 160; and Paul Patton's introduction to *Deleuze: A Critical Reader*, ed. Paul Patton (Cambridge, Mass.: Blackwell, 1996), 1–17.

9 See for example Isaiah Berlin, *Four Essays on Liberty* (Oxford: Oxford University Press, 1969), 46; and "Alleged Relativism in Eighteenth-Century European Thought," *The Crooked Timber of Humanity* (New York: Vintage, 1992), 70–90.

10 See William Connolly, *Identity\Difference: Democratic Negotiations of Political Paradox* (Ithaca: Cornell University Press, 1991), 174.

11 See Emmanuel Levinas, *Face to Face with Levinas*, ed. Richard A. Cohen (Albany: State University of New York Press, 1986). For an excellent elucidation and application of Levinas's ethical views see the work of another scholar influenced by Connolly's work, David Campbell: *Politics without Principle: Sovereignty, Ethics, and the Narratives of the Gulf War* (Boulder: Lynne Rienner, 1993).

12 A revised version of his comments appears as "Identity and Difference in Global Politics," *International/Intertextual Relations*, 323–42.

13 There does seem to be a peculiarly Anglo-Saxon intolerance for new words, which I regularly witnessed at meetings of the British International Studies

Association as well as the ISA. My first exposure came as a shock, when at a BISA panel organized in 1986 by John Vincent on Hedley Bull's influence in IR theory, a voice from the crowd cried out, "Shame!" when I used the word "heterologue" to describe Bull's style; it took me a moment of embarrassed silence to collect myself and reply that probably some of Bentham's peers took similar offense when he coined the word "international" in 1789.

14 Roland Barthes, *Criticism and Truth*, trans. K. Keuneman (Minneapolis: University of Minnesota Press, 1987), 32–33.

15 Ron Suskind, "Without a Doubt," *New York Times Sunday Magazine*, 17 October 2004.

16 Walter Kaufmann, ed., *The Portable Nietzsche* (New York: Viking, 1954), 71–72.

17 *New York Times*, 4 September 2005.

18 Connolly, commentary on panel presentations by Michael Dillon, Michael Shapiro, and R. B. J. Walker, annual meeting of the International Studies Association, Washington, 1990.

IDENTITY, DIFFERENCE, AND THE GLOBAL: WILLIAM CONNOLLY'S INTERNATIONAL THEORY

David Campbell

WRITING IN THE MID-1990S about the connection between democracy and territoriality, William Connolly surmised the constitutive relationship that bound political theory and international relations. "In late modernity," he wrote, "the nostalgic idealism of territorial democracy fosters the nostalgic realism of international relations. And vice versa. The nostalgia is for a time in the past when the politics of place could be imagined as a coherent possibility for the future."[1] With arguments such as this one, Connolly became one of few North American political theorists to appreciate and engage the critical shift that was under way in the study of international politics.

From the early 1980s onward the likes of Richard Ashley, James Der Derian, Michael Shapiro, and Rob Walker were retheorizing international relations by subjecting what had been an Anglo-American field to an engagement with continental philosophy.[2] Walker's seminal book *Inside/ Outside: International Relations as Political Theory* encapsulated the way this debate constituted a profound shift in the task of international theory as well as a profound shift in the subjects of international theory.[3] In this chapter I want to illustrate how Connolly's work has offered critical theorists of international politics some of the most significant articulations about the importance of identity and difference to global politics. In large part this is because, as I will demonstrate, the global condition has been an ever-present dimension of Connolly's thought over the last fifteen or more years. As such, Connolly's work sets the scene, effectively and productively, for approaching one of the key political conundrums of our time—how can we be with others in a period of increasing global tempo?

IDENTITY AND THE INTERNATIONAL

"Identity" has become one of the buzzwords of contemporary international relations theory. Constructivists, critical theorists, poststructuralists, feminists, postcolonial thinkers, and many others have fastened onto and worked with the concept in a number of ways.[4] Many of these efforts leave the larger ontological if not metaphysical issues in abeyance. There is no such forbearance from Connolly, who gets to the heart of the matter when he observes that "there is no identity without difference. Everything, my friends, depends upon how this paradoxical relationship is negotiated."[5]

Indeed, as both Bonnie Honig and Stephen White have noted in this book, Connolly's *Identity\Difference* (1991) offers an articulation of the problematic of identity/difference that explores the notion of human and social being in a manner productive for a number of fields. The dilemma of identity is that we cannot be without one. As Connolly argues, "it is probably impossible and surely undesirable to be human without some sort of implication in a particular identity."[6] Regardless of whether we are dealing with issues of personal identity or social order, for Connolly "identities are always collective and relational," with the fundamental relation being the relation with difference.[7] "The definition of difference is a requirement built into the logic of identity, and the construction of otherness is a temptation that readily insinuates itself into that logic."[8] Because it is a temptation rather than a necessity, we have the possibility of politics, especially a political imaginary that Connolly styled as "agonistic democracy"—"a practice that affirms the indispensability of identity to life, disturbs the dogmatization of identity, and folds care for the protean diversity of human life into the strife and interdependence of identity\ difference."[9]

From the outset this political imaginary was formed in a global context. It was designed to disturb the conviction that democracy was a condition achieved only by the institutions of government in a territorial state. This invoked the global because Connolly recognized that "the politics of identity\difference flows beneath, through, and over the boundaries of the state. It overflows state boundaries when the state constitutes a set of differences to protect the certainty of its collective identity and whenever the established identity of a sovereign state itself becomes an object of politicization."[10] Equally, from the outset it was clear that this political imaginary was not one that could be characterized as an idealism that seeks to go beyond the state, exceeding sovereignty and valorizing flow at the expense of fixity. To the contrary, Connolly's theorizations, rather than maintaining (as some have characterized it) that "the world is in a state of constant and unpredictable flux,"[11] are fixed firmly on the productive relationship of identity\difference, where settlements struggle with, and in, their contingent conditions of possibility.

Although Connolly maintained that his efforts in *Identity\Difference* to scramble the academic division of labor between political theory and international relations were no more than an interim report, with instances of the interstate outnumbered in his argument by a concern for individual and group examples, the second chapter of the book ("Global Political Discourse") offers a major reinterpretation of the international by foregrounding questions of identity\difference. Seeing Columbus's "discovery" of the new world as a paradigmatic encounter with otherness, Connolly details how this moment in world history, in which the "international" is produced from within the intertext of encounter, provides an understanding of how international relations theory comes to be superior to any social-science account of theory and evidence.[12]

What Columbus discovered, Connolly argued, was neither a new world that existed in and of itself (much less did he discover "America") nor a new world that was to be imagined from nothing. Rather, Columbus discovered an enigma—"an enigma that resists straightforward formulation while persistently demanding recognition: an enigma of otherness and knowledge of it, of otherness and the constitution of personal identity, of otherness and estrangement from it, of otherness and the consolidation of collective identity, of otherness and dependence on it, of otherness and the paradoxes of ethical integrity."[13] Of course, as is common in such encounters, Columbus and those whom he represented sorted and secured their cultural identity by concealing these enigmas. Indeed, through the strategies of military conquest or religious conversion with which Columbus operated, the enigma of otherness was contained by "strategies that enable a superior people to maintain its self-assurance by bringing an inferior people under its domination or tutelage."[14]

This reading of Columbus's "discovery," as a paradigmatic violent negotiation of the paradoxical relationship of identity and difference, established the cost borne by those who failed to engage the enigma of otherness. Although offered as a contestable and indirect insight, Connolly formulated the first lesson of the reading as a statement: "to deny the enigma of external otherness—to treat it simply as the innocent, primitive, terrorist, oriental, evil-empire, savage, communist, underdeveloped or pagan whose intrinsic defects demand that it is conquered or converted —is also to treat radical difference within one's own church or academy as otherness (as amoralism, confusion, evil or irrationalism) to be neutralized, converted or defeated. The definitions of the internal and the external compound each other, and both eventually seep into the definition given to the other within the interior of the self."[15]

The ethical consequence of this was equally clear. If a secure identity requires transforming external difference into otherness through the denial of its enigmatic effects on the self, that self will have to treat difference within through similar modalities of conversion or conquest. The result would unlikely be productive for democracy or enhance justice. Accordingly, Connolly formulated what was in effect the second lesson of this reading: "a lived conception of identity that takes itself to be both historically contingent and inherently relational in its definition might create possibilities for the strife and interdependence of identity\difference exceeding the models of conquest, conversion, community and tolerance."[16]

The significance of identity\difference for the international was further supported in the chapter by a reading of realist and neorealist international relations theory in terms of identity and the enigma of otherness. Through a critical examination of Kenneth Waltz and Robert Keohane— two of realism's avatars—Connolly disclosed the rhetorical strategies of their arguments through which identity and difference were dissolved into "the categories of theory, evidence, rationality, sovereignty and utility."[17] With mainstream international relations theory thus conceptually ill-equipped to address ethical issues raised by our inevitable global encounters with otherness, Connolly offered a sympathetic critique of Richard Ashley's deconstruction of sovereignty as an alternative. Although finding Ashley's position in close proximity to his own, Connolly was nonetheless critical of Ashley's comprehensive "postponism"—his fidelity to poststructural concerns with the positing of foundations, which prevented the articulation of alternatives. Arguing that Foucault was a practitioner of general and constructive (but not totalizing) social theories, Connolly saw Ashley's reticence as both misplaced and constraining to the task of formulating a theory of global politics that could address the paradoxical relationship of identity\difference.[18]

STATE AND SOVEREIGNTY

Within the problematic of identity\difference, and in common with the dominant perspectives in international relations, the state figures as a central concern. The nature of that concern differs radically, however. In place of the self-certitude of an existing and unitary actor, Connolly's conception of the state (by which he meant the political dimension of social order) placed it at the heart of the relationship between personal and collective identity. But collective identity is not theorized as naturally neat, seamless, and sorted. If successful it presents itself as such, but only after its internal challenges have been externalized. In this context "a collective identity recapitulates the contingent, conflict character of personal identity; it also *inflates* tendencies in the latter to dogmatize its configuration when confronted by disruptive contingencies."[19] Given the expansive and extensive disruptiveness brought on by the globalization of contingency, the dogmatic inclinations of the state (exemplified in its rendering of terrorism, which Connolly detailed a decade before 9/11) mean that "the state today is a ministry for collective salvation through a politics of generalized resentment. The ministry proceeds by making 'foreign' a variety of 'external' and 'internal' developments that would otherwise constitute signs of disruption within the collective identity."[20]

Having articulated a critique of the state in these terms, it would not have been surprising if Connolly believed that the state should be bypassed or superseded as one of the primary loci for negotiating personal and collective identity. Instead, and in line with the idea that one has to negotiate through, rather than flee from, the paradoxical relationship of identity\difference, Connolly argued that the issue was one of supplementing rather than supplanting the state as a center of sovereignty. Because late modernity is to be regarded as a "systematic time without a corresponding political place," the challenge is for the state to give ground to other modes of political identification, modes that flow from a globalization of politics to match the globalization of capital, labor, and contingency.[21] The power of the national-territorial political imaginary of the contemporary international order—which Connolly has elaborated as a "territorial unitarianism" in his latest book—means that the state cannot be wished away.[22] Nor is the question one of escaping the logic of territorialization. As Connolly argues, "the upshot is *not* to demand the deterritorialization of modern life. It is to support a more cosmopolitan, multidimensional imagination of democracy that distributes democratic energies and identification across multiple sites, treating the state as one site of identification, allegiance, and action amongst others."[23]

It is in this argument that Connolly's ongoing commitment to retheorizing and reworking pluralism meets the global condition. The renewal of pluralizing energies that Connolly seeks in personal and group relations by foregrounding the paradoxical relationship of identity\difference requires loosening the grip of the national, territorial state as the primary locus of collective identity. Doing so opens the way for and is made possible by the development of a "more diversified, nonnational pluralism" that will "denationalize the democratic state." Again, this is a strategy of supplementation, one meaning that "we experiment with another image of political attachment and communication within and around the state."[24]

These experiments are not easily conducted by the liberals who often function as Connolly's interlocutors. That is because the tendency of states to be presumptive nations means that the "secular ideals of individualism, minority rights, and democracy function simultaneously as important obstacles . . . and problematic sources" of the "cruel and dangerous modes of exclusionary politics" required to secure the nostalgia of bounded, homogeneous communities. With "secular liberalism . . . entangled in the nationalism its most valiant devotees also resist," the pursuit of what Connolly has most recently called a "deep, multidimensional pluralism" is a substantial ethico-political challenge to liberal theorists coming to terms with the contemporary global order.[25]

Thus the result of Connolly's state theorizations is the development of a "network image of the democratic state" that stands in contrast to—but is never liberated from—an "arboreal image of the democratic state." In these terms, "a democratic state now becomes a state with multiple, overlapping lines of identity, allegiance, and communication."[26] The arboreal image remains, because "we are all governed by states in a world whirling faster than heretofore."[27] The network image is developed by citizen action undertaken as an ethos of engagement that is generous in its presumptions about others. Citizens would have multiple loyalties, including ones that draw from "multiple constituencies in the same territory honoring different moral sources," as well as those that transcend the boundaries of the state, thereby remaking the categories of both citizenship and cosmopolitanism.[28] The network image is, though, open to action inimical to deep pluralism's ethos of engagement. After 9/11, Connolly notes, perhaps states should be treated as "unstable nodes of power traversed by a perverse anti-cosmopolitan network that subverts and disrupts the world of territorial states?"[29] In this context, those who do not respond to a presumption of generosity or recognize the relational dimension of identity\difference, and who are willing to engage in violence, might be subject to police and military actions designed to forestall violence—while those in home circles who advocate such actions by overstating danger need to be subject to critical work too. Deep, multidimensional pluralists thereby oppose, militantly if necessary, all "counterdrives to unitarianism."[30]

MICROPOLITICS, MARCROPOLITICS, AND THE "NEW INTERNATIONAL"

As the last points demonstrate, Connolly has been attentive to the changing global context, something he thinks that Georgio Agamben has not been. While Agamben's concern with sovereignty, the state, and sacrifice has had a largely positive reception in critical international relations scholarship, Connolly argues that Agamben fails to appreciate how sovereignty has always operated within a global context. To Connolly's mind, Michael Hardt's and Antonio Negri's general formulations in *Empire* better recognize the current situation. "The idea of Empire—as a loose assemblage of differentiated powers, not entirely under the thumb of a dominant state or a set of supranational corporations—is both timely and in need of further development," Connolly maintains. By detailing how "the elements of sovereignty are distributed in a complex assemblage with multiple sites, not concentrated in the single will of a people, a king or a dictator," Connolly believes that Hardt and Negri have encapsulated key features of the contemporary period.[31] Mainstream international relations theory—still bound by debates between imperialistic and anarchistic readings of international order—cannot grasp what is new about the present. For Connolly the contemporary world assemblage is marked by two tendencies: (1) neither state authorities, corporate élites, market mechanisms, nor international agencies possess sufficient foresight to govern the world intentionally as a system; (2) every state, corporation, labor movement, and supranational movement is nonetheless enabled, contained, and restrained by the larger world assemblage in which it is set. Ambiguities and uncertainties already discernable within sovereignty become magnified as its sites are extended to encompass the world.

However, having gone part of the way with Hardt and Negri, Connolly identifies how their conception of the *multitude* as the source of resistance—akin to the locus of citizen action in cross-state, non-national, and interfaith contestations that Connolly seeks—undercuts the ambiguities and uncertainties of Empire. By setting multitude against Empire, "rather than locating it ambiguously within and outside Empire and showing how various factions of it do and can act to press this global assemblage in new directions," Connolly argues that Hardt and Negri have articulated an either/or logic that drains Empire of its most provocative point. In effect, Connolly writes, the notion of the multitude as external to Empire "presupposes an architecture of Empire tighter than that presented in the author's best descriptions of the assemblage."[32]

In Connolly's terms, what Hardt and Negri have failed to allow for with this either/or logic is the relationship between micropolitics and macropolitics that animates large parts of Connolly's recent writings. Micropolitics—related to arts of the self, and techniques of the self in some formulations—involves those practices that work on us or are drawn on by us to establish us, individually or collectively. They are techniques through which existing identities can be stabilized, new identities permitted, or new formations enabled. They can be located in a multitude of cultural and social sites (clubs, families, neighborhoods, the media, the military, religious groups, and the like) though they always work at numerous "in-between" points, nodes, and lines of the network state. Micropolitics flows from the paradoxical relationship of identity\difference and is vital to a deep, multidimensional pluralism.[33]

Notwithstanding the term and its examples, micropolitics cannot be confined to a sense of the local, regional, or substate. It is not a conception that translates into the idea of a confined space or particular scale. Instead, micropolitics indicates the significance of the transversal rather than the transnational, highlighting how the global is simultaneously local and the local necessarily global. As Connolly maintains, therefore, there is a constitutive relationship between the micropolitical and the macropolitical, with the latter understood in more formal political and institutional terms. As he writes, "micropolitics operates below the threshold of large legislative acts and executive initiatives, even as it ranges widely and sets conditions of possibility for these more visible actions. Technique and micropolitics form connective links joining practices of memory, perception, thinking, judgment, institutional design and political ethos."[34] Although far from being the only transversal links—"market, antimarket practices (such as oligopolies, monopolies, and command systems), state decrees, and interstate agreements also play critical roles"—they do play an especially important role "below the threshold of political visibility inside every domain of life."

What the emphasis on the micropolitical points to is the significance of the visceral for contemporary thought and politics. In contrast to the epistemological register of intellectualism, where a sometimes narrow and shallow conception of reason governs thinking, the visceral is the densely layered register of political thought where affect—those dispositions to perceive, believe, associate, and decide—gives "texture and direction" to the "level of refined intellectuality." Although it is infused with ideas and not antithetical to the intellectual, the visceral register is "not susceptible to modification by argument, dialogue or conversation alone."[35] This is why methodological contests are often bitterly fought in the humanities and social sciences—each represents a question of faith as much as it does method.[36] Addressing the visceral register therefore means coming to terms with "the importance of relational techniques of the self and micro-politics. Such tactics *mix* image, movement, posture, concept and argument to new effect, simulating the process by which the habit in question became embodied the first time around."[37]

Paying attention to the affective and the visceral requires a new understanding of causality. Intellectualism implies a sense of what Connolly calls "efficient causality," in which "you first separate factors and then show how one is the basic cause, or they cause each other, or how they together reflect a basic cause."[38] In contrast—though not in place of effi-

cient causality—there is emergent causality, whereby elements have effects at multiple levels, infusing areas and issues beyond their domain,
and then, through adaptations, circuits, and feedback, themselves changing in response to these effects. Emergent causality thus refigures *causation* as *resonance*, whereby the elements affected fuse, "metabolizing into a
moving complex."[39]

For Connolly this recasting of causation as resonance is the basis
for a trenchant political critique of contemporary American politics at
home and abroad. Seeing the country governed by a "theo-econopolitical
machine"—the result of cowboy capitalism, evangelical Christians, the
electronic news media, and the Republican Party forming an assemblage
—Connolly offers a radical new way of explaining how (among other deg-
radations) "state practices of torture," "an international climate of fear
and loathing against the Islamic world," and "the Guantánamo Gulag"
have come to be accepted, with lies and distortions about alternatives
and those who promote them made equally acceptable. In large part, the
power of the "evangelical-capitalist resonance machine" is established by
"media presentations [that] do much of their work below the level of
explicit attention and encourage the intense coding of those experiences
as they do."[40] So while the objects of concern are micropolitical and American (at least in the first instance), the effects of concern are macropolitical and global.

Connolly's jeremiad is an appeal to "citizens who refuse to have their
thinking placed under the automatic purview of the regime in which they
reside, of religious authorities tied to the state, or corporate interests
linked to either."[41] The task for those citizens—both in and beyond America, united in cross-state, non-national movements—is to engage in their
own "micropolitical work on the subliminal register."[42] This is an especially challenging task, because given the idea of emergent rather than
efficient causality, and the techniques of the self employed below the level
of conscious politics by the evangelical-capitalist resonance machine, it
is not clear how this micropolitical resistance can be undertaken consciously and deliberately toward a desired outcome.

As Roland Bleiker argues in his chapter, while Connolly has highlighted
the potential contribution of transnational social activism to the micropolitics of democratic disturbance, there is considerable scope for an empirical investigation and extension of this thought. Nonetheless, what

Connolly has arrived at through this argument is an intersection with a number of contemporary thinkers, an intersection that contains the outlines of a new conception for global citizen action. The primary rallying point for this conception is the recognition that "we are all governed"—by states and other sites of sovereignty. Connolly identified this condition in his account of the arboreal image of the state. It resonates also with Stephen White's insightful argument in this book about the grounds upon which we can animate concern for global justice and human rights for those who live at the greatest distances from us.

White finds liberal justifications concerning the human rights of others to be uncertain and insufficient on a number of accounts. Politically, although they can prefigure *our* demand for protection, they cannot ground the claims of *others*. Conceptually, the moral sources for the modern self needed to secure the reasons for our protection cannot escape the deep reflection on their metaphysical and ontological dimensions that many liberals abhor. But White argues that this reflection does not warrant a return to theism. What is required in White's terms is a persuasive account of "the limits on agents" that nonetheless allows "the connectedness of agents." Drawing on Connolly's rendering of being in a world without God, White constructs this account in terms of subjection to a condition (mortality) giving rise to an ethos of finitude. The limits are thus clear, and the connectedness arises from awareness of the way this subjection to a condition of absolute vulnerability is shared. The challenge thus remains one of articulating a bond through the common experience of subjection that will extend this sense of connectedness "beyond cultural borders and across large geographical spaces onto settings which we have little or no experience of chairs at tables in common."[43]

In this task, both Michel Foucault and Jacques Derrida join the gathering at the intersection to move our thinking forward.[44] Foucault's most obvious articulation of this attitude came through his activism in association with Bernard Kouchner and Médecins sans Frontières (MSF) as part of the committee "Un Bateau pour le Vietnam" in the late 1970s and early 1980s.[45] Kouchner, a founder of MSF and later a French minister for humanitarian affairs in the administration of President Mitterrand, and most recently foreign minister in President Sarkozy's administration, had sent a team of doctors on board the ship *L'Île de lumière* to assist the "boat people" fleeing Vietnam.[46] In June 1981, as part of an alliance with

Médecins du Monde and Terre des Hommes under the banner of the Comité International contre le Piraterie, Foucault and others protested the violence of piracy against those who had fled Vietnam but had not yet been embraced by the regime of refugee protection. At a press conference in Geneva, Foucault offered a statement articulating the position of those protesting. At its heart was this claim: "There exists an international citizenry, which has its rights, which has its duties, and which promises to raise itself up against every abuse of power, no matter who the author or the victims. After all, we are all governed and, to that extent, in solidarity."[47]

This statement was not published until after Foucault's death, and it was the newspaper *Libération* which in June 1984 gave it the title "Face aux governements, les droits de l'Homme," describing it as a new declaration of the rights of man. Although this would seem to have reduced Foucault's argument to a liberal humanist understanding, the title accurately reflected that the "right" which Foucault theorized as productive came from no one or nothing except a recognition that "we are all governed and, to that extent, in solidarity." As such, it made clear how Foucault's perhaps surprising deployment of a discourse of rights was a revaluation of liberal and humanist terms, enabled by the agonistic and radically interdependent relationship with practices of governmentality rather than the existing character of subjects with inherent rights.

Foucault's argument therefore speaks to the idea of a political bond enabled by government's continuing power, and our implication in those practices of governmentality that traverse our life. It figures a new form of universality which does not rely on any a priori sense of essential sameness. Although it proceeds in the seemingly homogenizing language of a global "we," its emphasis on a common experience of subjection in a biopolitical age does not, as a matter of course, erase the radical asymmetries of power within, through, and across otherwise disparate societies. It is thus a political bond with some similarities to that identified by Derrida as marking "a new International":

> There is today an aspiration towards a bond between singularities [not "political subjects" nor even "human beings"] all over the world. This bond not only extends beyond nations and states, such as they are composed today or such as they are in the process of decomposition, but extends beyond the very concepts of nation or state. For example, if I feel in soli-

darity with this particular Algerian who is caught between F.I.S. and the Algerian state, or this particular Croat, Serbian or Bosnian, or this particular South African, this particular Russian or Ukrainian, or whoever—it's not a feeling of one citizen towards another, it's not a feeling peculiar to a citizen of the world, as if we were all potentially or imaginary citizens of a great state. No, what binds me to these people is something different than membership of a world nation-state or of an international community extending indefinitely what one still calls today "the nation-state." What binds me to them—and this is the point; there is a bond, but this bond cannot be contained within traditional concepts of community, obligation or responsibility—is a protest against citizenship, a protest against membership of a political configuration as such. This bond is, for example, *a form of political solidarity opposed to the political* qua *a politics tied to the nation-state*.[48]

With clear resonances to Connolly's articulation of a non-national pluralism, this political bond recognizes that we are connected by the practices of government, but that we struggle with the strategies of governmentality which discipline freedom, even though the context and content of those strategies of governmentality vary greatly. The claim is not that I am identical to an Algerian, Bosnian, or Darfurian or that our situations are identical (identifications which can elide other differences of race, class, ethnicity, and gender), but that if we think in terms of a form of solidarity organized around a critical engagement with "the political *qua* a politics tied to the nation-state" then a transversal activism is more readily conceivable. While this rendering recognizes the significant contribution of nonstate actors, it is a political bond that is not inherently anti-state but rather one activated by the reduction of the political to the state, and one that seeks to contest the imperatives associated with all specific political configurations (including, potentially, those of a nonstate kind). It is a political bond that draws attention to numerous sites of possible interventions, and requires decisions on the part of individual and collective subjects to be materialized in those sites, even though it cannot legislate for that decision making. In this sense it is a political bond which maintains that resistance is a choice, but only insofar as the sites, strategies, tactics, and techniques of resistance have to be decided upon by any number of potential resisters. What is not a choice is the requirement of resistance once the abundance of life, and its affirmation contra sovereignty and strategies of governmentality, are recognized. It is a political bond which might offer a more productive predicate for humanitarianism than any of the other codes, norms, or values currently in circulation. Therefore it is a political bond that might be the beginning for more creative practices about how we can be with others in a period of global tempo.

NOTES

1 William E. Connolly, *The Ethos of Pluralization* (Minneapolis: University of Minnesota Press, 1995), 135.
2 See Jim George and David Campbell, "Patterns of Dissent and the Celebration of Difference: Critical Social Theory and International Relations," *International Studies Quarterly* 34 (September 1990), 269–93.
3 R. B. J. Walker, *Inside/Outside: International Relations as Political Theory* (Cambridge: Cambridge University Press, 1993).
4 See David Campbell, Epilogue, *Writing Security: United States Foreign Policy and the Politics of Identity*, rev. edn (Minneapolis: University of Minnesota Press, 1998), for a discussion of these competing strands.
5 Connolly, *The Ethos of Pluralization*, xx–xxi.
6 Connolly, *Identity\Difference: Democratic Negotiations of Political Paradox* (Ithaca: Cornell University Press, 1991), 9.
7 Connolly, *The Ethos of Pluralization*, xvi.
8 Connolly, *Identity\Difference*, 9.
9 Ibid., x.
10 Ibid., xi.
11 Ian Shapiro, Rogers M. Smith, and Tarek E. Masoud, Introduction, *Problems and Methods in the Study of Politics*, ed. Ian Shapiro, Rogers M. Smith, and Tarek E. Masoud (Cambridge: Cambridge University Press, 2004), 11.
12 Connolly, *Identity\Difference*, 38.
13 Ibid., 36.
14 Ibid., 43.
15 Ibid., 40.
16 Ibid., 48.
17 Ibid., 49ff.
18 Ibid., 55ff. Connolly argued that "a constructive theory refuses to confine its task to the deconstruction of the totalitarian moment in established theories" (57). One of the few disagreements I have with Connolly lies in his occasional juxtaposition of construction and deconstruction. In *The Ethos of Pluralization* (36), Connolly argues that deconstruction, while "a related strategy of disturbance and detachment" which is "first and foremost an ethical project," nonetheless "refuses to pursue the trial of affirmative possibility

very far, out of a desire to minimize its implication in ontological assumptions it could never vindicate without drawing upon some of the same media it has just rendered ambiguous." I think we can explicate more fully the manner in which deconstruction's affirmations are better developed than is commonly recognized, especially by readings markedly less sensitive than Connolly's. For my attempt to do so see *National Deconstruction: Violence, Identity and Justice in Bosnia* (Minneapolis: University of Minnesota Press, 1998).

19 Connolly, *Identity\Difference*, 204.

20 Ibid., 207.

21 Ibid., 215.

22 Connolly, *The Ethos of Pluralization*, 135–36; Connolly, *Pluralism* (Durham: Duke University Press, 2005), 28–29.

23 Connolly, *The Ethos of Pluralization*, 137.

24 Connolly, *Why I Am Not a Secularist* (Minneapolis: University of Minnesota Press, 1999), 88, 91–92.

25 Ibid., 73; Connolly, *Pluralism*, Prelude.

26 Connolly, *Why I Am Not a Secularist*, 95.

27 Quoted in Bradley J. Macdonald, "Towards an Ethos of Freedom and Engagement: An Interview with William E. Connolly," *Strategies* 15, no. 2 (2002), 180.

28 Connolly, *Why I Am Not a Secularist*, 95.

29 Connolly, *Pluralism*, 13.

30 Ibid., 35, 41. This builds on Connolly's earlier caution that "engaging the paradox of ethicality by cultivating the experience of contingency in identity does not entail the celebration of any and every identity. It does not open itself to a politics of racism or genocide, for instance. For identities that must define what deviates from them as intrinsically evil (or one of its modern surrogates) in order to establish their own self-certainty are here defined as paradigmatic instances to counter and contest." Connolly, *Identity\Difference*, 14–15.

31 Connolly, "The Complexity of Sovereignty," *Sovereign Lives: Power in Global Politics*, ed. Veronique Pin-Fat, Jenny Edkins, and Michael J. Shapiro (New York: Routledge, 2004), 34–35.

32 Ibid., 35.

33 Connolly, *Why I Am Not a Secularist*, 148–49; Connolly, *Neuropolitics: Thinking, Culture, Speed* (Minneapolis: University of Minnesota Press, 2002), 20–21.

34 Connolly, *Neuropolitics*, 21.

35 Quoted in Macdonald, "Towards an Ethos of Freedom and Engagement," 168–69.

36 Connolly, "Method, Problem, Faith."

37 Quoted in Macdonald, "Towards an Ethos of Freedom and Engagement," 169.

38 Connolly, "The Evangelical-Capitalist Resonance Machine," *Political Theory* 33, no. 6 (December 2005), 869; Connolly, "Method, Problem, Faith," 342–43.

39 Connolly, "The Evangelical-Capitalist Resonance Machine," 870.

40 Ibid., 871, 877, 878, 880.

41 Quoted in Macdonald, "Towards an Ethos of Freedom and Engagement," 180.

42 Connolly, *Neuropolitics*, 130.

43 Stephen White, "Uncertain Constellations: Dignity, Equality, Respect and . . . ?," (in this volume).

44 I have discussed these arguments at greater length in "Why Fight: Humanitarianism, Principles and Poststructuralism," *Millennium: Journal of International Studies* 27, no. 3 (1998), 497–521.

45 Didier Eribon, *Michel Foucault*, trans. Betsy Wing (Cambridge: Harvard University Press, 1991), 267.

46 Ibid., 278–79.

47 Quoted in ibid., 279 n. 67.

48 "Nietzsche and the Machine: Interview with Jacques Derrida by Richard Beardsworth," *Journal of Nietzsche Studies* 7 (1994), 47–48 (italics added). See also the discussion in Jacques Derrida, *Specters of Marx: The State of the Debt, the Work of Mourning, and the New International*, trans. Peggy Kamuf (New York: Routledge: 1994), esp. 84–85.

AN INTERVIEW WITH WILLIAM CONNOLLY, DECEMBER 2006

Morton Schoolman and David Campbell

MS: Your concern with pluralism, as a mode of thinking as well as a theory and a political practice, has been present from your first book, *Political Science and Ideology*, published in 1967, through to your most recent *Pluralism*, published in 2005. With each study your examination of pluralism has become more expansive. You have reconsidered pluralism in the context of the history of philosophy and of political thought, but also in the context of major theoretical debates and approaches introduced into political theory during the period of time bounded by your work. Despite its increasingly expansive and multidimensional treatment, however, it is remarkable that pluralism has occupied your attention for forty years, and promises to do so into the future. How do you account for this intellectual commitment and its tenacity?

WC: My concern, I suppose, grew out of my childhood in a pro-union, working-class family, raised by nonreligious parents. They allowed me to go to church with my friends whenever I wanted. But it did not take. The neighborhood was full of Southern Baptists who had trekked north to Flint, Michigan, to work in the auto factories. I found myself hard-pressed to gain respect for my developing nontheism (as I call it now) in my neighborhood, school, extended family, and sports teams. Many friends, relatives, and teachers loved the sinner but not the sin. I must have been fairly articulate, however, because when friends from the day contact me after many years, they often ask, "Are you still an atheist?" The McCarthyism of the time, taking a heavy toll on adults I knew, also deepened my visceral commitment to diversity and my awareness of how intense opposition to it can be underneath generic expressions of support.

Another commitment was to explore how to reduce economic inequality. And I did not at first see how pluralism and the reduction of inequality are interconnected. In graduate school I was distressed by the logical empiricism of the day and unconvinced by a "descriptive" theory of interest-group pluralism that pushed the issues of participation, work life, economic inequality, and even religious diversity into the background. I wrote *Political Science and Ideology* to disclose how laced with ideological commitments the "analytical" concepts and "neutral" tests were that described the United States as a pluralist society, how the idea of "a power élite" could also be defended methodologically, and how the differences between the two theories depended as much upon different *contrast models* brought to research as upon those tests. The pluralists of the day had a constricted vision of possibility. They did not explore how new diversities simmering on the edge of becoming were blocked and how possible routes to reduce inequality were filtered out before they achieved public visibility. C. Wright Mills was informed by the image of a more participatory and egalitarian society.

My question, really, was how to spur debate between alternative contrast models, since each exerts an effect on the method adopted, the concepts formed, the test procedures accepted, and the conclusions reached. I concluded that political science was much more ideological than its practitioners appreciated. Fortunately for me, my dissertation was respected by some behavioralists in the department who disagreed with it. It appeared as a book at the moment mature scholars such as Peter Bachrach were exposing the ideological dimensions of political science.

I began my intellectual career, then, as a critic of "descriptive" pluralist theory, and I hovered uncertainly between a desire to achieve a more unified community and a desire to deepen and extend pluralism. George Kateb discerned the first disposition upon our initial meeting. It soon drifted away.

So the issue of pluralism has long been on the agenda, as your question suggests. But my thinking about it, as you also suggest, has changed. The first break occurred when I saw how different renderings of key concepts of political life—such as power, interests, legitimacy, freedom, democracy, and politics itself—express deeper onto-religious differences than I had heretofore imagined. I also began to suspect that while we could advance arguments on behalf of our conceptual selections, the debates over these terms are laced with onto-theological differences that might not be fully susceptible to definitive resolution. These are not simply "analytical" decisions, separated by a wall from theology and ontology. That judgment pushed me toward the pursuit of "deep pluralism," and later the critique of secular understandings of the private-public difference.

MS: I would like to follow up on your concept of "deep pluralism." While your thinking has evolved, pluralism seems gradually to have acquired a *value* resistant to the sorts of revisions that have accrued to other cultural ideals and theoretical concepts you have examined. It seems there is an irreducible value intrinsic to pluralism. This process started with the exploration of "contestable concepts," but it took a new turn in your later engagements with Nietzsche and Foucault, and once again with Deleuze and neuroscience. What is the value of pluralism? Does pluralism contain a depth, a value perhaps indeterminable, to which politics ought to be obligated?

WC: As you see, my idea of pluralism has been modified several times. With each modification concepts associated with the previous idea have faced revision. Here are a few of the changes.

First, a shift from the established theory of pluralism, in which diverse interests are brought to government and the whole culture is under-girded by a general consensus, to an ideal set in a context which is itself more pluralistic. This shift highlighted the need for a positive ethos of political engagement between diverse constituencies in a fast-moving world in which the assumption of a uniform center is either exaggerated or maintained through repression, forgetting, and displacement.

Second, the exploration of a torsion between existing pluralism and pluralization. Here the image of multiple minorities on the same territorial space is complicated by the *politics of becoming* through which emerging constituencies periodically press to allow a new identity, right, good, or faith to cross the threshold of legitimacy. Many such movements fail. But if a movement succeeds, the self-understanding of both it and existing constituencies is altered. While a politics of *agonistic respect* can inform an ethos of engagement between established constituencies, an ethos of *critical responsiveness* is needed to come to terms with the dicey politics of pluralization. A struggle may touch elements in established practices of morality, normality, God, identity, freedom, the good, rights, or reason. The politics of pluralization sometimes ushers a new right, good, or

identity into being, distressing those who think that the list of basic
rights is eternal.

What critics confuse with the refusal of principle is in fact the idea that
pluralists should periodically adopt a *double-entry orientation* to the principles that occupy them. We honor a set of principles, but a new movement
periodically asserts *a call* upon us to renegotiate aspects of them under
altered circumstances of being. This is a call to rethink something in the
established banisters of judgment. It often involves painful work on dimensions of your interpretation of principle.

Third, as these two ideas were fleshed out, I became more aware, through
engagements with phenomenology, genealogy, and neuroscience, of the
extent to which our identities, faiths, doctrines, creeds, and philosophies
become infused into the cruder brain systems and soft tissues of life, as
well as refined conceptual habits. The gut, for instance, has a complex
cortical organization of its own; it is in direct communication both with
direct tendencies to action and headstrong parts of thinking. These in-
stallations in the gut and lower brain networks—the subsystem in which
the amygdala participates is an example of the latter—do not merely inhabit the life of the individual. They possess *inter-corporeal powers of transmission*, as when, say, a thought-imbued feeling of disgust is first shared by
a large constituency and then amplified through reverberations back and
forth between them. Or when a traumatic event such as a hurricane, act of
terrorism, or crucifixion influences an entire tradition, or when collective
disciplines amplify the joy in living amidst suffering that already circulates through many much of the time. Attention to the visceral dimension
of cultural life presses advocates of shallow pluralism—that is, secular
pluralism—to come to terms with the case for *deep* pluralism, and with the
corollary need to supplement attention to the instrumental and deliberative aspects of politics with arts of the self and micropolitics. In micropolitics images, rhythms, concepts, smells, arguments, touch, and sound resonate together on the lower and higher registers of constituency life. The
power of mcropolitics is amplified when the media saturate cultural life.

These first three points carry over into the image of thinking one
adopts, not merely the thinking of theorists but that of citizens, teachers,
and journalists. A case can be made not only that there is a persistent
diversity in the commitments, identities, and faiths that infuse cultural
life, but also that each thought imbued creed or philosophy contains

some profoundly *contestable* assumptions and hopes. We are attached to these commitments by a thousand cords. They can be defended and adjusted through argument and evidence; but, as William James and Friedrich Nietzsche understood, specific hopes, anxieties and resentments sedimented into the visceral register infect the shape of arguments, the relative weight given to each, and our comparative representations of other creeds. The sharp separation between theology and philosophy—the division through which the secular academy is organized—subverts attention to these processes.

If you join appreciation of the persistent diversity of faiths to the idea that the affective intensity of each runs deep you take a step toward deep pluralism. If you link these two themes to the judgment that no single existential faith or philosophy has marshaled sufficient resources of argument, evidence, and inspiration to convince all reasonable people, you take another. But an additional step is needed. That is the quest to overcome the temptation to *resent* profoundly the plurality that marks the human condition. To feel such resentment is to seek to repress, or worse, others whose philosophy-creed challenges self-confidence in the universality of your own. So the judgment that the human condition is marked by deep plurality must be joined to strategies to overcome the all-too-human resentment of this condition. Today, as the world spins more rapidly, to bypass the pursuit of deep diversity is to fail an elemental test of fidelity to the world.

The next question—your question about the "irreducible value intrinsic to pluralism"—is from whence people draw the energy and sense of responsibility to translate the possibility into a quest. I imagine that you come to terms with this question through Adorno's idea of the disjunction between concept and world and his aesthetic theory. My response is, first, to identify positive strains in my partisan faith that encourage such a direction, trying to amplify them. It is, second, to try to open a line of connection between that faith and others across a pathos of distance. And it is, third, to identify specific features in the late modern age that might encourage others to strengthen such connections, so that positive resonances across these differences compete more successfully with the negative resonance machines carrying so much power today. That is how to proceed if you think that faith plays a role in theory and politics and that some critical differences between alternative faith-philosophies are unlikely to dissolve into an ecumenical creed or thick dogma of universal reason.

But what are these "positive strains in my partisan faith?" The nontheists I admire most do not in the first instance ground ethics in a law, a primordial debt, the intrinsic recognition of universal obligation, or an implied contract between self-interested agents. Rather, we seek to cultivate further a gratitude for being that already circulates in us to some degree, if we are lucky. We cultivate care for the abundance of life and the earth in a world ungoverned by a Transcendent Power. We then seek to weave this spirituality into our pursuit of self-interest, identity, judgment, and responsibility. It is from this reserve, for instance, that we draw the energy to affirm responsibility to others, with its specific content being adjusted as we meet unanticipated situations.

We sometimes hear that our agenda is "incoherent" because it is not grounded in a divine authority, an assumption of universal obligation, the subjective necessity of the categorical imperative, the counterfactual assumption of a general consensus, or at least the idea of the person as an intrinsically responsible agent. But we think that responsibility itself is a complex formation. And that its terms change over time. Besides, are critics in a perfect position to judge the capacity of our faith to inspire support for pluralism unless they themselves experiment with it? Since it is impossible for any individual or group to test every possibility, is it reasonable to presume that some other faiths embody strengths that you yourself do not plumb? It may be that others draw supplemental strength from the reserve we honor, even as some of their assumptions play a *secondary* role in our thinking. The proof may in the pudding, for both them and us. We agree, moreover, that we do not fully fathom the felt authority of existential orientations that do not inspire us. From this vantage point we solicit relations of agonistic respect with those who honor different onto-theological faiths, encouraging them too to come to terms without resentment with the comparative contestability and minority status of their onto-political creeds. Christianity, to which most western religious, secular, and neo-Kantian orientations are indebted, is professed by only about 30 percent of the world's populace. Millions and millions of people, for instance, do not accept the idea that morality takes the form of obedience to a law in the first instance.

Some critics reduce such an orientation to the embrace of mere "preference," ignoring the existential gratitude that on good days inhabits our preferences, interests, identities, and sense of responsibility. Others, who see through this misrepresentation, reduce arts of the self to "self-indulgence." But individual arts are critical to cultivation of a pluralist sensibility. And micropolitics, pursued in a positive key, carries such arts into collective endeavors. It forms a pervasive *part* of politics, as anyone can see who attends to the multimedia power of churches, the news media, film, corporate advertising, work disciplines, TV dramas, electoral campaigns, family dinners, school, professional associations, and above all the reverberations between them. A culture of deep pluralism requires not the transcendence of micropolitics but a turn in its dominant investments.

MS: Before returning to the politics of deep pluralism, I want to take a step back and inquire further about the approach you adopted in *The Terms of Political Discourse*. In that book, first published in 1974, you introduce the concept of "contestation," which anchors a critical apparatus. Among the most important, contestation is wedded securely to democracy. From *The Terms* on, contestation remains central to the critical approach taken. But by the early 1980s a change occurs in your thinking. Contestation is joined by genealogical and to some extent deconstructive strategies.

Now, it seems evident from the 1983 edition of *Terms*, to which you added a new final chapter, that you consider genealogy to be more relentless than contestation. You appear to signal your awareness of this tension between them when you conclude the new chapter to the 1983 edition of *Terms* with a fascinating last sentence. "To show the subject to be a construction," you argue, "is not to render its deconstruction imperative."

Is there a tension between these two critical approaches? Does your conception of "agonistic democracy" offer a common home for contestation, genealogy, and deconstruction?

WC: When I first came to terms with essentially contested concepts, of which "democracy" is one, I did not yet appreciate enough how the micropolitics of image, touch, smell, rhythm, words, caress, discipline, and music infiltrates cultural memory and presumptions of collective judgment. Our most refined concepts and affective dispositions are interinvolved, with neither being entirely exhausted by the other. Of course, I retain from that study the idea that only a few of the concepts that are potentially contest*able* can actually be contest*ed* at a particular time. For some provide the hinges upon which a contest turns, even though that initial contest may eventually carry you into territory heretofore ignored: from democracy to the will, from the will to the subject, from the subject to responsibility, from responsibility to established distinctions between God, nature, and culture. As such disputes emerge they touch chords of affect and feeling in our relational identities. To engage them is to put part of one's identity at risk. That's why "analytical" disputes are often so intense.

You could fashion a genealogy of gender practice, secularism, consumption practices, responsibility, morality, or the subject. The incentive to proceed, often, is an injury to a constituency in which you are involved, or the suffering of others brought forcefully to your attention. Is that suffering necessary or legitimate? You may have a preliminary suspicion that it is somehow bound up with something fishy in the practices of normality, morality, or responsibility in which you participate. You can't put your finger on it at first; for your thought is pulled back toward the established code of judgment. Now you seek to ascertain how the part of that code that applies to the issue in question was consolidated. A genealogy is often painful. As you come to terms with elements of contingency in the formation of this or that code you touch affective chords woven into your feelings, conceptual investments, and creedal commitments. The code may even be bound to hidden dispositions to revenge against the human condition. Carefully crafted, a genealogy can help people come to terms with contingencies in this or that aspect of their creed or identity; it can encourage us to appreciate an element of contestability that had previously escaped attention. So genealogy and conceptual contestation are bound together.

I do not assert, by the way, that a genealogy necessarily carries you to an ontology of immanence. That ontology too is contestable. It can, however, accentuate zones of contestability in the existential ontology you accept; it *may* even shake and disturb it so that you find yourself pressed to seek another. I say *may* to emphasize the element of uncertainty and variability here, uncertainties and variabilities that stalk the human condition.

I thus don't see a sharp break between the early exploration of essentially contestable concepts and the later exploration of genealogy. I see, retrospectively, a crooked path leading from the former to the latter, a path through which the readiness to engage the issues involved may become enhanced. Saying that, it is important to keep large chunks of agency, normality, and responsibility intact as you touch and test others. That is, I think, the tension your question identifies: you place some elements of your identity at risk, but you speak to democratic life in doing so by drawing upon others. Your sexual performance may have been tied to the implicit idea that normal sex is between a man and a woman. You panic upon encountering live challenges to that judgment. You may now bracket other aspects of your identity while working to recast that judgment, out of care for others. Or, your identity as a responsible being may be bound to the idea that morality is necessarily grounded in the revealed will of God. Again, close exposure to, say, Buddhists and atheists who seem to be ethical without recourse to such a Transcendent Being just might jostle that affect-imbued assumption, without immediately providing a route to reexamine it. You might then explore the contested history of your faith, and end up retaining a close relation between God and morality while appreciating the extent to which others proceed with nobility in different ways. Or it may be important to you, as a physicist, to see nature as a set of general laws open to full human knowledge. Then you encounter challenges to that view flowing from scientific experiments you respect. It now becomes pertinent to engage the history of how the lawlike model was consolidated, as you experiment with received categories of law and causality. It is interesting, for instance, how the philosophies of nature and time advanced by James, Bergson, and Whitehead early in the twentieth century have now made a comeback after a period when many thought they had been put to rest. As you proceed, you probe experiences that pulled you toward the lawlike model. And so on. Each time the conceptual and the affective are engaged together.

Often to jostle this or that sedimented disposition you *need to run little experiments on yourself*, treating yourself, as Nietzsche says, as your own guinea pig. Then you return to the issue to see how your thinking *now* proceeds. Thinking, historical genealogy, self-experiment, thinking: a circle that does not close in entirely upon itself.

We can now connect these themes to democracy. Democracy, to me, points in two directions. The root idea is having a hand in defining and shaping the culture that governs you. In one direction it involves citizens' participation in shaping policies that govern them, accepting a presumptive responsibility to obey them. In the other, it involves the periodic politics of agitation, protest, and new experiments by which hidden injuries in established norms, laws, and practices are exposed, contested, and sometimes changed. Democracy, to me, *consists in the torsion between these two dimensions*. This puts me at odds with the communitarian and individualist traditions. And it binds democracy and pluralism close together. Democrats committed to pluralism move back and forth on this plane. There is presumptive acceptance of an established pattern of diversity, in which you pursue relations of agonistic respect with constituencies of different faiths; and there is the uncertain engagement with new, unexpected movements that challenge something engrained in your identity and the established terms of diversity. I used to be surprised by those who reduce my conception of democracy to the second dimension. Now I see how people who concentrate on the politics of being are apt to slide over the torsion between being and becoming central to this vision.

If you think of human beings as essentially embodied and always already entangled in social life, you don't fear *too much* that a specific genealogy will reduce a collective identity to shambles. People plagued by that fear underplay the imbrications between thought and affect, the layered density of habit, and the thickness of intercorporeal relations. There is, though, some danger here. We must be cautious about seeking too much too soon in this domain, because of the fascist reactions the quest for a wholesale shift can trigger. Nonetheless, in a culture of democratic pluralism it is important to engage in genealogical practice from time to time. The acceleration of speed heightens this need. It means that we often encounter modes of suffering and possibility for which the established banisters of judgment have not adequately prepared us. Democratic pluralism would die on the vine, or devolve into a mere celebration of past achievements, if the experimental temper were dropped from it.

MS: "Agonistic politics" is oriented to problematizing the constructions of otherness and curtailing the violence these constructions entail, which would alter our relation to difference and enable us to cultivate opportunities for becoming different. By engaging what you have called the "paradox of ethicality," which highlights the ways the standards necessary for identity can also inflict violence on those to whom they are applied, agonistic politics weds a "care for being" and a "care for identity and difference" to the "politics of becoming." For you, politics must expose and challenge the exclusions individuals, groups, and social orders have built into their identities, so that pluralizing forces outside such identities can earn recognition, develop, and paradoxically contribute to fixing new standards. Agonistic politics, you make clear, requires a democratic form of public life that combines democratic contestation and genealogical modes of disturbance. This leaves one other dimension of agonistic politics to be considered, a dimension that cannot be easily formalized or formalized at all—namely, the plural sources of agonistic politics, the multiple sites from which the incitements to agonism flow, the public and private provocations that can set genealogy and contestation into motion at the macro- and micropolitical levels. You appear to want to insist that these sources and sites are irrepressible, and that it is being, ontologically grasped, that makes them so. What are the actual and virtual sources and sites of agonistic politics in the late modern democratic world, and how are they tied to being?

wc: I still prefer to speak of agonistic *respect* folded into a positive ethos of political engagement, rather than "agonistic democracy" or "agonistic politics." Some ideals of agonistic democracy are at odds with the pursuit of deep, multidimensional pluralism, to the extent they reflect the spirit of Carl Schmitt more than that, say, of Michel Foucault. The difference is one of ethos, sometimes brought to the same ontology of politics. So I understand the spirit of *your* question in the context of a politics of agonistic respect. I will speak of the sources of diversity first from my perspective and then ask how others might appreciate that diversity.

As an immanent naturalist I think the world comes equipped with strong pressures toward a diversity of being. In a world without a single, transcendent authority to which all bow, in which most children are imbued with the habits, creeds, and principles of their place and time before they reach maturity, and in which surprising events of multiple sorts periodically burst forth, a fundamental diversity of being keeps blooming and surging forth on its own. New faiths come into being as old ones die or mutate. The recurrence of such diversity indeed provides some evidence for the ontology of immanence embraced here, though it is not overwhelming. When a single faith or creed achieves an official lock over a political regime, many who are normalized, disciplined, punished, or repressed in its name find specific modes of resistance filtering into their lives. The emergence and reemergence of such resistance is to me a *sign* of the fundamental diversity of being. Those resistances, if given a chance, sow new movements of becoming. So the politics of pluralization periodically reasserts itself, even though it typically faces powerful counterpressures. And sometimes the carriers of the new message seek to universalize it in turn, even engaging in incredible violence to do so.

But if deep pluralism involves agonistic appreciation of a plurality of faiths, philosophies, and creeds on the same territory, how can one who embraces my political ontology make contact with those who embrace alternative creeds and doctrines? I start by agreeing that my creed (or ontology) contains a universal aspiration within it. But since neither it nor any other to date has been established by argument or revelation so definitively that everyone—despite differences of preliminary experience—must embrace it, I concede, hopefully without deep resentment, its contestability in the eyes of others. To the extent others reach a similar point—with a little help from critics who show them how far they would have to go to prove their creed to others—they too can proceed from their perspective to an appreciation of the fundamental diversity of being in the world. They embrace their faith at one level, and recoil back upon it at another to come to terms with the obdurate fact that it does not convince millions of others. Sometimes their own commitment is punctuated with a residual element of uncertainty. That seems noble to me, but perhaps not necessary to deep pluralism. What is needed is pursuit of *a bicameral orientation to citizenship and being,* in which you embrace your creed as you bring it into the public realm; and then recoil back without deep resentment on its contestability to open up negotiating space with others.

It is not *that* hard; millions and millions of people, imbibed with a variety of faiths, do it regularly. True, a number of priests, philosophers, preachers, journalists, and economists encounter difficulty here, because they are so invested in either proving the necessary rationality of their philosophy or the universal authority of their faith. But even here there are noble counterexamples, with William James, Kenneth Boulding, the Dalai Lama, Judith Butler, George Kateb, Dick Flathman, Charles Taylor, Cornel West, Stephen White, and Talal Asad representing a few examples from a variety of traditions. They seek to reduce violence in a world in which the human powers of rational and theological demonstration are less profound than many pretend. I find it amusing—on my good days—to encounter those who disparage as unphilosophical the readiness of William James to evangelize his philosophy of "a pluralistic universe" while leaving room for others to deny it. He is a deep pluralist whose doctrine of politics is not reducible to secularism.

But the politics of diversification is also grounded in more today. It also flows from tensions and dislocations that emerge between the fastest and slowest zones of life. An accelerated pace is apparent in the rapid flow of capital; a slower pace in the socialization processes by which children are drawn into a culture. It is the enlarged gap between the fastest and slowest zones that is important. Today population mobility, uneven economic development, global communication, managerial exchanges, new modes of transit, porous state borders, illegal immigration, the spread of religious movements, the migration of people with unsanctioned sexualities to large cities—all these move further and faster than heretofore. The acceleration of speed, though it contains counterpressures, amplifies trends toward diversity along multiple dimensions of being: in faith, economic interest, gender practice, ethnicity, household organization, language use, sensual affiliation, and more besides. Drives to pluralization have multiplied and intensified on numerous fronts; and attempts to attain them now generate bellicose and invasive counter-movements. That is why today is such a dangerous time, amidst its glimmers of promise.

My first systematic engagement with capitalism came in *The Politicized Economy* (1976, 83), written with Michael Best. A recent seminar Mark Blyth (a political economist) and I co-taught on Capitalism and Christianity has pulled me back into these issues. The idea that capitalism homogenizes the world is exaggerated, though it does produce such effects in the spheres of work and consumption. Nonetheless, the momentum and expansion of capitalism also generate, against the will of its leading publicists, powerful *pressures to minoritize the whole world*. Illegal immigration is just one example. The scope and speed of capitalization disrupts a (putative) world in which a national majority—organized around commonalities of faith, language, skin color, family structure, and so on—occupies the center of the territorial state. The cultural center around which diverse minorities are said to revolve becomes a symbolic site, deployed to whip multiple minorities into shape. The idea of such a definitive majority has always been an exaggeration, but it is more visibly so in many states today. Ours is increasingly a world of multiple minorities with no definitive national center, a world in which democratic politics can be saved only by forging a new ethos of engagement between minorities of multiple kinds.

The irony today is that the evangelical-capitalist right opposes minoritization of the world in the name of the centered stasis of the nuclear family, the Christian tradition, and the English language. To do so they must obscure the role of capitalism in the production of the minorities they demean or demonize. The political formula takes roughly the following form: idealization of a mode of economic life that contributes to minoritization; demonization of many minorities; and support for state-capital policies to bring the normative hierarchy and the distribution of life chances closer together. There are constituencies who fit the second category without falling into the third, but there is a discernible drive in this direction.

I agree with Deleuze and Guattari that modern capitalism is not a closed or autonomous mechanism, in the senses that some neoliberal economists, Marxists, and Weberians have imagined. Weber, for instance, recognized the element of contingency in the formation of capitalism, but found mature capitalism to be a closed "mechanism." We have in fact, though, a state-capitalist "axiomatic" that is not sufficient to itself. Today, for instance, the Christian right participates in the state-capital axiomatic, carrying it down paths it would not otherwise take. Capitalism is not a mechanism; it certainly is not an organism. It is a powerful machine with nomadic tendencies that helps to generate a world of interdependent minorities.

There is nothing further from my thinking than to search for "the autonomy of the political" as a way to control capitalism crudely defined as a mechanism. The idea of the autonomy of the political—either as actuality or dream—is a nonstarter for me. Those who push such a thesis, or who lament a world in which it has been lost, or who valorize the local alone to secure it, preach a message of despair. The ideas of capitalism as mechanism and the autonomy of the political haunt and track one another.

Today politics is *braided* into numerous practices, including labor-management relations, Christian-corporate relations, Christian-media relations, investment processes, corporate benefit packages, capital-military relations, consumption reform movements, military-gender practices, state-capital relations, church struggles, electoral campaigns, and the imbrications between all of them. It is because capitalism is both a powerful axiomatic and never sufficient to itself that politics is everywhere but not everything. The braided character of politics is merely suggested by saying that the state-capital machine has helped to generate a world of interdependent minorities, even though neither neoliberal economists nor the evangelical leaders on the right love the result.

The forces and ideas noted here work on each other. The acceleration of the capitalist machine draws attention to the *possibility* that the world itself has no intrinsic purpose; the production of new minorities further supports that projection. The reaction by the Christian right to this combination presses it to assume a prominent role in the boardrooms, think tanks, bureaucracies, courts, and media outlets of state-capitalism; and the consolidation of a capital-Christian right now poses the most dangerous threat of all to democratic pluralism, as it valorizes entrepreneurial creativity and delegitimizes the creativity of *any* other agency except God himself. To pretend that politics does not make a notable difference within numerous sites and junctures is to minimize the power of the evangelical-capitalist resonance machine.

MS: I would like to pursue your concept of politics a little further. From what you just have said the agonistic dimensions of your pluralism appear to place unusual demands upon politics. Theorists may inflate the role of the political in your thought. Yet your conception of politics seems underpinned by quite modest pretensions. On the one hand, your recognition of contingency in late modernity and your critique of the ideal of mastery, and on the other your belief that the task of politics is to open what is enclosed and stretch patterns of insistence, seem to restrain our expectations of what politics can achieve and what through politics we can hope for. Moreover, these restrained ambitions for politics are not then reassigned to other sorts of action. Is your political modesty rooted in some deeper modesty about the human condition?
WC: It is noble to cultivate modesty about human agency with respect to nature, politics, responsibility, divinity, life, and knowledge of the future. But such modesty does not mean that politics is always sharply limited in what can be achieved, for good or ill. A political movement periodically acquires a momentum that soars beyond the events, suffering, hopes, and

demands that triggered it. Sometimes overlapping modes of experience and multiple sites of action begin to resonate together in surprising ways, generating a movement with considerable range and power. Let's call that the politics of becoming. The hanging of James Connolly and the rise of the Irish rebellion; the consolidation of labor movements in several capitalist countries in the first half of the twentieth century; the formations of German Nazism and Italian fascism; the expansion of the civil rights movement and New Left into a set of interconnected movements; and the current specter of the state-evangelical-capitalist resonance machine—all reflect political movements that started small and became large. Neither a liberal understanding of procedural politics nor the dream of a general revolution suffices to come to terms with such phenomena.

An effective political movement foments a pattern of resonance between interdependent constituencies across multiple sites of action. If it grows, it is apt to do so in a topsy-turvy way. C. Wright Mills was almost alone in sensing the potential for a New Left before it became visible. Most other academics were talking about "the end of ideology" and "the politics of consensus." He was run out of sociology because his insights challenged the conventional wisdom of the day—what was called "logical empiricism." Jerry Falwell was an oddball preacher until evangelism and cowboy capitalism coalesced into a powerful movement. Up to the late 1970s he counseled against political involvement in the name of evangelical purity. Retrospectively, we can see that a theology infused with existential resentment, neglect of the grievances of the white working class by critical social movements of the day, and a predatory ethos in numerous corporate boardrooms set the context for this movement. Today it has acquired a major presence in church sermons, talk shows, government bureaucracies, court decisions, TV news, electoral campaigns, corporate boardrooms, investment decisions, consumption practices, think tanks, military ideology, and Republican Party "talking points."

That's why I agree when William James and Gilles Deleuze say that theory and action start in the middle of things, fanning out from there. You might eventually articulate a political ontology, or come to terms in a new way with the structure of capitalism, or find your cultural imagination stretched and enlivened. But you begin by stepping inside a contest, issue, or struggle, where latent energies, grievances, hopes, and ambitions are burning. You listen and participate; you feel where it is going; and you strive to make a difference in the world. My experiences, starting with labor, civil rights, and anti-Vietnam movements, through feminist and gay-lesbian movements that initially surprised me, to opposition to the Iraq war, to exploration of ways to contest the evangelical-capitalist resonance machine—all encourage thinking about politics in this way. These experiences, in turn, helped to trigger explorations of volatile elements in nature, time as becoming, and deep pluralism. You occasionally feel that you are working alone, but it typically turns out that others are charting a parallel course, waiting for you to catch up. That is another sense in which politics starts in the middle of things.

It is because capitalism is not a closed system—and there is no pure politics either—that we cannot chart with confidence the outside limit of politics. We can't see with confidence around the corner of a political movement. We make guesses, sometimes throwing ourselves into the mix. Who anticipated the collapse of the Soviet Union, or, shortly after that, the rise of powerful Islamic movements? Will global capitalism run up against insuperable resource, disease, or climatic limits? Or will it, after concerted struggle, retool its relations to nature, forging practices as different in the future as the early capitalism of steam, coal, and Taylorism was from the mercantile system? If it does so, will it be capitalism?

That's why it is periodically important to review the political situation, calling into question this or that assumption you had taken for granted. Working to modulate some passions and to intensify others. On my good days, I am neither an optimist nor pessimist about politics. Those are spectatorial stances. I seek to appreciate how fragile things are, in a world now stretched thin, how contingent the most complex social formations are—composed more of historical tangles, knots, and flows than by tightly defined structures, what dangers and possibilities exist on the horizon, and how susceptible this or that dangerous formation might be to a counter-movement. Indeed, as I formulate this sentence I hear myself echoing formulations by Foucault that inspired me three decades ago.

The most general wager I am willing to entertain is that pursuit of a reduction in economic inequality, the advance of deep pluralism, and a revamping of operational orientations to resource use and climate change could eventually catalyze a new resonance machine. Each party in it would inflect its priorities differently, and I do not know exactly how it will get rolling. But it is important to cultivate attunement to emerging issues that might foment such an assemblage. Attention to the grievances of white working-class males is one area to explore, something I have done in the past and will return to again. I also think that nontheists must seek active alliances with those in the Christian, Muslim, and Jewish traditions who manifest care for the future of the earth and fight against the violent, exclusionary voices that pretend to speak for them. We need such alliances. They may too.

I am unqualified to tackle yet larger issues. But even in these cases, it may be useful to ponder how little we now know with confidence about the outer reaches of historical contingency and political possibility, for good and ill. It is because politics is embedded in numerous events and processes that exceed it that we still have not plumbed its outer limit.

DC: You noted earlier some features characteristic of contemporary life, namely the acceleration of tempo and the tensions that emerge from different rates in different zones, as well as the countermeasures enacted by the unitarians who invest much faith in a spatially contiguous and culturally coherent community. These reflections foreground the global dimension of your thinking and the global context your ethico-political theorization engages. Yet as you've also observed, there has been a long established academic division of labor between "domestic" political theorists and "international relations" theorists, in which this sovereign intellectual partnership—where each side is to at least some extent productive of the other—has sought to contain cross-border and transversal interrogations. How do you read the relationship between political theory and international relations? At what stage, and how so, did you feel that the global context of political theory could no longer be partitioned off for others to deal with?

WC: I majored in political theory and minored in international relations as a graduate student at the University of Michigan. The tendency in IR theory was to state a few principles about the rationality of the state, and then to deduce theorems in a world of anarchy between states. "Realists" lumped "idealism" with "normative" political theory and identified themselves with the recognition of hard facts. The understanding, widely acknowledged today, that each explanatory theory secretes a set of normative priorities, was a radical idea at the time. It was shocking to me, for instance, to hear the thought of my "idealist" IR teacher, Inis Claude, summarized by realists indebted to Hans Morgenthau. That whole debate became scrambled, however, when both turned militantly against the Vietnam War.

In 1964 realist faculty members at UM, led by AFK Organski, attended a local meeting of the Democratic party, where some of us, led by a philosopher of participatory democracy named Arnold Kaufman, called upon the local party to condemn Lyndon Johnson's war policy. Organski and his allies gave a smooth, realist defense of the war, predicting that the local party would not be stupid enough to deny support during such a delicate moment. Kaufman said smart things too, but in less practiced concepts and in phrases punctuated by stutters. When the vote came, we were startled to find that we had just won by a large margin. Within a short period the first antiwar "teach-in" in the country was organized at the university.

Political theory and IR were enlivened by this debate, even as the Vietnam people, American soldiers, and the American economy suffered. Nonetheless, within a few years most theorists again retreated to the politics of place. The liberal-communitarian debate dominated, and experimental engagements between IR and political theory became moot. I found myself revisiting this territory while writing *Political Theory and Modernity* in the middle 1980s. Reviewing classic debates about the role of the state and capital, it became clear how a host of movements and practices now overflowed state boundaries and state-centered imaginaries of "international relations." I began to think about the global condition of late modernity itself, as a *time* connected by several interconnected contingencies, without a corollary *site* of action. Permit a quote from that book: "Late-modernity has become a systemic condition, without a corollary center of political action. *It is a time but not a place.* The internationalization of capital and ecological damage in a world of nation-states can serve as a symbol of this development, and acid rain, illegal aliens, drug traffic, non-state terrorism, corporate flight, resource shortages, disinvestment controversies, the accelerated pace of disease transmission across state lines and the nuclear capacity for global destruction can serve as some of its signs" (133). The idea of a late modern time without a corollary site of global action, which seems like a truism today, then encountered considerable opposition in place-centered political theory.

Now it became pertinent to explore actual and possible cross-state citizen movements that act simultaneously upon states, non-state actors, and international agencies. Attention to these questions led me to address the role that the acceleration of speed in the fastest zones of life plays in politics, to redefine classical images of cosmopolitan politics, and eventually to engage the issue of time itself. Luckily, several IR theorists were headed down a parallel path. I encountered your book, and you and I soon taught two seminars at Hopkins, one on sovereignty and another on territory and democracy. And I increasingly became engaged with IR theorists in a few countries. My sense is that the early momentum generated by people such as James Der Derian, Sandra Harding, R. B. J. Walker, Spike Peterson, Michael Shapiro, Richard Ashley, Michael Dillon, and you has lost some of its momentum in the States. But it is alive and kicking in England, Australia, Canada, India, Japan, and elsewhere.

Today, when the United States under George W. Bush has become the most dangerous state in the world, we need to fashion a new cosmopolitanism in which cross-state movements periodically apply pressure to dominant states from both inside and outside. It is unlikely that a just settlement between Israel and Palestine can be achieved without such a movement. It is equally unlikely that the United States will join the rest of the industrial world in curtailing global warming unless it faces a mix of internal and external pressures to do so.

Democracy contains two dimensions, with the second growing in importance as the globalization of contingency advances. There is the irreducible tension alluded to earlier between political representation and disruptions that call this or that settlement into question. There is also periodic citizen involvement in regional or global movements that transcend the level of the state. To limit citizen pressure to the interior of the state today would be to forfeit participation in a critical arena of politics, even while corporate élites, criminal rings, terrorist organizations, religious groups, and security forces increase their activity on this front. Today the Christian right is far better organized at this level than the democratic left.

Political theory, in the best sense, is democratic citizenship lifted to a high level of reflexivity. As reflection on the time of late modernity proceeds, it often becomes incumbent to challenge the gaze of the sovereign state, the priorities of capital, and the presumptions of international agencies. As such thinking and activism proceed, the lines between IR and political theory blur. So does the line between domestic citizenship and interstate politics.

Such a rallying call can devolve into the politics of witnessing. Yet witnessing itself occasionally grows into something larger. My mind rolls back to 1962 or '63, when the dissident economist Kenneth Boulding held a solitary, weekly vigil on the central square of the Ann Arbor campus. "What the hell is he doing?," we worldly graduate students asked. "Protesting the Vietnam War," we were told. Several of us found ourselves shifting slowly from ridicule through uncertainty to the conviction that we must join the opposition, as the war swept beyond anything the "containment" doctrine had led us to expect. Yes, witnessing is limited; it can be harnessed to retrograde demands; and it only occasionally bubbles into something pregnant with positive possibility. But in states where many academic, economic, and state officials still view the world through the lens of realist utopianism, it is also indispensable. It assumes multiple forms. Writing is witnessing.

DC: One prominent theme in your recent work—here I am thinking especially of *Neuropolitics*, has been a concern with "micropolitics," and the way this ensemble of practices takes us onto the visceral register. To what extent do you see this as a shift in your own thinking? To what extent has it been prompted by the workings of the "evangelical-capitalist resonance machine" that you excoriated in your December 2005 *Political Theory* article? Whether it is a shift or not, paying attention to the visceral in micropolitics raises a number of questions given the global context and concerns of your thought. How do you see the relationship between the micropolitical and the macropolitical? Is this something akin to, or different from, more conventional renderings of the local and the global, the national and the international? It also raises questions about how to conceive of progressive political action, because as I read the idea of a "resonance machine," and your figuration of "emergent causality" in contrast to "efficient causality," one of the features of this assemblage is that the relationship between its elements is not one of linear cause-effect, and therefore the operators of the machine cannot be sure of the outcomes their purchase on particular issues will have. But if the visceral register involves doing work at the subliminal level, how are we going to be able to have some idea about the possible effects of what we do, especially if the micropolitical exists in a relationship with the macropolitical?

WC: I recall a seminar Dick Flathman and I co-taught on Nietzsche and Wittgenstein in the middle 1990s. One agenda for me was to connect Nietzsche on how "the body is more profound than the soul" to Wittgenstein's oblique references to "nature," "life," and "training." What the former emphasized the latter treated as a reserve that did its work *in* language but was not available *to* language. Nietzsche agreed that bodily states were not translatable without remainder into language. But he also contended that "arts of the self"—by which you act tactically upon bodily processes below the reach of intellectual representation—could make a difference to the temper of your mood, feeling, language, and action. The topic mesmerized me. In the middle of that seminar a book appeared by the neuroscientist Joseph LeDoux. LeDoux focused on the amygdala, a little brain nodule participating in the production of fear, anxiety, and terror. On his reading, the rapid subsystem in which it participates operates below the linguistic register, even though it also communicates with the slower-moving and more linguistically rich neocortex. Once a trauma has been imprinted on the amygdala, intense feelings will arise again when the appropriate trigger is pulled—say the sound made by a tire blowout across the street. You are now driven back to a moment in a war or a holdup, reliving the pain, or, better, living it in a way that might not even have been so intense the first time. A neuroscientist can observe which brain-body areas are activated as you compulsively relive this agony.

We debated the issue in class, with some contending that attention to the observation of body-brain processes would discount the importance of language to life and others insisting that these experiments must be incorporated into cultural theory. LeDoux, whose work was too reductionist, soon gave way to Antonio Damasio, V. S. Ramachandran, and Francesco Varela in my exploration. It also seemed that an engagement with film could help. For film works on us subjectively *and* intersubjectively, and it does so on both the refined and visceral registers of being. The interplay in a film between images, words, background sounds, music, and rhythms recapitulates some of the processes by which our second natures were acquired. To bring neuroscience and film together is to proceed beyond intellectualism to the territory of micropolitics.

Micropolitics is certainly not reducible to the strategies an individual applies to himself or herself to affect thinking, mood, or action. It is intercorporeal politics in which collective dispositions on the visceral and intellectual registers are touched and mobilized. Out of these reverberations a new movement might bubble forth, or an old one become more intense. Campaign advertising participates in micropolitics; its effects might be local, national, or international in scope, intended or unintended. Take *Brokeback Mountain*, a film I saw at the Charles Theater in Baltimore twice over a four-day period. The second time I watched and listened to the audience as much as the film. We were engrossed together in the imbrications between music, gesture, words, kisses, punches, and plot surprises. The film, daily experience, and distressing news about crimes of hate resonated together that evening, as we responded to the screen, each other, and the larger culture—a love story, with the issues of same-sex love and gay marriage sometimes sliding into the background and then erupting as the agony of a love culturally denied becomes palpable. The closet is intolerable to the lovers and their wives, but coming out is also impossible in that setting. Our groans and occasional moments of relief were communicated back and forth intercorporeally, as was the seriousness of our composure as we trekked up the aisle at the end, in many cases heading to a coffeehouse to "talk about" the film and the world. A cultural event, a modern tragedy, an evening's entertainment, a conversation piece, all mixing together. A drop of micropolitics . . .

If a neuroscientist had attached refined instruments to our brains, skin, and guts, the interplay between these zones could have been observed as we experienced the film. And the interplay among us, the film, and the world could also be registered obliquely. It will happen soon, no doubt. As a "parallelist"—following Spinoza and Stuart Hampshire—I do not assert that third-person observation of body-brain processes captures our thought-imbued feelings. I do say that a change of observable body-brain state finds some expression in thought and feeling, that any change in thought and feeling finds some expression in body-brain states, and that these charges are communicated across individuals and constituencies in multiple ways. As we participate in these processes we make educated guesses about how they might escalate or turn in another direction. But we do not know entirely what we are doing, or what will happen. A period of relative equilibrium might give way rapidly to one of heightened disequilibrium. We thus must step back periodically, to see what is happening and where to turn. The ubiquity of micropolitics throws more cold water yet on a predictive science of politics.

Is the difference, then, that micropolitics is local and macropolitics state-centered? Not exactly, for most conceptions of macropolitics overplay the stability of self-interest and/or the autonomy of deliberation in politics. Both macro- and micropolitics work on the visceral and higher registers. Micropolitics is non-state-initiated politics enacted through multimedia modes such as film, TV, social movements, family struggles, the machinery of corporate life, the internet, church discipline, and patterns of gossip. Above all, it consists in resonances back and forth between these sites, resonances that set possibilities and limitations for macropolitics at the state level. The relation goes the other way too. A powerful machine generates multiple relays between micro- and macropolitics, each amplifying the other. That is how the evangelical-capitalist resonance machine works today. As I write, many in Congress are cowering before Attorney General Gonzales, as he defends a sinister conception of the presidency that would make Congress even more a tool of the executive. His assertions will become talking points to be spread far and wide through every medium available.

The complexity of micropolitics also suggests revisions in established concepts of causality. Empiricists typically adopt a restricted concept of cause, and headstrong theorists of narrative sometimes drop the concept itself to resist this reduction. But we can draw sustenance from recent work in complexity theory, evolutionary theory, and neuroscience to fashion a notion of emergent causality. Here movement back and forth between a current encounter and the multilayered past called up by it sometimes creates a new idea or possibility. Though imperfectly and incompletely, these elements infuse and infiltrate each other, as Proust saw so well. The results that emerge are often not predictable, particularly when a new period of disequilibrium has set in. At that point it would be like asking an evolutionary biologist to predict the next new species. That is why it is wise to step back from politics from time to time to see what is unfolding. Maybe something surprising has been tapped and now propels things in a new direction. Perhaps there is something positive in this turn, or dangerous. Since the standards and norms now sedimented into life may be insufficient to the new situation, it is time to think again. To think creatively, without assuming that established standards of judgment are already sufficient to the situation.

For some, this image of politics admits too much unpredictability and uncertainty. And perhaps it challenges their moral compass too much. But if you believe that an element of uncertainty is installed not just in the concepts and instruments of study but also in nature, bodies, and cultures, then this is a condition of life to address rather than to obscure, to affirm rather than to resent. James, Bergson, and Deleuze, who disagree on much else, agree that the flow of time carries real innovation and unpredictability, in culture, nature, and the intimate imbrications between them. And they also agree that classical conceptions of moral judgment need revision in the light of this condition. Perhaps it would be better for other sciences to model themselves upon the protean activity of politics than for the human sciences to mold themselves upon a classical image of science.

To participate in a cross-state citizen movement that deploys TV, the internet, mass rallies, films, divestment strategies, product boycotts, rock concerts, and church mobilization is to participate in micropolitics at the global level. We still have to catch up with advertisers, corporate élites, and evangelical leaders in this domain. And we face the additional burden of calling attention to the tactics through which we seek to inspire, contain, or shame others. For while there is never a vacuum in the domain of micropolitics, its mode of operation can be more or less conducive to democratic politics.

DC: I wonder if I could press you some more on how we can think about progressive political interventions in the context of being open to the visceral register where, as you suggest, doing work means operating at the subliminal level. This is related to, yet more than, the idea of micro- or macropolitics containing too much unpredictability and uncertainty for some. From the reading of William Bennett in *Why I Am Not a Secularist* to the diagnosis of the "evangelical-capitalist resonance machine" in *Political Theory*, you have exposed the strategies and tactics of the neoconservatives who currently seem so dominant. At one level their work involves a conscious politics, where the likes of Bennett seem to know what sort of effect (and affect) they are going to achieve. And yet one of the things that is attractive about your more recent critique of Bush and his gang is the recognition that they are "catalyzing agents" in, rather than omniscient controllers of, the resonance machine. This is where, in the world of the resonance machine, we move from conscious to subliminal politics. But if we make that move, as seems compelling, how does a political activist (whether film director, neighborhood organizer, or NGO worker) begin to think about his or her *modus operandi*? Obviously, there are no guarantees that action X will produce result Y, but given that the activist wants to have a chance that action X will get a hearing, how can we think about taking *conscious* steps when we are dealing with the *subliminal* register? Now in some respects this is already happening, as your experiences with the Charles Theatre audiences and the national conversation sparked by *Brokeback Mountain* demonstrate, though what I am asking is different. I guess, then, my question is, given this context of contemporary micropolitics working against the resonance machine, is why you think, as you say in the *Political Theory* article, that "an agenda of deep pluralism is not in the cards today, to say the least"? And, if it is not in the cards, how might it be consciously prompted at the subliminal level?

WC: The agenda of deep pluralism is not in the cards "today" because the right wing holds so many of those cards and because liberalism and secularism, as currently organized, are not reflective enough about how to proceed on the conscious and subliminal registers together. I understand this hesitancy. Because if you acknowledge that micropolitics is ubiquitous—that there is never a vacuum in this domain—you have to think about how to work on the subliminal register while respecting the integrity of those you seek to work upon. That is more difficult than saying, "The right is manipulative; but we appeal only to reason, deliberation and rational judgment."

How do you work consciously to tap the subliminal dimension of politics? Experimentation is essential. William Bennett understood this when he spoke of how much "freelancing" he did on behalf of forging a unitary culture. It seems important to look for issues opened up by surprising events or your adversaries, probing those that hit unanticipated chords in the populace. Take the Terry Schiavo case in the U.S. The right thought it had a wedge issue. The media were mobilized for weeks; religious and think-tank experts were engaged; Tom DeLay and George Bush were recruited. But the movement collapsed. The event triggered collective feelings about love, family, and dying unanticipated by the right. This collapse created an opportunity to amplify affirmative passions. The left, however, was ill prepared to respond to this opportunity. Why have we failed during similar moments such as the Guantánamo Gulag, the cultural pressure to produce, deregulate, and buy suvs, the appointment of right-wing judges, Abu Ghraib, domestic surveillance, the health crisis fostered by the fast food industry, and the huge layoffs by General Motors and Ford? Katrina poses a partial exception.

One reason is that between 1985 and today, the right wing has organized a huge battalion of well-financed think tanks. Experts in them are tutored about how to perform on the media; they are ready to appear at any time; and they keep in close touch with talk show producers. Take Regent University, the school Pat Robertson founded and runs. It has a degree program on how to use the media. A recent symposium in *theory & event* on think tanks covers this ground. It shows how far we have to go to engage media politics successfully. One source of the isolation of the academy has been the rapid growth of these media-centered think tanks. Another is that it is often easier to fan the flames of resentment and revenge than to inspire affirmative passions during a crisis.

But there is also a failure in the academic left itself to fold an existential dimension into its political appeals. The distribution of *ressentiment* and gratitude for being—a distribution within as well as between us—does not correspond neatly to any distribution of social positions. Moreover, traces of the one disposition among those with ample amounts of the other can be amplified by a powerful resonance machine. The evangelical-capitalist resonance machine is effective at activating those in a variety of positions attuned to its sensibility, and it draws in others who would break from its ethos if presented with an alternative. We are less effective in part because we avoid addressing the spiritual dimensions of life. We are tone-deaf to the role of spirituality in cultural practice.

Maybe some films can give us clues as how to proceed. Take *Far From Heaven, I Love Huckabees, Time Code, The Eternal Sunshine of the Spotless Mind, Memento, Waking Life, Run Lola Run,* and *Mullholland Drive.* These films focus on the role of duration in the organization of perception, scramble habits of perception in this way or that, challenge simple objectivism, and call the self-certainty of the linear image of time into question. Several take another turn as well. They activate a gratitude for being and care for the future that already circulates in many. For example, *I Love Huckabees* turns out to embrace things it first subjects to humor and mockery, including "existential detectives," ecological movements, media advertisements on behalf of ecological concerns, and the application of tactics by ourselves on ourselves to amplify attachment to this world. The attachment is folded into the humor. The attachment, in this film, is to a world in which temporality is open, human efficacy is fragile, perception is complex, and the myths of intellectualism and world mastery are bankrupt.

Consider theorists whose primary craft is writing. Some are too *singularly* committed to analytical modes of writing, or to a story of relentless disenchantment, or to a cold version of secularism, or to the sufficiency of negative critique, or to disclosing the heavy weight of primordial guilt. Others may be too embarrassed to express existential attachment. It feels naïve or childlike in a world with much suffering. But it is possible that inciting gratitude for being and seeking to embed care for the earth into specific critiques can help to stimulate positive responses to suffering. Some theorists do pursue such a course. I note Jane Bennett, Bonnie Honig, Brian Massumi, George Kateb, Tom Dumm, Philip Goodchild, Charles Taylor, and Cornel West, coming from different creedal traditions, as exemplars.

Writing is our craft. It is needful today for more to write in ways that delineate the complexity of the world while expressing sensibilities that resonate with artists, directors, movement leaders, novelists, poets, and religious prophets who inspire a gratitude for being. That is the sensibility to be amplified if care for the diversity of life and the future of the earth is to achieve higher political salience. Each contribution is minor, of course. But so, remember, is each appeal to neutrality, disenchantment, or primordial guilt. It is the resonances across expressions of attachment that count. Besides, we are teachers as well as writers. On all these fronts we do not make a sufficient contribution to the ethos from which a resonance machine on the democratic left could be fashioned.

We will perhaps disagree forever on this issue. But because we do it is imperative to seek alliances with those on the left proceeding from different sources of inspiration. To take just one instance, can the Levinasian focus on the debt to the Other also speak to a Deleuzian effort to deepen "belief in this world?" Does each, indeed, sound a minor chord that resonates with a major chord in the other? It is desirable to intensify these debates, to bring the question of spirituality front and center. And to seek lines of connection across these differences. The two thinkers identified above differ significantly, but each identifies an element of opacity in the source he honors.

Our most militant opponents are not shy about instilling revenge and *ressentiment*. They insinuate them into visceral judgments about entrepreneurial entitlement, capitalist necessity, male authority, court appointments, privatization of social security, welfare failure, curriculum design, the authority of God, preemptive wars, economic inequality, fast food, and a unitary presidency. They attract many who might be pulled in another direction if more of us contested these judgments without lapsing *entirely* into stories of disenchantment, neutrality, primal indebtedness, or secular coolness—if, that is, we infused a certain gratitude for being into our critiques, exposés, and calls for action.

I agree, with Spinoza I suppose, that life comes with suffering, that immense suffering can overwhelm people, that *ressentiment* is a risk that comes with life itself, that a degree of suffering is indispensable to cultivation of a noble sensibility, and that the pursuit of gratitude for being must take such obdurate facts into account. There is indeed much to be somber about. But if and when it is somber all the way down, the academic left fails to contribute positive energy to a counter-resonance machine. That is the self-indulgence I worry about.

I do not know how long "today" will last. But the democratic left still has a distance to go to make the most of the opportunities and "skill sets" with which it is endowed.

DC: Where do you think your craft of writing is taking you next? When you visited us at Durham in 2005 you drew upon Merleau-Ponty, Deleuze, and Foucault to address further some political contests in the age of the media-saturated resonance machines. Although there was much more in the paper than this, the challenge to notions of certainty and causality this reading made possible—especially the way the account of "intersensory perception" undid any reliance on "simple objectivity"—seemed to open up new ways to think about critical interventions for the democratic left. Is that what you had in mind, and where do you think you might go with this?

WC: In answering I bear in mind how a project sometimes changes in midstream. In the middle 1990s I was developing a critique of the nation, as it found expression in liberal, radical, and right-wing theories. But at some point that project bounced into a critical engagement with the secular tradition, a tradition that liberals and radicals invoke whenever they run into trouble.

Nonetheless, today I am working on three fronts. First, exploring the politics of perception, trying to learn more about it and the role the media play in it. The second is to challenge assumptions about nature, biology, and the mind-body relation adopted in several currents of cultural theory. The third is to explore key moments in the history of imbrications between capitalism and Christianity. Even to state the third in such bald terms sends a shiver down my spine. It is too grand, and beyond my grade level. But nonetheless, the hope is that these three zones of work will inform each other.

In a society saturated with electronic media and new modes of state surveillance, the logic of perception needs to be addressed again. Several traditions are pertinent here. But Merleau-Ponty is critical. Theorists in "my camp" exaggerate who locate a break between his thinking and that of Deleuze and Foucault. Each tradition needs infusions from the other. Merleau-Ponty draws attention to the intersensory dimension of perception. When you see, say, the face, skin, and demeanor of an old man looking at the picture of his deceased wife, a layered history of experience with touch, feeling, and voice becomes condensed into the visual image. The memory of words, colors, rhythms, and smells folds into visual perception. And indeed, the tactile sense of a word like "hard" affects you as you pick up the conceptual element. Such a condensation of the layered past fills perception with anticipation. The anticipatory structure of perception does not just prepare us to see something, it enters into the encounter itself, enabling some affect-imbued perceptions, discouraging others, and disabling still others.

Merleau-Ponty is superb at delineating these interconnections. But he was, understandably, less attuned to the role of the news media, films, and TV dramas in perception. He did not attend either to how state surveillance has become increasingly insinuated into the anticipatory structure of perception. Foucault helps here. And so does recent work in neuroscience and film theory.

A key task is to develop a positive alternative to the idea of simple objectivity in the fields of journalism, cultural studies, and political inquiry, an alternative that takes this complexity into account while providing journalists and social scientists with a model of responsible engagement. One reason that critical and liberal journalists dismiss the academic left today is that we took the simple model of objectivity away from them without providing an alternative mode of responsible conduct to follow—and to invoke when Fox News goes after them.

To get the most from this inquiry it is pertinent to reassess the images of nature and biology that prevail in cultural study. For those images hinder attention to the biocultural processes involved in perception and the organization of resonance machines. They discourage attention to intecorporeal contagion by cultural theorists and encourage biological reductionism by social scientists.

The idea is to learn how to refine our powers of perception, how better to expose and counter the politics of fear, surveillance, and aggression, and how to fold democratic sentiments into collective perception.

The third idea is the most ambitious. It is to study key moments in state/capital/Christian imbrications in Europe and America, exploring how shifts in the direction of each impinge upon the others. Weber provides a starting point, but so do Marx, Tawney, and even Werner Sombart. I say "even" with respect to Sombart because of his demonization of Judaism in reading the diaspora through the lens of the "nomadic" he despised and the "organic" he loved. I am also impressed with a recent study by Linda Kintz, *Between Jesus and the Market*.

You hear on the media that the founders of America were Christian. That leaves out a few figures. It is still not widely known that Thomas Jefferson retranslated the Gospels during the last years of his life, to separate the "diamonds" from the "dung hills" around them. His effort correlates with recent attempts by Jesus scholars to cull sayings that Jesus uttered from themes added after the crucifixion. Such studies speak to the politics of perception, as they challenge revenge themes on the Christian right. It is pertinent to remember that the *Left Behind* series, which has sold sixty million copies, visualizes the return of Christ to terrorize billions of nonbelievers. If a spirituality is composed of a set of institutionally embedded dispositions and existential beliefs, it is important to explore how people with similar dispositions and different beliefs can move and inspire each other, forming a common assemblage out of disparate parts. The result can be a resonance machine of the right or the left. So the idea is to explore how a particular spirituality becomes infused into institutional practices, and how these practices then work back and forth upon each other.

Only a minority will embrace an alternative reading of Jesus, or be drawn to the fascinating reading of Jesus and Yaweh that Harold Bloom advances in a recent book. But tunneling into these materials provides a way to address existential issues in state capitalism. That in turn may open the door to connections between the nontheistic and non-Christian left on the one hand and millions of Christians who chafe under the alliance between neoliberalism, neoconservatism, and the evangelical right on the other. The recent move by dissident evangelicals to address global warming carries some potential. That focus could eventually challenge the exclusive link advanced by the right between God as Creator and entrepreneurial entitlement. Support for equality and ecology will falter until the line of associations between God, cowboy capitalism, and providence is broken.

If capitalism is a relatively open axiomatic, insufficient to itself, then it is important to attend to the changing spiritualities inhabiting it.

So, a study of media and the politics of perception, of state/capital/Christian imbrications, and of operational conceptions of nature in capitalist culture—that should keep me busy.

BIBLIOGRAPHY

Agamben, G. 1998. *Homo Sacer: Sovereign Power and Bare Life*, trans. D. Heller-Roazen. Stanford: Stanford University Press.

Aguiar, M. 2001. "Decolonizing the Tongue: Reading Speech and Aphasia in the Work of Michelle Cliff." *Literature and Psychology* 47 1/2, 94–108.

Alexie, S. 1993. *First Indian on the Moon*. New York: Hanging Loose.

——. 1994. "Sherman Alexie, Literary Rebel: Interview with John and Carl Bellante." *Bloomsbury Review* 14, 13–17.

——. 1998. "Death in Hollywood." *Literary Cavalcade* 53, no. 8, 1–6.

——. 2000. "Indian Country." *New Yorker*, 13 March.

Allahwala, A., and R. Keil. 2005. "Introduction to a Debate on the World Social Forum." *International Journal of Urban and Regional Research* 29, no. 2, 409–16.

Alter, R. 2004. *The Five Books of Moses*. New York: W. W. Norton.

Arditi, B., and J. Valentine. 1999. *Polemicization*. Edinburgh: Edinburgh University Press.

Arendt, H. 1978. *The Life of the Mind*, ed. M. McCarthy. New York: Harcourt.

——. 1983. *On Revolution*. Westport: Greenwood.

Augustine. 1961. *Confessions*, trans. R. S. Pine-Coffin. New York: Penguin.

——. 1964. *On the Free Choice of the Will*, trans. A. S. Benjamin and L. H. Hackstaff. Indianapolis: Bobbs-Merrill.

——. 1972. *Concerning the City of God against the Pagans*, ed. D. Knowles, trans. H. Bettenson. Baltimore: Penguin.

Austin, J. L. 1962. *How to Do Things with Words*. Cambridge: Harvard University Press.

Bakhtin, M. M. 1984. *Problems of Dostoevsky's Poetics*, trans. C. Emerson. Minneapolis: University of Minnesota Press.

Balibar, E. 2004. *We the People of Europe? Reflections on Transnational Citizenship*, trans. J. Swenson. Princeton: Princeton University Press.

Ballard, J. G. 2000. *Super-Cannes*. London: Flamingo.

Bartelson, J. 1995. *A Genealogy of Sovereignty*. Cambridge: Cambridge University Press.

Barthes, R. 1987. *Criticism and Truth*, trans. K. Keuneman. Minneapolis: University of Minnesota Press.

Bartsch, I., C. DiPalma, and L. Sells. 2001. "Witnessing the Postmodern Jeremiad: (Mis)understanding Donna Haraway's Method of Inquiry." *Configurations* 9, no. 1, 127–64.

Benhabib, S. 1994a. "Deliberative Rationality and Models of Democratic Legitimacy." *Constellations* 1, 26–52.

——. 1994b. "Democracy and Difference: Reflections on the Metapolitics of Lyotard and Derrida." *Journal of Political Philosophy* 2, 1–23.

——. 2002. *The Claims of Culture: Equality and Diversity in the Global Era*. Princeton: Princeton University Press.

——. 2006a. "Democratic Iterations: The Local, the National and the Global." *Another Cosmopolitanism*, ed. R. Post, 45–82. Oxford: Oxford University Press.

——. 2006b. "The Philosophical Foundations of Cosmopolitan Norms." *Another Cosmopolitanism*, ed. R. Post, 13–44. Oxford: Oxford University Press.

Bennett, J. 2001. *The Enchantment of Modern Life: Attachments, Crossings, and Ethics*. Princeton: Princeton University Press.

Bennett, J., and W. Chaloupka, eds. 1993. *In the Nature of Things: Language, Politics, and the Environment*. Minneapolis: University of Minnesota Press.

Berlin, I. 1969. *Four Essays on Liberty*. Oxford: Oxford University Press.

——. 1992. *The Crooked Timber of Humanity*. New York: Vintage.

Bernstein, R. 1983. *Beyond Objectivism and Relativism: Science, Hermeneutics, and Praxis*. Oxford: Basil Blackwell.

Bigo, D., and E. Guild. 2002. "De Tampere à Seville: Vers une ultra gouvernementalisation de la domination transnationale?" *Cultures et Conflits: Sociologie politique de l'international* 45, 5–18.

Bird, C. 2004. "Status, Identity and Respect." *Political Theory* 32, no. 2, 207–32.

Bondurant, J. 1967. *Conquest of Violence: The Gandhian Philosophy of Conflict*. Berkeley: University of California Press.

Bourdieu, P. 1980. *The Logic of Practice*, trans. R. Nice. Stanford: Stanford University Press.

——. 1984. *Distinction: A Social Critique of the Judgement of Taste*, trans. R. Nice. Cambridge: Harvard University Press.

——. 1989. "Flaubert's Point of View." *Literature and Social Practice*, ed. P. Desan, P. P. Ferguson, and W. Griswold, trans. P. P. Ferguson. Chicago: University of Chicago Press.

——. 1991. *Language and Symbolic Power*, trans. G. Raymond and M. Adamson. Cambridge: Harvard University Press.

——. 1994. "Rethinking the State: Genesis and Structure of the Bureaucratic Field." *Sociological Theory* 12, 1–19.

Brown, W. 2003. "Neoliberalism and the End of Liberal Democracy." *Theory and Event* 7, no. 1, http://muse.jhu.edu/journals/theory_and_event/.

Burchell, G., C. Gordon, and P. Miller. 1991. *The Foucault Effect*. London: Harvester Wheatsheaf.

Burke, E. 1990. *A Philosophical Enquiry into the Origin of Our Ideas of the Sublime and Beautiful*. Oxford: Oxford University Press.

Bush, G. W. 2001a. "Address to the Nation," 11 September, http://www.american rhetoric.com/speeches/gwbush911addresstothenation.htm.

——. 2001b. "The Deliberate and Deadly Attacks . . . Were Acts of War," 12 September, http://www.americanrhetoric.com/speeches/gwbush911cabinetroomaddress .htm.

——. 2001c. "National Day of Prayer and Remembrance for the Victims of the Terrorist Attacks," 13 September, http://www.americanrhetoric.com/speeches/ gwbush911memonationaldayofprayerandrememberance.htm.

Butler, J. 1992. "Contingent Foundations: Feminism and the Question of 'Post-modernism.'" *Feminists Theorize the Political*, ed. J. Butler and J. W. Scott. New York: Routledge.

——. 2004. *Precarious Life: The Powers of Mourning and Violence*. London: Verso.

Campbell, D. 1993. *Politics without Principle: Sovereignty, Ethics, and the Narratives of the Gulf War*. Boulder: Lynne Rienner.

——. 1998a. *National Deconstruction: Violence, Identity and Justice in Bosnia*. Minneapolis: University of Minnesota Press.

——. 1998b. "Why Fight: Humanitarianism, Principles and Poststructuralism." *Millennium: Journal of International Studies* 27, no. 3, 497–522.

——. 1998c. *Writing Security: United States Foreign Policy and the Politics of Identity*, rev. edn. Minneapolis: University of Minnesota Press.

Camus, A. 1955. "The Myth of Sisyphus." *The Myth of Sisyphus and other Essays*, trans. J. O'Brien, 88–91. New York: Random House.

Cavell, S. 1988. *Conditions Handsome and Unhandsome: The Constitution of Emersonian Perfectionism*. Chicago: University of Chicago Press.

——. 1992. *The Senses of Walden*. Chicago: University of Chicago Press.

——. 1994a. "Opera and the Lease of Voice." *A Pitch of Philosophy: Autobiographical Exercises*, 129–70. Cambridge: Harvard University Press.

——. 1994b. "Philosophy and the Arrogation of Voice." *A Pitch of Philosophy: Autobiographical Exercises*, 1–52. Cambridge: Harvard University Press.

Cheah, P. 2007. *Inhuman Conditions: Cosmopolitanism and Human Rights in the Current Conjuncture*. Cambridge: Harvard University Press.

Christodoulidis, E. A. 2001. "The Aporia of Sovereignty: On the Representation of the People in Constitutional Discourse." *King's College Law Journal* 12, 111–33.

Cicci, R. 2001. "*The Gift of Dyslexia* by Ronald Davis." *Perspectives* 27, no. 3, 10–11.

Cliff, M. 1978. "Notes on Speechlessness." *Sinister Wisdom*, no. 5, 5–9.

——. 1987. *No Telephone to Heaven*. New York: Dutton.

——. 1988. "A Journey into Speech." *Graywolf Annual 5: Multicultural Literacy, Opening the American Mind*, ed. R. Simonson and S. Walker, 57–62. St. Paul: Graywolf.

——. 1993. *Free Enterprise*. New York: Dutton.

Coetzee, J. 2001. *The Lives of Animals*. Princeton: Princeton University Press.

Cohen, R. A., ed. 1986. *Face to Face with Levinas*. Albany: State University of New York Press.

Coles, R. 1997. *Rethinking Generosity: Critical Theory and the Politics of Caritas*. Ithaca: Cornell University Press.

Connolly, W. E. 1967. *Political Science and Ideology*. New York: Atherton.

——. 1969. *The Bias of Pluralism*. New York: Atherton.

——. 1974. *The Terms of Political Discourse*. Lexington, Mass.: D. C. Heath.

——. 1983. *The Terms of Political Discourse*, new edn. Princeton: Princeton University Press.

——. 1987. *Politics and Ambiguity*. Madison: University of Wisconsin Press.

——. 1991. *Identity\Difference: Democratic Negotiations of Political Paradox*. Ithaca: Cornell University Press; enlarged edn Minneapolis: University of Minnesota Press, 2001.

——. 1993a. *The Augustinian Imperative: A Reflection on the Politics of Morality*. Thousand Oaks, Calif.: Sage, rev. edn Lanham, Md.: Rowman and Littlefield, 2002.

——. 1993b. *Political Theory and Modernity*. Ithaca: Cornell University Press.

——. 1993c. *The Terms of Political Discourse*. Princeton: Princeton University Press.

——. 1995. *The Ethos of Pluralization*. Minneapolis: University of Minnesota Press.

——. 1997. "Debate: Reworking the Democratic Imagination." *Journal of Political Philosophy* 5, no. 2, 194–202.

——. 1999. *Why I Am Not a Secularist*. Minneapolis: University of Minnesota Press.

——. 2002. *Neuropolitics: Thinking, Culture, Speed*. Minneapolis: University of Minnesota Press.

——. 2004a. "The Complexity of Sovereignty." *Sovereign Lives: Power in Global Politics*, ed. V. Pin-Fat, J. Edkins, and M. J. Shapiro. New York: Routledge.

——. 2004b. "Method, Problem, Faith." *Problems and Methods in the Study of Politics*, ed. I. Shapiro, R. M. Smith, and T. E. Masoud. Cambridge: Cambridge University Press.

——. 2005a. "The Evangelical-Capitalist Resonance Machine." *Political Theory* 33, no. 6, 869–86.

——. 2005b. *Pluralism*. Durham: Duke University Press.

Connolly, W. E., and M. Best. 1976. *The Politicized Economy*. Lexington, Mass.: D. C. Heath.

Conway, J. 2005. "Social Forums, Social Movements and Social Change: A Response to Peter Marcuse on the Subject of the World Social Forum." *International Journal of Urban and Regional Research* 29, no. 2, 425–28.

Coons, J. E., and P. M. Brennan. 1999. *By Nature Equal: The Anatomy of a Western Insight*. Princeton: Princeton University Press.

Danner, M. 2004. "Torture and the Truth: America, Abu Ghraib, and the War on Terror." *New York Review of Books*, 10 June.

De Grazia, D. 2002. *Animal Rights: A Very Short Introduction.* Oxford: Oxford University Press.

De Grazia, V. 2005. *Irresistible Empire: America's Advance through Twentieth-Century Europe.* Cambridge: Harvard University Press.

Deibert, R. J. 2000. "International Plug 'n Play? Citizen Activism, the Internet and Global Public Policy." *International Studies Perspectives* 1, no. 3, 255–72.

De Landa, M. 1997. *A Thousand Years of Nonlinear History.* New York: Zone.

Deleuze, G., and F. Guattari. 1977. *Anti-Oedipus: Capitalism and Schizophrenia,* trans. R. Hurley, M. Seem, and H. R. Lane. New York: Viking.

——. 1983. *Anti-Oedipus: Capitalism and Schizophrenia,* trans. R. Hurley, M. Seem, and H. R. Lane. Minneapolis: University of Minnesota Press.

——. 1986. *Kafka: Towards a Minor Literature,* trans. D. Polan. Minneapolis: University of Minnesota Press.

——. 1994. *What Is Philosophy?,* trans. H. Tomlinson and G. Burchell. New York: Columbia University Press.

——. 1996. *A Thousand Plateaus: Capitalism and Schizophrenia,* trans. B. Massumi. London: Althone.

DeNuccio, J. 2002. "Slow Dancing with Skeletons: Sherman Alexie's The Lone Ranger and Tonto Fistfight in Heaven." *Critique: Studies in Contemporary Fiction* 44, no. 1, 86–96.

Der Derian, J., and M. J. Shapiro, eds. 1989. *International/Intertextual Relations: Postmodern Readings of World Politics.* Lexington, Mass.: Lexington Books.

Derrida, J. 1988. "Signature, Event, Context." *Limited Inc,* trans. S. Weber, 1–23. Evanston, Ill.: Northwestern University Press.

——. 1989. "Jacques Derrida: In Discussion with Christopher Norris." *Deconstruction,* ed. A. Papadakis et al. London: Academy.

——. 1994a. "Nietzsche and the Machine: Interview with Jacques Derrida by Richard Beardsworth." *Journal of Nietzsche Studies* 7, 7–66.

——. 1994b. *Specters of Marx: The State of the Debt, the Work of Mourning, and the New International,* trans. P. Kamuf. New York: Routledge.

——. 2005. *Rogues: Two Essays on Reason,* trans. M. Brault and P. A. Naas. Stanford: Stanford University Press.

Diamond, C. 2006. "The Difficulty of Reality and the Difficulty of Philosophy." *Reading Cavell,* ed. A. Crary and S. Shieh, 98–118. London: Routledge.

Dickman, G. E. 2002. "The Nature of Learning Disabilities through the Lens of Reading Research." *Perspectives* 29, no. 2.

Donnelly, J. 2003. *Universal Human Rights in Theory and Practice.* Ithaca: Cornell University Press.

Dryzek, J. S. 2000. *Deliberative Democracy and Beyond: Liberals, Critics, Contestations.* Oxford: Oxford University Press.

Dubey, M. 1999. "The Politics of Genre in *Beloved.*" *Novel: A Forum on Fiction* 32, no. 2, 187–206.

Eden, G. 2003. "The Role of Brain Imaging in Dyslexia Research." *Perspectives* 29, no. 2, 14–16.

Eglash, R. 1999. *African Fractals*. New Brunswick: Rutgers University Press.

Eribon, D. 1991. *Michel Foucault*, trans. B. Wing. Cambridge: Harvard University Press.

Eschle, C. 2002. "Engendering Global Democracy." *International Feminist Journal of Politics* 4, no. 3, 315–41.

———. 2005. "'Skeleton Women': Feminism and the Antiglobalization Movement." *Signs: Journal of Women in Culture and Society* 30, no. 3, 1741–60.

Eschle, C., and B. Maiguashca, eds. 2005. *Critical Theories, World Politics and the Anti-Globalisation Movement*. London: Routledge.

Euben, J. P. 2001. "The Polis, Globlization and the Politics of Place." *Democracy and Vision: Sheldon Wolin and the Vicissitudes of the Political*, ed. A. Botwinick and W. E. Connolly. Princeton: Princeton University Press.

Finkel, Andrew. 2000. "Food for Thought." CNN.com, 30 November.

Fisher, P. 1988. "Democratic Social Space: Whitman, Melville and the Promise of American Transparency." *Representations* 24, 60–101.

Flathman, R. 1976. *The Practice of Rights*. Cambridge: Cambridge University Press.

Fletcher, J. M. 2003. "Operationalizing Learning Disabilities: The Importance of Treatment-Oriented Models." *Perspectives* 29, no. 2, 23–25.

Foucault, M. 1981. "The Order of Discourse." *Untying the Text*, ed. R. Young. Boston: Routledge and Kegan Paul.

———. 1988. "The Thought from the Outside." *Foucault / Blanchot, trans.* J. Mehlman and B. Massumi. New York: Zone.

Freud, S. 1962. *Totem and Taboo*. New York: W. W. Norton.

Friedman, T. 2000. *The Lexus and the Olive Tree*. New York: Farrar, Straus and Giroux.

———. 2006. *The World Is Flat: A Brief History of the Twenty-First Century*. New York: Farrar, Straus and Giroux.

Fuchs, D. 2003. "On Responsiveness-to-Intervention as a Valid Method of LD Identification: Some Things We Need to Know." *Perspectives* 29, no. 2, 28–31.

Fuentes, C. 1982. "Writing in Time." *Democracy* 2, no. 1, 61–74.

Gallie, W. B. 1956. "Essentially Contested Concepts." *Proceedings of the Aristotelian Society* 56, 167–98.

George, J., and D. Campbell. 1990. "Patterns of Dissent and the Celebration of Difference: Critical Social Theory and International Relations." *International Studies Quarterly* 34, no. 3, 269–93.

Gilger, J. 2003. "Genes and Dyslexia." *Perspectives* 29, no. 2, 6–8.

Gorman, C. 2003. "The New Science of Dyslexia." *Time*, 8 September, http://www.time.com/time/magazine/article/0,9171,1005284,00.html?internalid=ACA.

Guenoun, S. 2000. "An Interview with Jacques Rancière: Cinematographic Image, Democracy and the Splendor of the . . ." *Sites* 4, no. 2, 1–7.

Gutmann, A. 2001. Introduction. *Human Rights as Politics and Idolatry*, ed. A. Gutmann, vii–xxviii. Princeton: Princeton University Press.

Habermas, J. 1988. *Theorie des kommunikativen Handelns*. Frankfurt: Suhrkamp.

——. 1989. *Between Facts and Norms: Contributions to a Discourse Theory of Law and Democracy*, trans. W. Rehg. Cambridge: MIT Press.

——. 1998. *Die postnationale Konstellation: Politische Essays*. Frankfurt: Suhrkamp.

——. 2001a. "Constitutional Democracy: A Paradoxical Union of Contradictory Principles?" *Political Theory* 29, no. 6, 766–81.

——. 2001b. *The Postnational Constellation: Political Essays*, trans. M. Pensky. Cambridge: MIT Press.

Haraway, D. 1988. "Situated Knowledges: The Science Question in Feminism and the Premise of Partial Perspective." *Feminist Studies* 14, no. 3, 575–99.

——. 2003. *The Companion Species Manifesto: Dogs, People, and Significant Otherness*. Chicago: Prickly Paradigm.

Hardt, M., and A. Negri. 2000. *Empire*. Cambridge: Harvard University Press.

——. 2002. "Today's Bandung?" *New Left Review*, no. 14, 112–18.

Hari, J. 2005. "McEurope." *New York Times*, 8 May.

Heidegger, M. 1968. *What Is Called Thinking*. San Francisco: Harper and Row.

Held, D. 1995. *Democracy and the Global Order: From the Modern State to Cosmopolitan Governance*. Cambridge: Polity.

Hitchens, C. 1998. "Morrison's True West." *Vanity Fair*, February, 144–45.

Hobbes, T. 1981. *Leviathan*, ed. C. B. MacPherson. London: Penguin.

Hollinger, D. 2001. "Debates with the PTA and Others." *Human Rights as Politics and Idolatry*, ed. A. Gutmann, 117–26. Princeton: Princeton University Press.

Holmes, S. 1998. "Precommitment and the Paradox of Democracy." *Constitutionalism and Democracy*, ed. J. Elster and R. Slagstad, 195–240. Cambridge: Cambridge University Press.

Honig, B. 1993. *Political Theory and the Displacement of Politics*. Ithaca: Cornell University Press.

——. 2001a. "Dead Rights, Live Futures: A Reply to Habermas's 'Constitutional Democracy.'" *Political Theory* 29, no. 6, 792–805.

——. 2001b. *Democracy and the Foreigner*. Princeton: Princeton University Press.

——. 2005. "Bound by Law? Alien Rights, Administrative Discretion, and the Politics of Technicality." *The Limits of Law*, ed. A. Sarat et al., 209–45. Stanford: Stanford University Press.

——. 2006. "Another Cosmopolitanism? Law and Politics in the New Europe." *Another Cosmopolitanism*, ed. R. Post, 102–27. Oxford: Oxford University Press.

——. 2007. "Between Decision and Deliberation: Political Paradox in Democratic Theory." *American Political Science Review* 101, no. 1, 1–17.

Honneth, A. 2000. *Das Andere der Gerechtigkeit: Aufsätze zur praktischen Philosophie*. Frankfurt: Suhrkamp.

Hunter, I. 2004. "Reading Thomasius on Heresy." *Eighteenth-Century Thought* 2, 39–55.

Ignatieff, M. 2001a. "Human Rights as Idolatry." *Human Rights as Politics and Idolatry*, ed. A. Gutmann, 53–100. Princeton: Princeton University Press.

——. 2001b. *Human Rights as Politics and Idolatry*, ed. A. Gutmann. Princeton: Princeton University Press.

——. 2001c. "Response to Commentators." *Human Rights as Politics and Idolatry*, ed. A. Gutman, 161–74. Princeton: Princeton University Press.

Jacobson, N. 1977. *Pride and Solace: The Functions and Limits of Political Theory*. Berkeley: University of California Press.

Joxe, A. 2002. *Empire of Disorder*, trans. A. Hodges. New York: Semiotext(e).

Kaldor, M. 2000. "'Civilising' Globalisation: The Implications of the 'Battle' for Seattle." *Millennium: Journal of International Studies* 29, no. 1, 105–14.

Kammen, M. 1997. *In the Past Lane: Historical Perspectives on American Culture*. New York: Oxford University Press.

Kant, I. 1987. *Critique of Judgment*, trans. W. S. Pluhar. Indianapolis: Hackett.

——. 1996. *Critique of Pure Reason*, trans. W. S. Pluhar. Indianapolis: Hackett.

Kariel, H. 1973. "Neither Sticks nor Stones." *Politics and Society* 3, no. 2, 179–99.

Kateb, G. 1994. *The Inner Ocean: Individualism and Democratic Culture*. Ithaca: Cornell University Press.

Keenan, A. 2003. *Democracy in Question: Democratic Openness in a Time of Political Closure*. Stanford: Stanford University Press.

Khayati, A. 1999. "Representation, Race and the "Language" of the Ineffable in Toni Morrison's Narrative." *African American Review* 33, no. 2, 313–24.

Kierkegaard, S. 1941. *Fear and Trembling: A Dialectical Lyric*, trans. W. Lowrie. Princeton: Princeton University Press.

——. 1980. *The Concept of Anxiety*, ed. and trans. R. Thomte and A. B. Anderson. Princeton: Princeton University Press.

Kompridis, N. 2006. "The Idea of a New Beginning: A Romantic Source of Normativity and Freedom." *Philosophical Romanticism*, ed. N. Kompridis, 32–59. New York: Routledge.

Kristeva, J. 1993. *Nations without Nationalism*, trans. L. S. Roudiez. New York: Columbia University Press.

Kymlicka, W. 1993. *Multicultural Citizenship: A Liberal Theory of Minority Rights*. Oxford: Clarendon.

LaFrance, E. B. 1997. "The Gifted/Dyslexic Child: Characterizing and Addressing Strengths and Weaknesses." *Annals of Dyslexia* 46, 163–82.

Larmore, C. 1999. "The Moral Basis of Liberalism." *Journal of Philosophy* 96, 599–625.

——. 2005. "Respect for Persons." *Hedgehog Review* 7, no. 2, 66–76.

Lauterbach, L. 1998. "Slaves of Fashion." *Boston Review* 23, no. 3, 13–17.

——. 1999. "On Flaws: Toward a Poetics of the Whole Fragment." *Theory and Event* 3, http://muse.jhu.edu/journals/theory_and_event/.

Lavoi, R. 2003. "On the Waterbed: The Impact of Learning Disabilities." Talk presented at Kapiolani Community College.

Layoun, M. N. 1990. *Travels of a Genre: The Modern Novel and Ideology*. Princeton: Princeton University Press.

Leet, M. 2004. *Aftereffects of Knowledge in Modernity: Politics, Aesthetics and Individuality*. Albany: State University of New York Press.

Levi, M. and D. Olson. 2000. "The Battles for Seattle." *Politics and Society* 28, no. 3, 309–29.

Levinas, E. 1986. *Face to Face with Levinas*, ed. R. A. Cohen. Albany: State University of New York Press.

Locke, J. 1960. *Second Treatise of Government*, ed. P. Laslett. Cambridge: Cambridge University Press.

———. 1993. "Letter on Toleration." *Political Writings of John Locke*, ed. D. Wooton, 94–109. New York: Penguin, 1993.

Luhmann, N. 1990. "Verfassung als evolutionäre Errungenschaft." *Rechtshistorisches Journal* 9, 176–220.

Lyon, G. R. 2003. "Reading Disabilities: Why Do Some Children Have Difficulty Learning to Read? What Can Be Done about It?" *Perspectives* 29, no. 2, 17–19.

Macdonald, B. J. 2002. "Towards an Ethos of Freedom and Engagement: An Interview with William E. Connolly." *Strategies: Journal of Theory, Culture and Politics* 15, no. 2, 165–80.

Maiguashca, B. 2006. "Making Feminist Sense of the 'Anti-globalization Movement.'" *Global Society* 20, no. 2, 115–36.

Mann, T. 1945. *The Tables of the Law* [Das Gesetz], trans. H. T. Lowe-Porter. New York: Alfred A. Knopf.

Marius, R. 1999. *Martin Luther: The Christian between God and Death*. Cambridge: Harvard University Press.

Marratti, P. 2001. "Against the Doxa: Politics of Immanence and Becoming Minoritarian." *Micropolitics of Media Culture: Reading the Rhizomes of Deleuze and Guattari*, ed. P. Pister, 205–20. Amsterdam: Amsterdam University Press.

Mason, S. 1998. "Fractal Aesthetics." *What Rain Internet Philosophy Journal*, http://www.whatrain.com/fractallogic/page44.htm.

Mill, J. S. 1978. *On Liberty*. New York: Hackett.

———. 1989. *On Liberty and Other Writings*, ed. S. Collini. Cambridge: Cambridge University Press.

Morris, B., L. Munoz, and P. Neering. 2002. "Overcoming Dyslexia." *Fortune*, http://money.cnn.com/magazines/fortune/fortune_archive/2002/05/13/322876/index.htm.

Morrison, Toni. 1990. *Playing in the Dark*. Cambridge: Harvard University Press.

———. 1993. Nobel lecture, http://nobelprize.org/nobel_prizes/literature/laureates/1993/morrison-lecture.html.

———. 1999. *Paradise*. New York: Plume.

Nancy, J.-L. 1993. *The Birth to Presence*, trans. B. Holmes et al. Stanford: Stanford University Press.

Neiman, S. 2001. "Theodicy in Jerusalem." *Hannah Arendt in Jerusalem*, ed. S. E. Asheim, 65–90. Berkeley: University of California Press.

Newton, J. 2001. "Sherman Alexie's Autoethnography." *Contemporary Literature* 42, no. 2, 413–28.

Nietzsche, F. 1968. *The Will to Power*, ed. W. Kaufmann. New York: Vintage.

——. 2006. *Thus Spoke Zarathustra: A Book for All and None*, ed. A. Del Caro and R. B. Pippin, trans. A. Del Caro. Cambridge: Cambridge University Press.

Noble, D. 1968. The Eternal Adam and the New World Garden. New York: George Braziller.

O'Brien, R., A. M. Goetz, J. A. Scholte, and M. Williams. 2000. *Contesting Global Governance: Multilateral Economic Institutions and Global Social Movements*. Cambridge: Cambridge University Press.

Patton, P., ed. 1996. *Deleuze: A Critical Reader*. Cambridge, Mass.: Blackwell.

——. 2000. *Deleuze and the Political*. New York: Routledge.

Perry, M. J. 1998. *The Idea of Human Rights: Four Inquiries*. Oxford: Oxford University Press.

Polletta, F. 2004. *Freedom is an Endless Meeting: Democracy in American Social Movements*. Chicago: University of Chicago Press.

Rancière, J. 1989. *The Nights of Labor: The Workers' Dream in Nineteenth-Century France*, trans. John Drury. Philadelphia: Temple University Press.

——. 1994. "Post-Democracy, Politics and Philosophy: An interview with Jacques Rancière," trans. Kate Nash. *Angelaki* 1, no. 3, 171–78.

——. 1995. *On the Shores of Politics*, trans. Liz Heron. New York: Verso.

——. 1998. *Dis-agreement*, trans. Julie Rose. Minneapolis: University of Minnesota Press.

——. 2000. "Literature, Politics, Aesthetics: An interview by Solange Guenoun and James H. Kavanagh." *SubStance* 29, no. 2, 3–24.

——. 2001. "Ten Theses on Politics." *Theory and Event* 5, no. 3, http://muse.jhu.edu/ journals/theory_and_event/.

Raskind, M. "Addressing the Needs of Youth with Disabilities in the Juvenile Justice System: The Current Status of Evidence-Based Research." *Research Trends: Is There a Link between LD and Juvenile Delinquency*, http://www.schwablearning .org.

Rawls, J. 1993. *Political Liberalism*. New York: Columbia University Press.

——. 1999. *The Law of Peoples*. Cambridge: Harvard University Press.

Richardson, R. Jr. 1995. *Emerson: The Mind on Fire*. Berkeley: University of California Press.

Rorty, R. 1998. *Truth and Progress, Philosopical Papers*, vol. 3. Cambridge: Cambridge University Press.

Rousseau, J. J. 1978. *On the Social Contract: With Geneva Manuscript and Political Economy*, ed. R. Masters, trans. Judith Masters. New York: St. Martin's.

——. 1988. *On the Social Contract*, ed. and trans. D. A. Cress. Indianapolis: Hackett.

Rowell, A. 1999. "Faceless in Seattle," *Guardian*, 6 October.

Rupert, M. 2005. "In the Belly of the Beast: Resisting Globalization and War in a Neo-imperial Moment." *Critical Theories, World Politics and the Anti-Globalisation Movement*, ed. C. Eschle and B. Maiguashca. London: Routledge.

Sandel, M. 1998. *Liberalism and the Limits of Justice*. New York: Cambridge University Press.

Santner, E. 2005. "Terry Schiavo and the State of Exception," http://www.press
.uchicago.edu/Misc/Chicago/05april_santner.html.

Sartre, J.-P. 1981. *The Family Idiot: Gustave Flaubert, 1821–1857*, trans. C. Cosman.
Chicago: University of Chicago Press.

Schmitt, C. 1985. *Political Theology: Four Chapters on the Concept of Sovereignty*, trans.
G. Schwab. Cambridge: MIT Press.

——. 1996. *The Concept of the Political*, trans. G. Schwab. Chicago: University of Chicago Press.

Schoolman, M. 2001. *Reason and Horror: Critical Theory, Democracy, and Aesthetic
Individuality*. New York: Routledge.

Schlosser, E., M. Nestle, M. Pollan, W. Berry, T. Duster, E. Ransom, W. LaDuke,
P. Singer, V. Shiva, C. Petrini, E. Coleman, and J. Hightower. 2006. *The Nation:
The Food Issue*, http://www.thenation.com/doc/20060911/forum.

Sensen, O. 2004. "How Human Dignity Grounds Human Rights: Two Paradigms."
Paper delivered at the Midwest Political Science Convention.

Shapiro, I., R. M. Smith, and T. E. Masoud, eds. 2004. *Problems and Methods in the
Study of Politics*. Cambridge: Cambridge University Press.

Shapiro, M. J. 1988. *The Politics of Representation*. Madison: University of Wisconsin
Press.

Shaviro, S. 1993. *The Cinematic Body*. Minneapolis: University of Minnesota Press.

Shaywitz, S. 2003. *Overcoming Dyslexia: A New and Complete Science-Based Program for
Reading Problems at Any Level*. New York: Alfred A. Knopf.

Sherman, G., and C. D. Cowen. 2003. "Neuroanatomy of Dyslexia through the
Lens of Cerebrodiversity." *Perspectives* 29, no. 2, 9–13.

Sieyès, E. J. 2003. "What Is the Third Estate?" *Sieyès: Political Writings*, ed. M. Sonen-
scher, 92–153. Indianapolis: Hackett Publishing.

Skinner, Q. 1994. "Modernity and Disenchantment: Some Historical Reflections."
Philosophy in an Age of Pluralism, ed. J. Tully, 37–48. Cambridge: Cambridge University Press.

Shiva, V. 1999. "This Round to the Citizens." *Guardian*, 8 December.

Silver, L. B. 2001. "Controversial Therapies." *Perspectives* 27, no. 3, 1, 4.

Singer, P. 1975. *Animal Liberation: A New Ethics for Our Treatment of Animals*. New
York: Avon.

Steger, M. B. 2005. *Globalism: Market Ideology Meets Terrorism*. Lanham, Md.: Rowman and Littlefield.

Stackhouse, M. 1999. "Human Rights and Public Theology: The Basic Validation
of Human Rights." *Religion and Human Rights: Competing Claims?*, ed. C. Gustafson and P. Juviler, 12–27. New York: M. E. Sharpe.

Stilles, A. 2001. "Slow Food." *Nation*, 20 August.

Strong, T. 2004. "The Tragic Ethos and the Spirit of Music." *International Studies in
Philosophy* 56, no.3, 23–41.

Sullivan, J. L., and J. C. Transue. 1999. "The Psychological Underpinnings of Democracy: A Selective Review of Research on Political Tolerance, Interpersonal Trust, and Social Capital." *Annual Review of Psychology* 50, 625–50.

Suskind, R. 2004. "Without a Doubt." *New York Times Sunday Magazine*, 17 October.

Taylor, C. 1989. *Sources of the Self: The Making of Modern Identity*. Cambridge: Harvard University Press.

——. 1999. "Conditions of an Unforced Consensus on Human Rights." *The East Asian Challenge for Human Rights*, ed. J. R. Bauer and D. Bell, 124–44. Cambridge: Cambridge University Press.

Thoreau, H. D. 1947. "Reading" [from *Walden*]. *The Portable Thoreau*, ed. C. Bode, 146–57. New York: Penguin.

Tully, J., ed. 1994. *Philosophy in an Age of Pluralism: The Philosophy of Charles Taylor in Question*. Cambridge: Cambridge University Press.

Varney, W., and B. Martin. 2000. "Net Resistance, Net Benefits: Opposing MAI." *Social Alternatives* 19, no. 1, 47–51.

Waldron, J. 2003. *God, Locke and Equality: Christian Foundations in Locke's Political Thought*. Cambridge: Cambridge University Press.

Walker, R. B. J. 1993. *Inside/Outside: International Relations as Political Theory*. Cambridge: Cambridge University Press.

Waltzer, M. 1981. "The Distribution of Membership." *Boundaries: National Autonomy and Its Limits*, ed. P. G. Brown and H. Shue. Totowa, N.Y.: Rowman and Littlefield.

White, S. K. 2000. *Sustaining Affirmation: The Strengths of Weak Ontology in Contemporary Political Theory*. Princeton: Princeton University Press.

——. 2003. "After Critique: Affirming Subjectivity in Contemporary Political Theory." *European Journal of Political Theory* 2, 217–25.

——. 2008. "Uncertain Constellations: Dignity, Equality, Respect and . . . ?" *The New Pluralism: William Connolly and the Contemporary Global Condition*, ed. D. Campbell and M. Schoolman. Durham: Duke University Press.

——. Forthcoming. "Reason and the Ethos of a Late-Modern Citizen." *Contemporary Debates in Political Philosophy*, ed. T. Christiano and J. Christman, 1–34. Oxford: Blackwell.

Wignaraja, P., ed. 1993. *New Social Movements in the South: Empowering the People*. London: Zed.

Williams, B. 1973. "The Idea of Equality." *Problems of the Self: Philosophical Papers, 1956–1972*, ed. B. Williams. Cambridge: Cambridge University Press.

Wittgenstein, L. 1967. *Philosophical Investigations*, trans. G. E. M. Anscombe. Oxford: Blackwell.

Woodbury, C. 1890. *Talks with Emerson*. New York: Baker and Taylor.

Woodward, B. 2004. *Plan of Attack*. New York: Simon and Schuster.

World Social Forum. 2006. "World Social Forum Charter of Principles," http://www.forumsocialmundial.org.br/main.php?id_menu=4&cd_language=2.

Zerilli, L. 2005. *Feminism and the Abyss of Freedom*. Chicago: University of Chicago Press.

ABOUT THE CONTRIBUTORS

WILLIAM E. CONNOLLY is the Krieger-Eisenhower Professor of Political Science at Johns Hopkins University. His recent books include *Pluralism* (Duke University Press, 2005), *Neuropolitics: Thinking, Culture, Speed* (University of Minnesota Press, 2002), *The Augustinian Imperative: A Reflection on the Politics of Morality* (new edition, Rowman and Littlefield, 2002), and *Why I Am Not a Secularist* (University of Minnesota Press, 1999).

ROLAND BLEIKER is a professor of international relations at the University of Queensland. His publications include *Popular Dissent, Human Agency and Global Politics* (Cambridge University Press, 2000) and *Divided Korea: Toward a Culture of Reconciliation* (University of Minnesota Press, 2005). He is currently finishing a book entitled *Aesthetics and World Politics* for Palgrave.

WENDY BROWN is a professor of political science at the University of California, Berkeley. Her most recent books are *Edgework: Essays on Knowledge and Politics* (Princeton University Press, 2005), and *Regulating Aversion: A Critique of Tolerance in the Age of Identity and Empire* (Princeton University Press, 2006). She is currently thinking about proliferating nation-state walls in relation to eroding sovereignty.

DAVID CAMPBELL is a professor of cultural and political geography at Durham University. His research deals with the visual culture of international relations, political theory and global geopolitics, and American security policy. The author of *Writing Security: United States Foreign Policy and the Politics of Identity* (revised edition, University of Minnesota Press, 1998) and *National Deconstruction: Violence, Identity and Justice in Bosnia* (University of Minnesota Press, 1998), he is currently working on a book on the visuality of geopolitics and international relations.

JAMES DER DERIAN is Research Professor of International Studies at Brown University, where he directs the Global Security Program (www.watsoninstitute .org), the Global Media Project (www.watsoninstitute.org/globalmedia), and the InfoTechWarPeace Project (www.infopeace.org) at the Watson Institute for International Studies. His most recent book is *Virtuous War: Mapping the Military-Industrial-Media-Entertainment Network* (Westview Press, 2001). He is also the producer of three documentaries, *VirtualY2K* (2000), *After 9/11* (2004), and *The Culture War* (2008).

THOMAS L. DUMM is a professor of political science at Amherst College. He is the author of many articles and four books, as well as the forthcoming *Loneliness as a Way of Life*. He was the founding co-editor of the journal *theory & event*, and currently serves as the nonfiction editor of *Massachusetts Review*. For his work on loneliness he was awarded a Guggenheim fellowship in 2001.

KATHY E. FERGUSON is a professor of political science and women's studies at the University of Hawai'i. She is the author of numerous books and articles, including *The Man Question: Visions of Subjectivity in Feminist Theory* (University of California Press, 1993) and, with Phyllis Turnbull, *Oh, Say, Can You See? The Semiotics of the Military in Hawai'i* (University of Minnesota Press, 1999), and a forthcoming book on Emma Goldman for Rowman and Littlefield. Her experiences raising two dyslexic sons have led her to bring the tools of political theory to bear on the world of learning "disabilities."

BONNIE HONIG is the Sarah Rebecca Roland Professor of Political Science at Northwestern University and a senior research fellow at the American Bar Foundation in Chicago. She is the author of *Political Theory and the Displacement of Politics* (Cornell University Press, 1993), awarded the Spitz Prize in 1994, and *Democracy and the Foreigner* (Princeton University Press, 2001). She has published articles in *Political Theory*, the *American Political Science Review*, *Social Text*, *New Politics*, and the *Boston Review*, and she is co-editor of the *Oxford Handbook of Political Theory* (with John Dryzek and Ann Phillips), Oxford University Press,2006. Her most recent book *Emergency Politics: Paradox, Law, Democracy* is forthcoming and she is now working on a book on Sophocles's *Antigone*.

GEORGE KATEB is the William Nelson Cromwell Professor of Politics, emeritus, at Princeton University. Among his publications are *Hannah Arendt: Politics, Conscience, Evil* (Rowman and Allanheld, 1984), *Emerson and Self-Reliance* (Rowman and Littlefield, 2002), *The Inner Ocean: Individualism and Democratic Culture* (Cornell University Press, 1992), *Mill's On Liberty*, edited with David Bromwich (Yale University Press, 2003), and *Patriotism and Other Mistakes* (Yale University Press, 2006).

MORTON SCHOOLMAN is a professor of political science at the State University of New York, Albany. His recent publications include *Reason and Horror: Critical The-*

ory, Democracy, and Aesthetic Individuality (Routledge, 2001), "The Next Enlightenment: Aesthetic Reason in Modern Art and Mass Culture," *Journal for Cultural
Research* (January 2005), and "Avoiding 'Embarrassment': Aesthetic Reason and
Aporetic Critique in *Dialectic of Enlightenment*," *Polity* (July 2005), the latter two
essays forming the basis of a work in progress entitled *Democratic Enlightenment:
The Politics of the Image, Memory, and Mass Culture*. He is also the editor of *Modernity
and Political Thought*, a series of volumes in contemporary political theory published by Rowman and Littlefield that examines the work of figures in the history
of political thought from the standpoint of their contribution to our understanding of modernity.

MICHAEL J. SHAPIRO is a professor of political science at the University of Hawai'i. Among his recent publications are *For Moral Ambiguity: National Culture and
the Politics of the Family* (University of Minnesota Press, 2001), *Methods and Nations:
Cultural Governance and the Indigenous Subject* (Routledge Press, 2004), and *Deform-
ing American Political Thought: Ethnicity, Facticity, and Genre* (University of Kentucky
Press, 2006).

STEPHEN K. WHITE is the James Hart Professor of Politics at the University of
Virginia. He is the former editor of *Political Theory*. His most recent books include
What Is Political Theory, edited with J. Donald Moon (Sage, 2004), and *Sustaining
Affirmation: The Strengths of Weak Ontology in Political Theory* (Princeton University
Press, 2000). He is currently working on a book provisionally entitled *The Ethos of a
Late-Modern Citizen*.

INDEX

Library of Congress Cataloging-in-Publication Data

The new pluralism : William Connolly and the contemporary global condition /
edited by David Campbell and Morton Schoolman.
p. cm.
Includes bibliographical references and index.
ISBN-13: 978-0-8223-4246-5 (cloth : alk. paper)
ISBN-13: 978-0-8223-4270-0 (pbk. : alk. paper)
1. Democracy—Philosophy. 2. Pluralism (Social sciences)—Political aspects.
3. Political science—Philosophy. 4. Connolly, William E.
I. Campbell, David, 1961– II. Schoolman, Morton.
JC423.N483 2008
321.8—dc22
2007043853